Examining the Impact of Deep Learning and IoT on Multi–Industry Applications

Roshani Raut
Pimpri Chinchwad College of Engineering (PCCOE), Pune, India

Albena Dimitrova Mihovska
CTIF Global Capsule (CGC), Denmark

A volume in the Advances in Web Technologies and Engineering (AWTE) Book Series

Published in the United States of America by
IGI Global
Engineering Science Reference (an imprint of IGI Global)
701 E. Chocolate Avenue
Hershey PA, USA 17033
Tel: 717-533-8845
Fax: 717-533-8661
E-mail: cust@igi-global.com
Web site: http://www.igi-global.com

Library of Congress Cataloging-in-Publication Data

Names: Raut, Roshani, 1981- editor. | Mihovska, Albena, editor.
Title: Examining the impact of deep learning and IoT on multi-industry applications / Roshani Raut and Albena Mihovska, editors.

Description: Hershey, PA : Engineering Science Reference, an imprint of IGI
   Global, [2021] | Includes bibliographical references and index. |
   Summary: "This book provides insights on how deep learning, together
   with IOT, will impact various sectors such as healthcare, agriculture,
   cyber security, and social media analysis applications offering
   solutions to various real-world problems using these methods from
   various researchers' point of views"-- Provided by publisher.
Identifiers: LCCN 2020046691 (print) | LCCN 2020046692 (ebook) | ISBN
   9781799875116 (hardcover) | ISBN 9781799875178 (ebook)
Subjects: LCSH: Internet of things--Industrial applications. | Machine
   learning--Industrial applications. | Automation.
Classification: LCC TK5105.8857 .H344 2021 (print) | LCC TK5105.8857
   (ebook) | DDC 006.3/1--dc23
LC record available at https://lccn.loc.gov/2020046691
LC ebook record available at https://lccn.loc.gov/2020046692

This book is published in the IGI Global book series Advances in Web Technologies and Engineering (AWTE) (ISSN: 2328-2762; eISSN: 2328-2754)

British Cataloguing in Publication Data
A Cataloguing in Publication record for this book is available from the British Library.

All work contributed to this book is new, previously-unpublished material. The views expressed in this book are those of the authors, but not necessarily of the publisher.

For electronic access to this publication, please contact: eresources@igi-global.com.

Advances in Web Technologies and Engineering (AWTE) Book Series

Ghazi I. Alkhatib
The Hashemite University, Jordan
David C. Rine
George Mason University, USA

ISSN:2328-2762
EISSN:2328-2754

MISSION

The **Advances in Web Technologies and Engineering (AWTE) Book Series** aims to provide a platform for research in the area of Information Technology (IT) concepts, tools, methodologies, and ethnography, in the contexts of global communication systems and Web engineered applications. Organizations are continuously overwhelmed by a variety of new information technologies, many are Web based. These new technologies are capitalizing on the widespread use of network and communication technologies for seamless integration of various issues in information and knowledge sharing within and among organizations. This emphasis on integrated approaches is unique to this book series and dictates cross platform and multidisciplinary strategy to research and practice.

The **Advances in Web Technologies and Engineering (AWTE) Book Series** seeks to create a stage where comprehensive publications are distributed for the objective of bettering and expanding the field of web systems, knowledge capture, and communication technologies. The series will provide researchers and practitioners with solutions for improving how technology is utilized for the purpose of a growing awareness of the importance of web applications and engineering.

COVERAGE

- Integrated Heterogeneous and Homogeneous Workflows and Databases within and Across Organizations and with Suppliers and Customers
- Metrics-based performance measurement of IT-based and web-based organizations
- Ontology and semantic Web studies
- IT readiness and technology transfer studies
- Mobile, location-aware, and ubiquitous computing
- Competitive/intelligent information systems
- Data analytics for business and government organizations
- Web systems performance engineering studies
- Human factors and cultural impact of IT-based systems
- Quality of service and service level agreement issues among integrated systems

IGI Global is currently accepting manuscripts for publication within this series. To submit a proposal for a volume in this series, please contact our Acquisition Editors at Acquisitions@igi-global.com or visit: http://www.igi-global.com/publish/.

Titles in this Series

For a list of additional titles in this series, please visit: http://www.igi-global.com/book-series/advances-web-technologies-engineering/37158

Result Page Generation for Web Searching Emerging Research and Opportunities
Mostafa Alli (Tsinghua University, China)
Engineering Science Reference • © 2021 • 126pp • H/C (ISBN: 9781799809616) • US $165.00

Building Smart and Secure Environments Through the Fusion of Virtual Reality, Augmented Reality, and the IoT
Nadesh RK (Vellore Institute of Technology, India) Shynu PG (Vellore Institute of Technology, India) and Chiranji Lal Chowdhary (School of Information Technology and Engineering, VIT University, Vellore, India)
Engineering Science Reference • © 2020 • 300pp • H/C (ISBN: 9781799831839) • US $245.00

The IoT and the Next Revolutions Automating the World
Dinesh Goyal (Poornima Institute of Engineering & Technology, India) S. Balamurugan (QUANTS Investment Strategy & Consultancy Services, India) Sheng-Lung Peng (National Dong Hwa University, Taiwan) and Dharm Singh Jat (Namibia University of Science and Technology, Namibia)
Engineering Science Reference • © 2019 • 340pp • H/C (ISBN: 9781522592464) • US $255.00

Integrating and Streamlining Event-Driven IoT Services
Yang Zhang (Beijing University of Posts and Telecommunications, China) and Yanmeng Guo (Chinese Academy of Sciences, China)
Engineering Science Reference • © 2019 • 309pp • H/C (ISBN: 9781522576228) • US $205.00

Semantic Web Science and Real-World Applications
Miltiadis D. Lytras (The American College of Greece, Greece) Naif Aljohani (King Abdulaziz University, Saudi Arabia) Ernesto Damiani (Khalifa University, UAE) and Kwok Tai Chui (The Open University of Hong Kong, Hong Kong)
Information Science Reference • © 2019 • 399pp • H/C (ISBN: 9781522571865) • US $195.00

Innovative Solutions and Applications of Web Services Technology
Liang-Jie Zhang (Kingdee International Software Group Co., Ltd., China) and Yishuang Ning (Tsinghua University, China)
Engineering Science Reference • © 2019 • 316pp • H/C (ISBN: 9781522572688) • US $215.00

701 East Chocolate Avenue, Hershey, PA 17033, USA
Tel: 717-533-8845 x100 • Fax: 717-533-8661
E-Mail: cust@igi-global.com • www.igi-global.com

Table of Contents

Detailed Table of Contents

Chapter 1
    Anshul, Chandigarh University, Mohali, India
    Raju Kumar, University Institute of Computing, Chandigarh University, Mohali, India

In this era of technology, for effective treatment of patients, clinical experts are getting great support from automated e-healthcare systems. Nowadays, one of the leading reasons of death is cancer. Some common cancers are breast cancer, prostate cancer, lung cancer, skin cancer, brain cancer, and so on. To save human lives from cancer, an effective and timely treatment is required. Many different types of image modalities like CT scan, ultrasound, x-ray, MRI can be used to determine the disease, but traditionally, this was purely dependent on the knowledge and experience of doctors. So, the death rate was quite high and increasing day by day. Machine learning and deep learning are providing robust solutions in this field. There are many deep learning techniques like RNN, CNN, DBN, autoencoders, generative adversarial networks which are providing robust solutions in cancer diagnosis and prognosis so that many human lives can be saved. The objective of this chapter is to give an insight into deep learning techniques in the field of a cancer diagnosis.

Chapter 2
    Anuja Rajendra Jadhav, Savitribai Phule Pune University, India
    Roshani Raut, Pimpri Chinchwad College of Engineering, India
    Ram Joshi, JSPM's Rajarshi Shahu College of Engineering, India
    Pranav D. Pathak, MIT School of Bioengineering Sciences and Research, Pune, India
    Anuja R. Zade, JSPM's Rajarshi Shahu College of Engineering, India

2020 started with the outbreak of the novel coronavirus (COVID-19) virus. In this panic situation, the combination of artificial intelligence (AI) can help us in fight against the deadliest virus attack worldwide. This tool can be used to control and prevention of the outbreak disease. The AI tool can be helpful in prediction, detection, response, recovery, drug discovery of the disease. The AI-driven tools can be used in identifying the nature of outbreak as well as in forecasting the spread and coverage worldwide.

In this case, so many AI-based tools can be applied and trained using active learning-based models for the detection, prevention, treatment, and recovery of the patients. Also, they can help us for identifying infected persons from the non-infected to stop the spread of the virus. This chapter mainly focuses on the AI-assisted methodology and models that can help in fighting COVID-19.

Chapter 3

Karuna Salgotra, CT Institute of Engineering, Management, and Technology, Jalandhar, India

Vikas Khullar, Chitkara University Institute of Engineering and Technology, Rajpura, India

Harjit Pal Singh, CT Institute of Engineering, Management, and Technology, Jalandhar, India

Suyeb Ahmed Khan, Baba Kuma Singh Ji Group of Institute, Amritsar, India

Attention deficit hyperactivity disorder (ADHD) is a complex neuropsychiatric disorder in which the diagnosed behavior of ADHD individuals reflects negligence and hyperactivity. Around 5% of young kids and 2–4% of grown-ups are found to have ADHD or ADHD-related symptoms. This study aims to provide a detailed review of neuroimaging technologies for ADHD diagnoses such as tomography, electroencephalography (EEG), magneto encephalography (MEG), magnetic resonance imaging (MRI), etc. In the present era, the number of artificial intelligent, machine learning, deep learning algorithms have been introduced along with available advanced technologies and found to be helpful in the identification of ADHD like neuropsychiatric disorders. The work presented in this chapter summarizes the ADHD diagnosing technologies in combination with evolutionary artificial intelligence techniques, which lead to smart possibilities in ADHD diagnosis.

Chapter 4

Mmathapelo Makana, University of Johannesburg, South Africa

Nnamdi Nwulu, University of Johannesburg, South Africa

Eustace Dogo, University of Johannesburg, South Africa

Traditional irrigation systems do not take into consideration the conservation of water. Therefore, automating the plant watering systems to reduce water wastage and loss would be key to water conservation as a means of making use of water wisely and responsibly. In this chapter, a smart irrigation system that helps control the amount of water applied to crops is proposed and developed. The system controls the ON/OFF state of the water pumping motor based on the soil moisture sensor reading. Other sensors incorporated in the system are the water level sensor and light dependent resistor. The system leverages on the Arduino Uno microcontroller development board to collect input signals from the three sensors. The water pump operates depending on the value of the output signal received by the relay module. This technique of watering is feasible and very affordable and reduces human intervention in field watering.

Irrigation is an ancient practice that evolved over the years. Irrigation is the method through which a controlled amount of water is applied to plants making the most important recourse of irrigation. Earth is composed of 70% of water of which only 2.5% is fresh. Most of it trapped in snowfields and glaciers with only 0.007% of the earth's water for the needs of mankind. Limited water resources had become the main challenge in farming. In the chapter, machine learning algorithms and neural networks are used to reduce the usage of water in crop irrigation systems. This chapter focus on four mainstream machine learning calculations (KNN [k-nearest neighbor], GNB [Gauss Naive Bayes], SVM [support vector machine], DT [decision tree]) and a neural networks technique (artificial neural networks [ANN]) to expectation models utilizing the huge dataset (510 irrigation cases), bringing about productive and precise dynamic. The outcomes showed that k-nearest neighbors and artificial neural networks are the best indicators with the most elevated effectiveness of 98% and 90% respectively.

Chapter 6

Livestock management is a critical issue for the farming industry as proper management including their health and well-being directly impacts the production. It is difficult for a farmer or shed owner to monitor big herds of cattle manually. This chapter proposes a layered framework that utilizes the power of internet of things (IoT) and deep learning (DL) to real-time livestock monitoring supporting the effective management of cattle. The framework consists of sensor layer where sensor-rich devices or gadgets are used to collect various contextual data related to livestock, data processing layer which deals with various outlier rejections and processing of the data followed by DL approaches to analyze the collected contextual data in detecting sick and on heat animals, and finally, insightful information is sent to shed owner for necessary action. An experimental study conducted is helpful to make wise decisions to increase production cost-effectively. The chapter concludes with the different future aspects that may be further explored by the researchers.

Online social media (forums, blogs, and social networks) are increasing explosively, and utilization of these new sources of information has become important. Semantics plays a significant role in accurate analysis of an emotion speech context. Adding to this area, the already advanced semantic technologies have proven to increase the precision of the tests. Deep learning has emerged as a prominent machine learning technique that learns multiple layers or data characteristics and delivers state-of-the-art output. Throughout recent years, deep learning has been widely used in the study of sentiments, along with the growth of deep learning in many other fields of use. This chapter will offer a description of deep learning and its application in the analysis of sentiments. This chapter will focus on the semantic orientation-based approaches for sentiment analysis. In this work, a semantically enhanced methodology for the annotation of sentiment polarity in Twitter/ Facebook data will be presented.

Chapter 8

This work represents a simple method for motion transfer (i.e., given a source video of a subject [person] performing some movements or in motion, that movement/motion is transferred to amateur target in different motion). The pose is used as an intermediate representation to perform this translation. To transfer the motion of the source subject to the target subject, the pose is extracted from the source subject, and then the target subject is generated by applying the learned pose to-appearance mapping. To perform this translation, the video is considered as a set of images consisting of all the frames. Generative adversarial networks (GANs) are used to transfer the motion from source subject to the target subject. GANs are an evolving field of deep learning.

Chapter 9

Moving object detection and tracking is the process of identifying and locating the class objects such as people, vehicle, toy, and human faces in the video sequences more precisely without background disturbances. It is the first and foremost step in any kind of video analytics applications, and it is greatly influencing the high-level abstractions such as classification and tracking. Traditional methods are easily affected by the background disturbances and achieve poor results. With the advent of deep learning, it is possible to improve the results with high level features. The deep learning model helps to get more useful insights about the events in the real world. This chapter introduces the deep convolutional neural network and reviews the deep learning models used for moving object detection. This chapter also discusses the parameters involved and metrics used to assess the performance of moving object detection in deep learning model. Finally, the chapter is concluded with possible recommendations for the benefit of research community.

Chapter 10

Social media analytics keep on collecting the information from different media platforms and then calculating the statistical data. Twitter is one of the social network services which has ample amount of data where many users used post significant amounts of data on a regular basis. Handling such a large amount of data using traditional tools and technologies is very complicated. One of the solutions to this problem is the use of machine learning and deep learning approaches. In this chapter, the authors present a case study showing the use of Twitter data for predicting the election result of the political parties.

Pradnya Sulas Borkar, Jhulelal Institute of Technology, Nagpur University, Nagpur, India
Prachi U. Chanana, Jhulelal Institute of Technology, Nagpur University, Nagpur, India
Simranjeet Kaur Atwal, Jhulelal Institute of Technology, Nagpur University, Nagpur, India
Tanvi G. Londe, Jhulelal Institute of Technology, Nagpur University, Nagpur, India
Yash D. Dalal, Jhulelal Institute of Technology, Nagpur University, Nagpur, India

The new era of computing is internet of things (IoT). Internet of things (IoT) represents the ability of network devices to sense and collect data from around the world and then share that data across the internet where it can be processed and utilize for different converging systems. Most of the organisation and industries needs up-to-date data and information about the hardware machines. In most industries, HMI (human-machine interface) is used mostly for connecting the hardware devices. In many manufacturing industries, HMI is the only way to access information about the configuration and performance of machine. It is difficult to take the history of data or data analysis of HMI automatically. HMI is used once per machine which is quite hard to handle. Due to frequent use of HMI, it leads to loss of time, high costs, and fragility, and it needs to be replaced, which was found to be costlier. An internet of things (IOT) is a good platform where all the machines in the industry are able to be handled from a single IoT-based web portal.

Arnab Mitra, Siksha 'O' Anusandhan (Deemed), India
Sayantan Saha, Siksha 'O' Anusandhan (Deemed), India

A lightweight data security model is of much importance in view of security and privacy of data in several networks (e.g., fog networks) where available computing units at edge nodes are often constrained with low computing capacity and limited storage/availability of energy. To facilitate lightweight data security at such constrained scenarios, cellular automata (CA)-based lightweight data security model is presented in this chapter to enable low-cost physical implementation. For this reason, a detailed investigation is presented in this chapter to explore the potential capabilities of CA-based scheme towards the design of lightweight data security model. Further, a comparison among several existing lightweight data security models ensure the effectiveness for proposed CA-based lightweight data security model. Thus, application suitability in view of fog networks is explored for the proposed CA-based model which has further potential for easy training of a reservoir of computers towards uses in IoT (internet of things)-based multiple industry applications.

Hydroponics farming is fast gaining acceptance globally as an alternative and viable method of farming, instigated by the contemporary challenges posed by climate change, exploding population growth, and global food insecurity. Hydroponics farming can be greatly improved by leveraging on innovative technological advances that will allow for the effective and efficient utiliza-tion of limited natural resources such as water, energy (sunlight), and dwindling agricultural farmlands, consequently resulting in higher yields. This paper presents the design and implementation of an automated flood and drain hydroponic system with internet of things and Android application functionalities. The design is an integrated and automatic plant-watering, water level, and pH measurement and control system using Android application with wi-fi communication technology. Tests carried out proved the worka-bility of the system in line with expected design considerations.

The current proposal of C++20 features suggests that the coroutines will have dedicated support for the native language. This chapter will provide an analysis that is performed based on a comprehensive survey of coroutines that are used in the development process of the embedded systems and how they are used on dedicated platforms based on their constrained resources. Another important aspect of the work consists of analyzing the performance of designing and implementation of coroutines in software applications related to IoT and embedded devices focusing on the security vulnerabilities of the devices within an IoT ecosystem. The research analysis that forms the basis of the current work is based on metrics, such as software and hardware platform requirements, computation power, scenarios, advantages, and designing user interfaces based on the programming language used. The current work will be completed by adding a comparison with C# 8 programming language and C++20.

Preface

The last two and a half centuries have brought about stunning technological changes. Disruptive technologies, such as artificial intelligence (AI), machine learning, deep learning and analytics, software and advanced computer technologies, together with concepts such as Internet of Things (IoT) have pushed forward the era of digitalization. New and more advanced equipment and methodologies have arrived to push industrial capabilities to new heights and bring an ongoing automation of traditional manufacturing and industrial practices, using modern smart technology, which is generally, known as the Industry 4.0 concept and is currently, at the time of the writing of this book, gaining a large research attention. Large-scale machine-to-machine communication (M2M) and the IoT are integrated for increased automation, improved communication and self-monitoring, and production of smart machines that can analyze and diagnose issues without the need for human intervention.

AI is a set of concepts and technologies, which allows machines and computers to imitate human intelligence. AI is a set of a broad range of technologies, frameworks, and subsets with different application possibilities and advantages. Two main subsets of AI are machine learning and deep learning with inclusive relations within the subsets. Deep learning is a subset of machine learning, which is a scientific discipline and model based on fewer assumptions about the used data than traditional machine learning. Therefore, the model can manage more complex data sets and tasks, such as speech recognition, image interpretation, and natural language understanding. Deep learning consists of a number of deep networks with multiple feature layers of artificial neurons between the input and output data, which would process the raw data and focus on clustering and detecting patterns. Deep learning models continuously improve by learning feature detectors optimized for detecting and classifying patterns that enables them to outperform other models in the analysis of highly complex data set.

A solution is only as good as the data we have and how well these data are trained. The ability to select the right tools for the processing and analysis of the data obtained from the sensing environment and how to make these data accessible to the end user in the form of user-friendly applications is what allows to generate the value of these applications. While deep learning gives us the advantage of performing complex data analysis, IoT gives us the possibility to collect a multitude of data to be analysed. It triggers a series of experiences and services increasing the amount of data exchanged in real time, that is collected sensors and many more. IoT takes the basic concepts of M2M and expands them outward by creating large "cloud" networks of devices that communicate with one another through cloud networking platforms. The technologies used by IoT devices allow users to create fast, flexible, high-performance networks that connect a wide variety of devices.

What we gain by AI and its subsets, including deep learning, is that there is no more a query-based approach to collecting data, humans do not enter the data, they validate it, and take decisions based on the data pushed to them by the machines. AI has allowed to have high-quality, well-structured data and to extract the relevant context, by performing complex calculations to be applied to predictive and real-time decision-making for the provisions of multi-industry applications.

The material collected in this handbook has been edited to provide knowledge about the current research achievements and challenges in the area of deep learning and IoT for multi-industry applications. The book targets senior and junior engineers, undergraduate and post-graduate students, and anyone else interested in the trends, development and opportunities for the Industrial IoT concept. IIoT is an updated version of IoT applied for multi-industry applications to improve efficiency, data collections, data analysis, and decision making.

This book comprises fourteen chapters. It was impossible to include all current aspects of the research in the targeted area. However, the book provides a useful tool in terms of various possible methodology to be applied for the provision of multi-industry applications through use of deep learning and IoT.

Each chapter reflects a various application field and methodology.

Chapter 1 explores how deep learning can be applied to the area of healthcare, and, in particular, to improve cancer diagnosis. Many different types of image modalities like CT SCAN, ULTRASOUND, X-RAY, Magnetic Resonance Imaging (MRI) can be used to determine the disease but traditionally this purely had been dependent on the knowledge and experience of medical doctors. Machine learning and deep learning are providing robust solutions in this field. There are many deep learning techniques like RNN, CNN, DBN, Autoencoders, generative adversarial networks, which are providing robust solutions in cancer diagnosis and prognosis so that many human lives can be saved.

Chapter 2 focuses on how a technology can help fight global pandemics, such as COVID-19, which has been ongoing during the writing of this book. AI tool can be helpful in Prediction, Detection, Response, recovery, drug discovery of the disease. AI-driven tools can be used in identifying the nature of the outbreak as well as in forecasting the spread and coverage worldwide. AI-based tools can be applied and trained using active learning based models for the detection, prevention, treatment and recovery of the patients. Also, they can help identifying infected persons from the non-infected in order to stop the spread of the virus. This chapter mainly focuses on the AI-assisted methodology and models that can help fighting COVID-19.

Chapter 3 focuses on how intelligent neuroimaging can help with the diagnosis of Attention Deficit Hyperactivity Disorder (ADHD). This is a complex neuropsychiatric disorder, in which the diagnosed behavior of ADHD individuals reflects negligence, hastiness, and hyperactivity. Around 5% of young kids and 2–4% of grown-ups are found to have ADHD or ADHD-related symptoms. This study aims to provide a detailed review of neuroimaging technologies for ADHD diagnosis such as Tomography, Electroencephalography (EEG), Magneto Encephalography (MEG), MRI, etc. AI, machine learning, deep learning algorithms along with other advanced technologies can be helpful in the identification of ADHD like neuropsychiatric disorders. The work presented in this chapter summarizes the ADHD diagnosing technologies in combination with evolutionary AI techniques.

Chapter 4 presents an automated microcontroller-based irrigation system. Traditional irrigation systems do not put into consideration the conservation of water. Therefore, automating the plant watering systems to reduce water wastage and loss would be key to water conservation as a means of making use of water wisely and responsibly. In this chapter, a smart irrigation system that helps control the amount of water applied to crops has been proposed and developed. The system controls the ON/OFF state of the water pumping motor based on the soil moisture sensor reading. Other sensors incorporated in the system are the water level sensor and Light Dependent Resistor. The system leverages on the Arduino

Uno microcontroller development board to collect input signals from the three sensors. The water pump operates depending on the value of the output signal received by the relay module. This technique of watering is feasible and very affordable and reduces human intervention in field watering.

Chapter 5 explores how machine learning algorithms and neural networks can be used to reduce the usage of water in crop irrigation systems. This chapter focuses on five mainstream machine learning calculations, namely, KNN (K-Nearest Neighbor), GNB (Gauss Naive Bayes), SVM (Support Vector Machine), DT (Decision Tree) and the ANN (Artificial Neural Networks) technique to design expectation models utilizing the huge dataset (510 Irrigation cases), and bringing about productive and precise dynamics. The outcomes of the performed research show that K-Nearest Neighbor and ANNs are the best indicators with the most elevated effectiveness of 98% and 90%, respectively.

Chapter 6 applies the concepts of IoT and deep learning for livestock management, which is a critical issue for the farming industry as proper management including the animals health and well-being, directly impacts the production. It is difficult for a farmer or shed owner to monitor big herds of cattle manually. This chapter proposes a layered framework that utilizes the power of IoT and deep learning to real-time livestock monitoring supporting the effective management of cattle. The framework consists of a sensor layer where sensor-rich devices or gadgets are used to collect various contextual data related to livestock, a data processing layer, which deals with various outlier rejections and the processing of the data. Deep learning allows for analyzing the collected contextual data and detect sick and on heat animals, as an insightful information for necessary action. The chapter presents an experimental study on how to make wise decisions to increase production cost-effectively.

Chapter 7 analyses the impact of deep learning on semantic sentiment analysis. Online social media (forums, blogs, and social networks) is increasing explosively and utilization of these new sources of information has become important. Semantics plays a significant role in the accurate analysis of an emotion speech context. The advanced semantic technologies have proven to increase the precision of the tests. Deep learning has emerged as a prominent machine learning technique that learns multiple layers or data characteristics and delivers state-of-the-art output. Throughout recent years, deep learning has been widely used in the study of sentiments, along with the growth of deep learning in many other fields of use. This chapter has a focus on the semantic orientation based approaches for sentiment analysis. In this context, a semantically-enhanced methodology for the annotation of sentiment polarity in Twitter/Facebook data has been presented.

Chapter 8 presents research on Generative Adversarial Networks (GANs) as an evolving field of deep learning and how it can be used to support the transfer of the motion from a source subject to a target subject. A pose is used as an intermediate representation to perform this translation. To transfer the motion of the source subject to the target subject, the pose is extracted from the source subject and then the target subject is generated by applying the learned pose to-appearance mapping. To perform this translation the video is considered as a set of images consisting of all the frames.

Chapter 9 shows the use of deep learning for moving object detection and tracking. Moving object detection and tracking is the process of identifying and locating the class objects such as people, vehicle, toy, and human faces in the video sequences more precisely without background disturbances. It is the first and foremost step in any kind of video analytics applications and it is greatly influencing the high-level abstractions such as classification and tracking. Traditional methods are easily affected by the background disturbances and achieve poor results. With the advent of deep learning, it is possible to improve the results with high-level features. The deep learning model helps to get more useful insights about the events in real time. This book chapter introduces the deep convolutional neural network and reviews the deep learning models used for moving object detection. It also discusses the parameters involved and the metrics used to assess the performance of moving object detection in deep learning model. Finally, the possible recommendations for the benefit of the research community are also provided.

Chapter 10 explores the use of deep learning in Social Media Analysis and presents machine and deep Learning models for Social Media Analysis in politics. The social media analytics keeps on collecting the information from different media platforms and then calculates the statistical data. Twitter is one of the social network services, which has ample amount of data where many users post significant amount of information on regular basis. Handling such big amounts of data using traditional tools and technologies is very complicated. One of the solution to this problem is the use of a machine learning and a deep learning approach. In this chapter, a case study is presented showing the use of twitter data for predicting the election result of the political parties.

Chapter 11 presents the model of an IoT platform that can be used in an industrial setting to handle all machines from an IoT-based web portal. In industry, it is very important that up-to-date data and information about the hardware machines is available. Human Machine Interfaces (HMI) are used mostly for connecting the hardware devices and still are the only way to access information about the configuration and performance of a machine. It is difficult to take the history of data or data analysis of HMI automatically. In addition, HMI is used for once per machine, which is quite hard to handle and the frequent use of HMI leads to loss of time, is more expensive and delicate to handle, which is mitigated by the proposed IoT-based platform.

Chapter 12 proposes a cellular automata-based lightweight data security model for use in fog networks. Lightweight security is crucial when the available computing units at the edge nodes are often constrained with low computing capacity and limited storage / availability of energy. The Cellular Automata (CA)-based lightweight data security model can enable low-cost physical implementation. This chapter explores the potential capabilities of a CA-based scheme towards the design of lightweight data security model. Further, a comparison among several existing lightweight data security models ensures the effectiveness for the proposed here CA-based lightweight data security model. The application suitability in fog networks is explored, which have further potential for easy training of reservoir computers towards uses in IoT-based multiple industry applications.

Chapter 13 presents an automated hydroponic system integrated with an android smartphone application. Hydroponics farming is fast gaining acceptance globally as an alternative and viable method of farming, instigated by the contemporary challenges posed by climate change, exploding population growth and global food insecurity. Hydroponics farming can be greatly improved by leveraging on innovative technological advances that will allow for the effective and efficient utilization of limited natural resources such as water, energy (sunlight) and dwindling agricultural farmlands consequently resulting in higher yields. The chapter presents the design and implementation of an automated flood and drain hydroponic system with IoT and android application functionalities. The design is an integrated and automatic plant-watering, water level and pH measurement and control system using Android application with Wi-Fi communication technology. The results of carried out tests are presented, which prove the workability of the system inline with expected design considerations.

Chapter 14 presents an analysis that is performed based on a comprehensive survey of coroutines that are used in the development process of embedded systems and how they are used on resources-constrained dedicated platforms. Another important aspect of the work consists of analyzing the performance of designing and implementing of coroutines in software applications related to IoT and embedded devices focusing on the security vulnerabilities of the devices within an IoT ecosystem. The research analysis that forms the basis of the presented research is based on metrics, such as software and hardware platform requirements; computation power; the scenarios; advantages; and designing user interfaces based on the programming language used. A comparison with C# 8 programming language and C++20 has been also included.

AI and its subsets, machine learning and deep learning, together with advances in IoT are keep driving the value of various applications into other increasingly connected environments where there are massive opportunities for improving operational effectiveness and productivity. These technologies enable IIoT connectivity, platforms, and analytics solutions that can boost productivity and cost-effectiveness, maximize revenues and unlock new business models such as products as a service. Harnessing data from connected products and systems can boost productivity and efficiency while lowering costs.

Many open challenges still remain, for example, how to make products, services, and operations more secure and scalable. There are still no end-to-end security solutions and many of the devices rely on open software platforms that makes them even more vulnerable. However, the technologies used by IoT devices and powered by AI and its subsets allow users to create fast, flexible, high-performance networks that connect a wide variety of devices and bring data to serve multiple purposes and applications to the end user.

Acknowledgment

We sincerely would like to thank the Authors for their perceptive and constructive contribution for completion of this project. Their persistent efforts made this book possible.

We extend our sincere thanks to all the reviewers of the book who contributed to the improvement in the quality and the contents of the book.

Our gratitude goes to our organizations, Pimpri Chinchwad College of Engineering, Pune, India and CTIF Global Capsule, Arhus University, Denmark for providing a healthy academic and research environment during the completion of this project.

We also deeply acknowledge the continuous guidance of Dr. P. R. Deshmukh, Government College of Engineering, Nagpur, India and Dr. G. V. Parishwad, Director, Pimpri Chinchwad College of Engineering, for their expertise, dedication and continuous support.

We are also immensely grateful to our family members, friends and colleagues for their support. We express our gratitude to all of them.

Introduction

This book will emphasize on both theories and experimental processes for the applications of Deep Learning in Internet of Things (IoT) in multi industry applications.

The currently enabling Deep learning techniques and IoT are overpowering in every domain and reaching its boundaries. In today's world, we always keep hoarding intelligent agents and AI bots around us. A most recent AI technique that proves itself to solve many real world problems in Deep Learning. Deep learning algorithms are known for considerably efficient, high performing and are now effective standards for solving numerous industrial and social problems. IoT discusses emerging and developing domains of computer technology, which supports the communication between human, human-things and between things. Deep Learning algorithms have brought a revolution in Computer Vision applications too by introducing efficient solution to several image processing related problems that has long remained unresolved or moderately solved. In the recent years Deep Learning and Internet of things have made its way for various industrial applications in the areas healthcare, agriculture, object detection, social media analysis, and industry.

In a manner appropriate to comprehensive range of readers, the book covers various research domains in Deep Learning and IoT over the vast range of applications which are at their heart of smart computing problem. The book provides a useful tool in terms of various possible methodology to be applied for the provision of multi-industry applications through use of deep learning and IoT. This book presents the capabilities of Deep Learning and Internet of things for various industrial applications and how these methods could be used to solve the real world problems related to health, agriculture, social and engineering applications.

The book is organised in a way that reflects its objectives of enlightening the readers on how deep leaning and IoT can be applied in various industry domains. The book chapters are focused on some specific applications of Deep Learning and IoT ranges from healthcare industry, agriculture industry including livestock management, social medial analysis, moving object detection and tracking, Human Machine Interface in industry, semantic analysis, an automated hydroponic system. Each chapter of this book makes the readers walk through the recent advancements in the deep leaning and IoT and their applications in industry.

We hope that the research highlighted in the area of Deep Learning and IoT for solving various industrial applications, using combination of theoretical and experimental knowledge will help the readers who are entering in this exciting research domains. We committedly recommend this book to anyone looking research in the area of Deep learning and IoT.

Chapter 1
Deep Learning Techniques in Perception of Cancer Diagnosis

Anshul
Chandigarh University, Mohali, India

Raju Kumar
University Institute of Computing, Chandigarh University, Mohali, India

ABSTRACT

In this era of technology, for effective treatment of patients, clinical experts are getting great support from automated e-healthcare systems. Nowadays, one of the leading reasons of death is cancer. Some common cancers are breast cancer, prostate cancer, lung cancer, skin cancer, brain cancer, and so on. To save human lives from cancer, an effective and timely treatment is required. Many different types of image modalities like CT scan, ultrasound, x-ray, MRI can be used to determine the disease, but traditionally, this was purely dependent on the knowledge and experience of doctors. So, the death rate was quite high and increasing day by day. Machine learning and deep learning are providing robust solutions in this field. There are many deep learning techniques like RNN, CNN, DBN, autoencoders, generative adversarial networks which are providing robust solutions in cancer diagnosis and prognosis so that many human lives can be saved. The objective of this chapter is to give an insight into deep learning techniques in the field of a cancer diagnosis.

1. INTRODUCTION

Cancer is not a single disease but it is a huge group of diseases, which can occur in any tissue or organ of the body. When the unhealthy cells cultivate hysterically and go beyond their borderlines and attack the other adjoining parts of the body then the situation becomes more critical (WHO, 2020). According to American cancer statics 2020, approximately 1.8 million new patients suffering from cancer will be diagnosed, and near about 606,520 deaths in the USA will occur (NIH National Cancer, 2020). In developing countries or semi-developed countries, the situation is more critical. According to WHO, in India, in the coming years, one from ten Indians will be diagnosed with any type of cancer and one from

DOI: 10.4018/978-1-7998-7511-6.ch001

fifteen will die because of it (WHO, 2020), which is a very alarming situation. In men, prostate cancer, brain cancer, colorectal cancer, liver cancer, lung cancer, and stomach cancer are common whereas, in women breast cancer, thyroid cancer, cervical, colorectal are common. Till the time, the death rate is high and it is increasing rapidly. Detection at an early stage, quality treatment, and survivorship care can lead to an improvement in the survival rate. So, there is always a requirement of some computer-aided system, which can accurately and timely detect cancer and help the doctors to save their patient's life. In today's scenario, many medical image modalities are there, which can be used in finding the accurate diagnosis of the disease. Medical experts mostly do this elucidation of the image data, which can be time-consuming, and also extensive disparities can occur between various interpreters. Machine learning and deep learning are providing many solutions in this area. There are many methods in machine learning like SVM, K-nearest neighbor, Random Forest, Decision tree, etc., which are showing good results in this area but the problem in all methods of machine learning is that feature learning cannot be done by the machine itself so it is quite a time consuming and costly process. Deep Learning is precipitously becoming a methodology of choice for medical image analysis as it is offering exciting solutions with good accuracy (Razzak, Naz, & Zaib, 2018).In deep learning, the neural network can learn the features automatically, which makes it more popular than machine learning techniques. Various deep learning techniques like RNN, DNN, CNN (Pereira, Pinto, Alves, & Silva, 2016), Fast RCNN (Girshick, 2015), Faster RCNN (Ren, He, Girshick, & Sun, 2017) which can be used in different application areas of medical image analysis like segmentation, disease categorization, abnormality exposure, etc (Anwar et al., 2018). This chapter is discussing the various deep learning techniques, evaluation criteria with the help of which deep learning techniques can be chosen for cancer diagnosis, applications of deep leaning in cancer diagnosis and problems in implementing deep learning.

2. RELATED WORK

Deep learning is showing its capabilities in attaining higher accuracy in diagnosis as compared to other domain experts. Several research-oriented entities are emboldening the companies to do work in the field of tumor detection using different deep learning techniques.

a) Breast Cancer

Breast cancer is an invasive tumor. Chemotherapy, surgery, radiations, hormone therapy can be used as a treatment. A deep neural network is providing good solutions in breast cancer detection. In a paper (Albayrak & Bilgin, 2017) deep neural network is used to detect the mitosis with the help of breast histopathological images. In this paper, for feature extraction, CNN is used followed by SVM used for mitosis detection. The paper (Gezahegn, 2020) used a faster R-CNN network to diagnose breast cancer. For this, for feature extraction, CNN is used then RPN(region proposal network) and ROI of faster RCNN is used for detection. The results showed 91.86% accuracy and 94.67% sensitivity in the detection of breast cancer. The paper (Ebg, 2016) used CNN to detect breast cancer using the histopathological image. The paper (Dhungel, Carneiro, & Bradley, 2015) concentrated on mass detection from mammograms as mass detection can be a challenging problem because of shape variations and variations in boundary, size, and texture. In the paper, (Dhungel et al., 2015) suggested a novel deep learning method using a cascaded deep convolutional method and random forest classifiers. The results show the true positivity rate of 0.96 ± 0.03 at 1.2 false positives for each image using dataset INbrest and 0.75 at 4.8 false positives for each image on the DDSM-BCRP dataset. In the paper (Swiderski, Kurek, Osowski, Kruk, & Barhoumi, 2017) used CNN to analyze the benign and malignant breast cancer. To improve the accuracy the non-negative matrix factorization and statistical self-similarity of the image are applied. Similarly stacked convolutional sparse autoencoder, RNN, autoencoders, DBN also applied by different researchers to improve the results. The paper (Guan, 2019) used GAN and CNN to detect breast cancer. They used GAN for data augmentation and then CNN for detection purposes. The paper (Danaee, Ghaeini, & Hendrix, 2017) suggested stacked denoising autoencoders for feature extraction followed by an evaluation done by a supervised classification model. The results showed that exceedingly interactive genes could be extremely convenient for cancer biomarkers.

b) Brain Cancer

Brain and central nervous system, which controls all the body functions. When the tumor grows in the brain it can impinge on the human being's thought processes. The brain tumor can be primary and secondary. Glioma is the most common primary brain cancer. Glioma and non-glioma are two categories of brain cancer. Some gliomas are Astrocytoma, Ependymoma, Brain stem glioma, Oligodendroglioma whereas Meningioma, Pineal gland, and pituitary gland tumors, Medulloblastoma, Craniopharyngioma, and Schwannoma lie under the non-gliomas category. There are four different grades are there grade -I, II, III, IV (Tandel et al., 2019). The first two grades I, II are slow-growing tumors also called the benign stage of tumor whereas grade III, IV are the stages in which tumor cells grow very aggressively, also called the malignant stage. The brain tumor is the 10th most customary reason of death. (Amin, Sharif, Anjum, Raza, & Bukhari, 2020) To diagnose brain tumor different tools like CT-SCAN, MRI, angiography (X-RAY), biopsy, nuclear medicine bone scan (capturing images of bones on film or computer) are used. Deep learning techniques use these image modalities to diagnose cancer. The paper (Ghassemi, Shoeibi, & Rouhani, 2020) used GAN and DNN for tumor classification. The paper (Amin et al., 2020) used CNN for glioma on different datasets. Li Li et al (Li, Li, & Wang, 2019) used an FCNN with U-NET for brain tumor segmentation. The paper (Lo, Chen, Weng, & Hsieh, n.d.) used deep learning techniques to grade the tumor. In the paper, (Kaldera, Gunasekara, & DIssanayake, 2019) used R-CNN to classify and segment the brain tumor using MRI images. Fast R-CNN (Girshick, 2015), V-net (Milletari, Navab, & Ahmadi, 2016), CNN (Albayrak & Bilgin, 2017; Pereira et al., 2016),3D CNN with fully connected CRF (Kamnitsas et al., 2017) are some recent research in which deep neural network used to segment, classify and grade the brain tumor.

c) Lung Cancer

Lung cancer is one of the most common cancers in the whole world. According to the American Cancer Society in the US approximately total new cases of lung cancer will be 228,820 (men and women both) and deaths will be 135,720 in 2020(American Cancer Society center (US), 2020). In Lung cancer, cancer starts from lungs and immediately spreads in the other portion of the body like breast, brain, prostate, etc. The paper (Lakshmanaprabu, Mohanty, Shankar, Arunkumar, & Ramirez, 2019) used optimal deep neural network and linear discriminate analysis (LDA) using CT imaging modalities. LDA is used for the feature's dimensionality reduction then ODNN classifies the lung cancer using Modified Gravitational Search Algorithm (MGSA). The precision is 94.56% in lung cancer classification. The paper (Tikade

& Rajeswari, 2018) used U-NET architecture and 3D multipath VGG like architecture in the detection and classification of lung cancer and gave 95.60% accuracy. In the paper, (Saba, 2019) used two deep 3D customized mixed link networks (CMixNet) for detection and classification with CT images to give sensitivity 94% and sensitivity 91%.

d) Skin Cancer

Skin cancer originates from the epidermics that is the superficial skin layer. This is cancer because of the unusual growth of the skin cell. Basal cell carcinoma (most common), squamous cell carcinoma, and melanoma are the most common type of cancer. American Cancer Society melanoma estimates about the melanoma cases 100,350 new cases and deaths 6850 will occur in the USA in 2020. If some suspicious changes occur then checking skin can detect skin cancer at its early stage which leads to a great chance of successful skin cancer treatment. Deep learning is also giving prominent results in skin cancer diagnosis. The paper (Kadampur & Al Riyaee, 2020) used a DL model to detect skin cancer and achieved AUC of 99.77% in cancer detection. The paper (Jafari et al., 2016) used a DCNN for accurate extraction of the lesion region. Dori et al (Dorj, Lee, Choi, & Lee, 2018) used AlexNet for feature extraction followed by ECOC SVM for skin cancer classification. The accuracy, sensitivity, and specificity achieved was 95.1%,98.9%, and 94.17% respectively. Another paper (Codella et al., 2017) used deep learning model for melanoma. The paper (Vasconcelos & Vasconcelos, 2017) also used a deep convolutional neural network to classify melanoma.

e) Prostate Cancer

Prostate cancer is especially found in men. Normally, men who are 65 or older suffer from this disease. According to a study, In the USA 6 out of 10 men who are more than 65 years old suffered from this disease. If prostate cancer is diagnosed at an early stage then the death rate can be very low due to the slow progression of cancer. So, Early detection and effective monitoring are vital for improving the patient's survival. The paper (Yoo, Gujrathi, Haider, & Khalvati, 2019) used a DCNN on diffusion-weighted magnetic resonance imaging and accomplished an area under the receiver operating characteristic curve (AUC) at slice level 0.87 and at patient level 0.84. The paper (Bulten et al., 2020) proposed a deep learning system to grade biopsies. The grading system followed was the Gleason grading system. In the paper (Schelb et al., 2019) used U-NET architecture for detection and segmentation of lesions suspicious for SPC using MRI images. To diagnose prostate cancer at the early stage Rela (Reda et al., 2018) developed a CAD system. For this, they used both prostates specific antigen and diffusion-weighted MRI imaging modalities. They consumed stacked nonnegativity constraint sparse autoencoders for the diagnosis of prostate cancer and achieved 94.4% accuracy, sensitivity 88.9%, and specificity 100%. In the paper, Liu et al (S. Liu, Zheng, Feng, & Li, 2017) compared deep learning techniques and non-deep learning techniques with the help of SIFT image feature and bag -of-word for image analysis and recognition. Results showed deep learning is giving better results than a non-deep learning technique.

3. MAIN FOCUS OF THE CHAPTER

The foremost objective of this chapter is to understand the field of oncology with the help of deep learning techniques. In the current era, the deep neural network is showing prominent results in the field of a cancer diagnosis. The focus is to understand the basic concept of cancer diagnosis and deep learning techniques with the help of medical image analysis which is helpful in cancer detection on time. This chapter is also focusing on the limitations of deep learning and giving some future directions in which research can be done so that more human lives can be saved.

4. MEDICAL IMAGE MODALITIES

Medical imaging insinuates to the procedures used to originate the images of different human body's organs for diagnostic and therapeutic purposes within digital life. These medical images allow doctors to look inside your body for clues regarding a medical condition. There are many types of image modalities, which can be used in the medical field some most popular modalities are:

a) Computed Tomography Imaging (CT-SCAN)

In CT scans, the X-ray beam rotates a portion of the body with a sequence of images taken at different angles. This information is used by the machine to create a 2-dimensional (2D) image frame of an image and then combine it to create a 3D (3D) image to provide a better view of the organs. Doctors use CT Scan For Fractures, Cancers, blood clots, heart disease, internal bleeding, etc. To visualize the internal organs, blood cells, upper body parts like spine, chest, sinuses, etc. this imaging modality can be used.

b) Magnetic Resonance Imaging

MRI is a radiation-free technique. In MRI images there are different sequences, each one having its features. The most common MRI sequences are Tl –weighted, T2-weighted, and FLAIR. (Abd-ellah, Ismail, Khalaf, & Hamed, 2019)

- **Tl -weighted** The scan is generated by a TE (short echo time) and TR (repetition time). The brightness and contrast of the image are determined by the T1 properties of the tissue.
- **T2-weighted** scans are produced by longer TE time and TR time. This MRI sequence is weak in water content so it is appropriate to the disorder where water accumulates inside the tissue.
- **Fluid attenuated recovery inversion (FLAIR)** analogous to a T2-weighted image without its detection protocol. For the early detection of cancer, this MRI sequence can be used.

c) Positron Emission Tomography (PET)

PET images stipulate an overview of the metabolic process in the body. The essence of PET imaging is that this method perceives in pairs of gamma radiation generated indirectly by a positron radionuclide. The tracer is inserted into the vein by an active molecule, usually the sugar used for cellular energy. PET imaging systems have weak scanning panels for capturing gamma emission inside the body and use software to program absorb emission sources, producing integrated 3-D images for future focus on the body.

d) Ultrasound Imaging

Ultrasound imaging uses high-speed sound waves to peer into the body and can show the internal organ's movement and blood flow through the blood vessels. Unlike X-ray imaging, no ionizing radiation is compatible with the concept of ultrasound.

On ultrasound examination, the transducer (probe) is placed directly on the skin or inside the opening of the body. A thin layer of gel is inserted into the skin so that ultrasound waves are transmitted from the probe through the gel to the body. (Anwar et al., 2018) Ultrasound images are generated based on the reflection of the waves from the physical structures. The amplitude of the sound signal and the time it takes for the wave to travel through the body provide the information needed to produce the image.

e) Histology Imaging

Histology imaging is pictures of cells, tissues, and organs that can be get with the help of a microscope. It explores the interplay between structure and function. The histology guide provides information about the visual arts of detecting the formation of cells and tissues and also understanding how this is determined by their functioning. Instead of duplicating the information contained in the histology text, the user is shown how to use this information to interpret cells and tissues as viewed by a microscope.

5. EVALUATION METRICS

The efficiency of the technique in detecting cancer can be evaluated on the different criteria. Some common performance measures are

a) Accuracy

Accuracy refers to closeness with real value. Mathematically, Accuracy can be calculated as

$$Accuracy = \left(TP + TN\right) / \left(TP + TN + FP + FN\right) \text{(Anwar et al., 2018)}$$

Where

TP= True Positive
TN= True Negative
FP=False Positive
FN=False Negative

b) Precision

Precision is how congruous the result is when the measurements are repeated.

$$Precision = TP / (TP + FP)$$ (Anwar et al., 2018)

c) Recall

The recall is used to find out the classifier's capability to calculate all relevant samples.

$$Recall = TP / (TP + FN)$$ (Anwar et al., 2018)

d) F_1 Score

Also called F-measure. F_1 score is generally used to check test accuracy.
The formula to calculate F_1 score is

$$F_1 \, score = 2 * \left(\frac{Precision * Recall}{Precision + Recall} \right)$$ (Anwar et al., 2018)

e) Sensitivity

In medical image analysis, it tells us how likely the result will be positive if the image has those characteristics. This is calculated as

Sensitivity= TP/(TP+FN)

f) Specificity

In medical image analysis, it tells us how likely the result will be positive if the image has those characteristics. This is calculated as

Specificity= TN/(TN+FP)

g) Dice Score

It is used to measure how the two objects are related. In medical images, the dice score is generally used in segmentation.

Dice Score = 2*TP/(2*TP+FP+FN)

Based on results shown by different deep learning techniques, CNN is showing promising results in all fields like segmentation, classification, registration, detection in medical images.

6. DEEP LEARNING TECHNIQUES FOR CANCER DETECTION

There are several deep learning techniques based on supervised learning and unsupervised learning, those are giving prominent results in the healthcare sector, especially in the diagnosis of cancer.

a) Convolutional Neural Network (CNN)

In the current era, CNN is the utmost popular deep learning technique, which is giving promising results in the healthcare sector especially in cancer detection. (Abd-ellah et al., 2019; Lo et al., n.d.; Mittal et al., 2019) In CNN, the signal is passed from layer to layer in forwarding direction without forming any cycle. Mathematically, it can be expressed as

$$F\left(a\right) = f_{.}(f)_{.1}(........(f)(a))) \text{ (Sun, 2018)}$$

Where

n = No of hidden layers
F_k = corresponding function at the layer k

In CNN, one functional layer includes a convolutional layer, activation layer, pooling layer, fully connected layer, and output layer.

Figure 1. Convolutional neural network (CNN)
(Hesamian, Jia, He, & Kennedy, 2019)

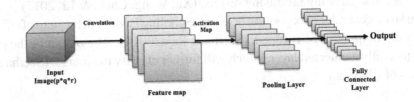

The first layer is a convolutional layer that yields the medical image as input, which is in the form of the pixel that can be expressed as a matrix (p*q*r) where 'p' stands for the height, 'q' stands for the width and 'r' for the image's depth. By convolving the filter map with the input image presents an effect called the activation map. In this layer, f is a combination of numerous convolutional kernel (x^1, x^2... x^{i-1}, x^i). Here each x^i is the linear function at i^{th} kernel. (Sun, 2018) Mathematically, it can be calculated as

$$x^i\left(a,b\right) = \sum_{p=-h}^{h}\sum_{q=-w}^{w}\sum_{r=-d}^{d}W_i\left(p,q,r\right)Y\left(a-p\right)\left(b-q\right)\left(c-r\right)\text{(Sun, 2018)}$$

In this equation

(a, b, c) = Pixel position in the input Y.
W_i = Weight at the ith kernel
(p, q, r) = length, breadth and depth of the filter respectively.

The **activation map** highlights how the filter is affecting the input. The activation layer lies between the convolutional layer and the pooling layer (Tandel et al., 2019). The activation function is a node that is placed either in between or at the end of the neural network. The main purpose of this function is to decide that either the neuron will activate or not. Some activation functions are there like sigmoid, tanh, ReLU.

Mathematical presentation of activation functions

1. Sigmoid function: $\left(\sigma\left(z\right)\right) = \dfrac{1}{1+e^{-z}}$

2. Tanh(z) = $\dfrac{2}{1+e^{2z}}$

3. ReLU Function f(z)= max(0,z) (Tandel et al., 2019)

4. Leaky ReLU function: f(z)= max(0.1z,z)

5. MaxOut function : f(z) = max $\left(w_1^T z + b_1, w_2^T z + b_2\right)$

6. ELU function = $\begin{cases} z \; if \; z \geq 0 \\ \alpha\left(e^z - 1\right) if \; z < 0 \end{cases}$

ReLU function is usually used as an activation function as it is computationally efficient, does not saturate at a positive region, and converts all negative inputs to zero. Leaky ReLU, parametric ReLU, randomize ReLU are also showing promising results. (Xu, Wang, Chen, & Li, 2015) .

In the pooling layer, generally max pooling or average pooling layer with the help of which dimensionality of convolution's output can be reduced. (Seetha & Raja, 2018) . The output of the pooling layer is finally provided to a fully connected layer, which will further classify the image. (Seetha & Raja, 2018).

Different types of CNNs are

1. **2D CNN**: In 2D CNN input images are used on which 2D filter is applied. It is the traditional CNN(Seetha & Raja, 2018). In 2D CNN, a 2D convolutional kernel is used which is capable to leverage context through the height and width of the slice to make the prediction.

2. **3D CNN**: The problem of not able to take the leverage context from adjacent slices in 2D CNN is solved by 3D CNN with the help of a 3D convolutional kernel. 3D CNN three parameters of image height, width, and depth are measured (Erden, Gamboa, & Wood, n.d.). This type of CNN is used, when more powerful volumetric representation is required (Erden et al., n.d.). 3D CNN provides better results in comparison to 2D CNN as the human body is also 3D in nature.in 3D CNN computational cost is still an issue.

3. **R-CNN**: In R-CNN instead of a pursuit of a colossal volume of information selective search t is done dependent on regions (Girshick et al. 2014) CNN first functions as an element extractor and contributes SVM to arrange the item. There are numerous issues in it like a specific hunt, a ton of preparing time required.

4. **Fast R-CNN**: In this, the medical image is straightforwardly given to CNN then identification of region followed by enveloping in the square is completed. At that point with the assistance of roll pooling layer reshaping is done which will be taken care of to the FC layer. At that point, the SoftMax function is normally used to foresee the proposed region class and boundary box's offset value. (Girshick 2015)

5. **Faster R-CNN:** Previous both R-CNN and Fast R-CNN used CPU dependent region proposal algorithm, which can affect the computational cost. To take care of this issue, a discrete convolutional organize is utilized for region proposal prediction which is additionally reshaped by the pooling layer to arrange the image. (Girshick et al. 2014)

Several CNN architecture is proposed by researchers from time to time to handle the problem of cancer detection. The already proposed are LeNet, AlexNet, ZFNet, GoogleNet/Inception V1, VGGNet, ResNet etc.

b) Fully Convolutional Networks (FCN)

In FCN, the up-sampling layer and deconvolutional layer replaced the fully connected layer of CNN. FCN produces the score map for each class, which has the same size, is of the input image, and also groups the image pixel by pixel. (Munir, Elahi, Ayub, Frezza, & Rizzi, 2019) The skip up connection (upsampling layer + deconvolutional layer) also improves the accuracy. FCN is used to develop many deep-learning algorithms to handle numerous applications. E.g. different types of FCN like Focal FCN, cascaded FCN can be used in brain tumor detection (Li et al., 2019), breast cancer detection, and so on.

Figure 2. Fully Convolutional Network
(Munir et al., 2019)

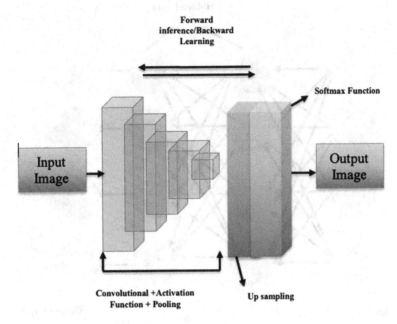

c) Recurrent Neural Network

RNN utilizes repetitive associations, which encourages the model to gain from past inputs. This neural network can remove the interslice context from the information. This type of neural network is entitled to RNN as they take the output from the last computation to perform the new operations. They can save precious results in memory. Many types of RNN are in use like LSTM(Shahzadi, Meriadeau, Tang, & Quyyum, 2019), Gated Recurrent Unit, Clockwork RNN.

Figure 3. Recurrent Neural Network

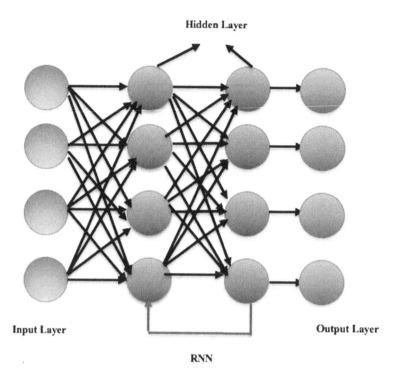

RNN model computes the function 'f' and output sequence 'c' using the equation

$$f_i = F(W_{af}a_i + W_{ff}f_{i-1} + b_f) \text{ (Munir et al., 2019)}$$

$$o_i = W_{fo} + b_{co} \text{ (Munir et al., 2019)}$$

Here,

'f' is the hidden vector sequence $(f_1, f_2, \ldots \ldots, f_i)$
'a' is the input sequence $(a_1, a_2, \ldots \ldots, a_i)$ by iteration of i =1 to I.
'o' is output sequence $(o_1, o_2, \ldots \ldots, o_i)$
'F' is hidden layer function generally sigmoid function

d) U-NET

Ronneberger proposed an architecture based on the fully convolutional network(FCN) called U-Net. (Ronneberger, Fischer, & Brox, 2015)This architecture is providing timely and accurate results. In this architecture upsampling is used in place of the pooling layer. Contraction, Bottleneck, and expansion are there in the U-Net architecture e.g. In U-Net architecture, the max pool follows convolutional layers. Similarly, in the bottleneck layer and expansion layer, up a max pool follows the convolutional layers.

The expansion layer and contraction layer are connected directly also which means the expansion layer will also be updated whenever the contraction layer will be reconstructed

e) V-NET

Milletari et al proposed V-Net (Milletari et al., 2016) in which convolutional as far as kernel size and stride are given to the contracting way for decreasing the resolution and extricating features. The extension part extracts the features, goes along with it with low-goals includes guide, and delivers yield.

f) Generative Adversarial Networks (GANS)

Goodfellow (Goodfellow, Pouget-abadie, Mirza, Xu, & Warde-farley, 2014) proposed a generative adversarial network(GAN). This network model has two neural networks, those are pitting against each other to produce novel and artificial instances that can work as real data. The two networks are called generator and discriminator respectively. The former is responsible to produce the new data instance and the latter one is used to check whether the data instance belongs to a real training dataset or not. The conditional generative adversarial network is also used in cancer detection

g) Auto-Encoder (AEs)

In Unsupervised learning, Autoencoders are used. These are feed-forward networks. Autoencoders learn the feature representation with dimensionality reduction from the data themselves (Munir et al., 2019). Encoder, Code, and decoder are the three components of AE. The encoder will encode the image data 'a' into 'c' by weight matrix and bias using equation

$$c = \sigma\left(W_{ac}a + b_{ac}\right) \text{(Sun, 2018)}$$

here 'σ' is an activation function.

At the decoder side, 'c' is decoded to regenerate the output $\hat{a}$ with the help of new weight $W_{c\hat{a}}$ (Transpose of weight matrix W_{ac}) and $b_{c\hat{a}}$ which is a new bias.

$$\hat{a} = \sigma'\left(W_{c\hat{a}}c + b_{c\hat{a}}\right) \text{(Sun, 2018)}$$

The min error on which autoencoder can be trained is

$$\arg\max_{Wb} \| a - \widehat{a} \|^2$$

In deep learning, some other types of autoencoders also exist.

1. In **Stacked Autoencoders,** for 'n' number of hidden layers, there is the stacking of 'n' autoencoders which is further followed by fine-tuning with the help of any supervised method. In this type of

autoencoder firstly, training is done and then a feature vector is formed which will act as an input to the next layer. (G. Liu, Bao, & Han, 2018)The process will repeat until the end of the hidden layer. Then backpropagation is used for cost minimization. (G. Liu et al., 2018)

2. In **Sparse Autoencoders** (SAE), sparsity is used in the hidden layers by increasing the count of nodes such that the hidden layer becomes loftier than the input layer. In this, the hidden layer is trained as SAE which will act as input to the next upcoming layer. In this at low-level SAE, feature extraction is done and then the number of SAE combined to act as an input to the high-level SAE on which further extraction can be performed.

3. In **Convolutional Autoencoders (CAE),** fully connected layers of AE are supplanted by a convolutional network(Cheng, Sun, Takeuchi, & Katto, 2018). As there is a spatial relationship that exists between the pixel so it is better than stacked autoencoders.to reconstruct the image essential features are extracted. CAE is more suited for high dimensional images as its parameter's count to develop an activation map never changed. (Cheng et al., 2018).

h) Restricted Boltzmann Machine (RBM)

Restricted Boltzmann machine has two layers: a visible layer and a hidden layer. These layers are arranged according to the bipartite graph means each node of a visible node is connected to each layer of the hidden layer but not within the same layer (Zhang, Ding, Zhang, & Xue, 2018). Using contrastive divergence algorithm performing Gibbs sampling, RBM is trained to amplify the multiplication of probabilities that are allocated to each pattern in the training set (Munir et al., 2019). RBM is showing good results not only with DBN (deep belief network), deep Boltzmann but also with the convolutional neural network it is performing well.

i) Deep Belief Network

A deep belief network is a model that can be demarcated as the stack of restricted Boltzmann machines. In this, each RBM layer (visible layer and hidden layer) communicates with the former and succeeding layer both. At the end of the RBM, softmax function can be there which can help in clustering the unlabeled data. The energy function used by RBM is

$$E\left(s,t\right) = x^{T}s - y^{T}t - s^{T}Yt \text{ (Zhang et al., 2018)}$$

Here,

x = visible layer's bias vector
y= hidden layer's bias vector

7. APPLICATIONS OF DEEP LEARNING TECHNIQUES IN CANCER DETECTION

Cancer is a life-threatening disease. It can originate anywhere in the body. Cancer cells are further distinguished according to their origin e.g. breast cancer, lung cancer, brain cancer, etc. According to all present studies, it is clear that the death rate increase as cancer goes to the advanced stages. So, to improve the survival rate early detection is a must. Manually, it is very time consuming and dependent on the doctor's experience. According to Nvidia, in breast cancer diagnosis deep learning drops an 85% error rate. (Nvidia, 2016). There are several examples to spectacle the impact of deep learning in the field of oncology e.g.

1. Deep learning is very helpful in detecting cancer at an early stage with the help of gene data. (Danaee et al., 2017) Gene data is very complex because of its high dimensionality but some researchers from Oregon state university was able to extract required features from gene expression data with the help of deep learning techniques for breast cancer (Danaee et al., 2017).

2. Deep learning can accurately segment the tumor and classify between malignant and benign tumors which can provide great help in oncology. CNN succeeds in performing in par with all specialists when classifying almost all types of cancer like skin cancer, brain cancer, breast cancer, etc. One example is Google CNN's system. It can distinguish the deadline skin cancer more accurately as compared to practitioners. The convolutional neural network is also giving a robust performance in lung cancer diagnosis, which is one of the leading cancer in the whole world. Deep learning techniques can detect the cancer cells in the very early stage which can lead to successful tumor diagnosis.

3. Traditionally examination through the microscope of tissues was used to examine the symptoms of the problem in the human body. By using deep learning techniques some researchers were also able to enhance the efficiency of histopathologic slide analysis such that diagnosis objectivity can be increased.

4. Deep learning is also useful in measuring the size of the tumor and to perceive the new metastases that might be ignored e.g. Google Research is working hard in developing deep learning tools using various image modalities like CT-SCAN, MRI, etc. that can surely complement the pathological workflow.

5. Prognosis means estimating the seriousness of cancer and also the possible chance of survival. Deep learning can also be used to develop a prediction model for the prognosis of the patient and undergoing treatment.

6. Deep learning techniques can also be used for the qualification of tumor-infiltrating immune cells in breast cancer which is considered as an emerging prognostic biomarker. (Turkki, Linder, Kovanen, Pellinen, & Lundin, 2016)

8. DISCUSSION AND FUTURE DIRECTIONS

Deep learning is playing a vigorous role in various health care areas such as the cancer cells and healthy cells, doctor's assistance, imaging diagnosis, digital pathology, and many more. Cancer prognosis is the probabilities of cancer reoccurrence and progression, estimation of cancer's fate, and to provide the survival estimation of the cancer patients. The accurate prediction of cancer prognosis will impressively advantageous in the treatment of cancer patients. Deep learning can also be linked to a multitude of emerging mobile health interfaces to develop digital biomarkers which are very helpful in the prediction of clinical outcomes. Although different deep learning techniques either supervised, unsupervised, or semi-supervised are showing effective results convolutional neural network is giving better results. CNN based models are giving almost the same results as a human in object detection and image classification. Different CNN architecture like LeNet-5, AlexNet (2012), ZFNet (2013), GoogLeNet/Inception, VGGNet, ResNet, U-Net, V-Net is used in the number of research paper to study and analyze the tumor.

Although, CNN is giving excellent results still there are some problems on CNN which are yet to be solved. CNN is performing well in structured data but in case of unstructured data it is not performing up to the mark. Deep learning techniques are black boxes in nature but in the case of cancer diagnosis, it is a problem. Deep Learning neural networks can also be used in protein structure prediction, classification of cells in the distinct stage of mitosis, and also in prediction of the future lineage of progenitor cells. Another deep learning future target in cancer diagnosis is drug development. A convolutional neural network is also very useful in implications for oncologic immunotherapy development. One of the major limitations in a deep neural network is the dataset as a deep learning model require a large amount of data for training purpose. Less availability of datasets can also lead to the problem of overfitting. Transfer learning, data augmentation, and GAN can solve the problem of less availability of the dataset. The establishment of public accessed databases like Cancer Genome Atlas (TCGA), Gene Expression Omnibus (GEO) and Genotype-Tissue Expression, BraT, ISLES, and many more are available for researchers to analyze the patients' multi-omics data and apply novel methods and perform predictions in cancer prognosis.

9. CONCLUSION

Deep learning suggests a generic model and requires comparatively less data engineering yet gives a prominent solution in detecting cancer more accurately. This chapter discussed various deep learning techniques, medical image modalities, the evaluation criteria that can be used to check the performance of deep learning algorithms. A literature survey showed that deep learning techniques on different types of cancers like brain cancer, breast cancer, lung cancer, etc. using different image modalities like CT-SCAN, MRI, X-Ray, etc. it is analyzed that convolutional neural network is leading among all of the currently present techniques. Deep learning overcomes the machine learning problems and with the support of graphics processing unit(GPU), massively parallel architecture, and burst of multi-omics data which includes genomics data, clinical information, and transcriptomics data, it gained tremendous success. Many organizations like the American Society of Clinical Oncology (ASCO) and American Society for Radiation Oncology (ASTRO), National Institutes of Health (NIH), and many more in this area helping the researchers in improving the cancer prognosis solutions.

REFERENCES

Abd-ellah, M. K., Ismail, A., Khalaf, A. A. M., & Hamed, H. F. A. (2019). A review on brain tumor diagnosis from MRI images : Practical implications, key achievements, and lessons learned. *Magnetic Resonance Imaging*, *61*(May), 300–318. doi:10.1016/j.mri.2019.05.028 PMID:31173851

Albayrak, A., & Bilgin, G. (2017). Mitosis detection using convolutional neural network based features. *CINTI 2016 - 17th IEEE International Symposium on Computational Intelligence and Informatics: Proceedings*, 335–340. 10.1109/CINTI.2016.7846429

American Cancer Society center (US). (2020). *Brain cancer statics*. Author.

Amin, J., Sharif, M., Anjum, M. A., Raza, M., & Bukhari, S. A. C. (2020). Convolutional neural network with batch normalization for glioma and stroke lesion detection using MRI. *Cognitive Systems Research*, *59*, 304–311. doi:10.1016/j.cogsys.2019.10.002

Anwar, S. M., Majid, M., Qayyum, A., Awais, M., Alnowami, M., & Khan, M. K. (2018). Medical Image Analysis using Convolutional Neural Networks: A Review. *Journal of Medical Systems*, *42*(11), 226. Advance online publication. doi:10.100710916-018-1088-1 PMID:30298337

Bulten, W., Pinckaers, H., van Boven, H., Vink, R., de Bel, T., van Ginneken, B., van der Laak, J., Hulsbergen-van de Kaa, C., & Litjens, G. (2020). Automated deep-learning system for Gleason grading of prostate cancer using biopsies: A diagnostic study. *The Lancet. Oncology*, *21*(2), 233–241. doi:10.1016/S1470-2045(19)30739-9 PMID:31926805

Cheng, Z., Sun, H., Takeuchi, M., & Katto, J. (2018). Deep Convolutional AutoEncoder-based Lossy Image Compression. *2018 Picture Coding Symposium, PCS 2018 - Proceedings*, 253–257. 10.1109/PCS.2018.8456308

Codella, N. C. F., Pankanti, S., Gutman, D. A., Helba, B., Halpern, A. C., Smith, J. R., & States, U. (2017). Deep learning ensembles for melanoma recognition in dermoscopy images. *IBM Journal of Research and Development*, *61*(4–5), 1–15. doi:10.1147/JRD.2017.2708299

Danaee, P., Ghaeini, R., & Hendrix, D. A. (2017). A deep learning approach for cancer detection and relevant gene identification. *Pacific Symposium on Biocomputing*, *0*(212679), 219–229. doi:10.1142/9789813207813_0022 PMID:27896977

Dhungel, N., Carneiro, G., & Bradley, A. P. (2015). *Automated Mass Detection in Mammograms using Cascaded Deep Learning and Random Forests*. Academic Press.

Dorj, U. O., Lee, K. K., Choi, J. Y., & Lee, M. (2018). The skin cancer classification using deep convolutional neural network. *Multimedia Tools and Applications*, *77*(8), 9909–9924. doi:10.100711042-018-5714-1

Ebg, F. G. (2016). Breast Cancer Histopathological Image Classification using Convolutional. *Neural Networks*, 2560–2567.

Erden, B., Gamboa, N., & Wood, S. (n.d.). *3D Convolutional Neural Network for Brain Tumor Segmentation*. Academic Press.

Gezahegn, Y. G. (2020). *Breast Cancer detection using Convolutional Neural Network*. Academic Press.

Ghassemi, N., Shoeibi, A., & Rouhani, M. (2020). Deep neural network with generative adversarial networks pre-training for brain tumor classification based on MR images. *Biomedical Signal Processing and Control*, *57*, 101678. doi:10.1016/j.bspc.2019.101678

Girshick, R. (2015). Fast R-CNN. *Proceedings of the IEEE International Conference on Computer Vision, 2015 Inter*, 1440–1448. 10.1109/ICCV.2015.169

Goodfellow, I. J., Pouget-abadie, J., Mirza, M., Xu, B., & Warde-farley, D. (2014). *Generative Adversarial Nets*. Academic Press.

Guan, S. (2019). Breast cancer detection using synthetic mammograms from generative adversarial networks in convolutional neural networks. *Journal of Medical Imaging (Bellingham, Wash.)*, *6*(03), 1. doi:10.1117/1.JMI.6.3.031411 PMID:30915386

Hesamian, M. H., Jia, W., He, X., & Kennedy, P. (2019). Deep Learning Techniques for Medical Image Segmentation: Achievements and Challenges. *Journal of Digital Imaging*, *32*(4), 582–596. doi:10.100710278-019-00227-x PMID:31144149

Jafari, M. H., Karimi, N., Nasr-Esfahani, E., Samavi, S., Soroushmehr, S. M. R., Ward, K., & Najarian, K. (2016). Skin lesion segmentation in clinical images using deep learning. *Proceedings - International Conference on Pattern Recognition, 0*, 337–342. 10.1109/ICPR.2016.7899656

Kadampur, M. A., & Al Riyaee, S. (2020). Skin cancer detection: Applying a deep learning based model driven architecture in the cloud for classifying dermal cell images. *Informatics in Medicine Unlocked*, *18*(November), 100282. doi:10.1016/j.imu.2019.100282

Kaldera, H. N. T. K., Gunasekara, S. R., & DIssanayake, M. B. (2019). Brain tumor Classification and Segmentation using Faster R-CNN. *2019 Advances in Science and Engineering Technology International Conferences, ASET 2019*, 1–6. doi:10.1109/ICASET.2019.8714263

Kamnitsas, K., Ledig, C., Newcombe, V. F. J., Simpson, J. P., Kane, A. D., Menon, D. K., Rueckert, D., & Glocker, B. (2017). Efficient multi-scale 3D CNN with fully connected CRF for accurate brain lesion segmentation. *Medical Image Analysis*, *36*, 61–78. doi:10.1016/j.media.2016.10.004 PMID:27865153

Lakshmanaprabu, S. K., Mohanty, S. N., Shankar, K., Arunkumar, N., & Ramirez, G. (2019). Optimal deep learning model for classification of lung cancer on CT images. *Future Generation Computer Systems*, *92*, 374–382. doi:10.1016/j.future.2018.10.009

Li, H., Li, A., & Wang, M. (2019). A novel end-to-end brain tumor segmentation method using improved fully convolutional networks. *Computers in Biology and Medicine*, *108*, 150–160. doi:10.1016/j.compbiomed.2019.03.014 PMID:31005007

Liu, G., Bao, H., & Han, B. (2018). A Stacked Autoencoder-Based Deep Neural Network for Achieving Gearbox Fault Diagnosis. *Mathematical Problems in Engineering*, *2018*, 1–10. Advance online publication. doi:10.1155/2018/5105709

Liu, S., Zheng, H., Feng, Y., & Li, W. (2017). Prostate cancer diagnosis using deep learning with 3D multiparametric MRI. *Medical Imaging 2017. Computer-Aided Diagnosis*, *10134*, 1013428. doi:10.1117/12.2277121

Lo, C., Chen, Y., Weng, R., & Hsieh, K. L. (n.d.). *Applied sciences Intelligent Glioma Grading Based on Deep Transfer Learning of MRI Radiomic Features*. Academic Press.

Mediun. (2020). *Convolutional Neural Network*. Author.

Milletari, F., Navab, N., & Ahmadi, S. A. (2016). V-Net: Fully convolutional neural networks for volumetric medical image segmentation. *Proceedings - 2016 4th International Conference on 3D Vision, 3DV 2016*, 565–571. 10.1109/3DV.2016.79

Mittal, M., Goyal, L. M., Kaur, S., Kaur, I., Verma, A., & Hemanth, D. J. (2019). Deep learning based enhanced tumor segmentation approach for MR brain images. *Applied Soft Computing*, *78*, 346–354. doi:10.1016/j.asoc.2019.02.036

Munir, K., Elahi, H., Ayub, A., Frezza, F., & Rizzi, A. (2019). Cancer diagnosis using deep learning: A bibliographic review. *Cancers (Basel)*, *11*(9), 1–36. doi:10.3390/cancers11091235 PMID:31450799

NIH National Cancer. (2020). Cancer Facts & Figures 2020. *CA: a Cancer Journal for Clinicians*, 1–76.

Nvidia. (2016). *Deep learning Breast Cancer Diagnosis*. Author.

Pereira, S., Pinto, A., Alves, V., & Silva, C. A. (2016). *Brain Tumor Segmentation Using Convolutional Neural Networks in MRI Images*. Academic Press.

Razzak, M. I., Naz, S., & Zaib, A. (2018). Deep learning for medical image processing: Overview, challenges and the future. *Lecture Notes in Computational Vision and Biomechanics*, *26*, 323–350. doi:10.1007/978-3-319-65981-7_12

Reda, I., Khalil, A., Elmogy, M., El-Fetouh, A. A., Shalaby, A., El-Ghar, M. A., ... El-Baz, A. (2018). Deep learning role in early diagnosis of prostate cancer. *Technology in Cancer Research & Treatment*, *17*, 1–11. doi:10.1177/1533034618775530 PMID:29804518

Ren, S., He, K., Girshick, R., & Sun, J. (2017). Faster R-CNN: Towards Real-Time Object Detection with Region Proposal Networks. *IEEE Transactions on Pattern Analysis and Machine Intelligence*, *39*(6), 1137–1149. doi:10.1109/TPAMI.2016.2577031 PMID:27295650

Ronneberger, O., Fischer, P., & Brox, T. (2015). U-net: Convolutional networks for biomedical image segmentation. Lecture Notes in Computer Science (Including Subseries Lecture Notes in Artificial Intelligence and Lecture Notes in Bioinformatics), 9351, 234–241. doi:10.1007/978-3-319-24574-4_28

Saba, T. (2019). Automated lung nodule detection and classification based on multiple classifiers voting. *Microscopy Research and Technique*, *82*(9), 1601–1609. doi:10.1002/jemt.23326 PMID:31243869

Schelb, P., Kohl, S., Radtke, J. P., Wiesenfarth, M., Kickingereder, P., Bickelhaupt, S., Kuder, T. A., Stenzinger, A., Hohenfellner, M., Schlemmer, H.-P., Maier-Hein, K. H., & Bonekamp, D. (2019). Classification of cancer at prostate MRI: Deep Learning versus Clinical PI-RADS Assessment. *Radiology*, *293*(3), 607–617. doi:10.1148/radiol.2019190938 PMID:31592731

Seetha, J., & Raja, S. S. (2018). Brain Tumor Classification Using Convolutional. *Neural Networks*, *11*(September), 1457–1461.

Shahzadi, I., Meriadeau, F., Tang, T. B., & Quyyum, A. (2019). CNN-LSTM: Cascaded framework for brain tumour classification. *2018 IEEE EMBS Conference on Biomedical Engineering and Sciences, IECBES 2018 - Proceedings*, (March), 633–637. 10.1109/IECBES.2018.8626704

Singh, S., Pandey, S. K., Pawar, U., & Janghel, R. R. (2018). Classification of ECG Arrhythmia using Recurrent Neural Networks. *Procedia Computer Science*, *132*(1), 1290–1297. doi:10.1016/j.procs.2018.05.045

Sun, Q. (2018). Deep Learning for Image-based Cancer Detection and Diagnosis— A Survey. *Pattern Recognition*, *83*, 134–149. Advance online publication. doi:10.1016/j.patcog.2018.05.014

Swiderski, B., Kurek, J., Osowski, S., Kruk, M., & Barhoumi, W. (2017). Deep Learning and Non-Negative Matrix Factorization in Recognition of Mammograms. *Icgip 2016*, 1–7. doi:10.1117/12.2266335

Tandel, G. S., Biswas, M., Kakde, O. G., Tiwari, A., Suri, H. S., Turk, M., Laird, J., Asare, C., Ankrah, A. A., Khanna, N. N., Madhusudhan, B. K., Saba, L., & Suri, J. S. (2019). A review on a deep learning perspective in brain cancer classification. *Cancers (Basel)*, *11*(1), 111. Advance online publication. doi:10.3390/cancers11010111 PMID:30669406

Tikade, R., & Rajeswari, P. D. K. (2018). Lung Cancer Detection and Classification using Deep learning. IEEE, 4, 5–9.

Turkki, R., Linder, N., Kovanen, P. E., Pellinen, T., & Lundin, J. (2016). Antibody-supervised deep learning for quantification of tumor-infiltrating immune cells in hematoxylin and eosin stained breast cancer samples. *Journal of Pathology Informatics*, *7*(1), 38. Advance online publication. doi:10.4103/2153-3539.189703 PMID:27688929

Vasconcelos, C. N., & Vasconcelos, B. N. (2017). Experiments using deep learning for dermoscopy image analysis. *Pattern Recognition Letters*, *0*, 1–9. doi:10.1016/j.patrec.2017.11.005

WHO. (2020)... *Cancer*.

Xu, B., Wang, N., Chen, T., & Li, M. (2015). *Empirical Evaluation of Rectified Activations in Convolutional Network*. Retrieved from https://arxiv.org/abs/1505.00853

Yoo, S., Gujrathi, I., Haider, M. A., & Khalvati, F. (2019). Prostate Cancer Detection using Deep Convolutional Neural Networks. *Scientific Reports*, *9*(1), 1–10. doi:10.103841598-019-55972-4 PMID:31863034

Zhang, N., Ding, S., Zhang, J., & Xue, Y. (2018). An overview on Restricted Boltzmann Machines. *Neurocomputing*, *275*, 1186–1199. doi:10.1016/j.neucom.2017.09.065

Chapter 2
Use of Artificial Intelligence (AI) in Fighting With the Novel Coronavirus (COVID–19)

Anuja Rajendra Jadhav
Savitribai Phule Pune University, India

Roshani Raut
Pimpri Chinchwad College of Engineering, India

Ram Joshi
JSPM's Rajarshi Shahu College of Engineering, India

Pranav D. Pathak
MIT School of Bioengineering Sciences and Research, Pune, India

Anuja R. Zade
JSPM's Rajarshi Shahu College of Engineering, India

ABSTRACT

2020 started with the outbreak of the novel coronavirus (COVID-19) virus. In this panic situation, the combination of artificial intelligence (AI) can help us in fight against the deadliest virus attack worldwide. This tool can be used to control and prevention of the outbreak disease. The AI tool can be helpful in prediction, detection, response, recovery, drug discovery of the disease. The AI-driven tools can be used in identifying the nature of outbreak as well as in forecasting the spread and coverage worldwide. In this case, so many AI-based tools can be applied and trained using active learning-based models for the detection, prevention, treatment, and recovery of the patients. Also, they can help us for identifying infected persons from the non-infected to stop the spread of the virus. This chapter mainly focuses on the AI-assisted methodology and models that can help in fighting COVID-19.

DOI: 10.4018/978-1-7998-7511-6.ch002

1. INTRODUCTION

In the month of December 2019, the spread of novel corona virus had begun from the most of the population of a large city in the Chinese province of Hubei, Wuhan. Presently, the corona virus is responsible over millions of deaths worldwide (Medical News Today, n.d.). SARS-CoV-2 is a coronavirus is responsible for causing novel coronavirus disease 2019 (hereafter named as COVID-19). After the successful isolation and identification, the virus mainly responsible for pneumonia was originally names as 2019 novel coronavirus (2019-nCoV) but then WHO officially named it as severe acute respiratory syndrome coronavirus 2 (SARS-CoV-2) and also declared outbreak of SARS-CoV-2 as a emergency for public health in the international concern on 30 January 2020. The cause of panick bout the SARS-CoV-2 is strong transmission capacity(Zheng et al., 2020). This virus has rapidly propagated due to widespread person-to-person transmission. This rapid transmission of virus makes the control and prevention very critical. The confirmation of COVID-19 is performed with the help of virus-specific RT–PCR, which takes up to 2 days for getting the results (Mei et al., 2020). Early detection of disease is very essential for individual penitents for its cure for rapid start of treatment and to stop its spread along large public groups. Also, after detection the infected person/group of person can be isolated from the healthy peoples and to prevent of disease spread (Medical News Today, n.d.; Mei et al., 2020).

Generally after getting infected with COVID-19 virus the patient shows common symptoms as cough, fatigue and fever. Some other symptoms like headache, hemoptysis, sputum production, lymphopenia, dyspnea and diarrhea are also observed in patients. After an incubation period of approximately 5.2 days, the symptom of COVID-19 appears in the infected person. Also, it takes 6-41 days with the average of 14 days for COVID-19 Symptoms to death in deadly affected person. This period is dependent on some several factors such as age of patient and his immune system. COVID-19 shows some of the similarities with earlier beta-coronavirus like dry cough, fever, dyspnea and bilateral ground-glass opacities on chest CT scans while it has some unique clinical symptoms which targets the lower airway as evident by upper respiratory track indications such as sneezing, sore throat and rhinorrhoea. In addition with this the CT scan of chest shows pneumonia but in several cases the it shows abnormal features such as acute cardiac injury, acute respiratory distress syndrome, RNAaemia, and incidence of grand-glass opacities which causes death (Huang et al., 2020) (Assiri et al., 2013; Ren et al., 2020; Rothan & Byrareddy, 2020).

To lower down affected patients and casualties due to COVID-19 it is necessary to prevent and control the widespread of virus among the healthy peoples. All government personals, NGO, volunteers, doctors, police and many other personals are fighting for monitoring, prevention and control of COVID-19. Besides this huge effort by the people's outbreak of COVID-19 is still continuous. On the other hand, these efforts only human efforts are not sufficient. Some of the computational tools like internet of things (IoT) and Artificial Intelligence (AI) can boost the human efforts to fight against the COVID-19 pandemic. This chapter focuses some of the methodologies and applications of IoT and AI in the fighting against the COVID-19. The collection of these strategies at single platform will definitely help corona worriers to fight with more strength against COVID-19.

2. USE OF COMPUTATIONAL TOOLS

2.1 Tools of Monitoring COVID-19

Monitoring of the spread of virus is first and most important step. The monitoring dashboards help in monitoring COVID-19 hotspots, increase and decrease in the cases, recovered cases and death casualties. Also, this type of dashboards gives bird's eye view of the status of particular city, state and country. This helps to government officials for formulating the containment response based on live status and situation for the targeted area. These dashboard uses GIS data and use AI to analyse and process the data. In this regard some of the live data dashboards are reported in this section.

Dong et. al. (2020) developed an online interactive dashboard and shared publically on 22 January 2020 which is hosted by Center for Systems Science and Engineering (CSSE) at Johns Hopkins University, Baltimore, MD, USA. The developed dashboard helps in track and visualizes the reported cases of COVID-19 in real time for all affected countries. The dashboard freely provides the data related to location, number of confirmed cases, recovered persons and deaths (Dong et al., 2020; Kamel Boulos & Geraghty, 2020). The dashboard is available at https://coronavirus.jhu.edu/map.html (Accessed at 10:00 PM; 11 June 2020)

The other important dashboard is provided by world health organization (WHO). WHO helps in fighting this situation with the continuous preparations, surveillance, and sue of GIS technologies. WHO launches this ArcGIS Operations Dashboard for COVID-19 on 26 January 2020. This platform demonstrates the country and region wise laboratory confirmed cases, recovered and deaths. The WHO dashboard automatically updates using ArcGIS GeoEvent Server to push updates multiple times per day. It also provides good map performance (10-12 zoom levels) (Kamel Boulos & Geraghty, 2020). The dashboard can be accessed at https://covid19.who.int/ (Accessed at 10:30 PM; 11 June 2020).

Platform from HealthMap (https://www.healthmap.org/covid-19/; Accessed at 10:45 PM; 11 June 2020) provides worldwide data for various diseases. Team of epidemiologists, researchers and software developers at Boston Children's Hospital, USA, runs the dashboard of HealthMap. The platform collects the data from various sources like social media, news media, expert-curated accounts and official alerts like WHO (Kamel Boulos & Geraghty, 2020).

Indian government also runs the nationwide dashboard. The government has two different dashboards. One is at https://www.mohfw.gov.in/ and other at https://www.mygov.in/covid-19/ (both was accessed at 11:30 PM; 11 June 2020). The database provides state wise lab confirmed active, confirmed and recovered cases along with the death and migrated cases. The dashboard offers various advisories, guidelines, state/UT's helpline number, live helpdesk, latest notification, FAQs and awareness about COVID-19 in English and Hindi language.

A drone, surveillance camera, health workers assists to generate the data from everywhere and the collected data is then uploaded to the servers of various dashboards which are then utilized for further processing.

2.2 Use of AI

Combating with COVID-19 is a huge challenge to the mankind. AI is powerful tool which can be used to fight against it effectively. AI can be used in many directions to produce an effortless and smooth conduction process for detection, prediction, forecasting, prevention, control, drug development and recovery related to COVID-19 patients. Machine learning, subclass of AI can be used to analyse the obtained data from various sources and platforms and extract the useful data from it (Shaikh, 2020). AI processes the data speedily and reduces the human efforts. According to Vaishya et al (2020) AL has lot of applications in COVID-19 pandemic. These application includes, early detection & diagnosis of the COVID-19 infection, treatment monitoring, tracing of the individuals, cases and mortality projection, drugs and vaccines development, disease Prevention and in reducing the workload of healthcare workers (Vaishya et al., 2020). Figure 1 shows the various applications of AI for COVID-19. Various applications of AI for COVID-19 are discussed in following sections.

Figure 1. Use of AI in fighting with COVID-19

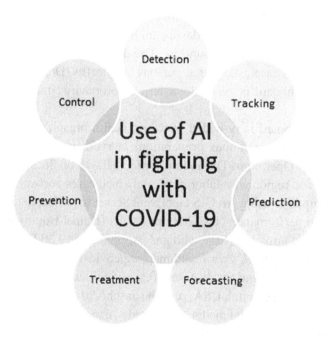

2.2.1 Detection, Prediction and Forecasting

The AI powered systems can be used for design of early warning systems using the algorithm and its available data. The available data is analyzed and mainly used to determine the epidemiological patterns. The data can be obtained by mining it from online content, information channels in different languages, mainstream news, governments' sites, etc. The detected patterns can be used to provide early warnings which are used to keep syndromic surveillance. For example, a global AI database company "BlueDot" uses machine learning, AI powered algorithm and natural-language processing to study and analyze the obtained information from multiple sources to track number of diseases. Similarly, WHO also provides early warnings using predicted data (OECD, 2020; Wu, 2020). In addition with this, a Chicago-based non-profit company, "Medical Home Network" implemented an AI platform to identify patients who are at risk from COVID-19 identified on the basis of complication in respiratory systems and social isolation (OECD, 2020) (Kent, 2020). According to Googal's DeepMind research in which deep learning is used to predict the protein structure associated with SARS-CoV-2 (Deep Mind, n.d.). This predicted data of COVID-19 can be used by the medical professionals, policy makers and general public to take the necessary precautions to restrict the spread of disease. Thus the AI and machine learning will play a crucial role in identification, detection and prediction of COVID-19 and thus can save the humans from infections as well as from deaths.

2.2.2 Diagnosis

Rapid diagnosis is very important to identify the infected patients so that they can be isolated form healthy once. This also helps in spread of disease within the huge populations. Also early detection of COVID-19 is very essential to control the spread. Traditionally teal time RT-PCR is used to detect the COVID-19 infections which uses primers genes and identifies infections based on the RNA sequence of the virus. But with this tests the major risk of eliciting false-negative and false-positive results especially when only samples of upper respiratory tract were tested. To get accurate results, multiple samples in different time points, and from upper and lower respiratory tract should be tested. Also for accurate readings real time RT-PCR readings should be combined with chest CT Scans (Tahamtan & Ardebili, 2020).

For rapid detection of COVID-19 AI can help by using the patient's symptom data and images. The only essential thing is that, the data should be collected for more populations as possible and the data should be accurate (OECD, 2020). Currently many attempts are made worldwide using AI in rapid detection of COVID-19.

In china, an AI algorithm announced by Alibaba, can diagnose suspected cases almost 45 time lesser than human detection i.e. only within 20 seconds with 96% accuracy. This algorithm is trained on more than 5000 confirmed COVID-19 cases. For the training, it uses CT Scans to diagnose the infected people within 20 -30 seconds. It also examines the diagnosed patients scan to determine fast health declines or progress depending on the symptoms like white mass in the lungs. Alibaba opens its cloud-based AI platform for all working medicinal professionals from all over the world who are working with local partners on unidentified data for utilization which includes modules for CT image analytics, epidemic prediction and analyzing genome sequence for COVID-19 (Lee, 2020).

Mei et al (2020) proposed AI algorithms in which the combines CT images and clinical history to get the area under curve of 0.92 and which gives good results in 84.3% sensitivity compared with 74.6% of senior thoracic radiologist with the application to a test set of 279 cases (Mei et al., 2020). Salman et al (2020), uses the chest X-ray images for simulated collected from GitHub, Kaggle and Open-i repository and applied deep learning features for COVID-19 detection. Using the features, the pre-trained CNN model was developed and the model (Inceptionv3) performance was checked using 6 parameters. The designed model (Inceptionv3) achieved 100% accuracy for detection (Salman, 2020). Zhang et al (2020) developed a model by collecting about 100 chest X-ray images (70 confirmed with COVID-19 from the Github repository) for more data acquisition, more 1431 chest X-ray images confirmed as other pneumonia of 1008 patients from the public ChestX-ray14 dataset. The developed model can give the accuracy about 96% (Zhang, 2020). Zhang et al (2020) developed a model to detect COVID-19 based on their chest CT Scans and find the sensitivity was 97.78% in which true positive 88, false positive 1, true negative 12 and false negative 2 cases were detected (Zhang, 2020). There are some other models are also available which shows good efficiency towards the COVID detection using AI. Table 1 shows some of the models developed to detect the COVID-19 worldwide. It shows that AI in assistance with

ML can successfully implement to diagnose COVID-19 more fastly and accurately. The only disadvantage is that, the model should be trained well with huge data base.

Table 1. Various models used for detecting COVID-19 worldwide

Model Used	Accuracy (%)	Reference
Inceptionv3	100	
ResNet Deep Anamoly detection model	96	
InceptionV2	80	
InceptionV3	96	
ResNet50	98	
VGG19	90	
DenseNet201	90	
ResNetV2	70	
InceptionV3	50	
InceptionResNetV2	80	
Xception	80	
MobileNetV2	60	
AlexNet	94.86	
DenseNet201	93.86	
GoogleNet	91.73	
InceptionResnetV2	91.13	
InceptionV3	30.26	
MobileNetV2	94.46	
ResNet18	94.26	
XceptionNet	93.00	
ResNet101	93.53	
ShuffleNet	65.26	
VGG16	94.20	
VGG19	94.13	
ResNet50	95.33	

2.2.3 Drug Development

AI powered drug development is attracting to all biologists, pharma companies to simplify their R & D efforts because the platforms can help in developing the precision medicine and reduces the cost and time for the development. In the COVID-19 situation this it is beneficial to used ability of AI powered tool for develop the drugs (vaccine, treatment drug) very efficiently, cost effective and in very less time. For this, deep learning can can help to find treatments or drugs from our old database or can forecast new treatment or drugs which can be helpful in combatting of COVID-19. The organizations like DeepMind uses the AI and deep learning to predict the structure of protein related to SARS-CoV-2 (OECD, 2020)

Abdulla et al (2020) reported an AI-based platform, Project IDentif.AI (Identifying Infectious Disease Combination Therapy with Artificial Intelligence). Using this database, the 12 possible drugs were selected which can be used treating infections in lung cells from the vesicular stomatitis virus (VSV). Also use of Project IDentif.AI remarkably reduces the experimentation required to obtained dosages and combination of these 12 possible drugs. The developed database can use to address COVID-19 and future pandemics (Abdulla, 2020).

2.2.4 Surveillance

Surveillance of the patients is also essential to control of spread of COVID-19. Many countries developed AI based platforms to tracing and surveillance of the infected as well as non-infecting peoples. Table 2 gives some of the mobile databases developed by the different countries to track and surveillance of infected and non-infected peoples.

Table 2. Various AI based mobile apps for surveillance of infected and non-infected peoples for COVID-19

AI Platform	Developed By	Reference
Aarogya Setu	The National Informatics Centre under the Ministry of Electronics and Information Technology. INdia	
Covid Care Kerala	Mobile App Development Competence Center, Kerala of National Informatics Centre, India	
TraceTogether	A Singapore Government Agency	
CovidWatch	In collaboration with Stanford University	
HaMagen	Ministry of health, Israel	
DataSpende	Germany	

There are some other efforts are also made for example in Korea the algorithm used surveillance-camera footage, geolocation data and the credit card records to trace COVID-19 patients. In china various color coading (red, yellow, green) are assigned to each person indicating their contagion risk using their mobile phones (OECD, 2020) .

2.3 Issues in Implementing AI

Though AI is proven itself as a powerful tool in fighting with COVID-19, it has some limitations for complete implementation. One of the major drawbacks is that, at initial stages for the model development huge relevant and accurate data points are needed so that the developed model can give better and reliable results (Shaikh, 2020). Also a patient shows concerns that AI that can totally replace the doctors, but that is not at all true with the development of AI. According to WHO, the peoples working on outbreak sites can collect the data related to risk factors, transmissibility, period of incubation and death rate for training of AI models. One more thing that we have to keep in mind that, for getting accurate and reliable results time to time, the AI models should be trained with fresh data every time with the most up-to-date data available (Kent, 2020). The AI powered system has one more challenge of ethical issues and privacy of the collected data of the patients (Bartoletti, 2019; Wahl et al., 2018).

CONCLUSION

COVID-19 pandemic creates major challenges towards the health care system all over the world. Due to the rapid spreading characteristics of the COVID-19 it is more difficult it to control from spreading with a only human efforts. To control it very efficiently its detection, prediction, diagnosis, drug development and surveillance of the infected people should be very fast. AI powered tool can facilities us for fighting with COVID -19 with its fact, reliable and convenient computing powers. In this AI can help humans with its high speed and accuracy to detect the patterns of outbreak so that the policy makers can take appropriate actions for the control. However for getting the complete benefits form AI, the developed models should be provided with maximum number of data points which are more accurate, reliable and up-to-date. Also the ethical and privacy of the patients are the other major issues of concern.

REFERENCES

Abdulla, A. (2020). Project IDentif.AI: Harnessing Artificial Intelligence to Rapidly Optimize Combination Therapy Development for Infectious Disease Intervention. Advanced Therapeutics.

Assiri, A., Al-Tawfiq, J. A., Al-Rabeeah, A. A., Al-Rabiah, F. A., Al-Hajjar, S., Al-Barrak, A., Flemban, H., Al-Nassir, W. N., Balkhy, H. H., Al-Hakeem, R. F., Makhdoom, H. Q., Zumla, A. I., & Memish, Z. A. (2013). Epidemiological, demographic, and clinical characteristics of 47 cases of Middle East respiratory syndrome coronavirus disease from Saudi Arabia: A descriptive study. *The Lancet. Infectious Diseases*, *13*(9), 752–761. doi:10.1016/S1473-3099(13)70204-4 PMID:23891402

Bartoletti, I. (2019). AI in Healthcare: Ethical and Privacy Challenges. In Artificial Intelligence in Medicine. AIME 2019. Springer. doi:10.1007/978-3-030-21642-9_2

Covid Watch. (n.d.). https://covid-watch.org/

Deep Mind. (n.d.). https://deepmind.com/research/open-source/computational-predictions-of-protein-structures-associated-with-COVID-19

Dong, E., Du, H., & Gardner, L. (2020). An interactive web-based dashboard to track COVID-19 in real time. *The Lancet. Infectious Diseases*, *20*(5), 533–534. doi:10.1016/S1473-3099(20)30120-1 PMID:32087114

Google Play. (n.d.). https://play.google.com/store/apps/details?id=org.nic.covidcarekannur&hl=en_IN&showAllReviews=true

Govextra. (n.d.). https://govextra.gov.il/ministry-of-health/hamagen-app/

Hemdan, Shouman, & Karar. (2020). *COVIDX-Net: A Framework of Deep Learning Classifiers to Diagnose COVID-19 in X-Ray Images.* arXiv preprint arXiv, 2020.2003.11055

Huang, C., Wang, Y., Li, X., Ren, L., Zhao, J., Hu, Y., Zhang, L., Fan, G., Xu, J., Gu, X., Cheng, Z., Yu, T., Xia, J., Wei, Y., Wu, W., Xie, X., Yin, W., Li, H., Liu, M., ... Cao, B. (2020). Clinical features of patients infected with 2019 novel coronavirus in Wuhan, China. *Lancet*, *395*(10223), 497–506. doi:10.1016/S0140-6736(20)30183-5 PMID:31986264

Kamel Boulos, M. N., & Geraghty, E. M. (2020). Geographical tracking and mapping of coronavirus disease COVID-19/severe acute respiratory syndrome coronavirus 2 (SARS-CoV-2) epidemic and associated events around the world: How 21st century GIS technologies are supporting the global fight against outbreaks and epidemics. *International Journal of Health Geographics*, *19*(1), 8. doi:10.118612942-020-00202-8 PMID:32160889

Kent, J. (2020). *Artificial Intelligence Identifies High-Risk COVID-19 Patients*. Academic Press.

Lee, K.-F. (2020). *Covid-19 Will Accelerate the AI Health Care Revolution*. Available from: https://www.wired.com/story/covid-19-will-accelerate-ai-health-care-revolution/

Medical News Today. (n.d.). https://www.medicalnewstoday.com/articles/novel-coronavirus-your-questions-answered

Mei, X., Lee, H.-C., Diao, K., Huang, M., Lin, B., Liu, C., Xie, Z., Ma, Y., Robson, P. M., Chung, M., Bernheim, A., Mani, V., Calcagno, C., Li, K., Li, S., Shan, H., Lv, J., Zhao, T., Xia, J., ... Yang, Y. (2020). Artificial intelligence–enabled rapid diagnosis of patients with COVID-19. *Nature Medicine*, *26*(8), 1224–1228. doi:10.103841591-020-0931-3 PMID:32427924

My Gov. (n.d.). https://www.mygov.in/aarogya-setu-app/

Narin, A., Kaya, C., & Pamuk, Z. (2020). Automatic Detection of Coronavirus Disease (COVID-19) Using X-ray Images and Deep Convolutional Neural Networks. arXiv preprint arXiv

OECD. (2020). *Using Artificial Intelligence to Help Combat COVID-19*, in *OECD*. http://www.oecd.org/coronavirus/policy-responses/using-artificial-intelligence-to-help-combat-covid-19-ae4c5c21/

Ren, L.-L., Wang, Y.-M., Wu, Z.-Q., Xiang, Z.-C., Guo, L., Xu, T., Jiang, Y.-Z., Xiong, Y., Li, Y.-J., Li, X.-W., Li, H., Fan, G.-H., Gu, X.-Y., Xiao, Y., Gao, H., Xu, J.-Y., Yang, F., Wang, X.-M., Wu, C., ... Wang, J.-W. (2020). Identification of a novel coronavirus causing severe pneumonia in human: A descriptive study. *Chinese Medical Journal*, *133*(9), 1015–1024. doi:10.1097/CM9.0000000000000722 PMID:32004165

Reuters. (n.d.). https://in.reuters.com/article/health-coronavirus-germany-tech/germany-launches-smartwatch-app-to-monitor-coronavirus-spread-idINKBN21P1US

Rothan, H. A., & Byrareddy, S. N. (2020). The epidemiology and pathogenesis of coronavirus disease (COVID-19) outbreak. *Journal of Autoimmunity*, *109*, 102433. doi:10.1016/j.jaut.2020.102433 PMID:32113704

Salman, F. M. (2020). COVID-19 Detection using Artificial Intelligence. *International Journal of Academic Engineering Research*, *4*(3), 18–25.

Sethy, P. K. (2020). *Detection of Coronavirus Disease (COVID-19)*. Based on Deep Features and Support Vector Machine. Preprints.

Shaikh, J. (2020). Role of Artificial Intelligence in Prevention and Detection of Covid-19. *International Journal of Advanced Science and Technology*, *29*(9), 45–54.

Tahamtan, A., & Ardebili, A. (2020). Real-time RT-PCR in COVID-19 detection: Issues affecting the results. *Expert Review of Molecular Diagnostics*, *20*(5), 453–454. doi:10.1080/14737159.2020.17574 37 PMID:32297805

Trace Together. (n.d.). https://www.tracetogether.gov.sg/

Vaishya, R., Javaid, M., Khan, I. H., & Haleem, A. (2020). Artificial Intelligence (AI) applications for COVID-19 pandemic. *Diabetes & Metabolic Syndrome*, *14*(4), 337–339. doi:10.1016/j.dsx.2020.04.012 PMID:32305024

Wahl, B., Cossy-Gantner, A., Germann, S., & Schwalbe, N. R. (2018). Artificial intelligence (AI) and global health: How can AI contribute to health in resource-poor settings? *BMJ Global Health*, *3*(4), e000798. doi:10.1136/bmjgh-2018-000798 PMID:30233828

Wu, J. (2020). *How Artificial Intelligence Can Help Fight Coronavirus*. Academic Press.

Zhang, J. (2020). *COVID-19 Screening on Chest X-ray Images Using Deep Learning based Anomaly Detection*. arXiv preprint arXiv:2003

Zhang, M. (2020). *Application of artificial intelligence image-assisted diagnosis system in chest CT examination of COVID-19*. Nuclear Medicine & Medical Imaging.

Zheng, Y.-Y., Ma, Y.-T., Zhang, J.-Y., & Xie, X. (2020). COVID-19 and the cardiovascular system. *Nature Reviews. Cardiology*, *17*(5), 259–260. doi:10.103841569-020-0360-5 PMID:32139904

Chapter 3
Diagnosis of Attention Deficit Hyperactivity Disorder:
An Intelligent Neuroimaging Perspective

Karuna Salgotra
CT Institute of Engineering, Management, and Technology, Jalandhar, India

Vikas Khullar
iD https://orcid.org/0000-0002-0404-3652
Chitkara University Institute of Engineering and Technology, Rajpura, India

Harjit Pal Singh
CT Institute of Engineering, Management, and Technology, Jalandhar, India

Suyeb Ahmed Khan
Baba Kuma Singh Ji Group of Institute, Amritsar, India

ABSTRACT

Attention deficit hyperactivity disorder (ADHD) is a complex neuropsychiatric disorder in which the diagnosed behavior of ADHD individuals reflects negligence and hyperactivity. Around 5% of young kids and 2–4% of grown-ups are found to have ADHD or ADHD-related symptoms. This study aims to provide a detailed review of neuroimaging technologies for ADHD diagnoses such as tomography, electroencephalography (EEG), magneto encephalography (MEG), magnetic resonance imaging (MRI), etc. In the present era, the number of artificial intelligent, machine learning, deep learning algorithms have been introduced along with available advanced technologies and found to be helpful in the identification of ADHD like neuropsychiatric disorders. The work presented in this chapter summarizes the ADHD diagnosing technologies in combination with evolutionary artificial intelligence techniques, which lead to smart possibilities in ADHD diagnosis.

DOI: 10.4018/978-1-7998-7511-6.ch003

1. INTRODUCTION

In today's scenario, a huge number of people occasionally suffer from various obstacles such as stay-stable, focusing, or controlling hasty behavior. In a certain population, these dilemmas occurred constant and extremely prevalent, which could intrude into each phase of their life at home, academic, social, and work. Attention Deficit Hyperactivity Disorder (ADHD) is one of the most common neuropsychiatric disorders in adolescence and adult in which individuals may not be able to stay-stable, focused, or controlling hasty behavior (Durston 2003). According to the Diagnostic and Statistical Manual of Mental Disorders 5th edition (DSM-V 2013), ADHD caused due to the development of unsuitable levels of carelessness, hasty, and overactive behavior(Boon 2020). This neurobehavioral disorder is considered to be a serious threat to the health of kids as well as adults since it causes consideration, center, and arranging troubles for them. It was found that around 5% of school-age children and 2–4% of adults were diagnosed with ADHD or ADHD-associated indications (Peng et al. 2013). In any case, without proof and legitimate medicine ADHD may have severe results which could lead to disappointment, strain, disturbance, sadness, challenges among connections, substance misuse, wrongdoing, unexpected offenses, etc. ADHD symptoms could make their lives considerably extra challenging on a cultural, educational, or professional level (Oj et al. 2019).

Early diagnosis of ADHD symptoms could help in handling this challenging behavior for making defecated individuals as better survivors. This chapter aims to summarize the technological developments in the diagnosis of ADHA diagnosis which included Tomography, Magnetic Resonance Technique, Electroencephalogram (EEG), etc. Further, the role of artificial intelligence in ADHA diagnosis is also highlighted in the present work.-

2. ADHD CAUSES, SYMPTOMS AND DIAGNOSIS

Due to the complexity of this disorder, ADHD cannot be associated with an individual basis but probably it is an outcome from a combination of unlike factors. The mandatory causes and risk factors associated with ADHA are unknown, but it has been considered that hereditary may be the prime cause leads to ADHD and the heritability of ADHD arises from various studies of the family-like: adoption studies, twin studies, and molecular genetics investigations. Some secondary causes may also lead to ADHA which included environmental factors, traumatic brain injury experienced in adolescence, focal sensory system diseases, premature birth, hypoxic-ischemic encephalopathy, fetal exposed with toxic components during pregnancy, etc (Thapar et al. 2012; Tran and Wu 2019). These factors can cause difficulties with carelessness, inadequate coordination of motor activity, and impulses. Besides, it is observed that premature conceived individuals also have additional perceptional and neurological dangers. It was also found that the consumption of alcohol and smoking during pregnancy leads to serious issues such as behavioral development, learning ability, and hyperactivity in newborn kids (Degiorgi et al. 2017; Greenway and Edwards 2020).

Inattention, hyperactive, and impulsive behavior are the major traits of ADHD and generally found in most of the infected persons. The individuals with inattentive behavior face difficulty in noting down the concrete details during tasks and also face various obstacles, such as, not listening to directions carefully, daydream or dawdle too much, forget essential details, and seem absent-minded, etc. Moreover, hyperactivity and impulsivity in behavior result in trouble while doing tasks which required patience to perform task smoothly (Chheda-varma 2010). As per DSM-5, various symptoms of ADHD begin in adolescence usually before the age of 12 years. In daily practice, the guardians have the keen observation about the extraordinary motor movement throughout childhood times of kids but the characteristics of ADHD disease could not be easy to differentiate from the Hasty, Carelessness, and Aggressive Conduct of the kids (DSM-V 2013; Greenway and Edwards 2020; Oj et al. 2019; Silverstein et al. 2018). In some cases, it was also observed that the mild characteristics of ADHA could be seen in childhood age but the severity increased with age which leads to interference in routine task ability of adults. The severe ADHA infected adults reflected other significant symptoms such as difficulty in multitasking, weak ability to tolerate frustration, short-temper, Poor time management skills, impulsiveness, depression, learning disabilities, and anxiety, etc.

The diagnosis guidelines of DSM-V for ADHD identification included six or more symptoms of Distraction and Hyperactivity-Impulsivity for children below the age of 12 and age of 17 or more, the ADHA diagnosis guidelines take account of five traits instead of six (Greenway and Edwards 2020; Silverstein et al. 2018). The trained mental-health experts utilize the DSM-V guidelines to diagnose ADHD through clinical interviews. DSM-V suggested three different levels of ADHD individuals as presented in Table 1 (DSM-V 2013).

Table 1. Different Levels of ADHD

ADHA Level(s)	Symptoms
Level-A	Both inattention and hyperactivity symptoms present with high significance for the last 6 months.
Level-B	Inattention symptoms without hyperactivity for the last 6 months.
Level-C	Hyperactive behavior symptoms without inattention for the last 6 months.

3. NEUROIMAGING TECHNOLOGIES FOR ADHD DIAGNOSIS

The neuroimaging or brain imaging techniques used to identify structure, function, or pharmacology of the nervous system by fetching brain image either directly or indirectly (Rostain and Ramsay 2006). It was observed form the behavioral observations of teenagers with ADHD individual groups that the dissimilar impairments in the brain with no common anomalies between them (Tran and Wu 2019). Several neuroimaging techniques detect the ADHD brain through structural and functional characteristics using Positron Emission Tomography (PET). In PET, radioactive glucose crosses the blood-brain obstacles and estimates the movement of the brain by using glucose metabolic motion and cerebral perfusion. Diffusion Tensor Imaging (DTI) is another non-invasive method used to produce a functional mapping of the connectivity of the brain through translational movement of water particles. A quantitative or Volumetric (QV) method for Magnetic Resonance Imaging (MRI) utilizes statistical interpretation to evaluate brain region sizes (Klein et al. 2017). There are distinct neuroimaging machines and techniques used by researchers to detail their study of ADHD brains. To support the topic, different technologies were discussed as follows:

3.1 Tomography

Single-Photon Emission Computed Tomography (SPECT) and Positron Emission Tomography (PET) are techniques to detect ADHD brain imaging and depend upon the calculation of a radionuclide's decay, during which a positron or an X-ray is released to generate photons (Durston 2003). Due to high sensitivity and boundless insertion intensity, PET and SPECT scan facilitate images to monitor metabolic movement, cerebral perfusion, neuro-synaptic transmitter turnover, receptor restricting possibilities, etc (Klein et al. 2017). PET and SPECT have been widely used to identify cerebral blood flow irregularities in brain areas in ADHD. Conducted studies with PET and SPECT helped to compare Striatal Dopamine Transporter availability among ADHD patients and controls (Tan et al. 2019). Figure 1 presented the commercial PET/CT scanners used in the field designed by four major vendors.

Figure 1. Commercial PET/CT imaging equipment
(Townsend, Beyer, and Blodgett 2003)

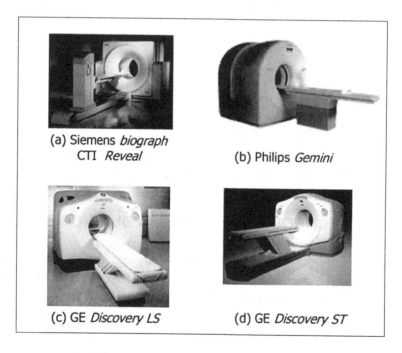

3.2 Electroencephalography

Electroencephalography (EEG) is a functional brain imaging technique used to study of ADHD brain. An EEG classifies electrical movement in your cerebrum using small, metal discs (electrodes) that joined to the scalp. Cerebrum cells communicate through electrical pulses and working all the time, even while an individual sleeps. While this criterion records as fluctuating formations on an EEG recording (Klein et al. 2017; Rodríguez-martínez et al. 2020). EEG was the earliest measure practiced to examine systematically human brain cortical activity, and now various investigations had tried to find be correlate ADHD to EEG. Most widely reported EEG variations, ADHD youngsters had raised the strength of slow fluctuations or diminished energy of quick flows or both. EEG signals obtained in various brain sections that describe the distinct brain functions and state (Richard, Lajiness-O'Neill, and Bowyer 2013). EEG experimental pieces of equipment are presented in Figure 2 (Laufs 2012).

Figure 2. EEG Experimental Equipments
(Laufs 2012)

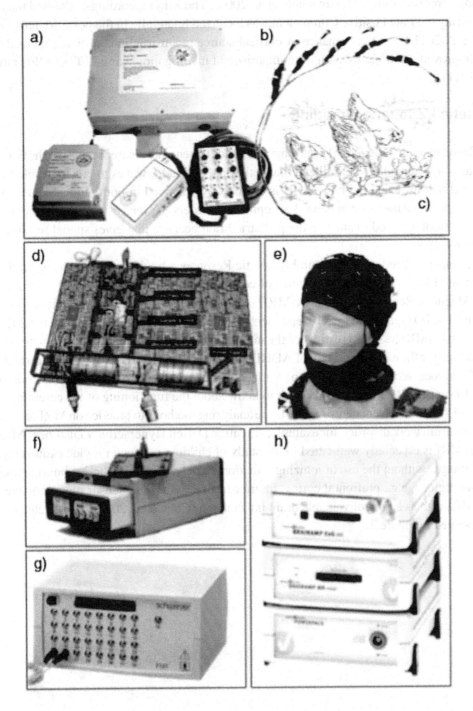

4.3 Magneto Encephalography

Magneto Encephalography (MEG) recognizes brain activity by measuring small magnetic fields produced by the brain. The endemic resolution of MEG is moderately better opposed to EEG, but MEG only estimates knowledge rigidly (Klein et al. 2017). MEG data could be collected by an inherently noisy recording procedure, which contains a combination of elements from various kinds of sources, along with working cerebrum sources (Demanuele et al. 2008). The MEG recordings exhibited the activation identified during the Late Positive Component was localized bilaterally in the posterior temporal cortex (Helenius et al. 2011). The performance of cortical source reconstructions utilizing merged EEG and MEG was improved significantly with the comparison of investigation using EEG or MEG alone (Ding and Yuan 2011).

4.4 Magnetic Resonance Imaging

Magnetic Resonance Imaging (MRI) uses magnetic fields to generate clearer images of the brain to study brain structure and function. MRI utilized magnetic field and radio waves to create detailed images of the organs and tissues inside the body. MRI is extensively practiced in both clinical and research perspectives to understand the brain in neurodevelopment disorders (Naveed et al. 2016). Anatomic MRI is the primary technology used to analyze the pediatric brain because that gives spatial resolution (Krain and Castellanos 2006).

Investigations practiced with Structural Magnetic Resonance Imaging (sMRI) scans produced non-obtrusive method to get a volumetric picture of cerebrum life structures, while others practiced with Functional Magnetic Resonance Imaging (fMRI) scans which measured cerebrum action by identifying variations in Blood Oxygenation Level-Dependent signals across time (Cubillo and Rubia 2010). Moreover, resting-state fMRI (rs-fMRI) estimates the internal cerebrum movements that promoted rs-fMRI as a primary device for the early prediction of ADHD (Kuang 2014). ADHD-200 consortium had gathered a dataset of preprocessed rs-fMRI data along with phenotypic detection of 947 subjects from 8 different institutions to support the investigation center to know about the functioning of the cerebrum (Aradhya and Ashfahani 2019). Different neuroscientists are analyzing methods to practice on MRI or fMRI data to recognize cerebrum work disorder, for example, Attention Deficit Hyperactivity Disorder (ADHD) (Sen et al. 2018). MRI is especially well-fitted to the study of children as it can provide exquisitely realistic anatomical images without the use of ionizing radiation. fMRI showed that brain abnormalities exist in various brain regions, e.g., prefrontal cortex, inferior frontal gyrus, and sensor motor cortexes to from functional MRI data as a kind of valuable brain information (Chen et al. 2020). A collected image MRI setup is presented in Figure 3.

Figure 3. Typical set up for MRI facility: (1) the MR scanner, (2) the projector, (3) optical tracker camera, (4) user interface console
(Blanco et al. 2005)

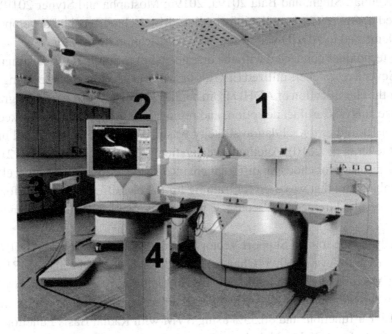

5. ARTIFICIAL INTELLIGENCE IN ADHD NEUROIMAGING

Artificial Intelligence (AI) facilitates various techniques for investigation with higher fairness and may have better-anticipating significance (Liu et al. 2018). AI tries to imitate human knowledge and to create another smart computer that would be ready to process data with individual awareness, conduct and thought to create a mind like humans in various domains such as Picture Examination, Regular Language Handling, Robotics, and Expert System (Liu et al. 2018).

Machine Learning (ML) was considered as the center of AI and the essential strategy for structuring smart devices. For the classification among healthy versus neurological patients, ML techniques implemented as valuable tools that identifying patterns in the data and utilizing them for identifying scenarios (Abraham et al. 2014). Different mental disorders such as Mild Cognitive Disorder, Alzheimer's disease, Psychomotor Epilepsy, Attention Deficit Hyperactivity Disorder (ADHD), can be smartly identified through Machine Learning calculation (Eslami and Saeed 2018). To best suit, the diagnosis characteristics, different types of ML algorithms are available, which can be further categorized based on feature selection and decision optimization tasks such as Supervised Machine learning, K-nearest Neighbor algorithm, Bayesian Network Classifiers (BNC), Support Vector Machines (SVM), Principal Component Analysis (PCA), and Multi-Kernel Learning.

Deep Learning (DL) prevailed remarkable success over conventional Machine Learning (ML) in the domain of clinical imaging research, because of its special capacity to study characteristics from raw data (Rim, Min, and Hong 2020). Sometimes Deep Learning referred to as Deep Neural Systems (DNS), which has multiple layers as compared to conventional Artificial Neural Networks. Deep learning has shown remarkable achievement and generalizability in the domain of medical by studying large information. The advancement of Deep Learning in PC Vision starts to its application in clinical image investigation, for Image Division, Image Enrollment, Image Combination, Tumor Identification, and PC Aided Analysis (Khullar, Singh, and Bala 2019a, 2019b; Mostapha and Styner 2019). Deep Learning methods performed a vital role, where the information-driven classifiers had developed for individual-specific data implemented to ADHD youngsters for identification decisions.

Brain imaging techniques connected with the diagnosing of technologies to distinguish ADHD from control subjects. Several researchers utilized EEG along with various Machine Learning and Deep Learning algorithms for the classification of ADHD from control subjects. SVM based program was practiced for automated spike analysis, artifact detection, and removal in EEG pattern for evoked possibilities. In this examination, a 10-fold cross-validation strategy was implemented that resulted in 92% classification exactness (Mueller et al. 2010). Another investigation (Abibullaev and An 2012) recommended a maximal disparity measure for choosing different characteristics of two groups as well as a semi-SVM based supervised algorithm that was used for training for the classification of EEG for ADHD associations. This method resulted tremendous accuracy, which was above 97% in the diagnostic procedure of ADHD disease.

Chang et al analyzed the trained Support Vector Machine (SVM) model for ADHD MRI classification and achieved accuracy was 0.6995 (Chang, Ho, and Chen 2012). Further, MRI images using an Extreme Learning Machine algorithm for ADHD classification were experimented by Peng et al (Peng et al. 2013). The results obtained for classification included accuracy of 90.18% using ELM, 84.73% using SVM with Linear function, and 86.55% using SVM with Radial Basis Function. Mahanand et al worked on a pilot study for ADHD which depends on the regional anatomy of the kid's mind, and that is done by MRI scans which acquired from the ADHD-200 consortium dataset. By utilizing ADHD-200 dataset, training of a Projection Based Learning algorithm for a Metacognitive Radial Basis Function Network (PBL-McRBFN) for classification was conducted and accuracy of 65 percent was achieved (Mahanand, Savitha, and Suresh 2013). Deshpande et al illustrated the efficiency of the Artificial Neural Network (ANN) structure for classifying ADHD individuals from typically developed and achieved accuracy between 90-95% (Deshpande et al. 2015). An investigation was conducted by Qureshi et al. using multiclass classification utilizing a hierarchical extreme learning machine (H-ELM) classifier. H-ELM classifier was examined with Support Vector Machine (SVM) and Extreme Learning Machine (ELM) based classifiers for cortical MRI data of ADHD subjects. As SVM was identified as a better approach which leads to implementing the SVM-based Recursive Feature Elimination (RFE-SVM) algorithm (Qureshi et al. 2017). The feature selected by this algorithm shows higher degrees of significance that depend on the internal linear SVM-based classification scores, consequently composing classification significantly more precise. By utilizing RFE-SVM, the binary classification accuracy of 85.29% and multiclass classification accuracy of 60.78% was achieved. Riaz et al. implemented the Elastic Net for feature extraction from ADHD-200 and then selected features based SVM was implemented. Support Vector Machine (SVM) was used for the classification of ADHD-200 data and achieved 81.8% of classification accuracy (Riaz et al. 2019). Felisa et al. highlighted the role of artificial intelligence for helping physicians to inquire about illness-related questions, which give a more individualized treatment for the sufferer and applied a deep convolutional neural network to detect mental disability using SPECT images of the cerebrum (Felisa et al. 2020). Kautzky et al. introduced a multivariate, genetic, and PET imaging model, which applied machine learning techniques to classify ADHD and healthy control. The mean accuracy was 0.82 (±0.09) with steady sensitivity (0.75) and specificity (0.86) was achieved with the implemented method (Kautzky et al. 2020).

Table 2. ADHD neuroimaging technologies with AI algorithms

Technologies	AI Algorithms	References
EEG	Used machine learning algorithm i.e. Support Vector Machine (SVM)	(Tenev et al. 2013)
EEG	Used deep learning algorithms	(Vahid et al. 2019)
EEG	Used a Multi-Layer Perceptron (MLP) neural network and Non-linear features to classify ADHD and healthy children.	(Mohammadi et al. 2016)
PET	Used deep learning-based Convolutional Neural Network algorithm.	(Hwang et al. 2018)
SPECT	Used deep learning techniques for the detection of mental illness.	(Felisa et al. 2020)
PET	Used machine learning for classification of ADHD and healthy control	(Kautzky et al. 2020)
EEG/ERP (Event-Related Potential)	Used machine learning methods to discriminate ADHD from a healthy control.	(Müller et al. 2019)
fMRI	Used deep learning models-deep belief network for extracting features and classification.	(Kuang 2014)
fMRI	Used fully Connected Cascade Artificial Neural Network Architecture for ADHD classification	(Deshpande et al. 2015)
MEG	Used Single channel Independent Component Analysis (ICA)	(Demanuele et al. 2008)
fMRI	Used multichannel deep neural network	(Chen 2019)
MRI	Used MRI to insights new changes in the brain structure and function in ADHD.	(Bush 2011)
fMRI	Used deep network optimizer based on CNN deep learning.	(Aradhya and Ashfahani 2019)
MRI	Used deep learning-based CNN algorithm.	(Mostapha and Styner 2019)

Several Deep Learning algorithms were additionally introduced for the diagnosis of ADHD neuroimages from control ones. The deep learning-based rs-fMRI classification using ADHD-200 dataset resulted in improved accuracy in comparison to SVM and RBF algorithms (Aradhya 2017; Aradhya and Ashfahani 2019). For ADHD characterization in time-frequency deterioration of EEG data, Deep Convolutional Neural Network (DCNN) was implemented and classification exactness of 88% was achieved, which was far better in contrast with other Machine Learning methods (Dubreuil-vall, Ruffini, and Camprodon 2019). Chen et al introduced a deep learning structure for the ADHD recognition dilemma by consolidating an EEG-based cerebrum connects by DCNN and achieved an accuracy of 98.17% during training (Chen et al. 2019). Table 2 presented the various ADHA diagnosis techniques which made the diagnosis smart with the help of different AI algorithms.

CONCLUSION

Since early and correct diagnosis is required in the treatment of ADHD, the role of neuroimaging technologies in ADHD diagnosis seems very crucial. The advancements in various neuroimaging technologies in combination with machine learning and deep learning algorithms had opened an era of intelligent and automatic diagnosis. The present work highlighted various intelligent algorithms that convert the traditional diagnosis into a smart and more accurate diagnosis. In the future, evolutionary combinations of artificial intelligence with neuroimaging technologies could open new arenas for research.

REFERENCES

Abibullaev & An. (2012). *Decision Support Algorithm for Diagnosis of ADHD Using Electroencephalograms*. Academic Press.

Abraham, Dohmatob, Thirion, Samaras, Abraham, Dohmatob, Thirion, Samaras, Varoquaux, Abraham, Dohmatob, & Thirion. (2014). *Extracting Brain Regions from Rest FMRI with Total-Variation Constrained Dictionary Learning To Cite This Version : HAL Id : Hal-00853242 Extracting Brain Regions from Rest FMRI with Total-Variation Constrained Dictionary Learning*. Academic Press.

Aradhya, A. M. S. (2017). *Deep Transformation Method for Discriminant Analysis of Multi-Channel Resting State FMRI*. Academic Press.

Aradhya, A. M. S., & Ashfahani, A. (2019). Deep Network Optimization for Rs-FMRI Classification. *IEEE International Conference on Data Mining Workshops, ICDMW*, 77–82.

Blanco, Ojala, Kariniemi, Per, Niinim, & Tervonen. (2005). *Interventional and Intraoperative MRI at Low Field Scanner – a Review*. Academic Press.

Boon, H. J. (2020). What Do ADHD Neuroimaging Studies Reveal for Teachers, Teacher Educators and Inclusive Education? *Child and Youth Care Forum*, *49*(4), 0123456789. doi:10.100710566-019-09542-4

Bush, G. (2011). Cingulate, Frontal, and Parietal Cortical Dysfunction in Attention-Deficit/Hyperactivity Disorder. *Biological Psychiatry*, *69*(12), 1160–1167. doi:10.1016/j.biopsych.2011.01.022 PMID:21489409

Chang, C. W., Ho, C. C., & Chen, J. H. (2012, August). ADHD Classification by a Texture Analysis of Anatomical Brain MRI Data. *Frontiers in Systems Neuroscience*, *6*, 1–35. doi:10.3389/fnsys.2012.00066 PMID:23024630

Chen, M. (2019). *A Multichannel Deep Neural Network Model Analyzing Multiscale Functional Brain Connectome Data for Attention*. Academic Press.

Chen, Y., Tang, Y., Wang, C., Liu, X., & Zhao, L. (2019). ADHD Classification by Dual Subspace Learning Using Resting-State Functional Connectivity. *Artificial Intelligence in Medicine*, 101786. PMID:32143793

Chen, Y., Tang, Y., Wang, C., Liu, X., Zhao, L., & Wang, Z. (2020). ADHD Classification by Dual Subspace Learning Using Resting-State Functional Connectivity. *Artificial Intelligence in Medicine*, *103*, 101786. doi:10.1016/j.artmed.2019.101786 PMID:32143793

Chheda-varma, B. (2010). *Attention Deficit Hyperactivity Disorder (ADHD): A Case Study and Exploration of Causes and Interventions Symptoms of ADHD*. Springer International Publishing.

Cubillo & Rubia. (2010). *Structural and Functional Brain Imaging in Adult Attention- Deficit / Hyperactivity Disorder*. Academic Press.

Degiorgi, M., Garzotto, F., Gelsomini, M., Leonardi, G., Penati, S., Ramuzat, N., Silvestri, J., Clasadonte, F., & Kinoe, Y. (2017). Puffy - An Inflatable Robotic Companion for Pre-Schoolers. *RO-MAN 2017 - 26th IEEE International Symposium on Robot and Human Interactive Communication*, 35–41. 10.1109/ROMAN.2017.8172277

Demanuele, C., James, C. J., Sonuga-Barke, E. J. S., & Capilla, A. (2008). Low Frequency Phase Synchronisation Analysis of MEG Recordings from Children with ADHD and Controls Using Single Channel ICA. *IET Conference Publications*. 10.1049/cp:20080428

Deshpande, G., Wang, P., Rangaprakash, D., & Wilamowski, B. (2015). Fully Connected Cascade Artificial Neural Network Architecture for Attention Deficit Hyperactivity Disorder Classification from Functional Magnetic Resonance Imaging Data. *IEEE Transactions on Cybernetics*, *45*(12), 2668–2679. doi:10.1109/TCYB.2014.2379621 PMID:25576588

Ding & Yuan. (2011). *Simultaneous EEG and MEG Source Reconstruction in Sparse Electromagnetic Source Imaging*. Academic Press.

DSM-V. (2013). *A.P.A., Diagnostic and Statistical Manual of Mental Disorders, 5th Ed.* Arlington, VA: American Psychiatric Association.

Dubreuil-vall, Ruffini, & Camprodon. (2019). *A Deep Learning Approach with Event-Related Spectral EEG Data in Attentional Deficit Hyperactivity Disorder*. Academic Press.

Durston, S. (2003). A Review f the Biological Bases of ADHD: What Have We Learned from Imaging Studies? *Mental Retardation and Developmental Disabilities Research Reviews*, *9*(3), 184–195. doi:10.1002/mrdd.10079 PMID:12953298

Eslami, T., & Saeed, F. (2018). Similarity Based Classification of ADHD Using Singular Value Decomposition. *2018 ACM International Conference on Computing Frontiers, CF 2018 – Proceedings*, 19–25. 10.1145/3203217.3203239

Felisa, Bernabel, Dufresne, & Sood. (2020). Deep Learning for Mental Illness Detection Using Brain SPECT Imaging. *Medical Imaging and Computer-Aided Diagnosis*.

Greenway, C. W., & Edwards, A. R. (2020). Knowledge and Attitudes towards Attention-Deficit Hyperactivity Disorder (ADHD): A Comparison of Teachers and Teaching Assistants Teaching Assistants. *Australian Journal of Learning Difficulties*, *00*(00), 1–19. doi:10.1080/19404158.2019.1709875

Helenius, P., Laasonen, M., Hokkanen, L., Paetau, R., & Niemivirta, M. (2011). *Neuropsychologia Impaired Engagement of the Ventral Attentional Pathway in ADHD*. Academic Press.

Hwang, Kim, Kang, Seo, & Paeng. (2018). *Improving Accuracy of Simultaneously Reconstructed Activity and Attenuation Maps Using Deep Learning*. Academic Press.

Kautzky, A., Vanicek, T., Philippe, C., Kranz, G. S., Wadsak, W., Mitterhauser, M., Hartmann, A., Hahn, A., Hacker, M., Rujescu, D., Kasper, S., & Lanzenberger, R. (2020). Machine Learning Classification of ADHD and HC by Multimodal Serotonergic Data. *Translational Psychiatry*, *10*(1), 104. doi:10.103841398-020-0781-2 PMID:32265436

Khullar, V., Singh, H. P., & Bala, M. (2019a). Autism Spectrum Disorders : A Systematic Review from the Perspective of Computer Assisted Developments. In S. P. And & C. Subudhi (Eds.), *Psycho-Social Perspectives on Mental Health and Well-Being*. IGI Global.

Khullar, V., Singh, H. P., & Bala, M. (2019b). IoT Based Assistive Companion for Hypersensitive Individuals (ACHI) with Autism Spectrum Disorder. *Asian Journal of Psychiatry*, *46*, 92–102. doi:10.1016/j.ajp.2019.09.030 PMID:31639556

Klein, A. M., Onnink, M., Van, M., Wolfers, T., Harich, B., Shi, Y., Dammers, J., & Arias-va, A. (2017). Brain Imaging Genetics in ADHD and beyond – Mapping Pathways from Gene to Disorder at Different Levels of Complexity. *Neuroscience and Biobehavioral Reviews*, *80*, 115–155. doi:10.1016/j.neubiorev.2017.01.013 PMID:28159610

Krain, A. L., & Xavier Castellanos, F. (2006). *Brain Development and ADHD*. Academic Press.

Kuang, D. (2014). *Classification on ADHD with Deep Learning*. Academic Press.

Laufs, H. (2012). NeuroImage A Personalized History of EEG – FMRI Integration. *NeuroImage*, *62*(2), 1056–1067. doi:10.1016/j.neuroimage.2012.01.039 PMID:22266176

Liu, J., Pan, Y., Li, M., Chen, Z., Tang, L., Lu, C., & Wang, J. (2018). Applications of Deep Learning to MRI Images W. *Survey (London, England)*, *1*(1), 1–18.

Mahanand, Savitha, & Suresh. (2013). *Computer Aided Diagnosis of ADHD Using Brain Magnetic Resonance Images*. Academic Press.

Mohammadi, Khaleghi, Nasrabadi, Rafieivand, & Begol. (2016). *EEG Classification of ADHD and Normal Children Using Non-Linear Features and Neural Network*. Academic Press.

Mostapha, M., & Styner, M. (2019). Role of Deep Learning in Infant Brain MRI Analysis. *Magnetic Resonance Imaging*, *64*, 171–189. doi:10.1016/j.mri.2019.06.009 PMID:31229667

Mueller, A., Candrian, G., Kropotov, J. D., Ponomarev, V. A., & Baschera, G. M. (2010). Classification of ADHD Patients on the Basis of Independent ERP Components Using a Machine Learning System. *Nonlinear Biomedical Physics*, *4*(S1), 1–12. doi:10.1186/1753-4631-4-S1-S1 PMID:20522259

Müller, A., Vetsch, S., Pershin, I., Candrian, G., Kropotov, J., Kasper, J., & Abdel Rehim, H. (2019). EEG/ERP-Based Biomarker/Neuroalgorithms in Adults with ADHD: Development, Reliability, and Application in Clinical Practice. *The World Journal of Biological Psychiatry*, 172–182. PMID:30990349

Naveed, Qureshi, Min, Jo, & Lee. (2016). *Multiclass Classification for the Differential Diagnosis on the ADHD Subtypes Using Recursive Feature Elimination and Hierarchical Extreme Learning Machine : Structural MRI Study*. Academic Press.

Oj, Elmose, Skoog, Hansen, Simonsen, Pedersen, Tendal, He, Faltinsen, & Gluud. (2019). *Social Skills Training for Attention Deficit Hyperactivity Disorder (ADHD) in Children Aged 5 to 18 Years (Review)*. Academic Press.

Peng, Lin, Zhang, & Wang. (2013). *Extreme Learning Machine-Based Classification of ADHD Using Brain Structural MRI Data*. Academic Press.

Qureshi, M. N. I., Oh, J., Min, B., Jo, H. J., & Lee, B. (2017). Multi-Class Discrimination of ADHD with Hierarchical Feature Extraction and Extreme Learning Machine Using Structural and Functional Brain MRI. *Frontiers in Human Neuroscience, 11*(157), 1–16.

Riaz, A., Asad, M., Alonso, E., & Slabaugh, G. (2019). DeepFMRI: End-to-End Deep Learning for Functional Connectivity and Classification of ADHD Using FMRI. *Journal of Neuroscience Methods*. PMID:32001294

Richard, A. E., Lajiness-O'Neill, R. R., & Bowyer, S. M. (2013). Impaired Prefrontal Gamma Band Synchrony in Autism Spectrum Disorders during Gaze Cueing. *Neuroreport, 24*(16), 894–897. doi:10.1097/WNR.0000000000000015 PMID:24077557

Rim, B., Min, S., & Hong, M. (2020). Deep Learning in Physiological Signal Data. *Survey (London, England)*. PMID:32054042

Rodríguez-martínez, E. I., Angulo-ruiz, B. Y., Arjona-valladares, A., Rufo, M., Gómez-gonzález, J., & Gómez, C. M. (2019, October). Research in Developmental Disabilities Frequency Coupling of Low and High Frequencies in the EEG of ADHD Children and Adolescents in Closed and Open Eyes Conditions. *Research in Developmental Disabilities, 96*, 103520. doi:10.1016/j.ridd.2019.103520 PMID:31783276

Rostain & Ramsay. (2006). *A Combined Treatment Approach for Adults With ADHD — Results of an Open Study of 43 Patients*. Academic Press.

Sen, Borle, Greiner, & Brown. (2018). *A General Prediction Model for the Detection of ADHD and Autism Using Structural and Functional MRI*. Academic Press.

Silverstein, Faraone, Leon, Biederman, Spencer, & Adler. (2018). *The Relationship Between Executive Function Deficits and DSM -5-Defined ADHD Symptoms*. Academic Press.

Tan, Qiu, Liu, Yan, Hai, Mei, Meng, Huang, Yu, He, & Liao. (2019). *Alterations of Cerebral Perfusion and Functional Brain Connectivity in Medication - Naïve Male Adults with Attention - Deficit / Hyperactivity Disorder*. Academic Press.

Tenev, A., Markovska-simoska, S., Kocarev, L., Pop-jordanov, J., Müller, A., & Candrian, G. (2013). Machine Learning Approach for Classi Fi Cation of ADHD Adults. *International Journal of Psychophysiology*, 1–5. PMID:23361114

Thapar, Cooper, Eyre, & Langley. (2012). *Practitioner Review : What Have We Learnt about the Causes of ADHD?* Academic Press.

Townsend, Beyer, & Blodgett. (2003). *PET/CT Scanners: A Hardware Approach to Image Fusion*. Academic Press.

Tran, K., & Wu, J. (2019). Case Report : Neuroimaging Analysis of Pediatric ADHD-Related Symptoms Secondary to Hypoxic Brain Injury. *Brain Injury: [BI]*, *33*(10), 1402–1407. doi:10.1080/02699052.2019.1641744 PMID:31307241

Vahid, Bluschke, Roessner, & Stober. (2019). *Deep Learning Based on Event-Related EEG Di Ff Erentiates Children with ADHD from Healthy Controls*. Academic Press.

Chapter 4
Automated Microcontroller–Based Irrigation System

Mmathapelo Makana
University of Johannesburg, South Africa

Nnamdi Nwulu
https://orcid.org/0000-0003-2607-7439
University of Johannesburg, South Africa

Eustace Dogo
University of Johannesburg, South Africa

ABSTRACT

Traditional irrigation systems do not take into consideration the conservation of water. Therefore, automating the plant watering systems to reduce water wastage and loss would be key to water conservation as a means of making use of water wisely and responsibly. In this chapter, a smart irrigation system that helps control the amount of water applied to crops is proposed and developed. The system controls the ON/OFF state of the water pumping motor based on the soil moisture sensor reading. Other sensors incorporated in the system are the water level sensor and light dependent resistor. The system leverages on the Arduino Uno microcontroller development board to collect input signals from the three sensors. The water pump operates depending on the value of the output signal received by the relay module. This technique of watering is feasible and very affordable and reduces human intervention in field watering.

INTRODUCTION

Water is an essential resource for agricultural crop farming. There is currently an increase in water demand because of the continuous increase in population, rapid urbanization, and climate change due to unpredictable weather patterns. Agriculture alone accounts for usage of nearly 70% of freshwater, this along with water losses in traditional irrigation system primarily due to variable soil moisture and water requirements on the farming field (Ahamed, 2019). Hence, the need to find better ways driven

DOI: 10.4018/978-1-7998-7511-6.ch004

by the technology of conserving, utilizing and management of water resource in all sectors including in agricultural use (Arvindan & Keerthika, 2016; Dogo et al., 2019).

Irrigation is the artificial administration of water to the soil using different systems of tubes, sprays and pumps at steady intervals so that plants can flourish quantitatively and qualitatively (Oregon State University, 2020). It is normally used in regions where there is little or no rainfall or areas where there are high chances of drought. Sources of irrigation water include wells, groundwater, treated wastewater and surface water sources such as lakes and rivers. Farmers must protect and sustainably use their water sources for high crop yields (Kamaruddin et al., 2019; Namala et al., 2016).

Previously, farmers have been using irrigation techniques that require manual control to irrigate fields at planned intervals. However, this technique sometimes results in under irrigation or over-irrigation. Water insufficiency can be harmful to crops. It may result in a slower growth rate and production of lightweight products. Over irrigation results in waterlogged soils and/or soil erosion which will result in low-quality soil for future use. These problems can be alleviated by automating the irrigation systems that will control the use of water in the agricultural fields to minimize wastage.

The following are the specific objectives:

1.   To design a system that allows automatic irrigation using engineering tools and techniques.
2.   To implement the designed system and test its performance and functionality.
3.   To evaluate the accuracy and reliability of the system based on the test results obtained.

LITERATURE REVIEW

Deep Learning and IoT in Irrigation System

Deep learning is an artificial intelligence concept and a sub-domain of machine learning algorithms based on artificial neural networks that allow the computer to learn from experience and data in terms of a hierarchy of concepts or multilayers representations (Goodfellow et al., 2016). Deep learning is inspired by the setup and working of the human brain in the form of many layers of depth in the architectural models (Goodfellow et al., 2016). A classic example of deep learning model is the multilayer perceptron (MLP), which is a mathematical function that maps input variables to the output variable. Over the years, other state-of-the-art deep learning architectural models have been developed to solve numerous complex real-life problems. The key deep learning architectural models are convolutional neural network (CNN) (LeCun et al., 1998), recurrent neural networks (RNN) (Rumelhart et al., 1985), stacked denoising autoencoder (SDAE) (Vincent et al., 2010), deep belief network (DBN) (Hinton et al., 2006), deep Boltzmann machine (DBM) (Salakhutdinov & Hinton, 2009) and their respective implementation variations. Generally, deep learning scales well in the presence of a large amount of data, which suits the massive IoT generated data. For interested readers, a detailed discussion of deep learning can be found in (Goodfellow et al., 2016).

IoT is a communication technology-based concept that enables a scenario where objects referred to as *things* are interconnected with one another, using standard communication protocols, with each object having its own uniquely identifiable addressing system, and forming an integral part of the internet (Atzori et al., 2017). IoT relates to the integration of people, machines, and information. The IoT functional stack architecture consists of the *Things* embedded with sensing capabilities, the *networking* layer, and the specific *application* layer (Minerva et al., 2015), as depicted in Figure 2. Wireless communication technology such as wireless sensor networks (WSN) plays a vital role in IoT implementation. It is also well documented in works of literature that IoT plays an important role in nearly all aspects of human life by enabling sensing and data generation capabilities necessary for the working of deep learning models to derive useful knowledge and decision-making.

Figure 1. Three-tier Architecture of IoT
(Minerva et al., 2015)

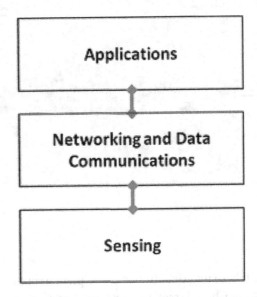

The synergy and application of deep learning and Internet of Things (IoT) enabled technologies offers viable and sustainable irrigation management solutions to farmers, by addressing the challenges associated with variable water requirement in farming fields due to differing soil moisture content level, soil type, organic content in the soil and slope of the farming land, with the overall aim of minimizing water losses and improved crop yield. The deep learning-IoT based system consists of numerous distributed sensors, such as soil moisture sensors, temperature and humidity sensors; water pumps, wireless communication modules, relays and microcontrollers, integrated to the internet via cloud computing platform (Ahamed, 2019). An advanced system depicted in Figure 2 would consist of water pumps connected to microcontrollers via relays, then the microcontrollers are in turn connected to wireless communication modules. The wireless modules transmit and receive signals generated by the numerous distributed wireless sensors, including sensing unmanned drones optimally placed across the entire farming field (Ahamed, 2019). The hardware and sensing components could then be integrated into a smartphone app via IoT-cloud architecture to allow for seamless remote control and management of the smart irrigation system. The deep learning system leveraging on the different learning algorithms uses the data generated by the sensors in tandem with other data sources such as remote sensing data, weather and climatic information, to derive useful information that is feed into the smart irrigation system to ensure that the water requirement of crops is meet optimally, in addition to the main objective of minimizing water losses during irrigation and improved crop production.

Figure 2. Example of deep learning IoT-based Irrigation system
(Source: (Ahamed, 2019))

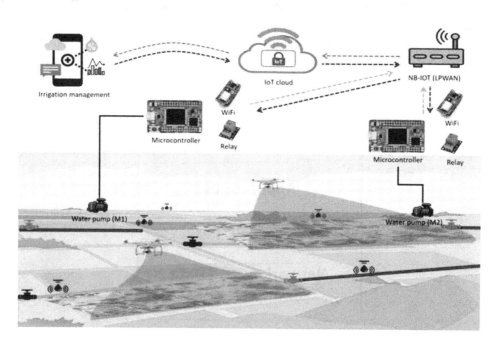

Related Work

This subsection reviews some of these microcontroller-based plant irrigation systems. There exist several implementations of microcontroller-based irrigation or plant watering systems with a different number of sensors, with incorporated with GSM module and cloud for remote monitoring, as well as with web and mobile App interfaces (Namala et al., 2016; National Geographic, 2020; Singh & Saikia, 2016; Thakare & Bhagat, 2018). From Table 1, it is observed that majority of the irrigation systems leverages on the Arduino Uno development board based on ATmega microcontroller as the preferred choice for implementing the system and integrated with WiFi or mobile capability. The soil moisture sensor is also a common hardware device design consideration in nearly all surveyed papers. Some recent work has attempted to incorporate machine learning into the irrigation system (Aggarwal & Kumar, 2019; Chang et al., 2019; Goap et al., 2018; Singh et al., 2019), fuzzy logic-based system (Alomar & Alazzam, 2018; Pezol et al., 2020) and solar-powered implementations (Aggarwal & Kumar, 2019; Mungale et al., 2020; Selmani et al., 2018).

However, the main aim of this current work is to design and implement a simple and cost-effective prototype automated plant watering system as an initial proof of concept, which allows the microcontroller to trigger the irrigation system using criteria as low soil moisture, medium to high water level and when there is no light detected. The prototype system will consist of a sample soil to be irrigated, a soil moisture sensor to detect the moisture content of the soil, a water level sensor to detect the availability of water in the tank, and a light-dependent resistor (LDR) to detect sunlight, a power supply and a water pumping system, as well as a buzzer to alert the farmer in case of any emergency. Even though this current design did not incorporate WiFi or smartphone app, the Arduino Uno development allows for future expansion to add these features including an interactive web interface.

Table 1. Comparative summary of some related works with this study

Reference	Microcontroller	Sensors	WiFi/GSM/Cloud
	Arduino	Flowmeter and soil moisture	Yes
	PIC 18F 4550	Soil moisture	Yes
	Arduino	Soil moisture, pH, temperature, humidity, light intensity, buzzer	Yes
	Arduino	Soil moisture, pH, temperature, humidity	Yes
	Arduino	Soil moisture, pH, temperature, humidity and flame	Yes
	Arduino	Soil moisture	Yes
	Arduino	Soil moisture, pH and temperature	Yes
	Arduino	Water flow, soil moisture and temperature	Yes
	Raspberry Pi	Soil moisture	No
	Arduino	Soil moisture	Yes
This study	Arduino	Soil moisture, water level, LDR (light intensity), buzzer	No

DESIGN AND IMPLEMENTATION

The proposed system aims to reduce human intervention in irrigation systems while making optimum use of irrigation water. This system would allow for automatic powering of a water pumping system via a relay module, depending on the status of the tested parameters. The proposed system continually monitors the soil moisture state, availability of water in the storage container and the presence of light. As long as it is powered on, the system operates the water supply automatically, irrespective of the presence or absence of the user. Hence, the duty of manually turning ON or OFF the pump motor is automated. This smart watering system can be placed in fields or home gardens to continuously monitor the soil moisture content. When the soil moisture of the soil is below a certain level, the system will turn on and start irrigating the field automatically. The system improves the livelihood of the user and help in saving water. Furthermore, it can also help ensure great crop yields since it can handle the occurrence of over-irrigation and under-irrigation. The Arduino microcontroller is the epicentre of the entire system. It serves as interlink between the sensors and the watering system. The system block diagram is shown in Figure 3 comprising the interconnection of the various hardware components utilized, namely the power supply subsystem, the control (microcontroller and sensing arrangement) subsystem and the water supply subsystem. The Arduino microcontroller is powered and programmed via a USB cable using the Arduino IDE software. The control unit, which consists of the water level sensor, the moisture sensors and the LDR records the all the output values showing the amount of water available, the moisture condition of the soil, the presence of sunlight. All these values are then displayed on the LCD. Finally, the water supply system controlled by a relay circuit is meant to trigger the motor pump ON/OFF depending on the signal received from the control unit.

Figure 3. The system block diagram

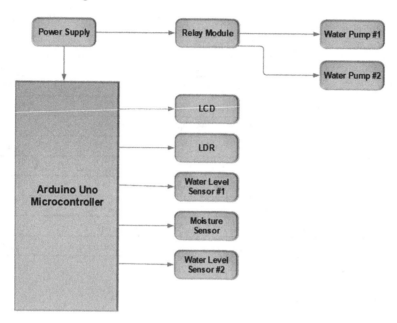

The circuit diagram of an automatic irrigation system is presented in Figure 4. The circuit includes 12V power supply, USB cable, Arduino UNO R3 board, water level sensor, two soil moisture sensor, LDR, two water pump, buzzer, 5V relay module board (4 Channel), 3.3k Ω resistors (5), potentiometer and transistor.

Figure 4. Circuit wiring diagram of the smart irrigation system

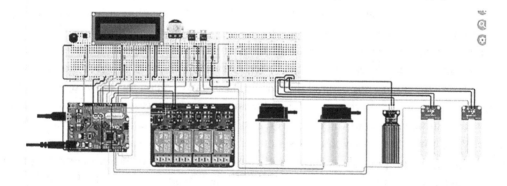

The entire system consists of the hardware and software subsystems, which will be described in subsequent subsections.

Table 2. Technical specification of the soil moisture sensor

Feature	Description and Rating
Colour	Red and Silver
Material	RF4
Power Supply	3.3V/ 5V
Working Current	> 20mA
Output Voltage	0~2.3V
Supply Voltage	5V
Sensor Type	Analogue output

Hardware Component

This section presents an overview of the hardware components utilized in implementing the prototype design.

Soil Moisture Sensor

In manual irrigation systems, visual observation and hand testing are used to test and monitor the moisture content of the soil. However, this is not an accurate and reliable method because human error may occur. To improve the monitoring of soil moisture content, a soil moisture sensor is used to measure the water volume of soil. This moisture is inserted into the soil to be tested and the volumetric water content of that soil will be detected and recorded in percentages. The two exposed pads of the moisture sensor together act as a variable resistor and function as probes for the sensor. A good conductivity between the two pads will result in a lower resistance. This is an indication of high moisture content in the soil. The system is configured such that if the analogue value detected is less than 200, then the soil is dry and if the recorded analogue value is between 200 and 500, the soil is moderately dry and lastly, if the analogue value is more than 500 it implies that the soil is extremely wet. The technical specification is outlined in Table 1.

Table 3. Technical specifications of the water level sensor

Feature	Description/Rating
Colour	Red and Silver
Material	RF4
Working Current	> 20mA
Output Voltage	3-5 V DC
Sensor Type	Simulation

Water Level Sensor

This sensor was included as part of the system to check the availability of water in the water storage. If low water levels are detected, the two motors are turned OFF, irrespective of the light and soil moisture conditions. This is done to prevent the motor from being destroyed because running it in the absence of water for a long time will result in overheat and the motor will eventually get damaged and stop working.

Light Dependent Resistor (LDR)

LDR is a component that varies its resistance based on the intensity of light that falls on it. When there is no light source falling on the LDR, the resistance increases. An increase in resistance will mean that there is no sunlight and the irrigation process can continue at this given time until sunlight is detected. The moment it detects the presence of sunlight, the irrigation process stops immediately because of low LDR reading. An LDR can function properly in any environment where visible light can penetrate through. For this work, the threshold analogue value for the LDR to start detecting sunlight was set to 200kΩ. The technical specification of the LDR used in the work is shown in Table 2.

Table 4. Technical specifications of an LDR

Feature	Rating
Dark Space Resistance	Dark Space Resistance
>1MΩ	>1MΩ
High light levels	High light levels
<1kΩ	<1kΩ

Relay Module

A relay module was used as the switching mechanism in the watering system. It switches ON or OFF the pumping motor, depending on the signal received. A relay switch was used because an Arduino cannot control higher voltage devices directly. The Arduino was used to control the relay, which in turn will control the water pump. The Arduino was programmed to turn on the relay when low soil moisture content, medium to high water level and no light were detected. If any of the three conditions are not satisfied, the Arduino is programmed to switch off the relay. The three high voltage terminals of the relay are connected to the water pump motor and the low side voltage pins connect to the Arduino.

Arduino UNO

Arduino UNO R3 is the epicentre of the whole system. To start the process, the Arduino is connected to a computer using a USB cable which will power on the system and upload the code from the computer to the board. An external wall-wart 12V power supply was plugged into the power jack of the Arduino board. Arduino Uno R3 was chosen as a microcontroller because it is affordable and has better specifications, which meet the requirements of this design as compared to the other alternative microcontrollers.

Table 5. Technical specifications of the diaphragm water pump

Feature	Description/Rating
Input Voltage	6-12 VDC
Flow Rate	1.5-2 L per minute
Operation Temperature	80 Degree C
Operating Current	0.5-0.7A
Suction Distance	Maximum of 2m
Signal Drive Current	15-20 mA
Maximum Output	DC 30V/10A, AC 250V/10A

Liquid Crystal Display (LCD) Screen

The LCD screen was used to display information such as the moisture content of the soil, water level, presence of light and the time it takes to irrigate. It also displayed important notifications that call for the user to take some action, such as filling up the water tank when a low water level is detected.

Water Supply System

A relay module was used as the switching mechanism in the water supply system. It switches ON or OFF the motor of the pump, depending on the signal received. A relay switch was used because an Arduino cannot control higher voltage devices directly. The Arduino was used to control the relay which in turn will control the pumps which are connected to a 12V external power supply. A relay module has a standard interface which a microcontroller can control directly. For safety requirements, the microcontroller is isolated from high voltage side and it also blocks the ground loop when the interface to a microcontroller. The Arduino was programmed to turn on the relay when low soil moisture content, medium to high water level and no light were detected. If any of the three conditions are not satisfied, the Arduino is programmed to switch off the relay.

A relay is a switch-like device which permits low current devices such as the Arduino microcontroller to control devices with high current requirements, such as a water pump. It makes use of an electromagnetic switch to switch and provide electrical isolation between the water pump and the power supply.

The relay module works from a signal of 12V and makes use of a transistor to switch ON the relay so that it can be directly connected to a microcontroller pin. The relay was used to interface the sensing subsystems with the microcontroller unit. An NPN transistor was used to connect the relay module to the Arduino microcontroller and a resistor was used to protect the transistor by limiting the current that will be flowing to the transistor while turning on. The relay module comes fully assembled and can support any microcontroller. The relay module switches up to 10A and is rated at up to 250V

For this work, a 2-channel relay could have been used in two watering systems. However, due to the constraint of budget, a 4-channel relay module was used as it was already available. A 4-channel relay has four mounting holes and an on-board switching transistor. Only two of the 4 mounting holes were used for the two watering pumps.

Software Component

The Arduino Integrated Development Environment (IDE) software is a simplified version of C/C++ for coding onto the physical Arduino board. The system functions in the following steps:

Step 1: Power supplied to the system via an external wall plug power supply.
Step 2: Scanning all sensors and display on LCD Screen.
Step 3: If the soil moisture content is low, and there is a medium to high water level available in the water storage and no sunlight present, start irrigation.
Step 4: If any of the following condition is detected, the system does not irrigate.
   ◦ High soil moisture content detected.
   ◦ Low water level.
   ◦ Presence of sunlight.

The system consists of two watering systems. It scans system 1 first, and then 2. This process of scanning happens in a small amount of time. If system 1 meets all the conditions for irrigation and system 2 does not, then the following will be observed:

- Motor 2 is turned ON and irrigation takes place for the next 10s in watering system 1 and then motor 2 turns ON for only 2 seconds since a dry condition was detected for system 2. After that, the system restarts and scan the sensors again.

If system 1 does not meet the conditions for irrigation, and system 2 meets all the conditions. The following will be observed:

- Motor 1 is turned ON for 2seconds and then switches OFF. After that, motor 2 is turned ON and irrigation will take place for the next 10 seconds since the soil is dry.
- Afterwards, the systems restart and scan the sensors again.

RESULT AND DISCUSSION

The watering system develop is based on soil moisture sensor, water level sensor and LDR. These sensors are installed in the field. The sensors and the Arduino microcontroller capture the soil moisture state, the water level and presence of light, and the results are displayed on the LCD screen. The system developed is expected to turn ON or OFF the water pump automatically, depending on the values detected by the sensors. This system thus includes less manpower where the only task of the user is to observe the LCD screen for results detected by the sensors and fill up the water storage only when low levels of water is detected. This system also reduced over-watering and under-watering, beneficial to the user in terms of optimum healthy crop production.

Figure 5 shows a screenshot obtained from the screen monitor of the Arduino IDE. In this experiment, the LDR was exposed to very little light and the Analog value detected was 14, which is much less than the threshold value thus a dark environment was displayed. The threshold value to detect light of this LDR was set to a higher value to avoid the detection of light in the environment. If set to a lower value, the LDR was always going to output, a light environment and the system would always be OFF as no irrigation is allowed whenever sunlight is detected.

Figure 5. Soil moisture output values for different light intensities

```
LUX: 14.00(Dark)
Water level: 0(EMPTY!)
Soil moisture 1: 0.00(DRY)
Soil moisture 2: 0.00(DRY)
Soil moisture 1: 0.00(DRY)
Soil moisture 2: 0.00(DRY)
Water level: 0(EMPTY!)
LUX: 12.00(Dark)
Water level: 0(EMPTY!)
Soil moisture 1: 0.00(DRY)
Soil moisture 2: 0.00(DRY)
Soil moisture 1: 0.00(DRY)
Soil moisture 2: 0.00(DRY)
Water level: 0(EMPTY!)
1023
LUX: 12.00(Dark)
Water level: 0(EMPTY!)
Soil moisture 1: 0.00(DRY)
Soil moisture 2: 0.00(DRY)
Soil moisture 1: 0.00(DRY)
Soil moisture 2: 0.00(DRY)
Water level: 0(EMPTY!)
LUX: 13.00(Dark)
Water level: 0(EMPTY!)
Soil moisture 1: 0.00(DRY)
Soil moisture 2: 0.00(DRY)
```

The two moisture sensors were placed in dry soil first and the Analog value detected was zero, which is what was expected. The water container had no water and the Analog input was zero shown by a water level of zero on the monitoring screen of Arduino IDE. As expected, no irrigation took place because there was no water in the water storage container.

Figure 6. Soil moisture reading in a dark environment and empty water storage

```
LUX: 13.00(Dark)
Water level: 0(EMPTY!)
Soil moisture 1: 140.00(DRY)
Soil moisture 2: 579.00(WET)
Soil moisture 1: 161.00(DRY)
Soil moisture 2: 568.00(WET)
Water level: 0(EMPTY!)
```

Figure 6 shows the results obtained when the LDR detected a dark environment, the water level sensor detected that there is no water in the storage container. Soil moisture sensor 1 was placed in a dry soil whilst soil moisture sensor 2 was placed in wet condition. Soil moisture sensor 1 gave an Analog output of 140 which is less than the threshold value to detect a moderate moisture soil which 200 to 500 or a wet soil condition where the threshold is an Analog value of 500 or more. Moisture sensor 2 gave an Analog value of 568 which is more than the threshold value for wet soil thus a wet soil condition was detected. As expected, even if the soil in the zone where moisture sensor 1 is placed is dry, irrigation will not take place because there is no water available.

Figure 7. Results with the dark environment, high-water level and dry soil

```
LUX: 18.00(Dark)
Started watering 1
LUX: 18.00(Dark)
Started watering 1
LUX: 18.00(Dark)
Started watering 1
LUX: 18.00(Dark)
Started watering 1
LUX: 19.00(Dark)
Started watering 1
LUX: 20.00(Dark)
Started watering 1
```

Figure 7 shows results obtained when a dark environment was detected, high water levels and dry soil. As expected, the watering system will be triggered ON as all the three conditions have been met. This process will continue for the next 10 seconds and then start scanning the sensors again.

Table 6. Results of sensors tested in different conditions and scenarios

Light Intensity	Water Level	Moisture 1	Moisture 1	Motor 1	Motor 2
0	0	0	0	OFF	OFF
0	279	724	0	OFF	ON
3	57	1	1	OFF	OFF
309	454	6	66	OFF	OFF
156	310	84	56	ON	ON
5	402	400	52	OFF	ON
8	410	58	578	ON	OFF
703	410	39	66	OFF	OFF

The overall completed prototype automated irrigation system is depicted in Figure 8

Figure 8. Complete prototype system

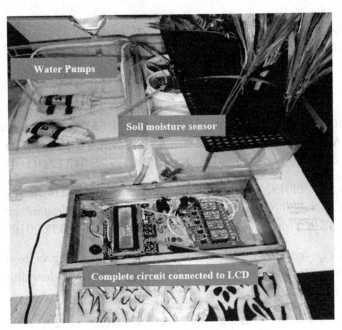

CONCLUSION AND RECOMMENDATION

An automated irrigation system was developed successfully, making use of a soil moisture sensor, a water level sensor, an LDR, a water pumping system and a 12V power adapter. The moisture sensor could test the moisture content of the soil and the water level sensor was able to detect the amount of water available in the container. The LDR was able to test whether there is sunlight or not. All this information from the sensors was stored as analogue input and output as digital for interpretation. The digital output information was then displayed on the LCD screen for the user. The most important information for the user is the water level status as detected by the water level sensor. The user must check for this information because if there is low or no water in the storage tank, the tank must be manually refilled.

Listed below are some recommendations, which can be incorporated to improve the project in future:

- Using a pump with two Input/output pins for lower costs
- Automating the water supply to the storage container by making use of additional water level sensor, which will be placed in another container that will function as a supply. This will, in turn, automate the whole process of irrigating with no human interference.
- Interfacing the system with a GSM module and the cloud to enable a user to control the water level and IoT devices through a smart mobile phone application using, for example, Arduino IoT Cloud Remote app.
- Integrating the system with more sensors as well as cameras for visual monitoring and analysis of the irrigation system.
- Incorporating artificial intelligence algorithms on the generated sensor data, as a way of predicting future occurrences in the system, assisting in mapping out the water-deficient part of the farming field and other advantages that could be derived from a deep learning-IoT platform.

ACKNOWLEDGMENT

We want to thank the University of Johannesburg for making the resources available to complete this work.

REFERENCES

Abba, S., Wadumi Namkusong, J., Lee, J. A., & Liz Crespo, M. (2019). Design and Performance Evaluation of a Low-Cost Autonomous Sensor Interface for a Smart IoT-Based Irrigation Monitoring and Control System. *Sensors (Basel)*, *19*(17), 3643. doi:10.339019173643 PMID:31438597

Aggarwal, S., & Kumar, A. (2019, March). A Smart Irrigation System to Automate Irrigation Process Using IOT and Artificial Neural Network. In *2019 2nd International Conference on Signal Processing and Communication (ICSPC)* (pp. 310-314). IEEE. 10.1109/ICSPC46172.2019.8976631

Ahamed, T. (2019). *Deep learning and IoT-based pump systems for precision irrigation.* Accessed August 8, 2020, at https://www.apo-tokyo.org/resources/articles/deep-learning-and-iot-based-pump-systems-for-precision-irrigation/

Akwu, S., Bature, U. I., Jahun, K. I., Baba, M. A., & Nasir, A. Y. (2020). Automatic plant Irrigation Control System Using Arduino and GSM Module. *International Journal of Engineering and Manufacturing*, *10*(3), 12–26. doi:10.5815/ijem.2020.03.02

Alomar, B., & Alazzam, A. (2018, November). A smart irrigation system using IoT and fuzzy logic controller. In 2018 Fifth HCT Information Technology Trends (ITT) (pp. 175-179). IEEE. doi:10.1109/CTIT.2018.8649531

Arvindan, A. N., & Keerthika, D. (2016, March). Experimental investigation of remote control via Android smartphone of Arduino-based automated irrigation system using moisture sensor. In *2016 3rd International Conference on Electrical Energy Systems (ICEES)* (pp. 168-175). IEEE.

Atzori, L., Iera, A., & Morabito, G. (2017). Understanding the Internet of Things: Definition, potentials, and societal role of a fast evolving paradigm. *Ad Hoc Networks*, *56*, 122–140. doi:10.1016/j.adhoc.2016.12.004

Chang, Y. C., Huang, T. W., & Huang, N. F. (2019, September). A Machine Learning Based Smart Irrigation System with LoRa P2P Networks. In *2019 20th Asia-Pacific Network Operations and Management Symposium (APNOMS)* (pp. 1-4). IEEE. 10.23919/APNOMS.2019.8893034

Dogo, E. M., Salami, A. F., Nwulu, N. I., & Aigbavboa, C. O. (2019). Blockchain and internet of things-based technologies for intelligent water management system. In *Artificial intelligence in IoT* (pp. 129–150). Springer. doi:10.1007/978-3-030-04110-6_7

Goap, A., Sharma, D., Shukla, A. K., & Krishna, C. R. (2018). An IoT based smart irrigation management system using Machine learning and open source technologies. *Computers and Electronics in Agriculture*, *155*, 41–49. doi:10.1016/j.compag.2018.09.040

Goodfellow, I., Bengio, Y., & Courville, A. (2016). *Deep learning*. MIT Press.

Hinton, G. E., Osindero, S., & Teh, Y. W. (2006). A fast learning algorithm for deep belief nets. *Neural Computation*, *18*(7), 1527–1554. doi:10.1162/neco.2006.18.7.1527 PMID:16764513

Kamaruddin, F., Abd Malik, N. N. N., Murad, N. A., Latiff, N. M. A. A., Yusof, S. K. S., & Hamzah, S. A. (2019). IoT-based intelligent irrigation management and monitoring system using Arduino. *Telkomnika*, *17*(5), 2378–2388. doi:10.12928/telkomnika.v17i5.12818

LeCun, Y., Bottou, L., Bengio, Y., & Haffner, P. (1998). Gradient-based learning applied to document recognition. *Proceedings of the IEEE*, *86*(11), 2278–2324. doi:10.1109/5.726791

Minerva, R., Biru, A., & Rotondi, D. (2015). Towards a definition of the Internet of Things (IoT). *IEEE Internet Initiative*, *1*(1), 1–86.

Mungale, S. C., Sankar, M., Khot, D., Parvathi, R., & Mudgal, D. N. (2020, February). An Effiecient Smart Irrigation System for Solar System by using PIC and GSM. In *2020 International Conference on Inventive Computation Technologies (ICICT)* (pp. 973-976). IEEE. 10.1109/ICICT48043.2020.9112431

Namala, K. K., & AV, K. K. PMath, AKumari, AKulkarni, S. (2016, December). Smart irrigation with embedded system. In *2016 IEEE Bombay Section Symposium (IBSS)* (pp. 1-5). IEEE.

National Geographic. (2020). *Resource Library*. Accessed February 20, 2020, at https://www.national-geographic.org/encyclopedia

Oregon State University. (2020). *Describe the importance of irrigation in producing forages*. Accessed February 18, 2020, at https://forages.oregonstate.edu/nfgc/eo/onlineforagecurriculum/instructormaterials/availabletopics/irrigation/importance

Pezol, N. S., Adnan, R., & Tajjudin, M. (2020, June). Design of an Internet of Things (IoT) Based Smart Irrigation and Fertilization System Using Fuzzy Logic for Chili Plant. In *2020 IEEE International Conference on Automatic Control and Intelligent Systems (I2CACIS)* (pp. 69-73). IEEE. 10.1109/I2CACIS49202.2020.9140199

Reghukumar, A., & Vijayakumar, V. (2019). Smart Plant Watering System with Cloud Analysis and Plant Health Prediction. *Procedia Computer Science*, *165*, 126–135. doi:10.1016/j.procs.2020.01.088

Rumelhart, D. E., Hinton, G. E., & Williams, R. J. (1985). *Learning internal representations by error propagation* (No. ICS-8506). California Univ San Diego La Jolla Inst for Cognitive Science.

Salakhutdinov, R., & Hinton, G. (2009, April). Deep Boltzmann machines. In Artificial intelligence and statistics (pp. 448-455). Academic Press.

Selmani, A., Outanoute, M., Alaoui, M. A., El Khayat, M., Guerbaoui, M., Ed-Dahhak, A., . . . Bouchikhi, B. (2018, April). Multithreading design for an embedded irrigation system running on solar power. In *2018 4th International Conference on Optimization and Applications (ICOA)* (pp. 1-5). IEEE. 10.1109/ICOA.2018.8370519

Singh, G., Sharma, D., Goap, A., Sehgal, S., Shukla, A. K., & Kumar, S. (2019, October). Machine Learning based soil moisture prediction for the Internet of Things based Smart Irrigation System. In *2019 5th International Conference on Signal Processing, Computing and Control (ISPCC)* (pp. 175-180). IEEE. 10.1109/ISPCC48220.2019.8988313

Singh, P., & Saikia, S. (2016, December). *Arduino-based smart irrigation using water flow sensor, soil moisture sensor, temperature sensor and ESP8266 WiFi module. In 2016 IEEE Region 10 Humanitarian Technology Conference (R10-HTC).* IEEE.

Thakare, S., & Bhagat, P. H. (2018, June). Arduino-based smart irrigation using sensors and ESP8266 WiFi module. In *2018 Second International Conference on Intelligent Computing and Control Systems (ICICCS)* (pp. 1-5). IEEE. 10.1109/ICCONS.2018.8663041

Vincent, P., Larochelle, H., Lajoie, I., Bengio, Y., Manzagol, P. A., & Bottou, L. (2010). Stacked denoising autoencoders: Learning useful representations in a deep network with a local denoising criterion. *Journal of Machine Learning Research, 11*(12).

Chapter 5
Performance Prediction for Crop Irrigation Using Different Machine Learning Approaches

Tarun Jain
SCIT, Manipal University Jaipur, India

Payal Garg
G. L. Bajaj Institute of Technology and Management, Greater Noida, India

Pradeep Kumar Tiwari
(iD) https://orcid.org/0000-0003-0387-9236

Manipal University Jaipur, India

Vamsi Krishna Kuncham
SCIT, Manipal University Jaipur, India

Mrinal Sharma
SCIT, Manipal University Jaipur, India

Vivek Kumar Verma
Manipal University Jaipur, India

ABSTRACT

Irrigation is an ancient practice that evolved over the years. Irrigation is the method through which a controlled amount of water is applied to plants making the most important recourse of irrigation. Earth is composed of 70% of water of which only 2.5% is fresh. Most of it trapped in snowfields and glaciers with only 0.007% of the earth's water for the needs of mankind. Limited water resources had become the main challenge in farming. In the chapter, machine learning algorithms and neural networks are used to reduce the usage of water in crop irrigation systems. This chapter focus on four mainstream machine learning calculations (KNN [k-nearest neighbor], GNB [Gauss Naive Bayes], SVM [support vector machine], DT [decision tree]) and a neural networks technique (artificial neural networks [ANN]) to expectation models utilizing the huge dataset (510 irrigation cases), bringing about productive and precise dynamic. The outcomes showed that k-nearest neighbors and artificial neural networks are the best indicators with the most elevated effectiveness of 98% and 90% respectively.

DOI: 10.4018/978-1-7998-7511-6.ch005

I. INTRODUCTION

Agriculture played a vital role in human society endeavors attempting to be self-sufficient in food (Faye et al, 1998) in history. Irrigation is essential for crop production in many parts of the world. Various studies have shown the irrigation practices utilized in the country are lacking, mainly in the uniformity of water application is very low. The main reason is the lack of farmers skills to manage irrigation. This directly results in the wastage of water and the reduction of crop yields. The economy is mainly based on agriculture in a country like India and with isotropic climate conditions, yet farmers are unable to utilize agricultural resources. Various irrigation methodologies are used by our farmers such as manual irrigation using watering cans and buckets, drip irrigation, flood irrigation, sprinkler irrigation, etc. The present system has several limitations and one which is water wastage which can directly lead to water scarcity in drought areas and unhealthy production of crops.

Improving the farmer's skill to manage and effectively control their irrigation system is as important as adopting the accurate irrigation scheduling methods. To address this problem, an automated irrigation system is developed by us where the irrigation takes place only when there is an acute requirement of water. Authors have made "PREDICTION OF CROP IRRIGATION SYSTEM", a model for controlling and predicting irrigation facilities to help millions of farmers. Authors have made an effort to compare various machine learning algorithms and give detailed analysis on the performance of each on our dataset. Authors have shown that KNN works better for the dataset and can be used for improving the irrigation systems in India thereby helping the farmers to manage their crops easily without much skill.

II. LITERATURE REVIEW

- A lot of research has been conducted in the Agriculture sector. They rectified some problems like power usage and water consumption. They have classified all soil categories like sandy, clay, loamy, chalky, peat, silt soils. They have used Time series analysis, Artificial Neural Networks (ANN), Multi Linear Regression and have also used WIFI module and the values of temperature, soil moisture, humidity is sent to farmer's mobile phone through the internet (Krishnan et al., 2020; Verma, & Jain, 2019).
- In this paper, sensors have been used to read the values of factors like soil, temperature, humidity, light intensity. A detailed explanation through flow charts has been given. The approach uses ID3 algorithm which selects the attribute that has the entropy of the smallest value. This algorithm produces a subset of the dataset by splitting the dataset by selected attributes (Kansara et al., 2015; Naghedifar, Ziaei, & Ansari 2020).
- Work also has been done in this field with the use of Machine Learning, the Internet of Things. Android Development is used for the approach to collect the data of humidity, air temperature, and soil moisture from sensors. This collected data is stored in the cloud and used for the training the machine learning algorithm. This is used to monitor the quality of air and the content of water for the soil. According to the data, a farmer is through the mobile app whether to irrigate the crop or not (Vaishali et al., 2017).
- The paper uses plant recognition through TensorFlow, ImageNet database, and android studio. The user has to take a photo of the plant and this is transferred to the cloud by the app. It is recognized by convolution neural networks (CNN) and the values which were recorded in the sensors

are processed by ML algorithm. The algorithm decides whether to irrigate the plant or not (Kwok & Sun, 2018; Shekhar et al., 2017; Goap et al., 2018).

- In this paper, the author talks about a knowledge based state management system to address the flaws in existing irrigation systems such as dry periods, device failure, or heavy rains. The proposed approach has three states i.e. supply, operation, and demand states. State transitions happen with the pre-defined set of rules validated by experts. Dynamically evaluating deliveries and inflows are permitted with a Global combined approach which is the major advantage of this idea (Faye et al., 1998).

- In this research work, they have explained the different processes to automate the agriculture by considering the factors like affordability, maintenance, and efficiency. Some methods such as automation canal delivery systems, automated surface irrigations, drip irrigation, and automation of micro-irrigation systems have also been used in the paper. (Rao & Sridhar, 2018).

- In this paper, the approach uses K means clustering and Support Vector Regression, a combination of unsupervised and supervised machine learning algorithms. The training data which includes parameters like soil moisture, air temperature, air relative humidity, soil temperature, and radiation are collected using an IoT approach that stores the data in the cloud to compute the results. (Velmurugan, 2020).

- This work is a comparative study on daily pan evaporation using Artificial Neural Networks (ANN), climate-based models like Penman, Priestley–Taylor and Stephens, and Stewart, which is used to estimate the daily pan evaporation and multilinear regression (Shirsath, & Singh, 2010).

- This paper talks about a generic weather-based decision system that can be used in various domains such as transport, agriculture, health, business etc. The approach is to find similar weather conditions for the similar domain based on the weather data collected over several years (Nikolaou et al., 2020).

- Authors of the paper have taken Temperature of the air, humidity in air, speed of the wind and radiation as training parameters. By taking the sensor readings and using only deep learning concept called artificial neural networks, it trains the given inputs and then the Arduino irrigates the field (Umair, & Usman, 2010)

- Work-based on smart farming using mobile phones. They have installed sensors in the soil. These sensors are used to read the values for a certain area. These sensors use a wireless sensor network (WSN). The data which is collected from sensors is sent through XBee to mobile phone. This model is used indoor plants in-home or office etc. (Kaewmard, & Saiyod, 2014)

- A lot of research on wheat crop has been made in the agriculture sector. They have separated the plants in two groups, one group contains manual watering plants and the other uses automatic electric sensors to water the plants. An experiment was conducted for 2 weeks. They have found out that an automated approach is showing great results than manual labor. Factors like effects on plants height, light received by the plant (photosynthesis), effect on plant fresh weight, effects on plants dry weight have been considered and these were explained in detail using the graphs (Boutraa et al., 2011)

- The paper describes using sensors which read the water level in paddy fields without even visiting them. They have used solar sensors which saves the electrical energy. Based on the current water level farmer controls the motor via mobile app from various places. They have explained the solar panel in detail and have used pictures for a better understanding of the readers (Uddin et al, 2012).

- In this paper, they used electrodes inserted inside the soil, raspberry pi is used to take pictures of the plant continuously for a few days to calculate the height, width of the plant and then sends messages through the internet. This model is cost-effective and can be used for indoor plants (Jadhav, & Hambarde, 2015)
- Most of the articles that have been studied as a part to initiate this project have been mentioned in the References. Most of these articles have been studied to understand their respective approaches, problems encountered, how problems were dealt with. Inspiration has been taken from most of them while working on the project.

III. METHODOLOGY

The majority machine learning techniques uses supervised learning. Supervised learning is wherever you have got input var X & an output var Y and you map an input to the output by employing an algorithmic program. The basic idea behind supervised learning is that the data provides the various example of situations and for every example, it defines an outcome. Then the machine uses the training data to build the model which will predict the outcome of the new data based on the previous examples.

$Y=f(x)$

It is known as supervised learning because the procedure of an algo learns from the trained dataset It can be pictured as a teacher supervising the learning process. All know the proper answers, the algorithmic program iteratively makes predictions on the data it has trained and is corrected by the teacher. Learning stops once the algorithmic program achieves a suitable level of performance.

Our approach includes the utilization of supervised algorithms like KNN (K-Nearest Neighbors), DT (Decision Tree), SVM (Support Vector Machine), GNB (Gauss Naive Bayes), ANN (Artificial Neural Networks). Authors acquired the agriculture irrigation dataset of 500 rows from "Kaggle" website and used Anaconda Jupyter Notebook as the coding environment.

A. Dataset

The following dataset is used to predict the favorable conditions for the irrigation. The authors have applied the above-mentioned machine learning algorithms to the dataset.

Attribute Information

1. **CropType:** fixed Numeric values (1-9)

Table 1. Numerical Values

Value	Crop
1	Wheat
2	Ground Nuts
3	Garden flowers
4	Maize
5	Paddy
6	Potato
7	Pulse
8	SugerCane
9	coffee

2. **CropDays:**

   a. **Wheat:-** Wheat is usually planted between March & may and should be harvested between July and September. That means a considerably shorter maturity time than winter wheat, around 120 days.

   b. **Ground nut:-**The groundnut usually grow slowly until about forty days after planting. Peanut plants start flowering about twenty-five to forty days after planting. Growth is more rapid between forty to a hundred days.

   c. **Garden Flower:-**Flower seed rarely list estimated days to mature but most flowers need about ninety-five days to grow from seed to flower.

   d. **Maize:-**Maize can take from 60-100 days to reach harvest it depends upon variety & the amount of heat during the growing season.

   e. **Paddy:-**Depending on the variety a paddy crop usually takes 105-150 days to mature after crop establishment.

   f. **Potatoes:-**It is exciting to harvest potatoes as soon as possible but to enjoy them in meals but different varieties of it may take anything from 70-120 days to grow.

   g. **Pulses:-**Pulses require a minimum of 6 hrs of sunshine every day. Its necessary to provide your crop with support. It takes about 40-45 days for the crop to mature and will be ready for harvest in about eighty days.

   h. **Sugarcane:-**In some states sugarcane is grown round the year but depending upon the variety and sowing time it takes about 12-18 months to mature. In general Jan- March is the period of planting and dec-march is the period of harvesting.

   i. **Coffee:-**Depending on the variety, it can take approx 3-4 years for the newly planted coffee trees to bear fruit and 90-100 days to harvest for mature coffee pant.

3. **Soil-moisture**: Moisture in soil is that the water stored on within the soil & is influenced by precipitation, temperature, soil characteristics, and more. These same factors facilitate verify the sort of biotic present, and therefore the quality of land for growing crops. The health of our crops depends upon in an adequate offer of water and soil nutrients, among different things. As water available declines, the general function and growth of plant area unit discontinuous, and crop yields decline. And, as our climate changes, water availability is turning into a lot of variables.

4. **Temperature:** Temperature affects varied growth processes in crops like seed dormancy breakage, photo-synthesis, transpiration, respiration, seed germination, and translocation. Plants mature earlier in hot areas with high temperatures as a result of photosynthate translocation happens quicker. Crops need a general temperature vary of zero to fifty degrees Anders Celsius. Most plants can't develop if the temperature falls beneath 6°C or the dirt is solidified for five back to back months. As a result, numerous territories are inadmissible for crop development.

5. **Humidity:** Humidity is vital to form photo-synthesis attainable. If it's in the case of anthurium, a good amount of humidity around a plant is even additional vital than for many alternative crops, as a result of the plant will solely absorb humidity in a reduced quantity and because of it has less water evaporation than most plants. If the plant loses an excessive amount of water, the stomata can shut with the result that photo-synthesis stops. If this happens, no more carbon-dioxide will be absorbed, and carbon-dioxide is needed to stay the photo-synthesis going.

6. **Irrigation:** 1 for Irrigation required 0 for not

B. Data Preprocessing

Any machine can't understand normal texts, Images, video recordings as they understand only 0's and 1's. Accuracies decrease if researchers put all the images or video recordings in a slide show and train our machine learning model by that.

In any machine learning process data preprocessing is essential where authors prepare the raw data in a way the machine learning model understands/interprets. In our dataset, every column is separated by the comma (,) and we have rescaled feature values if they are not in the same range.

IV. MODEL SELECTION

Model selection is an important stage in building the Deep Learning and Machine Learning (ANN) model for the determination of the calculations. It involves choosing between the best Machine Learning or Deep Learning Models. Accuracy, available resources and maintainability are many concerns while performing model selection beyond the model performance. Resampling methods and probabilistic measures are the two main classes of model selection.

There are many information mining strategies in machine learning. In elevated levels calculations can be classified into the unaided leaning and regulated learning.

In unaided learning he information which is not marked or order markings the machine are developed on these without concrete guidelines and directly applied on these are classification calculation

In regulated learning, the information and yields are all marked and machines are prepared on these. This model can also predict the future information and these are assembled to classification and regression strategies.

We have a total of 5 arrangement calculations in ML & DL they are

1.   SVM (Support Vector Machine)
2.   KNN (K-Nearest Neighbors)
3.   DT (Decision Tree)
4.   GNB(Gauss Naive Bayes)

5.   ANN (Artificial Neural Networks)

1. SVM (Support Vector Machine)

SVM (Support Vector Machine) is one of the most used supervised machine learning algorithms in classification problems. Classification or regression challenges are applied in this algorithm. The primary goal of this calculation is to find a hyperplane in N-Dimensional space that particularly orders the data points. These points which spread on either side can be attributed to various classes.

The straight separation which is determined between the nearest information focuses and the plane is implied to as edges. Maximal Marginal Hyperplane is the ideal line to isolate 2 classes in the line that has the biggest margin. It is best used with a non-linear solver.

$$h_{w,b}(x) = g\left(w^t x + b\right)$$

Class labels are denoted as +1 for positive class and -1 for negative class in SVM.

$$y \in \left\{-1, 1\right\}$$

The final optimization problem that we obtain fitting the best parameters:

$$\min \frac{1}{2}\left\|w^2\right\|$$

$$s.t.\, y_i\left(w.x_i + b\right) \geq 1, \forall x_i$$

Figure 1. SVM Visualization on train dataset (same irrigation dataset)

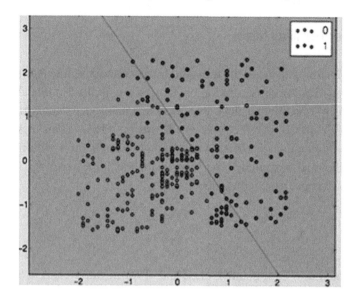

Figure 2. SVM Visualization on test dataset (same irrigation dataset)

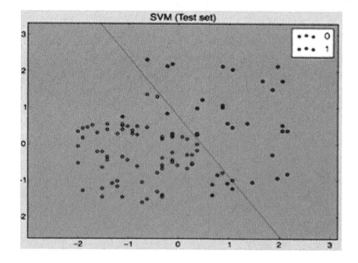

2. KNN (K Nearest Neighbor)

K-Nearest Neighbor, popularly known as KNN is a data classification problem in which the probability is estimated for a data point belonging to a member of one group than the other depending on K data points of a particular group nearest to it. This is achieved by calculation the Euclidian distance between the data points.

Euclidean distance between two points

Figure 3. Single Nearest point

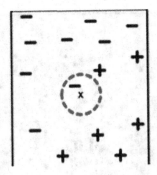

Figure 4. Double Nearest point

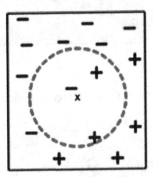

Figure 5. Triple Nearest point

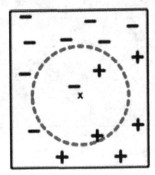

$$d\left(x_i, x_j\right) = sqrt\left[sum\ for\ r = 1\ to\ n \left(a_r\left(x_i\right) - a_r\left(x_j\right)\right)^2\right]$$

In KNN, choosing K is important as a smaller K can lead to noisy data points and a large value of K will lead to the inclusion of neighborhood points. Some of the factors to be considered to conclude the best K are cross-validation, parameter tuning, etc. In general practice, K is usually odd and close to the square root of N where "N" is the number of data points in the dataset.

Figure 6. KNN Visualization on train dataset (same irrigation dataset)

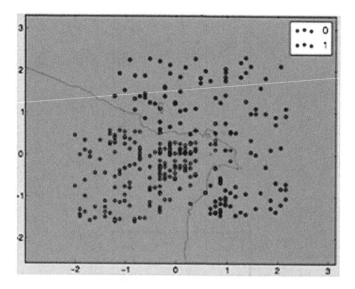

Figure 7. KNN Visualization on test dataset (same irrigation dataset)

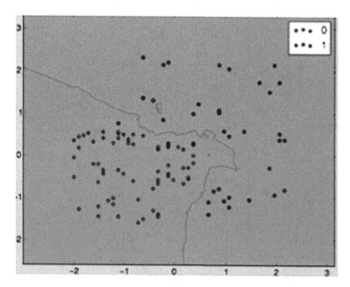

Figure 8. Decision tree

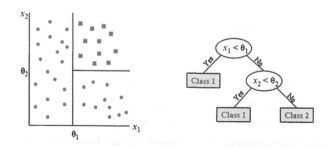

Figure 9. DT Visualization on train dataset (same irrigation dataset)

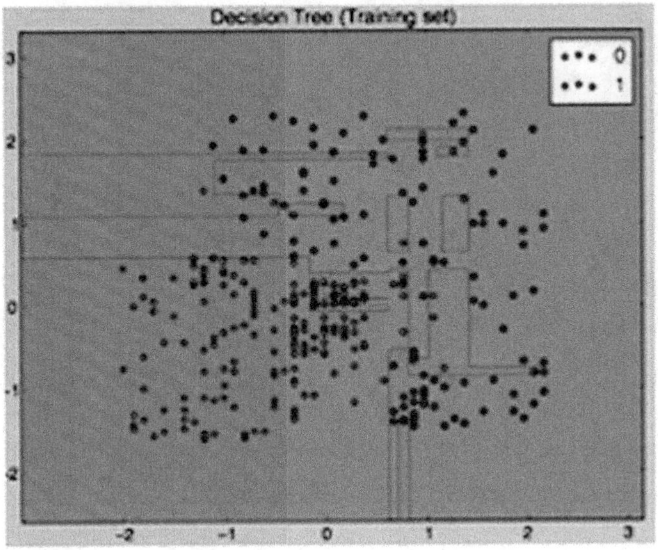

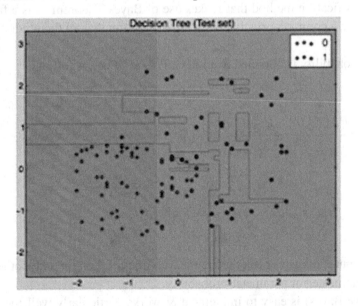

Figure 10. DT Visualization on test dataset (same irrigation dataset)

3. DT (Decision Tree)

DT (Decision tree) is a supervised learning algorithm. It comes under regression and classification problems. It solves the problem by using tree implementation where each node determines an attribute and leaf node determines a label. It is a non-parametric and hierarchical model. Decision trees prepare the learning rules from the tree nodes from the training data. It follows a greedy learning approach and finds the best split in recursive strategy.

Figure 11. GNB Visualization on train dataset (same irrigation dataset)

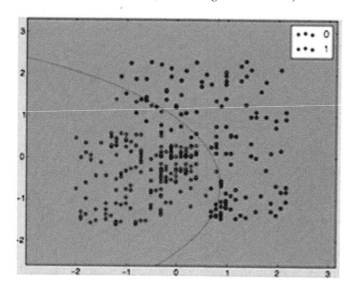

4. GNB (Gauss Naive Bayes)

Naive Bayes is a classification method that makes use of Bayes Theorem. It is a family of algorithms where all of them share a common principle with an assumption that all the predictors are independent of each other.

P(c|x) Posterior probability is obtained from P(x), P(c) & P(x|c) as follows.

$$\underset{\text{Posterior Probability}}{P}\left(C \mid x\right) = \frac{\overset{\text{Likelihood}}{P}\left(x \mid C\right)\ \overset{\text{Class Prior Probability}}{P\left(C\right)}}{\underset{\text{Predictor Prior Probability}}{P\left(x\right)}}$$

$$P\left(c \mid X\right) = P\left(x_i \mid c\right) \times P\left(x_2 \mid c\right) \times \ldots \times P\left(x_n \mid c\right) \times P\left(c\right)$$

Gauss Bayes computes the parameters using the Maximum Likelihood Hypothesis (MLH) i.e. calculating the maximum posterior parameter probability.

GNB(Gauss Naive Bayes) is easy to implement & works particularly well for huge data sets. It is also a robust classifier that works better for noisy points which are isolated. It is robust to irrelevant parameters. GNB does not just outputs the classification but runs probability across all the instances (classes). It is known for its simplicity & its nature of outperforming highly sophisticated classification methods in some real-world situations.

Figure 12. GNB Visualization on test dataset (same irrigation dataset)

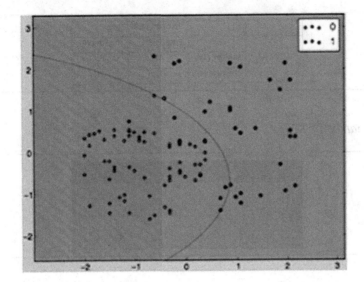

5. ANN (Artificial Neural Networks)

ANN (Artificial neural networks) are the computing systems that are built with a set of connected units just as neurons in the human brains which are called biological neural networks. The node in ANN can process and signal other nodes attached to it just like a neuron passing the signal in biological brains. They are doing this with no previous information and they involuntarily generate distinguishing characteristics from the data sample they process.

ANN is organized in layers specified that every unit receives input from the layer which is preceding immediately. A neural network consisting of one layer is called a single-layer network where every input unit connects to HIDDEN UNIT directly its outputs. Multilayer networks have one or additional layers of hidden units that don't seem to be connected to the outputs of the network. ANNs work well for the noisy, incomplete, outliers, or partial datasets. They can work with high speed in a distributed and parallel manner. Effectively, ANNs can be used in highly complicated systems such as cancer detection, image analysis like face detection, language modeling like machine translation, etc.

Figure 13. Mathematical model for Neuron

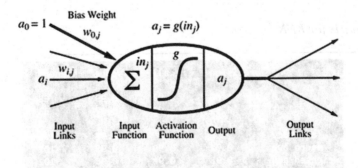

Table 2. Confusion Matrix

		PREDICTED	
		Positive (1)	Negative (0)
ACTUAL	Positive (1)	TP	FN
	Negative (0)	FP	TN

Table 3. Confusion matrix for KNN

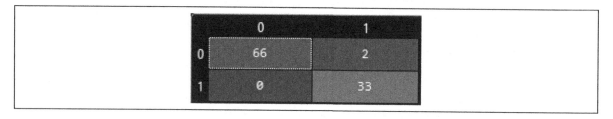

	0	1
0	66	2
1	0	33

The Activation function to give the output

$$a_j = g\left(in_j\right) = g\left(\sum_{i=0}^{n} w_i, ja_i\right)$$

V. RESULTS AND DISCUSSION

We have applied all 5 algorithms which are KNN (K-Nearest Neighbors), DT (Decision Tree), SVM (Support Vector Machine), GNB(Gauss Naive Bayes), ANN (Artificial Neural Networks) on our data-set containing 5 attributes. KNN (K-Nearest Neighbors) got the highest accuracy of 98% and Artificial Neural Networks (ANN) got the accuracy of 90% using the confusion matrix, so it is good to use KNN algorithm for the prediction.

Confusion Matrix is used to give a summary of a prediction results on classification problem by counting the number of correct (positive) or incorrect (negative) predictions and these values are broken down to respective classes.

Table 4. Accuracy Matrix for KNN

	precision	recall	f1-score	support
0	1.00	0.97	0.99	68
1	0.94	1.00	0.97	33
accuracy			0.98	101
macro avg	0.97	0.99	0.98	101
weighted avg	0.98	0.98	0.98	101

Table 5. Confusion matrix for SVM

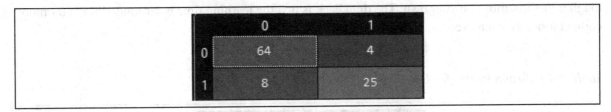

Now to get a better understanding authors made a classification report to compare the machine learning algorithms. It is used to measure the precisive prediction using a classification algorithm. Precision is a ratio of true positive to the sum of true positive and false positives.

- Accuracy = (TP+TN) / (TP+TN+FP+FN)
- Precision = (TP / (TP+FP)
- Recall = (TP / (TP+FN)
- F-measure = (2* Recall * Preccision) / (Recall + Precision)

1. K-Nearest Neighbor (KNN)

KNN has no model apart from storing the complete dataset, therefore there's no learning needed. Efficient implementations will store information using data structure like K-D Trees to create look-up and matching of recent patterns throughout predicted efficiency. As the complete trained dataset is kept, you'll wish to consider carefully concerning the consistency of your trained data. It'd be a decent plan to update it typically as new information becomes out there and take away inaccurate and outlier information.

The confusion matrix and classification report using the irrigation dataset of KNN is as shown in Tables 3 and 4.

Table 6. Accuracy Matrix for SVM

	precision	recall	f1-score	support
0	0.89	0.94	0.91	68
1	0.86	0.76	0.81	33
accuracy			0.88	101
macro avg	0.88	0.85	0.86	101
weighted avg	0.88	0.88	0.88	101

2. Support Vector Machine (SVM)

SVM is capable of doing classification and regression. Non-linear SVM means the boundary that the algorithmic rule calculates does not got to be a line. The advantage of this algorithm is that you simply will capture far more advanced relationships between your datapoints while not having to perform tough transformations on your own. The drawback is that the learning time is far longer as it's far more computationally intensive.

Table 7. Confusion matrix for DT

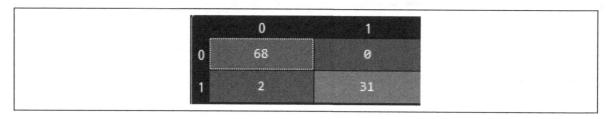

Table 8. Accuracy Matrix for DTv

	precision	recall	f1-score	support
0	0.97	1.00	0.99	68
1	1.00	0.94	0.97	33
accuracy			0.98	101
macro avg	0.99	0.97	0.98	101
weighted avg	0.98	0.98	0.98	101

Table 9. Confusion matrix for GNB

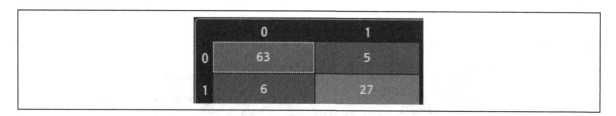

Table 10. Accuracy Matrix for GNB

	precision	recall	f1-score	support
0	0.91	0.93	0.92	68
1	0.84	0.82	0.83	33
accuracy			0.89	101
macro avg	0.88	0.87	0.88	101
weighted avg	0.89	0.89	0.89	101

Table 11. Confusion matrix for ANN

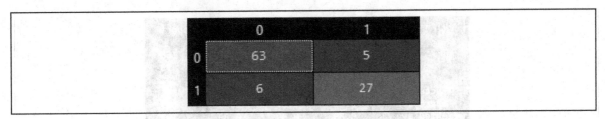

	0	1
0	63	5
1	6	27

The confusion matrix and classification report using the irrigation dataset of SVM is as shown in Tables 5 and 6.

3. Decision Tree (DT)

Decision trees have 3 main parts: a root node, leaf nodes, and branches. A Root node is that the start line of the tree, and each root and leaf nodes contain queries or criteria to be answered. Branches connect nodes, showing the result question to answer. Every node generally has 2 or a lot of nodes extending from it. As an example, if the question within the 1st node needs a "yes" or "no" answer, there'll be one leaf node for a "yes" response, and another node for "no."

The confusion matrix and classification report using the irrigation dataset of DT is as shown in Tables 7 and 8.

4. Gauss Naïve Bayes (GNB)

Gauss Bayes classifiers are highly scalable, requiring several parameters linear in the number of variables (features/predictors) in a learning problem. Rather than using expensive iterative approximation which is caused in majority classifiers, evaluating a closed-form expression can be used in maximum likelihood training which takes linear time.

The confusion matrix and classification report using the irrigation dataset of GNB is as shown in Tables 9 and 10.

5. Artificial Neural Networks (ANN)

The original goal of the ANN approach was to unravel issues within the same method that somebody's brain would. However, over time, attention captive to activity-specific tasks, resulting in deviations from biology. ANNs are used on a range of tasks, as well as laptop vision, speech recognition, computational linguistics, social network filtering, taking part in board and video games, diagnosing, and even in activities that have historically been thought-about as reserved to humans, like painting.

The confusion matrix and classification report using the irrigation dataset of ANN is as shown in Tables 11 and 12.

Table 12. Accuracy Matrix for ANN

```
             precision   recall  f1-score   support

         0      0.91      0.93      0.92        68
         1      0.84      0.82      0.83        33

  accuracy                         0.89       101
 macro avg      0.88      0.87      0.88       101
weighted avg    0.89      0.89      0.89       101
```

VI. CONCLUSION & FUTURE WORK

Water plays an important role in agriculture. Hence, it is crucial to know the water requirement for crops based on certain factors like temperature, moisture, and humidity.

In this work, the Authors automated the irrigation requirement for some crops grown in India. This wok also shows the application of various Machine Learning algorithms and the performance of each algorithm on our dataset. The examination of the outcomes resulted in the conclusion that KNN algorithm outperformed all the other algorithms (DT, GNB, SVM, ANN) with 98% accuracy. There are several opportunities for future work in this domain. The authors will conduct more experiments with varying weather conditions that will be performed in various locations and durations to automatically decide the quantity of water required for a crop at each time. It will benefit the farmers to choose the crop to be sown based on weather, climate of the location and duration of the year.

REFERENCES

Boutraa, T., Akhkha, A., Alshuaibi, A., & Atta, R. (2011). Evaluation of the effectiveness of an automated irrigation system using wheat crops. *Agriculture and Biology Journal of North America, 2*(1), 80–88.

Faye, R. M., Mora-Camino, F., Sawadogo, S., & Niang, A. (1998, October). An intelligent decision support system for irrigation system management. In *SMC'98 Conference Proceedings. 1998 IEEE International Conference on Systems, Man, and Cybernetics (Cat. No. 98CH36218)* (Vol. 4, pp. 3908-3913). IEEE. 10.1109/ICSMC.1998.726698

Goap, A., Sharma, D., Shukla, A. K., & Krishna, C. R. (2018). An IoT based smart irrigation management system using Machine learning and open source technologies. *Computers and Electronics in Agriculture, 155*, 41–49. doi:10.1016/j.compag.2018.09.040

Jadhav, S., & Hambarde, S. (2015). Automated Irrigation System using Wireless Sensor Network and Raspberry Pi. *International Journal of science and research, 4*(12), 2056-2058.

Kaewmard, N., & Saiyod, S. (2014, October). Sensor data collection and irrigation control on vegetable crop using smart phone and wireless sensor networks for smart farm. In *2014 IEEE Conference on Wireless Sensors (ICWiSE)* (pp. 106-112). IEEE.

Kansara, K., Zaveri, V., Shah, S., Delwadkar, S., & Jani, K. (2015). Sensor based automated irrigation system with IOT: A technical review. *International Journal of Computer Science and Information Technologies*, *6*(6), 5331–5333.

Krishnan, R. S., Julie, E. G., Robinson, Y. H., Raja, S., Kumar, R., & Thong, P. H. (2020). Fuzzy Logic based Smart Irrigation System using Internet of Things. *Journal of Cleaner Production*, *252*, 119902.

Kwok, J., & Sun, Y. (2018, January). A smart iot-based irrigation system with automated plant recognition using deep learning. In *Proceedings of the 10th International Conference on Computer Modeling and Simulation* (pp. 87-91). 10.1145/3177457.3177506

Naghedifar, S. M., Ziaei, A. N., & Ansari, H. (2020). Numerical Analysis of Sensor-Based Flood-Floor Ebb-and-Flow Sub-irrigation System with Saline Water. *Archives of Agronomy and Soil Science*.

Nikolaou, G., Neocleous, D., Christou, A., Kitta, E., & Katsoulas, N. (2020). Implementing Sustainable Irrigation in Water-Scarce Regions under the Impact of Climate Change. *Agronomy (Basel)*, *10*(8), 1120. doi:10.3390/agronomy10081120

Rao, R. N., & Sridhar, B. (2018, January). IoT based smart crop-field monitoring and automation irrigation system. In *2018 2nd International Conference on Inventive Systems and Control (ICISC)* (pp. 478-483). IEEE. 10.1109/ICISC.2018.8399118

Shekhar, Y., Dagur, E., Mishra, S., & Sankaranarayanan, S. (2017). Intelligent IoT based automated irrigation system. *International Journal of Applied Engineering Research: IJAER*, *12*(18), 7306–7320.

Shirsath, P. B., & Singh, A. K. (2010). A comparative study of daily pan evaporation estimation using ANN, regression and climate based models. *Water Resources Management*, *24*(8), 1571–1581. doi:10.100711269-009-9514-2

Uddin, J., Reza, S. T., Newaz, Q., Uddin, J., Islam, T., & Kim, J. M. (2012, December). Automated irrigation system using solar power. In *2012 7th International Conference on Electrical and Computer Engineering* (pp. 228-231). IEEE.

Umair, S. M., & Usman, R. (2010). Automation of irrigation system using ANN based controller. *International Journal of Electrical & Computer Sciences IJECS-IJENS*, *10*(02), 41–47.

Vaishali, S., Suraj, S., Vignesh, G., Dhivya, S., & Udhayakumar, S. (2017, April). Mobile integrated smart irrigation management and monitoring system using IOT. In *2017 International Conference on Communication and Signal Processing (ICCSP)* (pp. 2164-2167). IEEE.

Velmurugan, S. (2020). *An IOT based Smart Irrigation System using Soil Moisture and Weather Prediction*. Academic Press.

Verma, V. K., & Jain, T. (2019). Soft-Computing-Based Approaches for Plant Leaf Disease Detection: Machine-Learning-Based Study. In Applications of Image Processing and Soft Computing Systems in Agriculture (pp. 100-113). IGI Global.

Chapter 6
IoT and Deep Learning for Livestock Management

Rajiv Kumar
ⓘD https://orcid.org/0000-0001-7522-9078
Chandigarh University, India

ABSTRACT

Livestock management is a critical issue for the farming industry as proper management including their health and well-being directly impacts the production. It is difficult for a farmer or shed owner to monitor big herds of cattle manually. This chapter proposes a layered framework that utilizes the power of internet of things (IoT) and deep learning (DL) to real-time livestock monitoring supporting the effective management of cattle. The framework consists of sensor layer where sensor-rich devices or gadgets are used to collect various contextual data related to livestock, data processing layer which deals with various outlier rejections and processing of the data followed by DL approaches to analyze the collected contextual data in detecting sick and on heat animals, and finally, insightful information is sent to shed owner for necessary action. An experimental study conducted is helpful to make wise decisions to increase production cost-effectively. The chapter concludes with the different future aspects that may be further explored by the researchers.

INTRODUCTION

Livestock management in agriculture is a complex system that is affected significantly by several factors like regional weather conditions, livestock conditions, market share of livestock farming, and so on. The shed managers or farmers struggle to utilize available resources optimally to attain a good quality product with increased production. It is difficult for a farmer to keep track of the health and well-being of the cattle due to limited manpower and herds of cattle. Livestock production comprises various segments like cattle for milk, meat, eggs, wool, etc. It is observed by the agriculturists that the agriculture sector has major contributors as livestock around the globe. The shed owners or farmers should take care of the livestock owned. The prevalent traditional approaches are insufficient in achieving this goal with pace as desired. There arc various factors like monitoring movement of livestock, eating behavior,

DOI: 10.4018/978-1-7998-7511-6.ch006

continuous health monitoring, and the needs of medicines, etc. are major to be considered by the shed owners. It solely depended on the experience of the shed owners.

This chapter is focused to provide an efficient solution to the farmers. Nowadays the technical revolutions, the availability of various sophisticated sensors or wearable gadgets have witnessed the use of technology in various areas or industrial segments. Presently the companies are swiftly adopting the automated monitoring systems to achieve operational efficiency. Such automated systems are potentially helpful in devising effective methods to monitor and classify the various components of the companies. Internet of Things (IoT) and Deep Learning (DL) have been used to obtain these automated monitoring and responding system in different industrial segments. The use of IoT and artificial intelligence-based techniques like deep learning has also been witnessed in the field of cattle monitoring and farming. The automated method of tracking and recognizing the livestock to manage has been efficient ever than the existing manual method. The chapter is targeted to describe the importance of IoT and Deep Learning in Livestock Management through a proposed architecture organized in a layered format, where each layer is performing a specific activity to achieve effective livestock management – the primary motive of the author(s).

The proposed chapter will be divided into different sections to deal with i) problem definition ii) how IoT setup is helpful to handle the problem, iii) data collection and its analysis in real-time through well-drafted deep learning-based algorithms, iv) helping the livestock manager or shed keeper to decide the livestock feed and any medical administration if required. The chapter will start with section (i) that will provide a brief detail on the concept of Internet of Things (IoT), Deep Learning, and how both help dealing with the data heterogeneity to achieve insightful data analytics. With the inclusion of a concrete literature review, the problem will be defined based on the requirement analysis performed. Further, the achievable objectives, to solve the defined problem from the livestock management segment, will be defined. Section (ii) of the chapter will thoroughly discuss the proposed architecture to solve the problems at the side of shed owners or farmers, analytics and distribution of results at the other end. The heuristic-based algorithms using deep learning will be designed to analyze the logged or sensed data and the same will be implemented to handle real-time data for analysis and insightful decision making in the livestock field. The conclusion section will shed light on how the proposed architecture may be used to handle real-time problems faced during livestock management with careful allocation of resources. It will further explain the usefulness of the proposed system in a segment like livestock management, but later o may be scalable to be applied as an agricultural instrument for smart agriculture. Various untouched or yet to be explored areas will also be highlighted for the future scope of research work. At last, the chapter will include the most relevant references including the research work carried out not more than a decade.

The chapter is contributing through the achievement of selected objectives listed below:

- Justifying the use of IoT and Deep Learning as an effective methodology in dealing with real-time problems
- Proposing a multi-tier framework for livestock management using IoT and Deep Learning
- Designing algorithm for data analysis and recommendations to the shed owner or farmer
- Indicating the potential benefits of the proposed framework
- Suggesting future research scope in the same field or related

BACKGROUND

This chapter focuses on managing livestock using the alluring field of Internet of Things and Deep Learning. This section of the chapter discusses the meaning of all the three commonly used terms, *viz.* Livestock, Internet of Things, and Deep Learning. Livestock is a term primarily related to the agribusiness sector. It is one of the important constituents of agriculture business that includes livestock farming for milk production, meat production, poultry. Across the globe, agriculture is an important role player in the economic well-being of any nation where this sector has a major part from its constituent livestock farming. Managing livestock is a major challenge faced by most of the shed owners or farmers due to difficulty in managing a large livestock farm keeping the cost to a minimum possible. Further, the lack of expertise in every activity related to livestock farming hinders the mammoth work of livestock farming manually. Automated or gadget-assisted activity support is imperative to apply in livestock farming. Attaining this goal, the major industry segments are targeting the use of recent technologies like Internet of Things (IoT) and Deep Learning (DL). IoT is a paradigm that relates to a network of things connected over the Internet. (Sethi & Sarangi, 2017) explained the meaning of IoT clearly saying that there exists no precise definition for this term but is seen as connected things over the Internet. Similarly, the meaning, applications, architecture, and various future trends are discussed in (Patel & Patel, 2016). It is concluded that IoT is a connected network of various sensors, actuators, processing devices, and network devices, and Internet is the medium of communication among all. Various devices used in IoT paradigm can sense (collect), process, and transfer data to other devices. Deep Learning (DL) is an emerging subfield of artificial intelligence that extends its ancestor machine learning with hierarchical depth for more complex problem-solving scenarios. DL has the peculiarity to self-extract features from the raw data provided, as described in (Arel et al., 2010). DL involves multi-layered processing to learn data representations with abstraction performed at every layer. "It uses a backpropagation algorithm to update the internal parameters of a layer to compute data representation from the representation in the previous layer", (LeCun et al., 2015).

Internet of Things and Deep Learning – Role in Livestock Monitoring

After briefing about the concept of livestock, IoT, and DL, the author(s) is explaining how these terms fit in the bill of automated livestock management in this paragraph. With the advent of network technologies like Wi-Fi, 5G, and LTE, *etc.* a significant rise in the number of connected devices has been observed in the past decade. These devices are capable of exchanging information, without any human intervention, through connected physical objects over the internet. It has led to the increasing trend of using Internet of Things (IoT) technology in almost every walk of life including the industry. Various studies have been presented to highlight the use of IoT in various industrial segments like production, healthcare, agriculture, fleet management (transportation), smart city, smart traffic management. In each segment, the number of connected physical devices that are capable to generate a tremendous amount of data poses a great challenge to the industry experts in handling and analyzing this bulky data. Further, it is difficult to decide which data is important to log and which is to discard as the date is generated in a heterogeneous environment like different devices, different persons, and related to different contexts. The present statistical tools are insufficient to filter out noisy data and further, it is difficult to analyze such amount of data with speed as required in real-time applications. Thus, there is a need of introducing some heuristic-based algorithms as a solution that is capable to deal with the situation. It opens the opportunity to explore the use of machine learning in such industrial problems. In machine learning, there is a possibility to deal with the heterogeneity of data, spurious data resulting in better analytics. With a variety of algorithmic approaches in machine learning, Deep Learning has emerged as an effective approach in dealing with real-time problems due to its nature of efficiently handling the volume of data in solving the complex problems like the densely connected human neurons. The authors feel motivated to use deep learning concepts in this chapter to handle real-time problems related to livestock monitoring which is an inseparable and contributing segment in agriculture. Livestock monitoring is essential to keep the dairy production to the optimum while maintaining the quality of the products produced. The sensor rich IoT gadgets will be envisioned to use on the cattle and Deep learning algorithms will be applied to the data logged using a variety of sensors fixed as a gadget on the cattle. Data analytics will be performed to drive insightful metrics and recommend appropriate actions.

The chapter focuses on livestock monitoring involving cattle health and movement monitoring in the shed. As it involves a variety of data related to the cattle and the same can be obtained using different sensors. Here, IoT plays an important role to tie the sensors to the cattle for data collection. These sensing devices can process, store, and communicate the data to processing nodes or layers. Thus, IoT is suitable to use in the livestock monitoring where there is a need to continuously sense data from cattle and shed, process the sensed data to derive useful metrics those can be transferred to other devices or visualized to the farmer to inform about various contextual information related to livestock management. Further, the heuristic algorithms developed using DL methodology are helpful in precisely predicting the outcome of a contextual information analysis which may potentially benefit the shed owners to economical, efficient, and automated monitoring. A thorough literature survey on the use of IoT and DL into livestock farming favored the approach used in this chapter. This section of the chapter deals with the critical literature survey conducted. The use of IoT in smart livestock monitoring where "one mobile LoRa® gateway is used to monitor a small to moderate-sized livestock farm" as detailed in (Ikhsan et al., 2018). It uses neck-collar including heat, heartbeat, respiration, and humidity sensor to collect data that is transferred to LoRa® gateway for further analysis. The study focused on keeping energy consumption to a minimum possible while transmitting collected data and found that one static gateway is good for a small farm. It is further found that a mobile gateway is enough for monitoring a widely spread livestock farm. There is another study using "LoRa LPWAN" (Germani et al., 2019) proposed an IoT architecture for continuous livestock monitoring. Another interesting work witnesses the use of IoT and DL into the agriculture field to solve various problems to increase the productivity with the use of deployed sensors and analyzing of collected data through various DL algorithms, (Garg et al., 2020). So, the author(s) of this chapter feel motivated to use the combination of IoT and DL into livestock monitoring. (Lee, 2018) highlights the use of IoT and machine learning to detect movement-based estrus or calving period prediction in cows. It involved the data collection using an accelerometer and detect the increased movement to separate estrus period movement from a normal movement to increase the success rate of receptivity of cow to artificial insemination. (wa Maina, 2017) explored the use of sensors, IoT, and machine learning approaches to monitor cattle is on heat or sick. The system was useful to farmers to know about the events of interest like when cattle are ready for estrus or are sick. Use of IoT using smart weighing mats for measuring weight and gait of the pigs and applying machine learning approaches to perform gait analysis for "detecting lameness and next plan of gestation period", (Vaughan et al., 2017). Review of using IoT in agriculture and farming is presented with a focus that there is further scope to improve the farming including livestock with the use of sensors and IoT architecture for an efficient and autonomous management system. Recent technologies based on sensors, communication networks, and data analysis were used to detect the activity and heat in the cattle of a livestock farm in (Ariza-Colpas et al., 2019). Its focus is to design specific low-energy hardware devices for the study.

Deep learning has also played a vital role in livestock management and its allied areas like the agriculture field. From the past decade, there is an increase in the use of deep learning methods to enhance productivity in agriculture and livestock farming. (Kamilaris & Prenafeta-Boldú, 2018) reviewed the use of deep learning in the field of agriculture and found that the deep learning-based approaches have outperformed the traditional approaches used in the agriculture domain to detect crop diseases, soil fertility prediction, and recommender system to predict the expected crop yield. It was highlighted that deep learning effectively contributed to feature extraction, faster learning, and better performance. (Khamaysa et al., 2019) used deep learning concepts using a deep neural network to effectively detect the Mastitis in dairy cattle which is crucial in maintaining the well-being of the livestock. Deep learning-based framework has been used to identify individual cattle from a large image dataset obtained from a video clip. Convolutional Neural Network (CNN) and Long Short-Term Memory (LSTM) network methods have been used to conduct the study and achieve an accuracy of 81% (Qiao et al., 2019). Machine learning has been used to analyze the sensor data to detect cattle behavior to increase the production and well-being of the livestock. It is proved experimentally that the deep belief network *i.e.* deep learning is better in performance when compared against the machine learning methods like random forest and support vector machine (Suparwito & et al., 2019). A deep learning technique is used for feature extraction from images captured using quadcopters to classify livestock to cattle and sheep along with the count of each class. The approach used is potentially beneficial than existing methods to achieve better accuracy (Xu et al., 2020). A non-destructive thermal detection method should be adopted for the detection of cattle heat. (Zhang et al., 2020) has reviewed the possible use of infrared tomography to livestock production and diseases. The use of deep learning in the field of agriculture and its allied areas has been fortified by the review paper discussed in (Ünal, 2020). It reflected the studies carried out in various research papers targeting disease detection, precision livestock farming, object recognition, and many more. Precision livestock farming has been identified as a potential area to be explored using recent technologies including IoT and deep learning. Highlighting the need for precision livestock farming, various deep learning techniques to monitor behavior, health, pose detection and other production indicators have been listed.

The literature survey highlighted the importance of IoT and DL or machine learning in agriculture as well as in the livestock farming field which is targeted to autonomous monitoring for an efficient and economical framework. Further, it is reflected that many areas are yet to be explored and work is under progress like improving the efficiency of nodes, more efficient and faster processing algorithms may be developed. Keeping in view all these points, the author(s) has chosen the topic of livestock management using IoT and DL techniques to be addressed in this chapter. Moreover, the importance of the topic is fortified by the literature which is recent and is carried out in the previous five-six years from now. The literature also reflected the importance of a suitable framework for livestock management and author(s) are encouraged to include the framework proposal consisting of IoT and DL techniques in different stages.

MAIN FOCUS OF THE CHAPTER

This section of the chapter focuses on the highlights of the literature review to summarize the use of IoT and DL for various industrial segments and restricting the discussion to livestock monitoring. Forwarding to the economic growth through well-maintained livestock which is an integral part of the farming industry, it is clear that maintaining the livestock helps in boosting economical contribution of any nation and further this chapter focuses on the use of multiple fields like information technology through IoT, data analytics through analysis algorithms into livestock management. Hence, it is a multi-disciplinary approach to solve the real-time challenge in effectively managing the livestock. This section lists the various issues, controversies, problems faced for effective livestock management using technology implementations.

Issues, Controversies, Problems

The literature review performed and presented in the section introduction permits the author(s) to pinpoint specific issues related to livestock management. The livestock management is a work of an expert person who needs more time to decide on various factors like when the cattle are sick, on heat, or keeping good health. The human intervention makes it a daunting task to complete a big shed full of cattle. Checking the well-being of individual cattle, keeping the record of its healthy diet during the caring period, when it is ready for estrus or on heat, monitoring activity while grazing in the fields, etc. are a few points to take care for an effective livestock monitoring or management. There is a witness towards manual inspection for all the above issues. Various authors, during the literature review, highlighted the need for an automatic inspection system to increase efficiency and completing the task in a possible minimum period.

The automatic livestock management including monitoring activities, detecting cattle on heat or estrus, monitoring cattle health using sensors have opened new issues and controversies. The issues like usage of effective, durable, and energy-efficient sensors may be placed around the neck of the cattle. With the technological innovations manufacturing such sensors is possible but the exact place of placing the sensor becomes a controversy. The accuracy of the data recorded, and its analysis may be challenged by the experts so appropriate algorithms must be devised for the same using technology, and authors are motivated to suggest such an algorithm in this chapter. The problems in dealing with data acquired through sensors and its transmission to the analysis machine need to be addressed. The literature review sheds light on the use of Bluetooth, ZigBee, Wireless, and other connectivity equipment to connect sensors to collect data at a common place for further analysis. Further, it is observed that the automated livestock management helps in precision farming but has certain negative sides also. While considering the positive sides of automated livestock management, the benefits including better animal care, in-time disease detection due to continuous monitoring of the cattle using various sensors, improved quality of dairy and meat products may be listed. Despite these potential benefits, some negative factors include the deteriorated relationship between the shed owner/farmer and the animal, negative impact on the performance and expertise of the farmer being heavily dependent on the technology for the work, further, it may result to ignore those areas not covered by the sensors. These negative factors in the long run will drastically affect animal welfare, (Cornou C, 2019). Considering all the issues, controversies, and problems, the author(s) has selected the most relevant from each category to warrant the present chapter. The list of selected issues, controversies, and problems affecting the technology-dependent livestock management system are listed below, for the quick reference for the readers:

- Effective monitoring of cattle in the shed
- Maintaining overall animal welfare
- Monitoring the cattle entirely needs manual intervention
- The necessity of optimal use of resources to devise a foolproof system

- Faster detection of any disease in the cattle

The above-identified issues will be potentially addressed with the proposed system architecture detailed in this chapter. The author(s) are targeted to collect the data through an easy to use interface (hardware or application interface) that connects to the sensors and transmits collected data automatically to the analysis machine. The analysis machine will be equipped with deep learning algorithms to handle the continuous flow of sensor data, apply outlier rejections, and run analytical algorithms on the data. The processed data will be used to derive insightful inferences from the recorded data patterns. The following section of the chapter is designed to explain the proposed solution including data collection, transmission, and an effective way to analyze and visualize the data as insightful information that has the potential to handle the above-listed issues effectively. With the advent of technology, there is tremendous potential to solve various issues of agriculture and livestock monitoring. But it opens up a plethora of challenges handling heterogeneous data to dynamically align and process in real-time (Verma et al., 2020). The challenge of validation, verification, and ethical factors are to deal with. Enormous data generated from the sensors may pose challenges in visualization and more adaptive methods need to be explored. These challenges have been addressed to an extent in this chapter, but a few are not dealt with and are presented in the future research scope section of the chapter.

Major Highlights of the Chapter

- An architecture is proposed for real-time problems using IoT and Deep Learning techniques.
- The proposed architecture consists of different layers involving sensors, communication platforms as a client-side, and analysis followed with recommendation is performed at different layers as a server-side.
- A deep learning-based data analysis and recommendation system are proposed.
- Presentation of the performance of proposed architecture in real-time implementation and validating results with the ground reality.
- Various untouched factors are highlighted to be explored further as future research work.

The literature review and the issues highlighted above in this section justifies the author's stand with the topic of using IoT and Deep Learning as an effective methodology to handle real-time problems. The next section of the chapter discusses the proposed framework, algorithm for analysis while indicating the potential benefits of the proposed model to the livestock farmers. The untouched points which need further exploration will be provided in the last section of the chapter named future research directions.

PROPOSED SOLUTION AND RECOMMENDATIONS

Livestock management using technology like Internet of Things (IoT) and Deep Learning (DL) involves the use of sensor devices, communicating devices to transfer sensor data for processing, and the algorithm to analyze the collected data to infer insightful decisions about the cattle health and well-being, activity pattern of the cattle to predict the reediness for artificial insemination. The entire process is depicted in figure 1 as a layered architecture.

Figure 1. Proposed architecture of the system

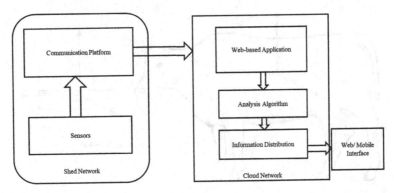

Figure 1 shows all the necessary modules of the proposed architecture. It contains two sections named as Shed Network (left section) and Cloud Network (right section).

The architecture consists of a client-side known as a shed network that consists of sensors deployed at the shed and the corresponding communication infrastructure to transmit the sensor information to the cloud network or server-side. The server-side known as cloud network comprises of three modules: i) to accept any client request, ii) deep learning algorithm to analyze sensor data and retrieve useful contextual information like healthy, on heat cattle, and iii) finally, the distribution module to disseminate information to various stakeholders like shed owners/ farmers, etc. The following subsections provide a detailed explanation of the proposed framework.

Client-Side or Shed Network – Sensors, Communication Network (IoT)

The left section includes the sensor layer and the communication layer. The sensor layer includes all the sensors required to tie around the neck of the cattle as a collar necklace or on the other parts of the body. The collar necklace consists of sensors like accelerometer, heat sensor, GPS sensor. The accelerometer sensor is used to detect the activity of the cattle viz. grazing, walking, standing, sitting, etc. With the prime objective of economic and efficient setup, the author(s) prefer to use the ADXL335 accelerometer that is economical tri-axial accelerometer with very less power consumption of 320µA (approx.). It has a sensitivity range of +/- 3g, a life period of 10,000g shocks, and operates on a 5V battery. Further, it has high resolution capable to measure up to 1degree tilt. Thus, it is a perfect sensor to use in livestock activity monitoring. The accelerometer is placed in line with the coordinates of the animal movement as shown in figure 2. The x-axis and y-axis are aligned with the horizontal movement of the cattle in the shed. Z-axis is typically used to measure vertical movements.

Figure 2. Axis alignment of cow and accelerometer

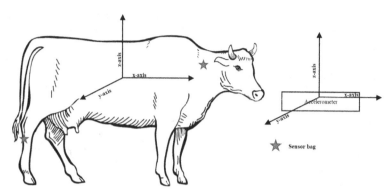

A GPS sensor is also used to locate the position of the cattle in the shed or outside while grazing. It will help to monitor the movement of the cattle in and outside the shed. It is most useful where the shed size is big enough and sprawled over acres of land. Then, the precise location of any diseased animal will help in the speedy medical administration to that cattle in the shed. Any standard GPS sensor is good for the location-sensing task. A standard heat sensor is used to detect the body temperature of the cattle. The prime objective of using a heat sensor to detect the body temperature in case of fever. Estrus or cattle on heat is detected by fusing the data obtained from the accelerometer and heat sensor both. It is an important challenge to decide the placement of sensors on the cattle body. The strategic location chosen is around the neck using a necklace elastic mounted with all the sensors. The objective is to protect the sensors from damage while the animal is laying down and to protect it from liquid like water, animal urine, and mud. The choice of using a water-resistant protective case, shown as a sensor bag in figure 2, containing sensors like GPS, accelerometer (in line with the axis of movement of the animal). This protective case is chosen to be fitted on the leg of the animal towards the outer side. It is placed to collect the activity of the cattle, especially movement. Another case is used to contain an extra accelerometer, heat sensor around the neck of the animal. It provides useful information to detect the movement while rumination, sensing body temperature, and detecting increased neck movement during the estrus period. The sensors are set to acquire the data at a 1Hz sampling rate.

The acquired data is transferred to the cloud side through a local or shed side communication platform. It composes of Bluetooth, antennas, Zigbee setup, but the author(s) use wireless connectivity of the sensor bag to the in shed transmitter (main device) through beaconing. The sensor data is periodically transmitted to the main device gateway in the shed which further transmits the data to the cloud, see figure 3. In figure 3, only one animal is shown but all present in the shed will be connected similarly. Each sensor bag is assigned an RFID tag to pinpoint the cattle that are sick or on heat. An additional sensor is shown as an intervaginal sensor to detect estrus or on heat precisely by fusing data with activity patterns. It further helps to identify the malfunctioning of the sensor bag due to damage or non-working, power failure and is repaired in time so that important event information about the livestock is not missed. The power failure is curtailed with a lithium battery in the sensor bag which is used to supply power to all the sensors. Challenges in charging the battery of the bag are still open and are not addressed in the present chapter. Maintaining the energy-efficiency of the sensor bag, the collected data is transmitted once every six hours to the main device. The main device has transmitters which directly transfers the data to the cloud side analytics machine. The collected data is pre-processed at the main device in the shed to identify important events that are further transferred to the cloud for analysis. The author(s) propose to select a time window and averaged the sensor data for the entire duration of the selected time window to generate a record <Temp, Ax, Ay, Az, Lat, Lon, RFID>. The record consists of averaged temperature, averaged tri-axial acceleration values recorded across the three-axis, GPS coordinates of the sensor bag, and the ID of the bag. The bag ID is also used to identify an individual animal in the shed.

Figure 3. Communication infrastructure for livestock management

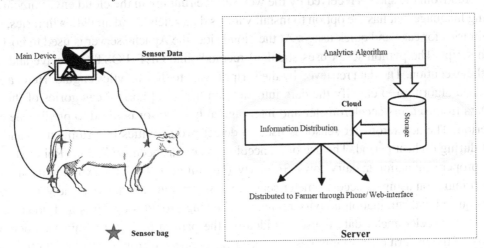

The data is collected by the main device and averages over a time window of 5 minutes (selected as a trial basis). The selected time window is sufficient enough to detect important events and will also reduce the data volume to be transmitted. The choice of an antenna (transmitter) at the main device is also a challenge. It is proposed to use LoRa® gateways of Semtech Corporation. It is selected due to its capacity to operate and perform a variety of functions like sensor data collection, transmission to the cloud, in an energy-efficient manner. Further, the operating range is to cover an area of 5-10kilometers which is sufficient for a moderate to big livestock farm. The data transferred is encrypted for better security against any intrusion or scribbling with the actual data. LoRa® technology has been used for livestock and agriculture monitoring through the Internet of Things (IoT) from the past decade as explained in (Abdullahi et al., 2019), (Citoni et al., 2019), and (Germani et al., 2019). LoRa® technology has the potential benefits of low-energy consumption, high encryption during data transmission, capacity to use unregistered radio frequency bands for faster transmission.

Server Side or Cloud Network – Analytics Algorithm and Distribution of Recommendations

The author developed the web script at the cloud side that accepts the sensor data transmitted by the gateway at the main device in the shed. The script is written as RESTful web technology using PHP. It is Representational State Transfer architectural style with features like scalability, reliability, and modifiable to achieve best results over the web. The livestock management needs such a web service for better management. A standardized interface and protocol - mainly HyperText Transfer Protocol (HTTP) is used throughout the framework. The important feature is to provide a variety of formats to access the content or information. It enables the RESTful web service to provide a standardized format that can be accessed from a mobile phone, desktop, or laptop. The format for sending data is JavaScript Object Notation (JSON) format. It is a light-weight text-based format for faster transfer and easily readable on a variety of devices including mobile phones. Author(s) propose to write the web script using Python as it is open source and has compatibility with various formats. A client-server architecture is followed where the client is the main node of the shed and the server is the cloud side analytic web service. The data transferred from the shed is received by the web service running in the cloud environment. Python is a scripting language that has the option to install various data science and analytics libraries, machine learning libraries for easy and quick usage. At the cloud side, the Apache server is used to host and run the Python script. The python script uses standard methods like GET, POST to receive and send the results of the execution. The data retrieved by the script is sent to the analytics engine. Here, a machine learning-based algorithm to classify the data into sick, on heat, and normal categories of the cattle is applied. Data from sensors accelerometer and intervaginal heat sensor is fused to predict the estrus or on heat period. The accelerometer sensor is used to detect two activities like rumination and restless movement during on heat period. The use of an accelerometer has been studied in (Reiter et al., 2018) to monitor proper rumination in dairy cows. Similarly, (Hamilton et al., 2019) explored the use of SVM to identify rumination using an accelerometer sensor. During rumination activity, the vertical axis data is mainly required and rumination activity related to chewing provides upwards and downwards motion. The z-axis accelerometer data is used to identify the pattern to detect rumination activity. The repeatability of the pattern over 30 minutes for sensor data collected from each cattle in the shed. The rumination activity is characterized by a continuous accelerometer signal for 30 minutes as averaged over 5 minutes window and the RFID. It helps to identify the livestock with a specific ID is following normal rumination activity or not. This is observed by computing the standard deviation (σ) for the accelerometer readings for 30 minutes, refer equation 1.

$$\sigma = \sqrt{\frac{\sum \left(az_i - \mu\right)^2}{N}} \tag{1}$$

Here, az_i is the vertical acceleration value along the z-axis, μ is the mean over a period for 30 minutes, N is the number of readings for 30 minutes. The computed value is stored along with ID as a rumination activity record in the database. On observing fall in the computed standard deviation, it indicates that the cattle are missing the normal rumination activity and is identified as a sick or problematic case which will be notified to the shed owner or farmer along with the ID, location of the diseased cattle. It helps in the early identification of the diseased cattle and immediately provides medicinal support to it.

Deep Learning Analytics Algorithm

The analysis algorithm is developed using a deep neural network (DNN). DNN is a neural network with three or more layers that uses unsupervised and supervised learning. It uses unsupervised learning to extract features from raw data through multiple hidden layers and supervised learning to optimize the output of the model. The model is a binary classifier, here, as it classifies the cattle as sick or healthy. The process of classification and the architecture of DNN is shown in figure 4 as parts 4a and 4b.

Figure 4. Classification process (4a) and DNN architecture (4b)

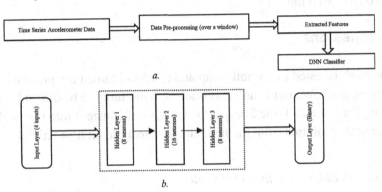

The DNN consists of one input layer with 4 values including acceleration, heat sensor data (from collar), the average time of rumination, window size. The hidden layers kept are three with 8 neurons at layer 1 and layer 3, 16 neurons are used in layer 2. The output layer produces a binary classification as a healthy or sick category which will be mapped to GPS and sensor bag ID of the observed animal. To implement DNN at the cloud side, Keras API (application programming interface) over TensorFlow is used. Keras works as the interface over neural network library TensorFlow in python environment. The rectified linear unit (ReLU) activation function is applied at the hidden layers. The ADAM optimizer which is the Stochastic Gradient Descent (SGD) function is used to produce the output, (Kingma & Ba, 2017). It is faster, memory efficient, and is most suited for large data sets. For modeling, the classifier data is divided into two parts 65% is used as a training data set and the remaining 35% is used as a test data set. The model is trained and tested for its accuracy using the validation process to classify the sick and normal behaving animals based on the rumination activity patterns. The same model is also trained to detect the estrus cycle or on heat period among the cattle to proceed for artificial insemination to increase the productivity of milk and calves. It is generally observed that cattle on the estrus cycle exhibits more activity as compared to others. Restlessness is experienced as an increased activity like movement in the shed, excessive mooing, head rubbing, and many more as described in (Welch, 2018). The heat period stays for 24 hours but may vary for the individual animal and is repeated every 21 days. During all these activities, an increased pattern of accelerometer readings is observed. It will be used in fusion with the data retrieved from the intervaginal heat sensor. When the timing period of the increased activity and heat data matches over time, it is easy to detect that the animal is on heat. The heat cycle is also observed through the use of video cameras installed in the shed and monitoring the activity of the cattle. Being targeted to use minimum sensors, author(s) detected the estrus cycle by analyzing accelerometer and heat sensor data only and the video camera is not used. The data is pre-processed to determine the alignment of excessive acceleration values and increase heat data continuously. If any animal in the herd is exhibiting increased heat and acceleration data simultaneously for more than 1 hour, an alert is sent to the shed owner or farmer to proceed with the artificial insemination leading to increased productivity. The date and time of the on heat detection is stored against the sensor bag ID of the identified cattle so that the same cattle are examined for the next cycle if the present is missed due to any reason. It will help to increase the chances of getting the artificial insemination done effectively to put the cattle into the gestation period. The responses generated by the classifier are encoded as JSON format data containing GPS coordinates, Sensor Bag ID, and Prediction to the mobile device and is also stored at the database to be referenced through a web interface.

Results and Discussions

The proposed framework is tested in a small setup and results obtained are present in this section. The target of the framework implementation and execution is to monitor the health and cattle heat detection for better production. Table 1 and Table 2 respectively shows the insight into the working of the model for detecting sick or healthy animal from the herd and to detect the on heat animal.

Table 1. Sample result obtained from the DNN model

Vertical Acceleration Az (in m/s^2)	Idle Rumination Period (in Minutes)	Temperature Data (Collar Sensor) in Degree Celsius	Classifier Output		Additional Information Provided by the Framework
			Sick (1)	Healthy (0)	
High Standard Deviation over a time window	>= 30 minutes	< threshold*		Healthy	GPS Location and Sensor Bag ID of identified cattle
Low Standard Deviation over a time window	< 15 minutes	> threshold*	Sick		GPS Location and Sensor Bag ID of identified cattle

* threshold is RT (Ractal Temperature) value 39.8°C, refer (Wenz et al., 2011)

Table 1 depicts the general input feature set to the DNN classifier model which produces 1 for the sick label and 0 for a healthy label for the animal under study. On detecting the sick, the corresponding GPS location in format <Latitude, Longitude>, and Bag ID is sent to the farmer or shed owner. It may be challenging to detect the identified animal from a herd with mere information of the GPS location and the Bag ID. The GPS location may be approximated to many cattle due to accuracy errors. Then the farmer needs to manually check the BagID and administer the sick cattle from livestock. To ease this task, the author(s) provide a glowing LED and sound alert from the bag ID of the identified cattle. It further helps during night times to exactly spot the identified sick animal from the shed. The estrus detection is based on the values of temperature recorded by the intervaginal sensor and accelerometer data. The increased acceleration pattern along with high-temperature value generally more than 39.8°C. The fused data is input to the model with acceleration data, temperature data, RT threshold, timestamps. The model predicts the estrus cycle if the high patterns are observed in the heat sensor data and accelerometer data continuously for 60 minutes. It should not be misled with the fever as during fever reduce activity is observed in the cattle. When the estrus event is detected, the date and time are recorded in the database along with the GPS coordinates and the sensor bag ID. This information is then transferred to the farmer or the shed owner to take necessary actions. Table 2 below shows the sample results obtained.

Table 2. Sample results for estrus cycle prediction

Vertical Acceleration Az (in m/s^2)	Temperature Data (Intervaginal Sensor) in Degree Celsius	Classifier Output		Additional Information Provided by the Framework
		On Heat (1)	Not on Heat (0)	
Normal Standard Deviation over a time window	< threshold*		Not on heat	Not recorded
High Standard Deviation over a time window	> threshold*	On heat (Estrus detected)		Date, Time, GPS Location data, and the Sensor Bag ID of identified cattle

* threshold is RT (Ractal Temperature) value 39.8°C, refer (Wenz et al., 2011)

It has been observed that the proposed framework using the Internet of Things and Deep Learning has potential applications to effective livestock management especially detecting sick and on heat cattle from the herd. It has potential benefits like low data volume, speedier communication, a higher rate of detection is also possible. Due to time restrictions, the real-time implementation at a vast level is not possible, but the author(s) feels motivated to carry forward the work for real-time testing in the cattle field or livestock shed to obtain more insightful results. During the implementation, there were certain challenges faced like improved and faster connectivity between sensors and the communication equipment, more non-destructive detection techniques can be explored to implement real-time detection of the well-being of the cattle. These challenges are beyond the scope of this chapter and are highlighted as future research directions in the following section.

FUTURE RESEARCH DIRECTIONS

Though the proposed framework exploits the use of IoT and DL to monitor livestock of any size effectively and in an energy-savvy manner, still many untouched parts are there to be further explored by the interested research fraternity. The important future research directions are highlighted below:

- Involvement of more sensors to study for effectivity and accuracy
- Real-time implementation is lacking due to constraints like time and Covid-19 outbreak. Author(s) are motivated to explore the real-time applicability of the system soon.
- The work is expandable to include pigs, hens in livestock management with a little addition of sensors and tweaking in the values of the algorithms for a different kind of animal.
- Psychological aspects of automated livestock monitoring are not discussed in the present chapter. The readers belonging to the field may carry forward this to study the impact of virtual no interaction between farmer and the cattle on the overall health of the cattle.
- The study of other faster machine learning approaches is further possible to explore.
- The inclusion of video cameras will warrant the accuracy of the model, but due to maintaining energy-efficiency livestock management, this is not included in this chapter. Good video compression and faster processing algorithms may be developed to fortify the claims of the present study.
- The present chapter has been designed for keeping in view the regional cattle characteristics, but the same work applies to other regions with a minimal setup change.

CONCLUSION

The chapter is focused on presenting a multi-layered framework to monitor the livestock in real-time. The use of client/server architecture is used in the framework, where the client-side is the shed network of sensors connected to the LoRa® routers. These routers are connected to the server-side cloud network. The Cloud network is chosen to target the scalability and availability of the framework when used in real-time. The use of energy-efficient routers and open source technology to design the cloud-side analytics and deep learning network script using python is an advantage of the proposed chapter. It helps to keep it cost-effective and compliant with a variety of interacting devices like farmer's mobile phones or web-based interface to get the insightful information derived after the analytics and executing the classifier model. The deep neural network is efficient to extract the features from the raw data itself and the ADAM function used as an optimizer to predict the results with greater accuracy. The results are targeted to the local region of the authors, but the proposed framework is liable to be used in other regions with a minimal setup change. The chapter highlighted the methodology to predict the sick and on heat cattle in a shed. Due to constraints like time and COVID-19 outbreak, the real-time implementation becomes difficult, but the system proposed is liable to handle the two problems effectively.

Despite the advantages to monitor the livestock farm effectively and efficiently, there are a few challenges to implement the proposed framework. The acceptability by the framers is a big challenge. Further, various aspects like the use of more sensors to study the impact on efficiency need to be explored. The proposed framework is expandable to apply in a bigger livestock farm including hens and pigs. Thus, it is not only suited for the dairy industry but is useful for the poultry and meat industry also. The effective management of livestock leads to an increase in the overall well-being of the animal that is directly linked to the increase in production. The increased production is an economy booster to the nations which are highly dependent on dairy, poultry, and meat market. Thus, it is an interdisciplinary effective management of livestock to increase economic growth.

ACKNOWLEDGMENT

It is acknowledged that the work carried in this chapter is not funded by any agency.

REFERENCES

Abdullahi, U. S., Nyabam, M., Orisekeh, K., Umar, S., Sani, B., David, E., & Umoru, A. A. (2019). *Exploiting iot and lorawan technologies for effective livestock monitoring in Nigeria*. Academic Press.

Arel, I., Rose, D. C., & Karnowski, T. P. (2010). Deep machine learning-a new frontier in artificial intelligence research. *IEEE Computational Intelligence Magazine*, 5(4), 13–18. doi:10.1109/MCI.2010.938364

Ariza-Colpas, P., Morales-Ortega, R., Piñeres-Melo, M. A., Melendez-Pertuz, F., Serrano-Torné, G., Hernandez-Sanchez, G., & Martínez-Osorio, H. (2019, September). Teleagro: iot applications for the georeferencing and detection of zeal in cattle. In *IFIP International Conference on Computer Information Systems and Industrial Management* (pp. 232-239). Springer. 10.1007/978-3-030-28957-7_19

Citoni, B., Fioranelli, F., Imran, M. A., & Abbasi, Q. H. (2019). Internet of Things and LoRaWAN-Enabled Future Smart Farming. *IEEE Internet of Things Magazine, 2*(4), 14–19. doi:10.1109/IOTM.0001.1900043

Cornou, C. (2009). Automation systems for farm animals: Potential impacts on the human—animal relationship and on animal welfare. *Anthrozoos, 22*(3), 213–220. doi:10.2752/175303709X457568

Garg, D., Khan, S., & Alam, M. (2020). Integrative Use of IoT and Deep Learning for Agricultural Applications. *Proceedings of ICETIT, 2019*, 521–531. doi:10.1007/978-3-030-30577-2_46

Germani, L., Mecarelli, V., Baruffa, G., Rugini, L., & Frescura, F. (2019). An IoT Architecture for Continuous Livestock Monitoring Using LoRa LPWAN. *Electronics (Basel), 8*(12), 1435. doi:10.3390/electronics8121435

Hamilton, A. W., Davison, C., Tachtatzis, C., Andonovic, I., Michie, C., Ferguson, H. J., & Jonsson, N. N. (2019). Identification of the rumination in cattle using support vector machines with motion-sensitive bolus sensors. *Sensors (Basel), 19*(5), 1165. doi:10.339019051165 PMID:30866541

Ikhsan, M. G., Saputro, M. Y. A., Arji, D. A., Harwahyu, R., & Sari, R. F. (2018, November). Mobile LoRa Gateway for Smart Livestock Monitoring System. In *2018 IEEE International Conference on Internet of Things and Intelligence System (IOTAIS)* (pp. 46-51). IEEE. 10.1109/IOTAIS.2018.8600842

Kamilaris, A., & Prenafeta-Boldú, F. X. (2018). Deep learning in agriculture: A survey. *Computers and Electronics in Agriculture, 147*, 70–90. doi:10.1016/j.compag.2018.02.016

Khamaysa Hajaya, M., Samarasinghe, S., Kulasiri, G. D., & Lopez Benavides, M. (2019). *Detection of dairy cattle Mastitis: modelling of milking features using deep neural networks.* Academic Press.

Kingma, D. P., & Ba, J. (2017). *Adam: A method for stochastic optimization.* Available at: https://arxiv.org/abs/1412.6980v9

LeCun, Y., Bengio, Y., & Hinton, G. (2015). Deep learning. *Nature, 521*(7553), 436-444.

Lee, M. (2018). *IoT Livestock Estrus Monitoring System based on Machine Learning.* Academic Press.

Maina, C. (2017, May). IoT at the grassroots—Exploring the use of sensors for livestock monitoring. In 2017 IST-Africa Week Conference (IST-Africa) (pp. 1-8). IEEE.

Patel, K. K., & Patel, S. M. (2016). Internet of things-IOT: definition, characteristics, architecture, enabling technologies, application & future challenges. *International Journal of Engineering Science and Computing, 6*(5), 6122-6131.

Qiao, Y., Su, D., Kong, H., Sukkarieh, S., Lomax, S., & Clark, C. (2019). Individual Cattle Identification Using a Deep Learning Based Framework. *IFAC-PapersOnLine, 52*(30), 318–323. doi:10.1016/j.ifacol.2019.12.558

Reiter, S., Sattlecker, G., Lidauer, L., Kickinger, F., Öhlschuster, M., Auer, W., & Iwersen, M. (2018). Evaluation of an ear-tag-based accelerometer for monitoring rumination in dairy cows. *Journal of Dairy Science, 101*(4), 3398–3411. doi:10.3168/jds.2017-12686 PMID:29395141

Sethi, P., & Sarangi, S. R. (2017). Internet of things: Architectures, protocols, and applications. *Journal of Electrical and Computer Engineering, 2017*, 1–25. doi:10.1155/2017/9324035

Suparwito, H., Wong, K. W., Xie, H., Rai, S., & Thomas, D. (2019, November). A hierarchical classification method used to classify livestock behaviour from sensor data. In *International Conference on Multidisciplinary Trends in Artificial Intelligence* (pp. 204-215). Springer. 10.1007/978-3-030-33709-4_18

Ünal, Z. (2020). Smart Farming Becomes Even Smarter With Deep Learning—A Bibliographical Analysis. *IEEE Access : Practical Innovations, Open Solutions, 8*, 105587–105609.

Vaughan, J., Green, P. M., Salter, M., Grieve, B., & Ozanyan, K. B. (2017). *Floor sensors of animal weight and gait for precision livestock farming. In 2017 IEEE SENSORS*. IEEE.

Verma, S., Bhatia, A., Chug, A., & Singh, A. P. (2020). Recent Advancements in Multimedia Big Data Computing for IOT Applications in Precision Agriculture: Opportunities, Issues, and Challenges. In *Multimedia Big Data Computing for IOT Applications* (pp. 391–416). Springer. doi:10.1007/978-981-13-8759-3_15

Welch, S. (2018). *How To Determine When A Cow Is In Heat - Farm And Dairy*. https://www.farmanddairy.com/top-stories/how-to-determine-when-a-cow-is-in-heat/464746.html

Wenz, J. R., Moore, D. A., & Kasimanickam, R. (2011). Factors associated with the rectal temperature of Holstein dairy cows during the first 10 days in milk. *Journal of Dairy Science, 94*(4), 1864–1872.

Xu, B., Wang, W., Falzon, G., Kwan, P., Guo, L., Sun, Z., & Li, C. (2020). Livestock classification and counting in quadcopter aerial images using Mask R-CNN. *International Journal of Remote Sensing*, ▪▪▪, 1–22.

Zhang, C., Xiao, D., Yang, Q., Wen, Z., & Lv, L. (2020). Application of Infrared Thermography in Livestock Monitoring. *Transactions of the ASABE, 63*(2), 389–399.

Chapter 7
Impact of Deep Learning on Semantic Sentiment Analysis

Neha Gupta

https://orcid.org/0000-0003-0905-5457

Manav Rachna International Institute of Research and Studies, Faridabad, India

Rashmi Agrawal

https://orcid.org/0000-0003-2095-5069

Manav Rachna International Institute of Research and Studies, Faridabad, India

ABSTRACT

Online social media (forums, blogs, and social networks) are increasing explosively, and utilization of these new sources of information has become important. Semantics plays a significant role in accurate analysis of an emotion speech context. Adding to this area, the already advanced semantic technologies have proven to increase the precision of the tests. Deep learning has emerged as a prominent machine learning technique that learns multiple layers or data characteristics and delivers state-of-the-art output. Throughout recent years, deep learning has been widely used in the study of sentiments, along with the growth of deep learning in many other fields of use. This chapter will offer a description of deep learning and its application in the analysis of sentiments. This chapter will focus on the semantic orientation-based approaches for sentiment analysis. In this work, a semantically enhanced methodology for the annotation of sentiment polarity in Twitter/ Facebook data will be presented.

1. INTRODUCTION

1.1 Introduction to Deep Learning

G.E Hinton in 2006 proposed the concept of deep learning & was also the founder of the Deep Neural Network machine learning (Day & Lee, 2016). The human brain is influenced by the neural network and contains many neurons which make up an impressive network. Deep learning (DL) simulate the structure of the human brain hierarchically, processes data from the lower to the upper level and gradu-

DOI: 10.4018/978-1-7998-7511-6.ch007

ally produces more and more semantic concepts. In developing the technology of big data and artificial intelligence, deep learning has been increasingly explored as a machine learning paradigm. Deep learning networks can provide both supervised and unsupervised training (Vateekul & Koomsubha, 2016). The architecture of deep learning demonstrates maximum potential when dealing with different functions and involves large numbers of labeled samples to collect data across deep architectures. Deep learning networks and techniques are widely implemented in various fields such as visual recognition, pedestrian tracking, off-road robot navigation, category artifacts, acoustic signaling & in the prediction of time series (Arnold et.al, 2011). In natural language processing the dynamic multi-tasking, including syntactic and semantic labeling, can be highly performed using deep architectures.

1.2 Introduction to Sentiment Analysis

Opinions or ideals have become an essential component in making judgement or alternatives for people or businesses. The rapid boom of Web 2.0 over the last decade has improved online organizations and enabled humans to put up their reviews or evaluation on a variety of topics in public domains. This user-generated content (UGC) is an essential statistics supply to help clients make shopping decision, however also provided treasured insights for shops or manufacturers to enhance their marketing strategies and products (Pang & Lee, 2008) . Sentiment evaluation deals with the computational treatment of critiques expressed in written texts (Kalra & Agrawal, 2017) .In the era of Information explosion, there may be a huge quantity of opinionated statistics generated each day. These generated statistics leads to unstructured records and the analysis of these records to extract useful information is a hard to achieve task. The need to address these unstructured opinionated statistics naturally causes the upward push of sentiment analysis. The addition of already mature semantic technologies to this subject has increased the consequences accuracy. Evaluation of semantic of sentiments is precisely essential method in the internet now days. Discovering the exact sense and understanding in which a specific sentence was written on the net is very important as there might not be any physical interaction to discover the significance of the sentence. There are a number of techniques to classify the specified sentiment as bad or terrible. This categorization helps us honestly discover the context of a sentence remotely (Gupta & Verma, 2019). The crucial troubles in sentiment evaluation is to express the sentiments in texts and to check whether or not the expressions indicate superb (favorable) or negative (unfavorable) opinions toward the challenge and to evaluate the correctness of the sentences that are classified.

1.3 Sentiment Analysis and Deep Learning

Deep learning plays a major role in both unsupervised and supervised learning, and many researchers use deep learning to perform sentiment analysis. Deep learning model is comprised of numerous efficient and common models, which are used to effectively solve the various problems (Ouyang, 2015). The most prominent example of deep learning is used by Socher where he has used Recursive Neural Network (RNN) to analyze the sentiments in film reviews (Socher et.al, 2011). Following the efforts of (Mikolov, 2013), many researchers have carried out a sentiment classification using neural networks, for instance, Kalchbrenner (Kalchbrenner et.al, 2014) anticipated a complex DyCNN(Dynamic Convolution Neural network) that uses an activity of pooling, i.e., dynamic k-max pooling on linear sequences. Similarly, Kim (Kim, 2014) uses CNN to learn sentence vectors of sentiments.

The motivation of writing this chapter is to understand the concepts related to deep learning, sentiment analysis and the importance of semantic in sentiment analysis. The present chapter starts with introduction to deep learning, basic of ontologies and their relation to sentiment analysis. The chapter further discusses semantic ontologies with concept forms and their relationships along with steps to develop a baseline model for simple analysis of sentiment using NLP. At the end of the chapter case study related to the sentiment analysis using R programming on the protests for CAA and NRC in India during December 2019 has been presented. The corpus of the case study has been built by collecting related articles from the Times of India and other leading newspapers of the India. Real time data has been extracted from twitter by applying the most frequent words as hash tags. Finally sentiment analysis techniques have been applied on twitter data to know the opinions of the people of country on the issue of NRC and CAA protest.

2. ONTOLOGY AND THE SEMANTIC WEB

Today the Internet has become a critical human need. People depend heavily on the Internet for their day-to-day tasks. World Wide Web (WWW) has rapidly become a massive database with some information on all of the interesting things. Most of the web content is primarily designed for human read, computers can only decode layout web pages (Kaur & Agrawal, 2017). Machines generally lack the automated processing of data collected from any website without any knowledge of their semantics.

This has become a concern because users spend a great deal of time comparing multiple websites. Semantic Web provides a solution to this problem. Semantic web is defined as a collection of technologies that enable computers to understand the meaning of metadata based information, i.e., information about the information content. Web Semantic can be applied to integrate information from heterogeneous sources and improve the search process for improved and consistent information (Jalota & Agrawal, 2019). The Semantic technologies allow the ontology to refer to a metadata.

Ontology is a description of a domain knowledge that includes various terminologies of a given domain along with the relationship between existing terms.

Ontology is designed to act as metadata. Ontologies can help to create conceptual search and navigation of semantics for integration of semantically in-order feature. The language structures used to constructs ontologies include: XML, XML Schema, RDF, OWL, and RDF Scheme.

OWL has benefits over other structure languages in that OWL has more facilities to express meaning and semantic than XML and RDF / s. Ontologies built using RDF, OWL etc. are linked in a structured way to express semantic content explicitly and organize semantic boundaries for extracting concrete information (Kalra & Agrawal, 2019).

A semantic ontology can exists as an informal conceptual framework with concept forms and their relationships named and described, if at all, in natural language, Or it may be constructed as a formal semantic domain account, with concept types and systematically defined relationships in a logical language.

However, within the Web environment ontology is not merely a conceptual construct but a concrete, syntactic structure that models a domain's semantics – the conceptual framework – in a machine-understandable language (Gupta & Verma, 2019).

For the purpose of comprehensive and transportable machine understanding, the semantic web relies heavily on the structured ontologies that structure underlying data. Consequently, the performance of the semantic Web is highly dependent on the proliferation of ontology that requires quick and easy ontology engineering and the avoidance of a bottleneck of information gain (Pang & Lee, 2008). Conceptual structures which define the underlying ontology are German to the concept of machine processable data on the semantic Web. By identifying mutual and specific theories of the domain, ontology lets both people and machines interact precisely in order to facilitate semantic exchange. Ontology language editors aid in the development of semantic Web. Thus, the cheap and rapid creation of a domain-specific ontology is crucial to the semantic Web's success.

2.1 Limitations of Semantic Ontologies

Ontology helps in delivering solutions for database identification, end-to-end application authentication, authorization, data integrity, confidentiality, coordination and exchange of isolated pieces of information issues (Agrawal & Gupta, 2019). Some of the drawbacks of semantic ontologies are

1. Natural language parsers can function on only single statement at a particular time.
2. It is quite impossible to define the ontology limits of the abstract model of a given domain.
3. Automatic ontology creations, automatic ontology emergence to create new ontologies, and the identification of possible existing relationships between classes to automatically draw the taxonomy hierarchy are needed.
4. Ontology validators are limited and unable to verify all kinds of ontologies, e.g. validation of ontologies on the basis of complex inheritance relations.
5. Domain-specific ontologies are highly dependent on the application domain, and it is not possible to determine the general purpose ontologies from them because of this dependency.
6. The reengineering of semantic enrichment processes for web development consists of relational metadata, which must be built at high speed and low cost based on the abundance of ontologies, which is not currently possible (Agrawal & Gupta, 2019).

Because of these limitations in ontology, it is not currently possible for Semantic Web to achieve the actual objectives of completely structured information over the web in a computer process-able format and making advanced knowledge modeling framework.

3. NLP AND SENTIMENT ANALYSIS

Sentiment analysis (Pang and Lillian 2008) is a kind of text classification that is used to handle subjective statements. Natural language processing (NLP) is used to gather and study opinion or sentiment words. Determining subjective attitudes in big social data maybe a hotspot in the field of data mining and NLP (Hai et al. 2014). Makers are additionally intrigued to realize which highlights of their items are increasingly well known out in the open, so as to settle on profitable business choices. There is an immense archive of conclusion content accessible at different online sources as sites, gatherings, internet based life, audit sites and so forth. They are developing, with increasingly obstinate content poured in constantly. In the past, manual strategies are used to investigate millions of sentiments & reviews and aggregated them toward a quick and efficient decision making (Liu, 2006). Sentiment analysis strategies carry out the project via automated procedures with minimum or no consumer support. The datasets that are available online may also comprise of objective statements, which no longer make effective contributions in sentiment analysis. These Type of statements are usually segregated at pre-processing stage. Binary Classification can be used to recommend the outcome of sentiment analysis. It may be considered as a multi-class classification problem on a given scale of likeness. Because text is considered as a complex community of words which might be uniquely related to every sentiment therefore graph based definitely evaluation techniques are used for NLP tasks. Opinion mining involves NLP, to retrieve semantics from phrases and words of opinion. NLP will, however, have open problems that may be too challenging to be handled quickly and correctly up to date. Because sentiment analysis frequently uses NLP really well in large scale, it reflects this complicated behavior (Agrawal & Gupta, 2019). NLP's definitions for categorizing textual source material now don't fit with opinion mining, because they are different in nature. Documents with vastly disproportionate identical frequency of words do not always have the same polarity of sentiment. This is because, a fact can be either morally right or wrong in categorizing textual content, and is commonly accepted by all. Because of its subjective existence, a number of opinions may be incorrect about the same thing. Another distinction is that opinion mining is responsive to individual words, in which an unmarried word like NOT can change the meaning of the entire sentence. The transparent challenging conditions are prepositional phrases without the use of NOT words, derogatory and hypothetical sentences, etc. The latter section includes an in-depth overview of NLP problems surrounding the assessment of sentiments. The online resources consists of subjective content material having basic, composite, or complex sentences. Plain sentences have approximately one product's unmarried view, whereas complex sentences have multiple opinions on it (Agrawal & Gupta, 2019). Long sentences have an implied mean and are difficult to test. Standard assessments pertain only to an unmarried person, even though comparative articles have an object or a variety of its aspects examined as opposed to some other object. Comparative viewpoints may be either empirical or contextual. An example of a subjective comparison sentence is "Game X's visual effects are much better than game Y's," while an example of objective comparison expression is

"Game X has twice as many control options as that of Game Y". Opinion mining anticipates an assortment of sentence types, since individuals follow different composing styles so as to communicate in a superior manner.

Normally, conclusion examination for content information can be figured on a few levels, remembering for an individual sentence level, section level, or the whole archive in general. Frequently, notion is registered on the archive overall or a few collections are done subsequent to processing the supposition for singular sentences. There are two major approaches to sentiment analysis (Gupta & Verma, 2019).

- Supervised machine learning or deep learning approaches
- Unsupervised lexicon-based approaches

Usually we need pre-labeled facts for the first strategy, although we do not also have the luxury of a well-labeled training dataset in the second technique. We would therefore want to use unsupervised approaches to predict sentiment through the use of knowledge bases, ontologies, databases, and lexicons with distinctive details, primarily curated and prepared for analysis of sentiment. A lexicon is an encyclopedia, a wordbook or an e-book. Lexicons, in our case, are special dictionaries or vocabularies created to interpret sentiments (Gupta & Agrawal, 2020). Some of these lexicons provide a list of wonderful and terrible polar terms with a few grades aligned with them along with the use of different techniques such as the position of terms, phrases, meaning, sections of expression, phrases, and so on, .

Rankings are given to the text documents from which we need to determine the sentiments. After these scores have been aggregated we get the very last sentiment.

TextBlob, along with sentiment analysis, is an excellent open-supply repository for efficient working of NLP tasks. It is additionally a sentiment lexicon (in the form of an XML file) that enables to offer rankings of polarity as well as subjectivity. The polarity rating is a float inside the [-1.0, 1.0] range. The subjectivity is a float in the range [0.0, 1.0] where zero.0 could be very objective and 1.0 may be very subjective.

Following the trends of artificial intelligence, the number of programs built for the processing of natural languages is growing every day with aid of the day. NLP-developed applications would allow for a faster and more effective implementation of infrastructures to remove human strength in many jobs (Niazi & Hussain, 2009). The following are common examples of NLP applications

- Text Classification (Spam Detector etc)
- Sentiment Analysis & Predictions
- Author Recognition systems
- Machine Translation
- Chatbots

3.1 Steps to Develop a Baseline Model for Simple Analysis of Sentiment Using NLP

Following steps needs to be followed to develop a baseline model for analysis of sentiment using NLP. The implementation is in python with standard libraries and tools:

1. Identifcation of Dataset
2. Name of the data set: Sentiment Labelled Sentences Data Set
3. Source of data set: UCI Machine Learning Library
4. Basic Information about the data set: 4.This information kit was generated through a user analysis of 3 websites (Amazon, Yelp, Imdb). Such remarks include impressions of restaurants, movies and goods. Two separate emoticons appear in each record in the data set (PORIA & GELBUKH 2013). These are 1: good, 0: bad.
5. Creation of a model of sentiment analysis with the above-mentioned data.
6. Create a Python based Machine Learning model with the sklearn and nltk library.
7. Code writing by library imports. For instance:

```
import pandas as pnd
import numpy as nmp
import pickle
import sys
import os
import io
```

8. Now upload and view the data set. For Example:

```
input_file = "../data/amazon_cells_labelled.txt"
amazon = pnd.read_csv(input_file,delimiter='\t',header=None)
amazon.columns = ['Sentence','Class']
```

9. Statistical analysis of the data on the basis of following parameters.
    a. Total Count of Each Category
    b. Distribution of All Categories
10. For a very balanced dataset that is having almost equal number of positive and negative classes then pre processing the text by removing special characters, lower string, punctuations, email address, IP address, stop words etc
11. Data pre-cleaning makes the data inside the model ready for use..
12. Build the model by splitting the dataset to test (10%) and training(90%).
13. Test the model with test data and examine the accuracy, precision, recall and f1 results.
14. To test the accuracy of the calculations, create the confusion matrix. Link to plot a confusion matrix can be seen at

```
#source: https://www.kaggle.com/grfiv4/plot-a-confusion-matrix
```

4. SEMANTIC SEARCH ENGINE

Current keyword-based search engines such as Google can identify internet pages by matching correct tokens or words with tokens or words in internet content inside the consumer's query (Ye & Zang, 2009). There are many disadvantages to this method.

1. Tokens or tokens-like words inside the User Search shall not be taken into account when looking for net sites.
2. The key-word based search engine gives equal importance to all key phrases whereas consumers challenge them as they think of one category of keywords as important.
3. To get the correct applicable end result, customers might also also want to enter numerous synonyms on his very own to get the desired records which would possibly result into the omission of many treasured net pages.
4. Another trouble is of information overloading. The traditional keyword based absolute search engines like google make it very tedious for user to locate the useful facts from a massive list of search results.

To remedy the above mentioned problems that the customers face, Ontology based semantic steps were developed.

Ontology is primarily based on Semantic Search Engine that which recognizes the meaning of the consumer query and gives the results in a comparative sense.

It is not principally easy to return built-in keyword pages but also the pages which can be used to provide the means available by using the Ontological synonym dataset, created using WordNet, to enter keywords from the user. First the Ontology Synonym Collection uses WordNet and then invokes the provider. In addition, if the similarity is 100%, extra keywords are taken into account to provide the user with the appropriate and accurate results. Approximately the meta facts like URL is provided by the meta-processor.

Following are the components of a basic semantic search engine:

1. Development of Ontology: Ontology with. OWL or. DAML extensions are developed in plain text format.
2. Crawler for Ontology: Ontology crawler discovers new ontological content on the web and add it to the library of ontology.
3. Ontology notepad: It is used for the purpose of annotating and publishing web pages to ontologies.
4. Web Crawler: Crawls across the web to find Web pages annotated with ontologies and create knowledge base on Ontology instances.
5. Semantic Searching: understands the context and logical reasoning of the content on the website and offers objective results.
6. Query Builder: Query builder is used to construct the user search queries.
7. Query Pre-processor: It pre-process the queries and send the queries to the inference engine.
8. Inference Engine: Reasoning of the search queries using ontology database and the knowledge base is done by the inference Engine.

5. SEMANTIC RESOURCES FOR SENTIMENT ANALYSIS

Sentiment and Semantic analysis is an important resource in our network today. It is necessary to find a suitable context and meaning for a selected sentence on the internet because the real meaning of the sentence can not be discovered by physical contact (Tsai & Hsu, 2013). There are large variety of methods and techniques used to identify and classify the argument as good or bad in quality. Such classification virtually helps in defining the context of the sentence (Liu, 2006). The essential questions of sentimental analysis is to identify the expressions of feelings in texts and to check whether the expressions indicate wonderful (favorable) or negative (unfavorable) opinions closer to the subject and how successfully and efficaciously sentences are classified. In the detailed interpretation of the meaning of the expression, Semantics plays a critical role. The role of semantics is studied from two perspectives:

1. The manner in which semantics is represented in sentimental tools like lexica, corpora and ontology.
2. The manner in which automatic systems conduct sentiment evaluations of social media data.

For example, context-dependence and a finer detection of feelings that lead to the assignment of feeling values to elements or to the layout and use of an extensive range of effective labels or to the use of current techniques for finer-grained semantical processing. In the case of semantics, lexical elements should be paired with logical and cognitive problems and other aspects that are concerned about emotions.

Many works in sentiment evaluation try to utilize shallow processing techniques. The not unusual element in a lot of these works is that they merely attempt to pick out sentiment-bearing expressions. No effort has been made to discover which expression simply contributes to the overall sentiment of the text.

Semantic evaluation is critical to recognize the exact meaning conveyed inside the textual content. Some words generally tend to mislead the which means of a given piece of text. For Example:

I like awful boys.

Here the phrase 'like' expresses fine sentiments while the word awful represent negative sentiments.

WSD (Word Sense Disambiguation) is a technique that could been used to get the right sense of the word. Syntactic or structural homes of textual content are used in many NLP applications like gadget translation, speech recognition, named entity recognition, etc.

In general, techniques that are using semantic analysis are high-priced than syntax-based techniques because of the shallow processing involved within the latter. Therefore it is incredibly essential for us to ascertain the precise significance of the expression or else it may result in unfortunate knowledge (in many cases altogether different) on the matter. The key issues in the sentiment assessment are the manner in which sentiments are interpreted in texts and how words indicate a positive or negative (un-favorable) view of the subject. In the present situation, feelings of good or bad polarities for particular topics are extracted from a report instead of the whole document being marked as good or bad in order to include a massive quantity of statistics from one individual paper.Most of their applications aim to classify an entire report into a file subject, which is either specifically or implied. For example, the film form evaluates into wonderful or terrible, implies that all the expressions of sentiment in the evaluation directly represent sentiments towards that film and expressions that contradict it. On the contrary, by studying the relationships between expressions of sentiment and subjects, we can investigate in detail what is and is not required (Niazi & Hussain, 2009). These approaches, therefore, provide a wide variety of incentives for different applications to reach beneficial and unfavorable views on particular topics. It provides strong functions for aggressive research, reputation assessment and the identification of undesirable rumours. For example, huge sums are spent on the evaluation and examination of customer satisfaction. However, the efficacy of such surveys is usually greatly limited (Pang and Lee 2008), con-sidering the amount of money and attempts spent on them, both due to sample length limitations and due to the problems associated with making successful questionnaires. There is thus natural preference for detecting and evaluating inclination, instead of making specific surveys, inside online archives, includ-ing blogs, chat rooms and news articles. Human views of these electronic files are easy to understand. Therefore there may have been also significant issues for some organisations, as these documents may have an impact on the general public and terrible rumors in online documents. Let us take an example to interpret the realistic application of sentiment investigation: "Product A is good however expensive." This declaration incorporates a aggregation of statements: "Product A is good" "Product A is expensive" We suppose it's smooth to agree that there is one assertion, Product A is good, it gives a good strong impression, and another statement, product A, is expensive and it has a negative thought. Therefore, we seek to extract any assertion of support additionally to research the benefit of the full context and present it to abandon users who use the findings in line with their program requirements. Sentiment Analysis research therefore involves:

- Sentiment expressions recognition.
- Polarity and expressive power.
- Their relation to the subject.

They are interrelated elements. For example, "XXX beats YY" refers to a positive meaning for XXX and a negative sense for YYY. The word "beats" refers to XXX.

6. SEMANTIC ORIENTATION AND AGGREGATION

6.1 Semantic Orientation

The semantic response to a function f shows whether the view is positive, negative or neutral. Here the view represent the opinion of the user. Wide variety of literature has been studied for semantic approach to sentiment analysis that classify the semantic orientation into two kinds of approches, i.e.

1.   corpus based
2.   dictionary or lexicon or knowledge based.

Figure 1. Sentiment Classification Techniques

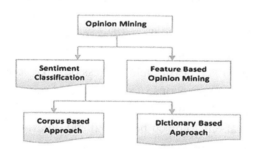

Corpus-based approach suggests data-driven approaches that not only have access to the sentiment labels, but can also be used for the advantage in an ML algorithm. This may simply be a rule-based technique or even a combination of NLP parsing. Corpus also has some specific domain, which will tell the Machine learning algorithm about the variety of the sentiment label for a word depending on its context / domain. Full semantic orientation requires large data sets to satisfy the polarity of the phrases and hence the feeling of the text.

The key drawback with the method is that it is based on the polarity of words contained within the training corpus, and the polarity of word is determined according to the terms in the corpus. Because of the simplification of this approach, this method was well studied in the literature. This method first eliminates sentiment expressions from the unstructured text and then measures the polarity of the words. Most of the sentiment-bearing terms are multi-phrase features in contrast to bag-of-words, e.g., "good movie," "satisfactory cinematography," "satisfactory actors," etc. In literature, the efficiency of a semantic orientation based technology was restricted because of by an insufficient availability of multi-word features.

Dictionary based approach suggests the judging of sentiment based on presence of signaling sentiment words (and perhaps some shorter context, like negations in the front of them) + some kind of counting mechanism to reach at sentiment prediction. In literature, dictionary based method is usually called the most effective (and subsequently of much less accuracy) one. Word based sentiment analysis is a statistical method for evaluating the feeling of a document. In the most successful case, feelings are binary: high or low, but they can be extended to more than one dimension, like anxiety, depression, rage, happiness, etc. This approach is largely based on the predefined list of sentences (or dictionary).

Dictionary-based approach works by identifying the words (for which an opinion has been given), from reviewed textual content then reveals their synonyms and antonyms from dictionary. WordNet or SentiWordNet or any another word network can be used as a dictionary. Corpus based approach helps locate the words of opinion in a particular context orientation, begin with the list of the words of opinion and then locate another word of opinion in a broad corpus. The most useful dictionary to use is Senti-WordNet 3.0. It is publicly accessible lexical tools consisting of "synsets," each with a positive and a negative numerical score of 0 to 1. This score is allocated from the WordNet automatically. This uses a semi-supervised learning process and an iterative algorithm for random walks. The above mentioned method works as follows:

First of all, the system needs to collect the simple and easy to understand sentiment words that have well defined positive or negative orientations. This collection is further extended by the algorithm by searching for its synonyms and antonyms in the WordNet or another online dictionary. The words searched by the algorithm are further added into the seed list to enlarge the collection. Included in the seed list are the following terms. The algorithm continues with the iterations. The cycle stops when new words can no longer be identified. A manual inspection is conducted to clean the list after the cycle had been completed.

6.2 Semantic Aggregation

Every review related to a product (shall we take an example of a camera) is mapped with its precise polarities in the product ontology. Product attributes that are at the higher level of the tree overpower the attributes that are at the lower level. When a reviewer talks about certain features of the product that are more advantageous or terrible within the ontology, he is weighting that feature more in comparison to other statistics of all child nodes (ex- light, resolution, coloration and compression). This is because the function of the parent class abstracts data and the characteristics of its child class. The value of the function is captured in the ontological tree by increasing the height of the characteristic node. In case of neutral polarity of the parent function, the polarity of the characteristic node is attributed to the polarities of its younger nodes. Thus data in a particular node is generated by his own data and by the weighted information of all its younger nodes.

In order to assess the record content of the base ode and the polarity of the analysis, the accurate propagation is carried out from the bottom to the top.

Let us create an ontology tree $TR(V1, E1)$ where $V1_i \in V1$ which is used for setting up a product attribute.

attribute.

The attribute set of a product V1i consists of the V1i tuple

$$V1_i = \{f1_i, p1_i, h1_i\}$$

Where $f1_i$ is represented as the feature of the product

$P1_i$ represents the polarity score of the product recieved after the review in relation to $f1_i$ and $h1_i$

$H1_i$ represents the height attribute of the product

$E1_{ij} \in E1$ is s a relationship attribute

$$F1_i \in V1_i,$$

$$F1_i \in V1_j$$

$$V1_i, V1_j \in V1 \,.$$

Let $V1_{ij}$ be the jth child of $V1_i$

The positive sentiment weight (PSW) and negative sentiment weight (NSW) of a vertex $V1_i$ can be calculated using the formula:

$$PSW(V1_i) = h1_i * p1_i$$

$$NSW(V1_i) = h1_i * p1_i$$

The product review polarity is estimated using expected sentiment-weight (ESW) of the ontology tree defined as,

$$ESW\ (root) = PSW\ (root) + NSW\ (root)$$

7. SEMANTIC APPROACH TO LEXICON ADAPTATION

The sentiment of a term isn't always static, as located in general-cause sentiment lexicons, however rather relies upon at the context wherein the term is used, i.e., it relies upon on its contextual semantics (Liu, 2006). Therefore, the lexicon adaptation technique functions in two predominant step

First, given a corpus and a sentiment lexicon, the approach builds a contextual semantic representation for each particular term in the corpus and ultimately uses it to derive the time period's contextual sentiment orientation and strength. The SentiCircle representation version is used to this end. Following the distributional inference, the words co-occurring in specific ways appear to have a common meaning, with certain words within the same corpus, SentiCircle derives the word's contextual semantics from its co-occurrence-styles. Such patterns are then interpreted as a Geometric Circle & are used to measure the word's conceptual meaning, using simple trigonometric identities. For each single duration m within the corpus in particular, we are constructing a two Dimensional geometric circle, in which the center of the circle is the time span m and each factor is described as a background c_i (i.e., a time period that happens with m inside the identical context).

Secondly, rules are applied, mostly in line with the correspondent contextual sentiments, in order to change the previous feelings of the words within the lexicon.

The adaptation process uses a series of antecedent-consistent regulations which determine how their previous feelings in Thelwall-Lexicon are to be up to date in accordance with their SentiMedians' positions (i.e. their contextual feelings). For a term m, it checks, particularly,

1. the prior SOS value of the SentiCircle quadrant in Thelwall-Sexicon and
2. the SentiMedian of m.

The method then chooses the most suitable rule to update the previous feeling and/or opinion of the word.

8. CASE STUDY: SENTIMENT ANALYSIS ON CAA AND NRC PROTESTS IN INDIA - 2019

To perform the sentiment analysis on the protests held for CAA and NRC in India during December 2019, we created one corpus by collecting related articles from the Times of India and other leading newspapers of the India. The corpus was created for the articles of December 2019 and January 2020 during the peak of the protest.

The aim of this case study is to show the technique of sentiment analysis using R programming. The first objective of this study is to plot a word cloud and identify the most frequent words from the corpus along with the sentiments of these words. These words are used as hash tags to extract the data from the twitter. We extracted real time data from twitter by applying the most frequent words as hash tags. Then we applied sentiment analysis on twitter data to know the opinions of the people of country on the issue of NRC and CAA protest.

a) Installing Packages and Library

First step for implementing sentiment analysis on R is to install the relevant packages and their corresponding libraries. Some of the important packages which are used in sentiment analysis are-tm, SnowballC, SentimentAnalysis and wordcloud. We read the corpus as text file and loaded the data as corpus.

```
docs <- Corpus(VectorSource(text))
First few lines of corpus is shown below-
<<SimpleCorpus>>
Metadata:  corpus specific: 1, document level (indexed): 0
Content:  documents: 192
[1] 20-12-2019 25,000 Citizens Protest CAA At August Kranti
[2] Call for "azaadi" or freedom dominated the student-driven protest of over
25,000 Mumbaikars, including 7,000 women, against the Citizenship Amendment
Act (CAA) and the proposed National Register of Citizens (NRC) at the historic
August Kranti Maidan at Grant Road on Thursday. The protest was supported by
political parties and activists.
[3] While organisers said more than one lakh protesters had turned up, police
pegged the number at over 25,000.
```

[4] Students from Tata Institute of Social Sciences (TISS), IIT-Bombay and Mumbai University mobilised their peers and other citizens from across the city. "The first call was given on my Twitter handle on December 11 and though I have only a few thousand followers, the tweet was seen by over one lakh individuals," said Fahad Ahmad, PhD student of TISS who was one of the main organisers. "I am on 24 WhatsApp groups coordinating with students from across the city."

The sample text is an evidence for the extracted article from Times of India dated 20-12-2019. Before applying the text analysis, the text needs to be transformed. Hence text transformation is an important step while analyzing the text. Here we applied the tm_map() function for text transformation to replace the special characters like- "/", "@" and "|" with space in the text. Subsequent to changeover of special characters with space, text cleaning is done with the same tm_map() function where the content_transformer(tolower) is used to convert all capital letters into lowercase letters and removeNumbers is used to remove the digits from the text.

To remove the common stop words, an inbuilt English stopwords dictionary is used by R which can be accessed as –

```
stopwords("english")
```

The common stopwords are-

```
'but' 'if' 'or' 'because' 'as''we\'re' 'they\'re'  'until' 'while' 'of' 'at'
'by' 'for' 'with' 'about' 'against' 'between' 'into' 'i' 'me' 'my' 'myself'
'we' 'our' 'ours' 'ourselves' 'you' 'your' 'yours' 'yourself' 'yourselves' 'he'
'him' 'his' 'through' 'during' 'before' 'after' 'above' 'below' 'to' 'from'
'up' 'down' 'in' 'out' 'on' 'off' 'over' 'more' 'most' 'other' 'some' 'such'
'no' 'nor' 'not' 'only' 'own' 'same' 'so' 'than' 'too' 'very' 'under' 'himself' 'she''her' 'hers' 'herself' 'it' 'its' 'itself' 'they' 'them' 'their'
'theirs' 'themselves' 'what' 'which' 'who' 'whom' 'this''that' 'these' 'those'
'am''is' 'are''was' 'were' 'be' 'been' 'being' 'have' 'has' 'you\'ll' 'he\'ll'
'she\'ll' 'we\'ll' 'they\'ll' 'isn\'t' 'aren\'t''wasn\'t' 'weren\'t' 'hasn\'t'
'haven\'t' 'hadn\'t' 'had' 'having' 'do''does' 'did' 'doing' 'would' 'should'
'could' 'ought' 'i\'m' 'you\'re' 'he\'s''she\'s' 'it\'s' 'i\'ve' 'you\'ve'
'we\'ve' 'they\'ve' 'i\'d' 'you\'d' 'he\'d' 'she\'d' 'we\'d' 'they\'d' 'i\'ll'
'again' 'further' 'then' 'once' 'here' 'there' 'when' 'where' 'why' 'how'
'all' 'any' 'both' 'each' 'few'
'doesn\'t' 'don\'t' 'didn\'t' 'won\'t' 'wouldn\'t' 'shan\'t' 'shouldn\'t'
'can\'t' 'cannot' 'couldn\'t' 'mustn\'t'
'let\'s' 'that\'s' 'who\'s' 'what\'s' 'here\'s' 'there\'s' 'when\'s' 'where\'s'
'why\'s' 'how\'s' 'a' 'an' 'the' 'and'
```

To add more stopwords we need to specify our stopwords as a character vector. In this case we find "said" and "also" as the stopwords and we removed them by applying the following function-

```
docs <- tm_map(docs, removeWords, c("said", "also"))
```

Subsequently punctuation and white spaces are also eliminated. First few lines of the transformed corpus are shown below-

```
<<SimpleCorpus>>
Metadata:  corpus specific: 1, document level (indexed): 0
Content:  documents: 192
 [1]  citizens protest caa august kranti


 [2] call "azaadi" freedom dominated studentdriv-
en protest mumbaikars including women citizenship amendment act
caa proposed national register citizens nrc historic august kranti
maidan grant road thursday protest supported political parties activists

 [3]  organisers one lakh protesters turned police pegged number


 [4] students tata institute social sciences tiss iitbombay mum-
bai university mobilised peers citizens across city " first call giv-
en twitter handle december though thousand followers tweet seen
one lakh individuals" fahad ahmad phd student tiss one main or-
ganisers " whatsapp groups coordinating students across city"

 [5] apart three institutions organis-
ers got support students st xavier's college internation-
al institute population sciences iips wilson college among others



 [6] appeals attend rally made protests places " can see people mumbra mira
road govandi bhendi bazaar outraged know allow inequality constitution stop "
activist teesta setalvad
```

To build a term document matrix we applied the following function-

```
D_t_m <- TermDocumentMatrix(docs)
mat <- as.matrix(d_t_m)
var<- sort(rowSums(mat),decreasing=TRUE)
doc <- data.frame(word = names(var),freq=var)
head(doc, 10)
```

This has resulted the output as frequency of each word in descending order. We have shown only first 10 lines of the output by via head().

Table 1. Word frequency table

Word	Freq	
caa	caa	32
citizenship	citizenship	29
nrc	nrc	28
police	police	27
india	india	26
modi	modi	24
people	people	23
delhi	delhi	23
law	law	20
minister	minister	19

Using this word frequency table we plotted the frequency table of words as shown in figure and generated the word cloud as shown in Figures 2 and 3.

Figure 2. Word Frequency Plot

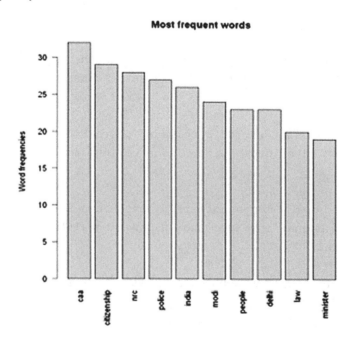

Figure 3. Word cloud

To carry out sentiment analysis of these frequent words we used the SentimentAnalysis package and its library where we used the above generated document term matrix. First few lines of sentiments generated are-

Table 2. Sentiment Analysis of Frequent Words

WordCount	SentimentGI	NegativityGI	PositivityGI
5	-0.20000000	0.20000000	0.00000000
30	0.00000000	0.06666667	0.06666667
8	0.00000000	0.00000000	0.00000000
42	0.04761905	0.00000000	0.04761905
18	0.05555556	0.00000000	0.05555556
24	0.12500000	0.00000000	0.12500000

Every document has a word count, a negativity score, a positivity score, and the overall sentiment score. The distribution of overall sentiment can be seen as-

```
summary(sent$SentimentGI)
Min.   1st Qu.   Median    Mean  3rd Qu.    Max.     NA's
-0.33333  0.00000  0.00000  0.01538  0.05518  0.33333      34
```

After adding the column of words with the sentiment score-

Table 3. Sentiment score of the words

d[1:6, 1]	WordCount	SentimentGI	NegativityGI	PositivityGI
protest	5	-0.20000000	0.20000000	0.00000000
caa	30	0.06666667	0.10000000	0.16666667
citizenship	8	-0.25000000	0.25000000	0.00000000
india	44	0.06818182	0.00000000	0.06818182
nrc	18	0.11111111	0.00000000	0.11111111
police	26	0.07692308	0.11538462	0.19230769

b) Performing Sentiment Analysis on Twitter Data Based on Hashtags

In 21st century, there has been an exponential rush forward in the online commotion of people across the world. One of the online social platforms is Twitter when people freely express their sentiments. There are several challenges in performing sentiment analysis on the data extracted from the twitter as inhabitants have a dissimilar way of writing and while posting on Twitter, people are least bothered about the correct spelling of words or they may use a lot of slangs which are not proper English words but are used in casual conversations. Hence it has been an interesting research area among researchers from one decade.

By motivating from the above, we have generated the most frequent words from the corpus collected in the above section from various articles in news papers during December 2019 and January 2020 on NRC and CAA and these words have been used as hashtags to extract the relevant data from twitter. Using the twitter API in R we performed data extraction by passing most frequent word as hashtag and extracted top 250 tweets. These tweets were stored as a data frame. First few lines of text of this dataframe can be seen as-

```
head(tweets.df$text)
```

1. 'RT @ShayarImran: Participated in KSU protest march and public meeting against #CAA #NRC at Calicutt, Kerala \n@RamyaHaridasMP \n@srinivasiyc…'
2. '@hfao5 @AnjanPatel7 @SyedAhmedAliER @KTRTRS @trspartyonline @TelanganaCMO @asadowaisi Hyderabadi\'s must protest KCR… https://t.co/T53DB7do14'
3. 'RT @GradjanskiO: Novi protest ce obeleziti puteve Vesicevih rusevina.\n\nUrbicid! Mrznja prema gradjanima!\n\n15.02.2020\n\u23f0 18h\nPlato\n\nDo pobede…'
4. 'RT @SwamiGeetika: #DelhiAssemblyElections2020 \n\nYouth gathered in large numbers to protest after TMC barred distributing Hanuman Chalisa an…'
5. 'RT @anyaparampil: Workers w Venezuelan airline Conviasa tell @ErikaOSanoja their protest of Guaidó\'s arrival in Venezuela is part of "defen…'

6.   'RT @JamesRu55311: We've known for a long time that BBC is already lost, and that they were complicit in their own downfall. Watching them s…'

This data frame is first converted into a vector and then preprocessing is applied before sentiment analysis. The function get_nrc_sentiment() is used to identify the positive and negative words. We then computed the total positive and negative words in the twitter text and the a plot is drawn as shown in figure below. This plot shows the sentiments attached with the corresponding text.

Figure 4. Total Positive And Negative Words In The Twitter Text

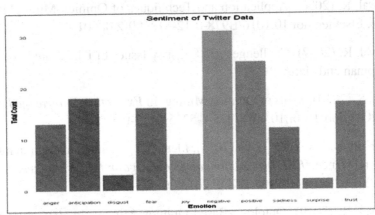

As we can discover here, in the given case more number of negative words are found hence it represents the negative sentiments of the people. Thus we can easily identify and analyse the sentiments of the people based on the key words.

CONCLUSION

The chapter discusses the concepts related to deep learning, sentiment analysis and the importance of semantic in sentiment analysis. The present chapter has illustrated the basic of ontologies and their relation to sentiment analysis. The chapter has further discussed semantic ontologies with concept forms and their relationships along with steps to develop a baseline model for simple analysis of sentiment using NLP. At the end of the chapter case study related to the sentiment analysis using R programming on the protests for CAA and NRC in India during December 2019 has been presented. The corpus of the case study has been built by collecting related articles from the Times of India and other leading newspapers of the India. Real time data has been extracted from twitter by applying the most frequent words as hash tags. Finally sentiment analysis techniques have been applied on twitter data to know the opinions of the people of country on the issue of NRC and CAA protest. This work can be extended further by applying various sentiment analysis techniques to improve the accuracy of the predicted words. More work is also required to preprocess the data in order to improve the accuracy.

REFERENCES

Agrawal, R., & Gupta, N. (Eds.). (2018). *Extracting Knowledge from Opinion Mining*. IGI Global.

Arnold, L., Rebecchi, S., Chevallier, S., & Paugam-Moisy, H. (2011) An Introduction to Deep Learning. *ESANN 2011 Proceedings, European Symposium on Artificial Neural Networks, Computational Intelligence and Machine Learning*, 477-488.

Day, M., & Lee, C. (2016). *Deep Learning for Financial Sentiment Analysis on Finance News Providers*. Academic Press.

Gupta, N., & Agrawal, R. (2020). Application and Techniques of Opinion Mining. In *Hybrid Computational Intelligence*. Elsevier. doi:10.1016/B978-0-12-818699-2.00001-9

Gupta, N., & Agrawal, R. (2017). Challenges and Security Issues of Distributed Databases. In *NoSQL* (pp. 265–284). Chapman and Hall/CRC.

Gupta, N., & Verma, S. (2019). Tools of Opinion Mining. In *Extracting Knowledge From Opinion Mining* (pp. 179–203). IGI Global. doi:10.4018/978-1-5225-6117-0.ch009

Hai, Z., Chang, K., Kim, J. J., & Yang, C. C. (2013). Identifying features in opinion mining via intrinsic and extrinsic domain relevance. *IEEE Transactions on Knowledge and Data Engineering*, 26(3), 623–634. doi:10.1109/TKDE.2013.26 doi:10.1109/TKDE.2013.26

Jalota, C., & Agrawal, R. (2019). Ontology-Based Opinion Mining. In Extracting Knowledge From Opinion Mining (pp. 84-103). IGI Global. doi:10.4018/978-1-5225-6117-0.ch005 doi:10.4018/978-1-5225-6117-0.ch005

Kalchbrenner, N., Grefenstette, E., & Blunsom, P. (2014). *A convolutional neural network for modelling sentences*. arXiv preprint arXiv:1404.2188. doi:10.3115/v1/P14-1062

Kalra, V., & Aggarwal, R. (2017). Importance of Text Data Preprocessing & Implementation in RapidMiner. In *Proceedings of the First International Conference on Information Technology and Knowledge Management–New Dehli, India* (Vol. 14, pp. 71-75). 10.15439/2017KM46

Kalra, V., & Agrawal, R. (2019). Challenges of Text Analytics in Opinion Mining. In *Extracting Knowledge From Opinion Mining* (pp. 268–282). IGI Global. doi:10.4018/978-1-5225-6117-0.ch012

Kaur, S., & Agrawal, R. (2018). A Detailed Analysis of Core NLP for Information Extraction. *International Journal of Machine Learning and Networked Collaborative Engineering*, 1(01), 33–47. doi:10.30991/IJMLNCE.2017v01i01.005

Kim, Y. (2014). *Convolutional neural networks for sentence classification*. arXiv preprint arXiv:1408.5882. doi:10.3115/v1/D14-1181

Liu, B. (2006). Mining comparative sentences and relations. In AAAI (Vol. 22). Academic Press.

Medhat, W., Hassan, A., & Korashy, H. (2014). Sentiment analysis algorithms and applications: A survey. *Ain Shams Engineering Journal*, 5(4), 1093–1113. doi:10.1016/j.asej.2014.04.011

Mikolov, T., Chen, K., Corrado, G., & Dean, J. (2013). *Efficient estimation of word representations in vector space.* arXiv preprint arXiv:1301.3781.

Niazi, M., & Hussain, A. (2009). Agent-based tools for modeling and simulation of self-organization in peer-to-peer, ad hoc, and other complex networks. *IEEE Communications Magazine, 47*(3), 166–173. doi:10.1109/MCOM.2009.4804403

Ouyang, X., Zhou, P., Li, C. H., & Liu, L. (2015). *Sentiment analysis using convolutional neural network. In 2015 IEEE international conference on computer and information technology; ubiquitous computing and communications; dependable, autonomic and secure computing; pervasive intelligence and computing.* IEEE.

Pang, B., & Lee, L. (2008). Opinion mining and sentiment analysis. *Foundations and Trends in Information Retrieval, 2*(1–2), 1–135. doi:10.1561/1500000011

Poria, S., Gelbukh, A., Hussain, A., Howard, N., Das, D., & Bandyopadhyay, S. (2013). Enhanced SenticNet with affective labels for concept-based opinion mining. *IEEE Intelligent Systems, 28*(2), 31–38. doi:10.1109/MIS.2013.4

Socher, R., Lin, C. C., Manning, C., & Ng, A. Y. (2011). Parsing natural scenes and natural language with recursive neural networks. In *Proceedings of the 28th international conference on machine learning (ICML-11)* (pp. 129-136). Academic Press.

Tsai, A. C. R., Wu, C. E., Tsai, R. T. H., & Hsu, J. Y. J. (2013). Building a concept-level sentiment dictionary based on commonsense knowledge. *IEEE Intelligent Systems, 28*(2), 22–30. doi:10.1109/MIS.2013.25

Vateekul, P., & Koomsubha, T. (2016). A Study of Sentiment Analysis Using Deep Learning Techniques on Thai Twitter Data. *13th International Joint Conference on Computer Science and Software Engineering (JCSSE)*, 1-6. 10.1109/JCSSE.2016.7748849

Ye, Q., Zhang, Z., & Law, R. (2009). Sentiment classification of online reviews to travel destinations by supervised machine learning approaches. *Expert Systems with Applications, 36*(3), 6527–6535. doi:10.1016/j.eswa.2008.07.035

Chapter 8
Motion Imitation for Monocular Videos

Priyanka Nandal
Maharaja Surajmal Institute of Technology, India

ABSTRACT

This work represents a simple method for motion transfer (i.e., given a source video of a subject [person] performing some movements or in motion, that movement/motion is transferred to amateur target in different motion). The pose is used as an intermediate representation to perform this translation. To transfer the motion of the source subject to the target subject, the pose is extracted from the source subject, and then the target subject is generated by applying the learned pose to-appearance mapping. To perform this translation, the video is considered as a set of images consisting of all the frames. Generative adversarial networks (GANs) are used to transfer the motion from source subject to the target subject. GANs are an evolving field of deep learning.

INTRODUCTION

Wide opportunities are originated by Generative adversarial networks (GANs) in the field of image manipulation (Goodfellow et al, 2014), human novel view synthesis and motion imitation. Applications offered by GANs in the field of image manipulation include appearance transfer i.e. changing one's face in some way (Raj et al, 2018; Zanfir et al, 2018): make it younger/older, add beard, glasses, etc. Such translations are performed by two types of network architecture i.e. deep neural networks trained on either paired or unpaired datasets. Unpaired datasets are mostly used in practical applications. Another potential application of GANs includes human novel view synthesis (Zhu et al, 2018; Zhao et al, 2018). The aim of human novel view synthesis is to create new images of the human body which are captured from contrasting viewpoints such as movie or game making, virtual clothes try-on, character animation, re-enactment and so on. As the GANs emerged with its variant conditional GANs (cGANs) (Mirza & Osindero, 2014), many works based on GAN achieved huge success. An application employing GAN technique is popularly known as talking-head video generation in which one or few facial images are given and a piece of audio speech is given, the task is to synthesize a realistic-looking, animated

DOI: 10.4018/978-1-7998-7511-6.ch008

talking-head video. A wide range of practical applications for talking-head video generation exist such as lip synchronization in re-dubbing videos with other languages, telepresence for video-conferencing or role-playing video games, bandwidth-limited video transformation, and virtual anchors, assistive devices for hearing impaired people, enhancing speech comprehension while maintaining privacy or natural spontaneous motion. Another successful achievement of GAN is in human video motion transfer (HVMT) (Chan et al, 2014; Wang et al, 2018; Liu et al, 2019; Zhou et al, 2019; Aberman et al, 2019). In HVMT or simply known as motion imitation, a video is synthesized in which the actions of the person in the source video are imitated by the person in a target video. Applications of HVMT include movies, games, videos (converting black-and-white videos to color) and robotics (teaching robots from human demonstration). For instance, in VR/AR games and movies, a key role is played by the animation of virtual characters. Plausible visual results are rendered by animating the virtual game roles or movie actors freely to perform user-defined mimetic movements (Xu et al, 2018; Shysheya et al, 2019).

The problem consisting of human motion transfer based on video is an alluring but exigent research problem. An approach for video retargeting is presented here in which the sequential content is transferred from one domain to other through the use of GANs. Two monocular video clips are accepted as input. One video clip acts as the source subject and another act as the target subject. The objective of present problem is to transfer the motion from the source person to the target, at the same time preserving the target person's appearance. The subject should have the identical motion as the source person particularly, in the synthesized video. This is accomplished by translating the frames image-to-image, and to produce high-quality frames while ensuring temporal coherence essentially. The video is decomposed and deep neural network design and training techniques are applied so that approximate human motion can be transferred from one video to another. This problem is approached as video-to video translation via pose as an intermediary representation. The poses are extracted from the source subject and the learned pose-to-appearance mapping is applied to generate the target subject in order to transfer the motion. For temporally coherent video results, two consecutive frames are predicted and a different pipeline for realistic face generation is introduced. Even though the approach is fairly elementary, it yields surprisingly fascinating results. The revelation is that the target person not at all executed the similar precise order of motions as the source, and in fact does not know how to dance. The target video clip contains the individual carrying out a set of standard moves, devoid of any allusion to the exact motions of the source. The source and the target have dissimilar builds, can be of separate genders, and wear distinct clothing. A personalized dancing video can be generated of a person who does not have any dancing experience with the help of such methods. Motion imitation has been recently studied in the literature using GAN technique (Garcia Ricardez et al, 2020; Ding, 2020; Zuo et al, 2020).

The proposed algorithm can be used in industry. Vast scope of implementation is in movie industry where new and difficult forms of dance can be imitated for movie actors/actresses where the target persons i.e. the movie actors/actresses do not know any particular form of dance. The human motion can be transferred to humanoid robot. This is done in order to train the robots. Techniques for transferring the human motion directly to the robots exist but greater accuracy can be achieved in robot motion generation by using the GANs employing the key poses and transferring the motion from source to the target (Liu et al, 2020; Oh et al, 2020).

RELATED WORK

In the recent years extensive attempts have been made towards fast video content production. Earlier, existing video footage was realigned in accordance with the resemblance to the desired pose (Bregler, Covell & Slaney, 1997; Efros et al, 2003; Mori et al, 2004). It was a tedious task to find resemblance for various actions of different subjects.

Image-to-Image Translation

Image-to-image translation uses paired training data to transfer an image from original domain to other and introduces encoder-decoder architecture with skip connections. The architecture and training methods have been widely adopted in follow-up work. One of the pioneering works is pix2pix (Isola et al, 2017) which is based on a cGAN framework. It involves learning the mapping of images from input to output. First model was proposed to synthesize images of resolution 2048x1024 (Chen & Koltun, 2017). CycleGAN (Zhu et al, 2017) further illustrates the notion of applying cycle consistency to train on unpaired data for learning to translate between two domains. Recycle-GAN integrates both spatial and temporal constraints for video retargeting tasks (Bansal et al, 2018). The methods of unpaired image-to-image translation can be either single mode GANs (Yi et al, 2017; Zhu et al, 2017a; Li et al, 2018; Choi et al, 2018) or multimodal GANs (Zhu et al, 2017b; Huang et al, 2018; Lee et al, 2018, 2019; Liu et al, 2019; Choi et al, 2019). FUNIT (Liu et al, 2019) supports multi-domain image translation by means of employing handful of reference images from a target domain. StarGAN v2 (Choi et al, 2019) provide both latent-guided and reference-guided synthesis. All of the above-mentioned methods operate at resolution of at most 256x256 when applied to human faces. Gender swap is one of well-known tasks of unsupervised image-to-image translation (Liu, Li & Sun, 2019; Choi et al, 2018, 2019). Face aging/ rejuvenation is a special task which gets a lot of attention (Song et al, 2018; Zhang, Song & Qi, 2017; He et al, 2019). Formulation of the problem can vary. The simplest version of this task is making faces look older or younger (Choi et al, 2018). More difficult task is to produce faces matching particular age intervals (Li et al, 2018; Wang et al, 2018; Yang et al, 2019; Liu, Li & Sun, 2019). S^2GAN (He et al, 2019) proposes continuous changing of age using weight interpolation between transforms which correspond to two closest age groups. In SPADE (Park et al, 2019) generator, all normalization layers adopt the segmentation mask to modulate the layer activations. So its usage is limited to the translation from segmentation maps.

Video-to-Video Translation

The counterpart of image based pose transfer is the video based human motion transfer. A mapping is learned in generative human motion transfer from input images of a person to construct images displaying the person in new poses. Video generation in video based human motion transfer is considered with access to more appearance information contained in a whole video, leading to a higher level of temporal coherence and visual quality. Video synthesis model is a hard-won task for a long duration video because temporally coherent frames are produced in it along with ensuring that each video frame looks photorealistic. With the latest developments in deep learning, particularly generative adversarial networks (GANs) and its variants like cGAN, CoGAN (Liu & Tuzel, 2016), CycleGAN, Recycle-GAN, DiscoGAN (Kim at al, 2017), ProgressiveGAN (Karras et al, 2017), StyleGAN (Karras, Laine & Aila,

2019) and BigGAN (Brock, Donahue & Simonyan, 2018) exciting results have been generated for video-to-video translation. A lot of methods (Chan et al, 2018; Balakrishnan et al, 2018; Ma et al, 2017, 2018; Esser, Sutter & Ommer, 2018) have been suggested for human motion transfer amid two domains on the basis of variations of these GANs. To extract the pose information from the input image and utilize it as the input of a GAN network to produce a realistic output image is the fundamental idea of these approaches. Parametric face models are used to transfer facial expression in some models (Thies et al, 2016; Averbuch-Elor et al, 2017). Image generation neural networks were also used to transfer human body motion (Kim at al, 2018). Future frames were predicted using the pose to generate a new human video (Villegas et al, 2017, 2018). Given a target pose, a novel view is synthesized using a reference image (Ma et al, 2017, 2018). The approach is improved by employing deformable skip connections in the generative network architecture (Siarohin et al, 2018). A spatial transformation sub-module is used to synthesize unseen poses after segmenting the human body parts according to the target pose (Balakrishnan et al, 2018). Generally blurry videos are produced owing to the classic regress-to-the-mean problem by several of these models as these models are trained with image reconstruction losses. An input person image and an estimation of surface map i.e. DensePose (Guler, Neverova & Kokkinos, 2018) were used to generate images that combine the pixel-level prediction and UV texture mapping (Neverova et al, 2018). Despite the contrary, these approaches are extremely susceptible to problems like self-occlusions as a result of the lack of 3D semantic information.

BACKGROUND

Generative Adversarial Networks (GANs)

The model is built on GANs. A zero sum game is played by the generator and discriminator during the training of GAN. This is done in order to minimize the difference amid the synthesized and the real data. Realistic synthetic data is produced by the generator. Different modes of data can be employed as input to the generator like textual descriptions (Zhang et al, 2017; Reed et al, 2016), categorical labels (Miyato & Koyama, 2018; Odena, Olah, & Shlens, 2017) and images (Isola et al, 2017; Zhu et al, 2017; Liu, Breuel & Kautz, 2017) along with noise distribution (Goodfellow et al, 2014; Radford, Metz & Chintala, 2015; Denton et al, 2015). These are defined as conditional GANs. Flexible command over the output of the model is allowed in these cGANs. The work presented here utilizes conditional GANs for video generation.

SOLUTIONS AND RECOMMENDATIONS

Methodology

Data distribution P_{data} contains a sequence of source video frames. Sequence of video frames of source is represented as $s_1^T \equiv \{s_1, s_2, s_3, \ldots s_T\}$. Sequence of corresponding real video frames is represented as $x_1^T \equiv \{x_1, x_2, x_3, \ldots x_T\}$. The objective of motion imitation is to find out a mapping function so as to convert s_1^T to a sequence of output video frames $\tilde{x}_1^T \equiv \left\{ \tilde{x}_1, \tilde{x}_2, ..., \tilde{x}_T \right\}$. Thereby the conditional distribution of $\tilde{x}_1^T$ given s_1^T is equivalent to the conditional distribution of x_1^T given s_1^T.

$$p\left(\tilde{x}_1^T \mid s_1^T \right) = p\left(x_1^T \mid s_1^T \right) \tag{1}$$

Photorealistic and temporally coherent sequences are generated as output by the model by means of coordinating the conditional video distributions. It looks as if the output sequences were taken by the camera. A conditional GAN framework is proposed here in order to accomplish the matching task for video distribution.

A generator G is learned, the purpose of which is to map an input source sequence to a matching output frame sequence $x_1^T = G\left(s_1^T \right)$. The generator is trained to optimize the following cost function.

$$\min_{G} \max_{D \in (0,1)} \mathrm{E}_{\left(x_1^T, s_1^T \right)} \log\left(D\left(x_1^T, s_1^T \right) \right) + \mathrm{E}_{s_1^T} \log\left(1 - D\left(G\left(s_1^T \right), s_1^T \right) \right) \tag{2}$$

Here D is the discriminator. By solving (2) the Jensen-Shannon divergence among $p\left(\tilde{x}_1^T \mid s_1^T \right)$ and $p\left(x_1^T \mid s_1^T \right)$ is minimized. It is a well recognized challenging task to solve the minmax optimization problem stated in (2). Good performances have been achieved in the literature by carefully designing the network architectures (Denton, Chintala & Fergus, 2015; Miyato & Koyama, 2018; Radford, Metz & Chintala, 2015). A new variation of design is proposed here for motion imitation.

To generate photo-realistic videos and allow more fine-grain controls, the conditional video generation methods have shown great potential. Given monocular videos of source and target person, the aim is to generate a novel video of the target imitating the motion of the source. The solution for the problem is categorized into different following parts: first pose detection is performed, then the pose is normalized globally, and at the end mapping is done from normalized pose stick figure to the target subject.

1. Pose Estimation and Normalization

In this step, the motion/movement of the source and target subjects is extracted from each frame of the video, by employing the pre-trained model for pose detection. The pre-trained model is capable of efficiently detecting the 2D pose (2D keypoints of the human body structure) of the person in a video. The extracted poses for each frame is then saved as pose stick figures, which is formed by joining the key-points returned by this model. As target and source subject may have either dissimilar limb measurements or may stand near or at a greater distance from the camera; consequently the pose key points are transformed by evaluating the ankle and height positions for the poses of every subject and a linear mapping is used amidst the nearest and extreme ankle positions in the two videos while retargeting motion between the both.

2. *Pose to Video Translation*

Now final mapping is done with the target object, i.e. the normalized pose stick figures which make the motion of the target subject like source subject. This process is accomplished in two steps:

a. *Training Phase*

The images of a person are generated by the generator when pose stick figure is given. With pre-trained very deep convolutional networks, this adversarial preparation is carried out using a discriminator and a perceptual loss function for reconstruction. In the training process, the target person's generated pose stick figures are passed on to the generator, whose task is to create images from the abstract pose stick images. More detailed images are generated by the generator so as to deceive the discriminator that consecutively determines the dissimilarity amid the generated output and the original data. The two networks are improved by each other as they are trained simultaneously. The discriminator is unable to differentiate among the original images and the images generated by the generator. This helps to optimize the generated image to match the target image.

b. *Transfer Phase*

The source object pose is extracted to yield target object pose. But since the location, limb positions and environment of the source entity are not sure; therefore to make it compatible with the location of the target individual, a global position normalization model is used during this step. The distance between the positions of the ankle and the height is considered to linearly map the position of the source object to that of the target object which is then passed to the previously trained model to generate the target person.

The video frames are generated sequentially. A huge volume of superfluous information appears in successive frames. The subsequent frame can be estimated by warping the present frame provided that the optical flow among successive frames is familiar. Apart for the occluded areas, this estimation is mostly correct. The generation of a particular frame relies upon the factors such as the current source frame, past L source frames and the past L generated frames. Two successive frames are predicted at a time. The first output frame is conditioned on its analogous pose stick figure and as there is no previously generated frame at time $t - L$, a zero image is used. The second output frame is conditioned on its analogous pose stick figure and the previous output frame. As a consequence, the discriminator has now the task of determining both the variation in realism and temporal coherence among the "fake" sequence and "real" sequence. To model this conditional distribution a feed forward network is trained. The final output is obtained by applying this network is a recursive manner. The value of L should be kept optimum as the lesser value causes training instability, at the same time larger value of L leads to increase in training time and GPU memory resulting in the slightest improvement in quality. The value of L is kept 2 in the work presented here. To generate fine details and realism to the face, conditional GAN was applied to face region also. The full image scene is generated with the generator G. A minor portion of the image centered in the vicinity of the nose key point and the pose stick figure sectioned in a similar way is input to a different generator G_f. Therefore the final face region is synthesized from the integration of the output of the two generators. A different discriminator D_f is used for the face region. This discriminator output 1 for a true face and 0 for a fake one. The objective during the training of the generator and discriminator is

$$\min_G \left[\left(\max_{D_i} \sum_{k_i} L_M\left(G, D_k\right) \right) + \lambda_F \sum_{k_i} L_F\left(G, D_k\right) + \lambda_P \left(L_P\left(G\left(x_{t-1}\right), y_{t-1}\right) + L_P\left(G\left(x_t\right), y_t\right) \right) \right] \qquad (3)$$

Here x, y are the joint coordinates of the pose. L_M defines the GAN loss on images by the conditional image discriminator D.

$$L_M\left(G, D\right) = E_{(x,y)}\left[\log D\left(x, y\right)\right] + E_x\left[\log\left(1 - D\left(x, G\left(x\right)\right)\right)\right] \qquad (4)$$

L_F defines the discriminator feature matching loss, L_P is the perceptual reconstruction loss. λ_P and λ_F are the GAN weights.

A benefit is provided by GANs that they automatically learn the appropriate loss between the data and generated distributions.

Implementation

The network was trained in a spatio-temporally progressive manner. Initially low resolution videos with few frames were generated. The model is trained for 40 epocs. During the training 30 frames per second for a video were used. Python is used as the programming language. The GPU used is NVIDIA Tesla K80. A 'CUDA_VISIBLE_DEVICES' environment variable is defined to let the internal modules to recognize and utilize the GPU to be used. The monocular videos of about 5 minutes in length are taken from the YouTube. The resolution of the frames is 512×720. One of the video files serves as the source and another as the target object. It is ensured that the person in both the videos is performing different motions in each corresponding different frames. Pose stick figure is generated corresponding to each frame.

After extracting the poses from both subjects we normalize the pose stick figures to reasonably match the poses, by determining an appropriate transformation among the source and target poses using the method described heretofore. In the training phase, the target image's set of frames with their corresponding pose stick figure is passed to train the generator G.

After the final phase i.e. after transferring the motion we finally get the results as expected, though with some limitations. Below are some images of the results (with different sets of subjects).

Impressive results have been shown by deep Convolutional GANs. The results are presented for the natural YouTube videos. The transferred motion i.e. target (subject's) new motion appears to be almost identical to the motion of the source subject.

Comparative Performance Analysis

In PoseWarp (Balakrishnan et al, 2018), a new pose of target subject is generated. Single image is synthesized in this method. The author synthesized a frame-by-frame video for comparison purpose.

To evaluate the videos two metrics are used. First metric used is Structural Similarity Index Measure (SSIM). The perceived image quality degradation amid the real and synthesized frames is measured by this index (Wang et al, 2004). The second metric used is Learned Perceptual Image Patch Similarity (LPIPS). This index measures the perceptual similarity amid the real and generated images (Zhang et al, 2018).

Figure 1. Source Subject at Frame No. 412

The scores of both the metrics i.e. LPIPS and SSIM are similar on the body regions for the model variations as can be seen in Table 1. Full images scores were also quite similar as the static background can be generated with no complication.

Figure 2. Pose stick figure of Source Subject at Frame No. 412

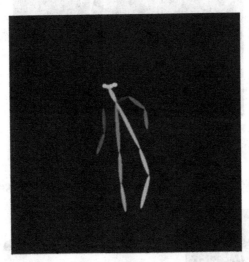

For LPIPS metric lower value is considered as better and for SSIM metric higher value is considered as better.

Figure 3. Target Subject at Frame No. 412

Figure 4. Pose stick figure of Target Subject at Frame No. 412

Figure 5. Pose Stick Figure, Synthesised image and Original Target Image at epoch 1

Figure 6. Pose Stick Figure, Synthesised image and Original Target Image at epoch 15

Figure 7. Pose Stick Figure, Synthesised image and Original Target Image at epoch 30

Figure 8. Pose Stick Figure, Synthesised image and Original Target Image at epoch 40

FUTURE TRENDS AND CONCLUSION

An imitation learning is proposed using conditional GAN framework. The input used is the raw YouTube monocular videos. The motion was transferred from the source video to the target video successfully. Temporally consistent videos were synthesized. It is demonstrated by the experiments that conditional GAN framework can be applied to synthesize a video which transfers the motion from the source subject to the target subject. The work presented here depicts the use of conditional GAN to synthesize high resolution photo-realistic videos. The pose information is extracted and a conditional GAN is employed to learn a mapping from a 2D pose figure to a frame. However the work suffers from several limitations.

Figure 9. Final results, displaying source subject, its motion pose stick figure and target subject (a human) after transferring motion.

Figure 10. Final results, displaying source subject, its motion pose stick figure and target subject (a cartoon) after transferring motion.

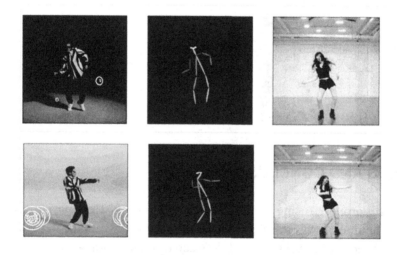

Table 1. Metric comparison for PoseWarp and the work presented here (video2video)

Metric	PoseWarp	video2video (Current Work)
SSIM	0.816.	0.816
LPIPS	0.051	0.050

Figure 11. Resulted target subject does not have second palm in the generated frame.

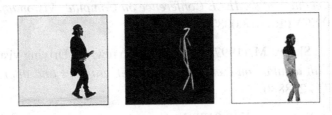

As the resulting video seems to be convincing but occasionally there are anomalies like stuttering, disappearing parts of the body, also one can discover that regions near the face, hand palm need some more work so that the content looks more realistic. As shown in the above image (Figure 11), the generated frame of the target subject does not have a second palm and lacks some details over that region. Therefore the model presented here needs some additional algorithms or networks to work over these problems. Many previous trained models suffer from image reconstruction losses, generally synthesizing blurry videos owing to the classic regress-to-the-mean issue (Denton & Birodkar, 2017; Finn, Goodfellow & Levine, 2016; Kalchbrenner et al, 2016; Lee et al, 2018; Liang et al, 2017; Mathieu, Couprie, & LeCun, 2016; Villegas et al, 2017; Walker et al, 2016, 2017; Xue et al, 2016; Lotter, Kreiman & Cox, 2017). Further, long duration videos are not generated even with adversarial training (Liang et al, 2017; Mathieu, Couprie, & LeCun, 2016). However, the model presented here is able to generate new motions fairly well employing the training data. Videos with good-resolution and long-duration are synthesized by this model.

Thus one can conclude that GANs are promising approach towards such problems where content needs to be created. In future, further refinement can be done using GAN to the regions which adds more detail and realism over the face and hand palm. More complex videos can also be synthesized in future where rather than solo, multiple people perform the movements. The results can be further improved in future. To improve the results target videos can be combined with scene lighting or diverse clothing, refining pose detection systems, and alleviating the artifacts induced by high frequency textures in hair or loose/wrinkled clothing.

REFERENCES

Aberman, K., Shi, M., Liao, J., Lischinski, D., Chen, B., & Cohen-Or, D. (2019, May). Deep Video-Based Performance Cloning. *Computer Graphics Forum*, *38*(2), 219–233. doi:10.1111/cgf.13632

Alp Güler, R., Neverova, N., & Kokkinos, I. (2018). Densepose: Dense human pose estimation in the wild. In *Proceedings of the IEEE Conference on Computer Vision and Pattern Recognition* (pp. 7297-7306). IEEE.

Averbuch-Elor, H., Cohen-Or, D., Kopf, J., & Cohen, M. F. (2017). Bringing portraits to life. *ACM Transactions on Graphics*, *36*(6), 196. doi:10.1145/3130800.3130818

Balakrishnan, G., Zhao, A., Dalca, A. V., Durand, F., & Guttag, J. (2018). Synthesizing images of humans in unseen poses. In *Proceedings of the IEEE Conference on Computer Vision and Pattern Recognition* (pp. 8340-8348). 10.1109/CVPR.2018.00870

Bregler, C., Covell, M., & Slaney, M. (1997, August). Video rewrite: Driving visual speech with audio. In *Proceedings of the 24th annual conference on Computer graphics and interactive techniques* (pp. 353-360). 10.1145/258734.258880

Brock, A., Donahue, J., & Simonyan, K. (2018). *Large scale gan training for high fidelity natural image synthesis.* arXiv preprint arXiv:1809.11096

Chan, C., Ginosar, S., Zhou, T., & Efros, A. A. (2019). Everybody dance now. In *Proceedings of the IEEE International Conference on Computer Vision* (pp. 5933-5942). IEEE.

Chen, Q., & Koltun, V. (2017). Photographic image synthesis with cascaded refinement networks. In *Proceedings of the IEEE international conference on computer vision* (pp. 1511-1520). 10.1109/ICCV.2017.168

Choi, Y., Choi, M., Kim, M., Ha, J. W., Kim, S., & Choo, J. (2018). Stargan: Unified generative adversarial networks for multi-domain image-to-image translation. In *Proceedings of the IEEE conference on computer vision and pattern recognition* (pp. 8789-8797). 10.1109/CVPR.2018.00916

Choi, Y., Uh, Y., Yoo, J., & Ha, J. W. (2019). *StarGAN v2: Diverse Image Synthesis for Multiple Domains.* arXiv preprint arXiv:1912.01865.

Denton, E. L. (2017). Unsupervised learning of disentangled representations from video. In Advances in neural information processing systems (pp. 4414-4423). Academic Press.

Denton, E. L., Chintala, S., & Fergus, R. (2015). Deep generative image models using a laplacian pyramid of adversarial networks. In Advances in neural information processing systems (pp. 1486-1494). Academic Press.

Ding, Z. (2020). Imitation Learning. In *Deep Reinforcement Learning* (pp. 273–306). Springer. doi:10.1007/978-981-15-4095-0_8

Efros, A. A., Berg, A. C., Mori, G., & Malik, J. (2003, October). Recognizing action at a distance. In Null (p. 726). IEEE. doi:10.1109/ICCV.2003.1238420

Esser, P., Sutter, E., & Ommer, B. (2018). A variational u-net for conditional appearance and shape generation. In *Proceedings of the IEEE Conference on Computer Vision and Pattern Recognition* (pp. 8857-8866). 10.1109/CVPR.2018.00923

Finn, C., Goodfellow, I., & Levine, S. (2016). Unsupervised learning for physical interaction through video prediction. In Advances in neural information processing systems (pp. 64-72). Academic Press.

Garcia Ricardez, G. A., Koganti, N., Yang, P. C., Okada, S., Uriguen Eljuri, P. M., Yasuda, A., El Hafi, L., Yamamoto, M., Takamatsu, J., & Ogasawara, T. (2020). Adaptive motion generation using imitation learning and highly compliant end effector for autonomous cleaning. *Advanced Robotics, 34*(3-4), 189–201. doi:10.1080/01691864.2019.1698461

Goodfellow, I., Pouget-Abadie, J., Mirza, M., Xu, B., Warde-Farley, D., Ozair, S., Courville, A., & Bengio, Y. (2014). Generative adversarial nets. *Proceedings of the International Conference on Neural Information Processing Systems*, 2672–2680.

He, Z., Kan, M., Shan, S., & Chen, X. (2019). S2GAN: Share Aging Factors Across Ages and Share Aging Trends Among Individuals. In *Proceedings of the IEEE International Conference on Computer Vision* (pp. 9440-9449). 10.1109/ICCV.2019.00953

Huang, X., Liu, M. Y., Belongie, S., & Kautz, J. (2018). Multimodal unsupervised image-to-image translation. In *Proceedings of the European Conference on Computer Vision (ECCV)* (pp. 172-189). Academic Press.

Isola, P., Zhu, J. Y., Zhou, T., & Efros, A. A. (2017). Image-to-image translation with conditional adversarial networks. In *Proceedings of the IEEE conference on computer vision and pattern recognition* (pp. 1125-1134). IEEE.

Kalchbrenner, N., van den Oord, A., Simonyan, K., Danihelka, I., Vinyals, O., Graves, A., & Kavukcuoglu, K. (2017, August). Video pixel networks. In *Proceedings of the 34th International Conference on Machine Learning-Volume 70* (pp. 1771-1779). JMLR. org.

Karras, T., Aila, T., Laine, S., & Lehtinen, J. (2017). *Progressive growing of gans for improved quality, stability, and variation.* arXiv preprint arXiv:1710.10196.

Karras, T., Laine, S., & Aila, T. (2019). A style-based generator architecture for generative adversarial networks. In *Proceedings of the IEEE Conference on Computer Vision and Pattern Recognition* (pp. 4401-4410). 10.1109/CVPR.2019.00453

Kim, H., Garrido, P., Tewari, A., Xu, W., Thies, J., Nießner, M., Pérez, P., Richardt, C., Zollhöfer, M., & Theobalt, C. (2018). Deep video portraits. *ACM Transactions on Graphics*, *37*(4), 1–14. doi:10.1145/3197517.3201283

Kim, T., Cha, M., Kim, H., Lee, J. K., & Kim, J. (2017, August). Learning to discover cross-domain relations with generative adversarial networks. In *Proceedings of the 34th International Conference on Machine Learning-Volume 70* (pp. 1857-1865). JMLR. org.

Lee, A. X., Zhang, R., Ebert, F., Abbeel, P., Finn, C., & Levine, S. (2018). *Stochastic adversarial video prediction.* arXiv preprint arXiv:1804.01523.

Lee, H. Y., Tseng, H. Y., Huang, J. B., Singh, M., & Yang, M. H. (2018). Diverse image-to-image translation via disentangled representations. In *Proceedings of the European conference on computer vision (ECCV)* (pp. 35-51). Academic Press.

Lee, H. Y., Tseng, H. Y., Mao, Q., Huang, J. B., Lu, Y. D., Singh, M., & Yang, M. H. (2020). Drit++: Diverse image-to-image translation via disentangled representations. *International Journal of Computer Vision*, *128*(10-11), 1–16. doi:10.100711263-019-01284-z

Li, P., Hu, Y., Li, Q., He, R., & Sun, Z. (2018, August). Global and local consistent age generative adversarial networks. In *2018 24th International Conference on Pattern Recognition (ICPR)* (pp. 1073-1078). IEEE. 10.1109/ICPR.2018.8545119

Liang, X., Lee, L., Dai, W., & Xing, E. P. (2017). Dual motion GAN for future-flow embedded video prediction. In *Proceedings of the IEEE International Conference on Computer Vision* (pp. 1744-1752). 10.1109/ICCV.2017.194

Liu, L., Xu, W., Zollhoefer, M., Kim, H., Bernard, F., Habermann, M., . . . Theobalt, C. (2018). *Neural Rendering and Reenactment of Human Actor Videos.* arXiv preprint arXiv:1809.03658.

Liu, M. Y., Breuel, T., & Kautz, J. (2017). Unsupervised image-to-image translation networks. In Advances in neural information processing systems (pp. 700-708). Academic Press.

Liu, M. Y., Huang, X., Mallya, A., Karras, T., Aila, T., Lehtinen, J., & Kautz, J. (2019). Few-shot unsupervised image-to-image translation. In *Proceedings of the IEEE International Conference on Computer Vision* (pp. 10551-10560). IEEE.

Liu, M. Y., & Tuzel, O. (2016). Coupled generative adversarial networks. In Advances in neural information processing systems (pp. 469-477). Academic Press.

Liu, Y., Li, Q., & Sun, Z. (2019). Attribute-aware face aging with wavelet-based generative adversarial networks. In *Proceedings of the IEEE Conference on Computer Vision and Pattern Recognition* (pp. 11877-11886). 10.1109/CVPR.2019.01215

Liu, Y., Zhang, W., Pan, S., Li, Y., & Chen, Y. (2020). Analyzing the robotic behavior in a smart city with deep enforcement and imitation learning using IoRT. *Computer Communications*, *150*, 346–356. doi:10.1016/j.comcom.2019.11.031

Lotter, W., Kreiman, G., & Cox, D. (2016). *Deep predictive coding networks for video prediction and unsupervised learning.* arXiv preprint arXiv:1605.08104.

Ma, L., Jia, X., Sun, Q., Schiele, B., Tuytelaars, T., & Van Gool, L. (2017). Pose guided person image generation. In Advances in Neural Information Processing Systems (pp. 406-416). Academic Press.

Ma, L., Sun, Q., Georgoulis, S., Van Gool, L., Schiele, B., & Fritz, M. (2018). Disentangled person image generation. In *Proceedings of the IEEE Conference on Computer Vision and Pattern Recognition* (pp. 99-108). IEEE.

Mathieu, M., Couprie, C., & LeCun, Y. (2015). *Deep multi-scale video prediction beyond mean square error.* arXiv preprint arXiv:1511.05440.

Mirza, M., & Osindero, S. (2014). *Conditional generative adversarial nets.* arXiv preprint arXiv:1411.1784.

Miyato, T., & Koyama, M. (2018). *cGANs with projection discriminator.* arXiv preprint arXiv:1802.05637.

Mori, G., Berg, A., Efros, A., Eden, A., & Malik, J. (2004). Video based motion synthesis by splicing and morphing. *Computer Science*.

Neverova, N., Alp Guler, R., & Kokkinos, I. (2018). Dense pose transfer. In *Proceedings of the European conference on computer vision (ECCV)* (pp. 123-138). Academic Press.

Odena, A., Olah, C., & Shlens, J. (2017, August). Conditional image synthesis with auxiliary classifier gans. In *Proceedings of the 34th International Conference on Machine Learning-Volume 70* (pp. 2642-2651). JMLR. org.

Oh, J., Sim, O., Cho, B., Lee, K., & Oh, J. H. (2020). Online Delayed Reference Generation for a Humanoid Imitating Human Walking Motion. *IEEE/ASME Transactions on Mechatronics*, 1. doi:10.1109/TMECH.2020.3002396

Park, T., Liu, M. Y., Wang, T. C., & Zhu, J. Y. (2019). Semantic image synthesis with spatially-adaptive normalization. In *Proceedings of the IEEE Conference on Computer Vision and Pattern Recognition* (pp. 2337-2346). IEEE.

Radford, A., Metz, L., & Chintala, S. (2015). *Unsupervised representation learning with deep convolutional generative adversarial networks.* arXiv preprint arXiv:1511.06434.

Raj, A., Sangkloy, P., Chang, H., Hays, J., Ceylan, D., & Lu, J. (2018, September). Swapnet: Image based garment transfer. In *European Conference on Computer Vision* (pp. 679-695). Springer.

Reed, S., Akata, Z., Yan, X., Logeswaran, L., Schiele, B., & Lee, H. (2016). *Generative adversarial text to image synthesis.* arXiv preprint arXiv:1605.05396.

Shysheya, A., Zakharov, E., Aliev, K. A., Bashirov, R., Burkov, E., Iskakov, K., Ivakhnenko, A., Malkov, Y., Pasechnik, I., Ulyanov, D., & Vakhitov, A. (2019). Textured neural avatars. In *Proceedings of the IEEE Conference on Computer Vision and Pattern Recognition* (pp. 2387-2397). IEEE.

Siarohin, A., Sangineto, E., Lathuilière, S., & Sebe, N. (2018). Deformable gans for pose-based human image generation. In *Proceedings of the IEEE Conference on Computer Vision and Pattern Recognition* (pp. 3408-3416). 10.1109/CVPR.2018.00359

Song, J., Zhang, J., Gao, L., Liu, X., & Shen, H. T. (2018, July). Dual Conditional GANs for Face Aging and Rejuvenation. In IJCAI (pp. 899-905). doi:10.24963/ijcai.2018/125

Thies, J., Zollhofer, M., Stamminger, M., Theobalt, C., & Nießner, M. (2016). Face2face: Real-time face capture and reenactment of rgb videos. In *Proceedings of the IEEE conference on computer vision and pattern recognition* (pp. 2387-2395). 10.1145/2929464.2929475

Villegas, R., Yang, J., Ceylan, D., & Lee, H. (2018). Neural kinematic networks for unsupervised motion retargetting. In *Proceedings of the IEEE Conference on Computer Vision and Pattern Recognition* (pp. 8639-8648). 10.1109/CVPR.2018.00901

Villegas, R., Yang, J., Hong, S., Lin, X., & Lee, H. (2017). *Decomposing motion and content for natural video sequence prediction.* arXiv preprint arXiv:1706.08033.

Walker, J., Doersch, C., Gupta, A., & Hebert, M. (2016, October). An uncertain future: Forecasting from static images using variational autoencoders. In *European Conference on Computer Vision* (pp. 835-851). Springer. 10.1007/978-3-319-46478-7_51

Walker, J., Marino, K., Gupta, A., & Hebert, M. (2017). The pose knows: Video forecasting by generating pose futures. In *Proceedings of the IEEE international conference on computer vision* (pp. 3332-3341). 10.1109/ICCV.2017.361

Wang, T. C., Liu, M. Y., Zhu, J. Y., Liu, G., Tao, A., Kautz, J., & Catanzaro, B. (2018). *Video-to-video synthesis.* arXiv preprint arXiv:1808.06601.

Wang, Z., Bovik, A. C., Sheikh, H. R., & Simoncelli, E. P. (2004). Image quality assessment: From error visibility to structural similarity. *IEEE Transactions on Image Processing, 13*(4), 600–612. doi:10.1109/TIP.2003.819861 PMID:15376593

Wang, Z., Tang, X., Luo, W., & Gao, S. (2018). Face aging with identity-preserved conditional generative adversarial networks. In *Proceedings of the IEEE Conference on Computer Vision and Pattern Recognition* (pp. 7939-7947). IEEE.

Xu, W., Chatterjee, A., Zollhöfer, M., Rhodin, H., Mehta, D., Seidel, H. P., & Theobalt, C. (2018). Monoperfcap: Human performance capture from monocular video. *ACM Transactions on Graphics, 37*(2), 1–15. doi:10.1145/3181973

Xue, T., Wu, J., Bouman, K., & Freeman, B. (2016). Visual dynamics: Probabilistic future frame synthesis via cross convolutional networks. In Advances in neural information processing systems (pp. 91-99). Academic Press.

Yang, H., Huang, D., Wang, Y., & Jain, A. K. (2019). Learning continuous face age progression: A pyramid of gans. *IEEE Transactions on Pattern Analysis and Machine Intelligence, 1*. doi:10.1109/TPAMI.2019.2930985 PMID:31352335

Yi, Z., Zhang, H., Tan, P., & Gong, M. (2017). Dualgan: Unsupervised dual learning for image-to-image translation. In *Proceedings of the IEEE international conference on computer vision* (pp. 2849-2857). 10.1109/ICCV.2017.310

Zanfir, M., Popa, A. I., Zanfir, A., & Sminchisescu, C. (2018). Human appearance transfer. In *Proceedings of the IEEE Conference on Computer Vision and Pattern Recognition* (pp. 5391-5399). IEEE.

Zhang, H., Xu, T., Li, H., Zhang, S., Wang, X., Huang, X., & Metaxas, D. N. (2017). Stackgan: Text to photo-realistic image synthesis with stacked generative adversarial networks. In *Proceedings of the IEEE international conference on computer vision* (pp. 5907-5915). 10.1109/ICCV.2017.629

Zhang, R., Isola, P., Efros, A. A., Shechtman, E., & Wang, O. (2018). The unreasonable effectiveness of deep features as a perceptual metric. In *Proceedings of the IEEE conference on computer vision and pattern recognition* (pp. 586-595). 10.1109/CVPR.2018.00068

Zhang, Z., Song, Y., & Qi, H. (2017). Age progression/regression by conditional adversarial autoencoder. In *Proceedings of the IEEE conference on computer vision and pattern recognition* (pp. 5810-5818). 10.1109/CVPR.2017.463

Zhao, B., Wu, X., Cheng, Z. Q., Liu, H., Jie, Z., & Feng, J. (2018, October). Multi-view image generation from a single-view. In *Proceedings of the 26th ACM international conference on Multimedia* (pp. 383-391). ACM.

Zhou, Y., Wang, Z., Fang, C., Bui, T., & Berg, T. (2019). Dance dance generation: Motion transfer for internet videos. In *Proceedings of the IEEE International Conference on Computer Vision Workshops* (pp. 0-0). IEEE.

Zhu, H., Su, H., Wang, P., Cao, X., & Yang, R. (2018). View extrapolation of human body from a single image. In *Proceedings of the IEEE Conference on Computer Vision and Pattern Recognition* (pp. 4450-4459). 10.1109/CVPR.2018.00468

Zhu, J. Y., Park, T., Isola, P., & Efros, A. A. (2017). Unpaired image-to-image translation using cycle-consistent adversarial networks. In *Proceedings of the IEEE international conference on computer vision* (pp. 2223-2232). 10.1109/ICCV.2017.244

Zhu, J. Y., Zhang, R., Pathak, D., Darrell, T., Efros, A. A., Wang, O., & Shechtman, E. (2017). Toward multimodal image-to-image translation. In Advances in neural information processing systems (pp. 465-476). Academic Press.

Zuo, G., Chen, K., Lu, J., & Huang, X. (2020). Deterministic generative adversarial imitation learning. *Neurocomputing*, *388*, 60–69. doi:10.1016/j.neucom.2020.01.016

Chapter 9
Deep Learning for Moving Object Detection and Tracking

Kalirajan K.

KPR Institute of Engineering and Technology, India

Seethalakshmi V.

KPR Institute of Engineering and Technology, India

Venugopal D.

KPR Institute of Engineering and Technology, India

Balaji K.

SNS College of Engineering, India

ABSTRACT

Moving object detection and tracking is the process of identifying and locating the class objects such as people, vehicle, toy, and human faces in the video sequences more precisely without background disturbances. It is the first and foremost step in any kind of video analytics applications, and it is greatly influencing the high-level abstractions such as classification and tracking. Traditional methods are easily affected by the background disturbances and achieve poor results. With the advent of deep learning, it is possible to improve the results with high level features. The deep learning model helps to get more useful insights about the events in the real world. This chapter introduces the deep convolutional neural network and reviews the deep learning models used for moving object detection. This chapter also discusses the parameters involved and metrics used to assess the performance of moving object detection in deep learning model. Finally, the chapter is concluded with possible recommendations for the benefit of research community.

DOI: 10.4018/978-1-7998-7511-6.ch009

INTRODUCTION

Video surveillance is an emerging field with more advent for anonymous activity monitoring in the restricted areas and it greatly becomes a part of the life today. Usually, the video surveillance systems observe and analyze the huge amount of visual information to find out the suspicious activities in the given image frame. However, it is difficult to store and analyze the substantial surveillance data manually due to boredom and exhaustion. Alternatively, an intelligent video surveillance system can support the manual operations in case of event detection and other activity based analysis. A typical video frame comprises both foregrounds as well as backgrounds information. The pixel points which describe the target features in the region of interest are considered as foreground information and the rest of the feature points are treated as background information. In most of the cases, existing moving object detection approaches concentrate only on the foreground information and frequently ignored the background information. As a result, trackers will be deviated away from the target and detect the non-foreground objects. Figure 1 shows a typical smart video surveillance system which includes major steps such as object detection, object classification, object tracking, and event analysis.

Figure 1. Typical video surveillance systems

Moving object detection is the first and foremost step in any kind of video processing applications such as video surveillance, traffic monitoring, human-computer interaction, people monitoring, military and border security service, and vehicle navigations etc… The moving object detection is the process of identifying and locating the target more appropriately in all image frames without background intervention. Any particular region of interest within a frame such as a vehicle, animal, people and other moving objects can be considered as a target to be identified by the vision system. Commonly used moving object detection methods include background subtraction, a mixture of Gaussians, an adaptive mixture of Gaussians, optical flow based approach, and temporal differencing. Since the performance of moving object detection algorithm is greatly influencing the high-level abstractions such as classification, tracking, and event analysis, an intelligent video surveillance system requires more appropriate and robust object detection algorithms. Object classification is the second step in smart video surveillance system. It will classify the objects into people, vehicle, animal and other targets such as toys, buildings etc. In event analysis, the actions and behaviors of the tracked objects will be analyzed and described in the final decision. The optimal and feasible decision about the event will lead to early effective precautions and corrective measures to avoid the event before occurring. Recently, several contributions have been proposed for moving object detection and tracking. However, the robustness and novelty are still difficult to achieve because of the complex environments including illumination changes, rapid variations in target appearance, similar objects in the background, occlusions, target rotations, scaling, fast and abrupt motion changes, moving soft shadow, flat surface regions, and dynamic backgrounds. For an example, in people tracking, people will give an ID and it is forwarded in subsequent frames. If any person does not appear, then that particular person's ID will be dropped out. On the other hand, if any new person appears, then new ID will be assigned. This is a difficult task because of people may get occluded with others or similar persons may appear and so on. Deep learning that uses multi-layer neural networks is dramatically improving the performance of computer vision and video analytics. Deep neural network is a powerful programming paradigm which learns multiple levels of representation and abstraction of data such as images, sound, and text. Due to remarkable successes of deep learning techniques, it is possible to obtain valuable insights about video content and the performance of object detection can significantly be improved with deep learning algorithms such as region based convolutional neural networks (RCNN), fast RCNN, single shot detector (SSD), you only look once (YOLO). Figure 2 shows CCTV surveillance system for specific event detection such as car accidents, and trigger alerts accordingly. Usually, this system performs real-time monitoring in which objects, object attributes, movement patterns, or behavior related to the monitored environment are detected. The use of deep neural network (DNN) has made it possible to train systems that mimic human behavior and it is capable of identifying and tracking specific person in an image. Training models from scratch requires considerable effort. However, there are several pre-trained models available for tasks such as image classification, object detection, and facial recognition and it allows for parameter tuning of a model for a given use case.

Figure 2. Example of moving object and tracking system

BACKGROUND

More contributions have been presented in the literature of moving object detection algorithms. Every one of these endeavours concentrates on a few diverse examinations in the context of object detection and tracking problems. Hence, it is necessary to survey the existing methodologies in different aspects. This section deliberates the detailed literature review of moving object detection methods.

Temporal Differencing

In the temporal differencing method, the object motion is estimated by intensity difference calculation between the successive frames followed by thresholding. Keck et al. (2013) use three-frame differencing method for moving object detection. Cheng et al. (2011) employ the temporal difference method to detect the moving objects in each block of the image frame. Usually, the temporal differencing method does not prefer for moving object detection because of its inability to provide the complete object outliers.

Background Subtraction and Background Modeling

The background subtraction method aims to separate the stationary background from the moving objects in a scene with the assumption that the camera is stationary and the background is static in nature. The basic idea of background subtraction method is to subtract the background frame with the current frame for moving object detection. Bhaskar et al. (2015) use dynamic inverse analysis for background modeling and thereby update the dynamic background variations. However, it is not able to update the rapid variations due to low frame rate. Sajid & Cheung (2015) employ multiple background models to improve the robustness of background subtraction. Kim & Kim (2012) adapt a clustering-based feature, called fuzzy color histogram (FCH), which has an ability of greatly attenuating color variations generated by background motions. Lanza et al. (2011) consider only two non-parametric mixture components for background subtraction to handle the illumination changes and camera jitter. Ko et al. (2010) propose warping background subtraction algorithm in which the background is modeled by a set of warping layers. It effectively handles the background motion and illumination changes. However, it does not work for rapid background motion changes. Zhao et al. (2012) improved the background subtraction results by including the spatial-temporal constraints with type-2 fuzzy GMM. Barnich & Droogrnbroeck (2011) proposes visual background extraction algorithm (Vibe) in which the first frame is used to model the background and the background model consists of a set of arbitrarily selected background pixels. While updating the background model, a new pixel replaces the pixel in the background sphere. This method does not require any tuning algorithm. However, it does not produce the deterministic background model and the moving object in the first frame will not be identified.

Segmentation Based Methods

Segmentation based approaches are desired to accomplish moving object detection by separating the foreground objects from the non-foreground objects. Tsai & Luo (2011) use mean-shift method for foreground segmentation. However, the segmented results are significantly affected by the dynamic backgrounds. Chen et al. (2012) propose the hierarchical background model for better accuracy. In this model, initially the background is segmented by the mean-shift algorithm and the hierarchical background model is created using the region models and pixel models. The region models are obtained from the histogram of a particular region and the pixel model is obtained using the co-occurrence of pixels in each region. Kim et al. (2005) use codebook model for background modeling and temporal filter for moving object detection. But the codebook model is not suitable to detect the objects with a similar background color.

Object Detection Based on Feature Extraction

Recently, several researchers involve local image features such as color, pixel intensity, edges and texture for moving object detection and tracking. These local image features share the similar properties among the foreground objects and they are invariant to object rotation, image scaling, occlusions and partially invariant to illumination changes. Wu et al. (2014) present a novel Center Symmetric Scale Invariant Local Ternary Patterns (CS-SILTP) descriptor in which spatial and temporal relationships within the neighborhood are explored. Choi et al. (2012) proposed the feature-level fusion of color local Gabor wavelets and color LBP for face recognition. In order to reduce the dimensional space, the authors employed the low-dimensional feature extraction techniques. Zhou et al. (2013) combine the color and texture information and create Spatial-Color Binary Pattern (SCBP) which gives good results than the LBP. Lee et al. (2011) develop an Opponent Color LBP (OCLBP) that incorporates both color and texture information to handle the illumination variations and smooth surface regions. However, the detection result easily gets affected by illumination noises and it involves more computational complexity. Zhu et al. (2010) use multi-scale color LBPs for object detection. The author applies the ordinary LBP operator independently to different color channels and the individual results are concatenated to each other. Ma & Sang (2013) proposes the Multichannel-Scale Invariant Local Ternary Pattern (MC-SILTP) for foreground object detection. This approach stays invariant in flat areas as a result of different channel thresholding. However, MC-SILTP cannot be bounded by the spatial non-saliency and still keep sensitive in featureless areas. Balcilar & Sonmez (2013) integrate the color and texture features using the Choquet integral for foreground object classifications and achieved good results against the background challenges. Despite the fact that the moving object detection approaches have been studied for many years, still it remains an open research problem and it is a great challenge to achieve robust, precise and superior methodology. Moving object detection methods are based on the assumption that the video frames are of noise free, good quality and faster. However, it is not possible to have such video frames in practice and these assumptions may become violated. Several algorithms have been presented in the literature to attempt the visual challenges pertaining to moving object detection. Yet, still there is a wide scope for further improvements.

The next section presents the deep convolutional neural network, the parameter settings and the training process for convolutional networks. Further, the performance metrics are discussed and the conclusion and future scope are deliberated at the end.

DEEP NEURAL NETWORK MODEL

Basically, neural networks are computing systems with interconnected nodes that can recognize hidden patterns and their correlations in input data. It can assist the people to solve more real- life problems. It can predict unknown class and make inferences by learning the features and hidden relationships present in input patterns. A simple neural network model consists of an input layer, a hidden layer and an output layer. Each input layer is connected to the every nodes of the hidden with weights and these weights are increased or decreased based on the relevancy with output. For strong correlation, the weights are increased and vice-versa. A group of samples applied to the neural network during training is often referred to as training set whereas a group of unobserved samples used to test the performance of neural network is known as validation set. Usually, the dataset will be divided into training dataset and test dataset in the ratio of 80: 20. Further, 20% of the training dataset will be assigned to validation process. One of the foremost challenge in deep learning is dataset and it is important to note that the lack of dataset leads poor classification accuracy. In such cases, own dataset can be created with the help of data augmentation technique before building the neural network model. The error function estimates the error for training dataset and this error mimics how far the actual predictions done by the neural network. Bias measures the ability of the model to predict known training samples output. Variance tells about the fitting of concealed samples in the validation set. For high bias and high variance, the neural network suffers from Underfitting problem. That is, the model will not be able to classify the training data even with low probability of error. Conversely, if low bias and high variance are used, then Overfitting problem occurs. Overfitting is a problem at which the model gives high test error rate even it is fully trained. Overfitting can also occur in case of non-availability of large training dataset. In order to alleviate this issue, the dataset can be created manually through data augmentation process.

Choosing a Model

There are several deep learning models such as linear model, deep feed forward network, convolutional neural network (CNN) and recurrent neural network (RNN). Among these models, convolutional neural network is best suited for object detection and recognition in image and video sequences. If the input data has dependent sequences such as speech signal, natural language sentences, then the RNNs are more suitable for processing these data. The basic deep models can also be combined to create more complex models. For example, the combination of CNNs and RNNs works well in case of correlated two dimensional and three dimensional data sequences. A convolutional neural network is a neural network that has one or more convolutional layers. It consists of different types of layers such as input layer, convolution layers, pooling layer, fully connected and output layers. Convolutional neural networks are mostly used for object classification and object detections. On the other hand, RNNs use sequential data in which all inputs are dependent to each other and the output for each input element depends on the previous elements. RNNs are mainly used for forecasting, sentiment analysis and natural language processing applications. Deep convolutional neural networks are paramount technique used for moving object detection and it involves more complex neural networks. A network with more than two layers is called a deep neural network (DNN). The word "deep" refers to the number of layers through which the data is transformed. A DNN can achieve human-like accuracy in such tasks as image classification, object detection and classification, speech recognition, handwriting recognition, and computer vision. A convolutional neural network (CNN) is a subtype of DNN, a multi-layered algorithm that is widely used for image, video, and language processing. The region-based convolutional neural network (R-CNN) is a new category of CNN created specifically for object detection. Types of R-CNN includes Fast R-CNN, Faster R-CNN, and Mask R-CNN. A CNN can recognize emotions, gestures, speech, and handwriting, detect and classify objects, and detect and recognize actions in video. In practice, the hidden and output layers are considered to name the model and the input layer is not taken into account (see Figure 3). For example, the neural network shown in Figure 3(b) is also called as two layer neural network because it consists of one hidden layer and output layer. On the other hand, the model shown in Figure 3(d) is called as 6 layers neural network because of 5 hidden layers and 1 output layer are present in the model. As compared to Figure 3(a), the model shown in Figure 3(d) is deeper and complex. Therefore, it is referred to deep neural network model. This kind of deep network can able to predict the deep features whereas the shallow model shown in Figure 3(a) cannot do it.

Figure 3. Example of neural networks: (a) logistic regression model (shallow model), (b) neural network with single hidden layer, (c) and (d) neural network with two hidden layers and 5 hidden layers respectively.

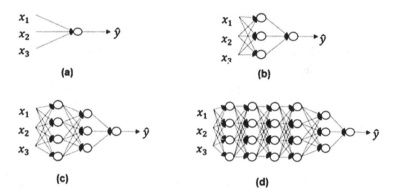

Notations Used for Deep Neural Network

Consider the deep neural network shown in Figure 4. Let L be the number of layers in the network, $n^{[l]}$ be the number of nodes or number of units in l^{th} layer. Here, there are five hidden layers and one output layer and hence,

$$L = 6, \ n^{[1]} = 4, n^{[2]} = 4, n^{[3]} = 4, n^{[4]} = 4, n^{[5]} = 3.$$

The number of units in the output layer is $n^{[6]} = n^{[L]} = 1$ and the number of nodes in the input layer is $n_x = 3$. For each layer L, the term $a^{[l]}$ is used to denote the activations in l^{th} layer and it is given by $a^{[l]} = g^{[l]}\left(z^{[l]}\right)$.

Figure 4. Notations of deep neural networks (DNNs).

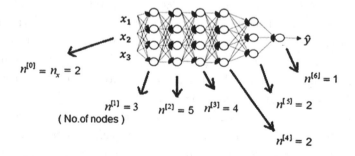

The weights for computing the value $z^{[l]}$ in layer l is denoted by $w^{[l]}$. Here, X is also the activations of layer zero, so $a[0] = X$ and the activation of the final layer, $a[L] = y'$. So, $a[L]$ is equal to the predicted output in the neural network.

Forward and Backward Propagation in a Deep Neural Network

Figure 5. Forward propagation.

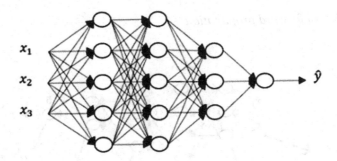

Consider the deep neural network shown in Figure 5. First, the forward propagation is carried out for a single training example X and later it is carried out for the entire training set. The activation for first layer is computed as $z^{[1]} = w^{[1]}a^{[0]} + b^{[1]}$ and $a^{[1]} = g^{[1]}\left(z^{[1]}\right)$. Here, the parameters $W^{[1]}$ and $b^{[1]}$ (bias vector) affect the activations in first layer. For the second layer, the activation is computed as $z^{[2]} = w^{[2]}a^{[1]} + b^{[2]}$, $a^{[2]} = g^{[2]}\left(z^{[2]}\right)$. In similar way, the activations are computed for third and fourth layers. Thus, the general forward propagation equation can be written as $z^{[l]} = w^{[l]}a^{[l-1]} + b^{[l]}$ and $a^{[l]} = g^{[l]}\left(z^{[l]}\right)$. The activations can be calculated in a vectored way for the whole training set at a time. In this case, the forward propagation equation can be written as follows.

$$Z^{[1]} = W^{[1]}A^{[0]} + b^{[1]},\ A^{[1]} = g^{[1]}\left(Z^{[1]}\right) \tag{1}$$

$$Z^{[2]} = W^{[2]}A^{[1]} + b^{[2]},\ A^{[2]} = g^{[2]}\left(Z^{[2]}\right) \tag{2}$$

$$Z^{[3]} = W^{[3]}A^{[2]} + b^{[3]},\ A^{[3]} = g^{[3]}\left(Z^{[3]}\right) \tag{3}$$

The predicted output y' for the deep neural network shown in Fig is given by

$$y' = g\left(Z^{[4]}\right) = A^{[4]}. \tag{4}$$

Parameters of DNN ($W^{[l]}$ & $b^{[l]}$)

Figure 6 shows the implementation of forward propagation. Figure 7 shows the process involved in forward and backward propagation in deep convolutional network. For the implementation of forward propagation, the first step will be $Z^{[1]} = W^{[1]}X + b^{[1]}$. Let's ignore the bias term b for now, and focus on the parameters W. From Figure 6, it is observed that the first hidden layer has three hidden units and so the dimension of Z is 3 by 1.

Figure 6. Implementation of forward propagation

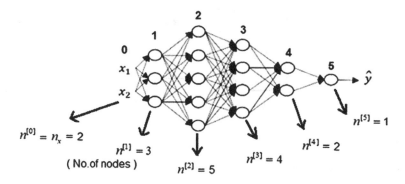

Figure 7. Process of forward and reverse propagation

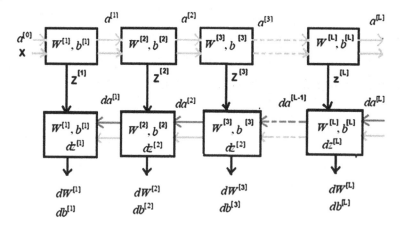

The input layer has two input features. So, the input feature vector has a dimension of 2 by 1. Now, the weight matrix W is calculated as follows.

$$Z^{[1]} = W^{[1]}X + b^{[1]}$$
$$[3,1] = W^{[1]}.[2,1] + b^{[1]}$$
$$[n^{[1]},1] = W^{[1]}.[n^{[0]},1]$$

$$W^{[1]} = [n^{[1]}, n^{[0]}] \tag{5}$$

By the rules of matrix multiplication, the weight matrix W must be 3 by 2 matrix. Therefore, the above equation is expressed in matrix as follows.

$$\begin{bmatrix} \cdot \\ \cdot \\ \cdot \end{bmatrix} = \begin{bmatrix} \cdot & \cdot \\ \cdot & \cdot \\ \cdot & \cdot \end{bmatrix} \begin{bmatrix} \cdot \\ \cdot \end{bmatrix}$$

In vector form, weight W must be 3 by 2 dimensional vector $W^{[1]} = [n^{[1]}, n^{[0]}]$. Generally, the weight W should be $W^{[l]} = [n^{[l]}, n^{[l-1]}]$ and $b^{[l]} = [n^{[l]}, 1]$. For layer L, the model has some parameters $W^{[l]}$ and $b^{[l]}$ for the forward propagation (See Figure 7). The input takes the activations $a^{[l-1]}$ from previous layer and output $a^{[l]}$. So, the hidden layer computes $Z^{[l]} = W^{[l]} a^{[l-1]} + b^{[l]}$ and then $a^{[l]} = g\left[Z^{[l]}\right]$. In this way, the forward propagation goes from the input $a^{[l-1]}$ to the output $a^{[l]}$. For back propagation, the computation starts to implement a function that inputs $da^{[l]}$ and outputs $da^{[l-1]}$ by using the parameters $W^{[l]}$, $b^{[l]}$ and $dZ^{[l]}$. So, one iteration of training through neural network involves starting with a [0] which the input X and going through forward propagation, computing the predicted output y' and then back propagation and weight *w* and bias *b* would get updated as follows.

$$W^{[l]} = W^{[l]} - \alpha dW^{[l]} \tag{6}$$

$$b^{[l]} = b^{[l]} - \alpha db^{[l]}. \tag{7}$$

Thus, in each layer there is a forward propagation step and corresponding backward propagation step.

Optimization in Deep Neural Network

Parameter Initialization

The accuracy of any deep neural model depends on the parameters and hyper parameters used for training a model. The parameters are the coefficients of the model selected by the model itself in such a way that the chosen parameters should minimize the loss function. The loss function will be differed case-by-case and it depends on the desired output. Consider the task to predict the location of a car in an image. In this case, the loss function depends on the weights as well as the ground truth corresponding to the input image. The choice of parameters' initialization (weights and bias) for deep neural model determines the convergence speed of optimization algorithm. The unscrupulous parameter initialization will lead to early stopping of training with all activations and gradients to zero. Specifically, the seed point of initialization predicts the convergence speed, end of loss function, accuracy and so on. For effective training of deep neural network (DNN), parameters such as $W^{[1]}, b^{[1]}, W^{[2]}, b^{[2]}, \ldots .. W^{[l]}, b^{[l]}$ are properly initialized. For any deep neural network, these model parameters are the deciding factors to predict how far the model works accurately for particular task. Initially, good parameter values are unknown. However, good parameters are obtained by minimizing the cost function using gradient descent optimization algorithm. For gradient descent optimization, the parameter values are initialized and then the parameters values are adjusted iteratively in opposite direction where the cost of the gradient reduces. Based on the desired output, the cost function will be dissimilar for different task. The value of cost function will be varied either closer to or far away from the target point by updating the parameter values. It can be done through feeding a training dataset into the model and adjust the parameters iteratively to minimize the cost function as small as possible. Figure 8 illustrates the optimization procedures for moving object detection task. Here, a task is to draw a bounding box around a car. This process starts by defining the loss function that reflects the task. This loss function will be used to find the good parameters. The training dataset for this task is the variety of cars in the real world. The loss function is optimized such that the loss is minimized on the training data. The loss function takes as input the predictions of the model and compares them to ground truth. The model processes images from the training dataset one at a time, updating the parameters each time until the loss is optimized. In general, the average of loss function for the entire training dataset, called cost function, is considered instead of single example loss function. The aim of optimization algorithm is to find the good parameter values that minimize the cost function. In this context, finding the minimum of the cost function is equivalent to finding the best model for the assigned task.

Figure 8. Optimization in DNN propagation

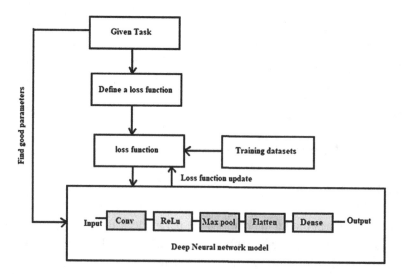

Hyper Parameter Tuning

In addition to parameters, there are some hyper parameters to improve the training accuracy. The most important hyper parameters are learning rate (α), number of iterations, number of hidden layers (L), number of hidden units $(n^{[1]}, n^{[2]}...)$ and the choice of the activation function. These hyper parameters are the parameters that control the ultimate parameters W and b of deep neural network. There are also other hyper parameters in deep learning model such as momentum, mini-batch size, stopping time and regularization parameters and so on. For any particular task, it is difficult to know in advance exactly the best value of the hyper parameters. So, the best practice is to try out with different values of the hyper parameters iteratively to see the best results.

Learning Rate

The learning rate has great impact on the gradient descent back propagation algorithm. If it is too large, the algorithm converges faster. But, the large step size causes more oscillations and parameter overshoot problem occurs. If it is too small, the algorithm takes longer time to converge. Therefore, learning rate must be adapted in such a way that it is high at the initial stage and gets reduced later when it approaches to the minimum. In gradient descent, it is difficult to find the best decay schedule. However, adaptive learning rate algorithms including stochastic gradient descent, Momentum, Adam and RMSprop can be used to adjust the learning rate during the optimization.

Mini-batch Size

Mini-batch size is the number of samples used to train a model in each iteration. Mini-batch size can be 32, 64, 128, 256, 512, whereas large batch size involves thousands of examples. The selection of right batch size plays a major role in the process of convergence of the cost function and parameter values. If large size is used, then it becomes generalized model and it does not fit for new data. In addition to that, the computation of cost function at every iteration becomes slow because it inputs the entire training set. Therefore, small batch size is often considered to speed up the parameter update process.

Choice of Activation Function

The activation function is a transformation function which is used by the neuron to turn on and off the neuron output based on the threshold value (See Figure 9). Mostly, the activation function used by the DNN is a non-linear function which maps the complex data such as images, video, and audio to the model outputs learn any complex data with accurate predictions. The choice of the activation function has a great impact on the training process of deep neural network.

Figure 9. Activation function in Neuron

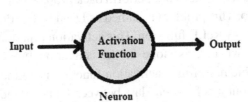

Figure 10. Types of Activations in Neuron: (a) Sigmoid, (b) tanh, (c) ReLU, (d) Leaky ReLU, (e) ELU

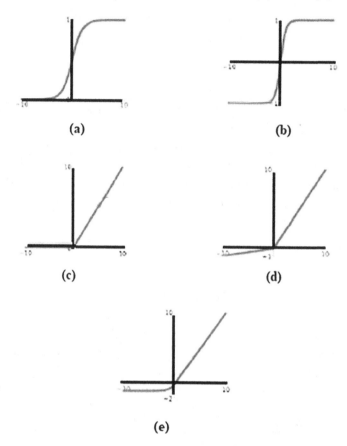

(a)

(b)

(c)

(d)

(e)

There are several types of activation functions (see Figure 10) such as sigmoid, tanh, Rectified Linear Unit (ReLU), Leaky ReLU, maxout and ELU. The sigmoid and tanh activations create vanishing gradient problem. That is, the network model refuses further learning or takes long time to get accurate prediction for very high or very low values of input. On the other hand, ReLU is computationally efficient and allows the network to converge very quickly. ReLU is a linear function which has a slope for $x > 0$ and zero for $x < 0$. Thus, it is not affected by the vanishing gradient problem as long as the input is greater than zero. However, the model does not perform back propagation and it will not do the learning when the input approaches zero. This problem is named as Dead ReLU Problem. The dead ReLU problem can be avoided by using Leaky ReLU function. This activation function takes the mathematical form as $Z = \max(ca, a), 0 \leq c < 1$, where c is slope of the activation function for $a < 0$. Therefore, it eliminates the dead ReLU problem. Softmax activation function is a function only used for neurons in output layer. It normalizes the outputs for each class between 0 and 1, and classify the inputs into multiple classes. Among all non-linear activations, sigmoid is used at the last layer and ReLU is used for hidden layers. The use of more hidden layers in the model relatively improves the training accuracy to some extent. Softmax is used for output layer in case of multiclass classifications.

Epochs

In DNN model, the number of data passes is called as epochs and the number of epochs need to be adjusted. If it is too low, under fitting problem occurs and if it is too large, over fitting problem occurs. The choice of Epochs decides the training time of entire dataset and when to stop the training. The selection of epochs depends on the dataset and task to be completed. It is good practice that start with small number of epochs, gradually increase the epoch number and track the performance. In addition to the number of epochs, it is good practice to choose whether the weight should be updated after each epoch, sample, or mini-batch during modeling the algorithm.

Dropout

Dropout is one of the regularization concept in which some of the redundant nodes are randomly removed from the model on each pass to make the model as simple and more adaptable. During the training phase, some redundant and useless nodes can be removed from the model in order to simply the network model instead of over burdening. So, while building a model, the user can decide the probability to keep the node or drop it.

DNN Architectural Model for Moving Object Detection

Figure 11. DNN for Moving object detection and tracking

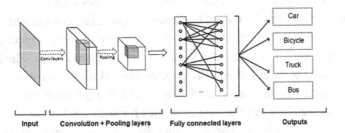

Deep neural networks (DNNs) are mainly used for video analysis, face detection image classification, moving object detection and tracking. Figure 11 shows the architectural model of deep convolutional neural network (CNN) for moving object detection and tracking. It consists of several convolutional layers, pooling layer and fully-connected layer. The input layer receives a structured data such as image and video and outputs a single vector of class scores. The convolutional layers generate a volume of feature maps by computing a dot product between the weights used and the region connected to the input volume. The pooling layer will down sample the feature map along the spatial dimensions. The fully-connected layer will create the class scores according to the given categories. A CNN may include hundreds of concealed layers to identify different features of the input images called feature maps. The feature learning has multiple stages each having one convolutional layer and one pooling layer. First, the model needs to know the shape of the input data and hence the input shape is passed to the first convolutional layer. The convolution layer acts as a filter with a kernel of 3×3 matrix that convolves around the original input to 3×3 filters to produce a feature map. That is, at each location, the product of kernel elements and input elements are computed and all products are added together to produce the output at that location.

Figure 12. Max pooling process

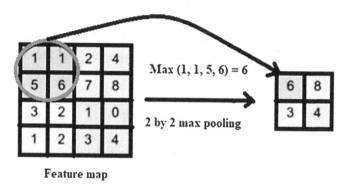

The pooling layer is used to reduce the spatial size of feature map to get most important features without over fitting issue. Mostly maximum pooling and average pooling methods are used for feature reduction. In maximum pooling layer, the highest value is taken from each pixel area as demonstrated in Figure 12. In this example, each 2 by 2 image grid is considered on the given feature map and it is replaced by the highest value among four pixels. In case of average pooling, the average of four pixels are used to replace the 2 by 2 image grid on the feature map. A CNN with more convolutional layers and pooling layers gives an improved performance because of appropriate complex feature detections. In this case, the first convolutional layer fragments the input image into different object parts such as a person and road. The second layer identify the features such as face, hands and so on. The third layer will deeply analyze the features within the face. Finally, the pooling layer does dimensionality reduction and fully connected layer investigates the ultimate probabilities and takes decision about the image class. Alex Net and Google Inception network are the best examples for such kind of deep neural network models. These model are designed to classify independent input data for object localization. A deep convolutional auto encoder is used to pre-train the feature extraction part of the proposed model. This allows the feature extractor to be trained in an unsupervised manner, which is needed when annotated data is scarce.

The proposed model will be trained and tested with the input dataset. Subsequently, fine-tuning of the earlier further training with labelled data. The input dataset is divided into two groups, the first group is an 80% of the data chosen randomly and used to train the predictive model by extracting the most important features. The second group comprises 20% of the data unlabeled which is used only to test the proposed model. The proposed model is trained based on statistical gradient descent (SGD) optimization in which the weights are adjusted in order to minimize the loss function. The model starts with an input layer and an initialized weight for each node, then the weights are adjusted through several epochs (passes) over the entire training data in an iterative process. At the beginning, the number of epochs, the number of nodes and the activation functions for the nodes are all defined by the model. At the end of each epoch the loss function is minimized, the weight values are adjusted and the accuracy is maximized. This iterative process continues until all epochs are completed.

Fully connected layer needs activation function to trigger the nodes and calculate the weights. The proposed model employs Rectified Linear Unit (ReLU) activation function in order to make the CNN model robust. In addition to that, a dropout layer is utilized after the pooling layer to prevent over fitting and to improve regularization by omitting a random portion of processing units. After the network is trained, the last hidden layer outputs are used as object characterizations to construct the classification. The final output is a vector of probability scores, representing how likely each of the features is to be part of a class. In feature extraction phase, the proposed CNN model gives precise landmark (ex. facial points) estimations of the object based on the attribute inference. This model outputs a confidence map for each landmark and the final estimated position for each landmark is obtained by finding the maximum of the confidence map. Then, all detected points with less confidence score are eliminated. Finally landmark refinement is done and the valid detections are recorded. If neither detection is able to locate a point with sufficient confidence, then the landmark locations with the highest score are used. The proposed model ends with more than one fully-connected layer to create the class scores according to the given image features.

Region Based Convolutional Neural Network (R-CNN) Model

Figure 13 shows another deep neural model used for object detection problem. A strong CNN classifier, trained on ImageNet dataset, can be used for multi-class object detection problem. A pre-trained CNN classifier can be used as a feature extractor, train and support external machine classifier on these features and then use it in a sliding window framework. Nevertheless, the training process will be too slow because CNN has to be applied for hundreds of thousands of windows. To overcome this limitation, a region-based convolution network (R-CNN) can be used for moving object detection problem.

Figure 13. R-CNN Model for moving object detection

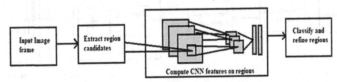

In this method, external object proposals generator is used to obtain object candidate regions. Then, features are extracted using CNN and then classified using support vector machine (SVM). The training of R-CNN involves three steps such as pre-training, parameter tuning and image classification. In first step, CNN is pre-trained on ImageNet. In second step, it is adjusted on limited data set and in third step, linear classifier and bounding box are used for object detection. The R-CNN method performs well even pre-trained model is used for feature extraction because it uses fine tuning and bounding box regression. However, all features are independently computed and it involves more complex training procedure. The basic R-CNN model requires fixed resolution input images and it should be re-scaled after the object regions are extracted. But, it can adapt any CNN classifier to various image resolutions by changing last pooling layer, to the Spatial Pyramid Pooling (SPP) layer. Here, the spatial pyramid is constructed on top of the region of interest. First level of the pyramid is a region of interest itself. On second level, the region is divided into four cells with two by two grid. On third level, region is divided into 16 cells on four by four grid. Average pooling is applied to each cell. So, if the last convolutional layer has 256 maps, then pooling in each cell produce one vector with length of 256. Feature vectors for all cells are concatenated, and then passed as input to the fully convolutional layer for object classification.

Fast R-CNN Model

Figure 14 shows the fast R-CNN deep model for moving object detection and tracking. In Fast R-CNN, the Region of Interest (ROI) Pooling layer is used in which there will be only one pyramid layer. In addition to Region of Interest Pooling, two more modifications have been introduced. First, Softmax classifier is used instead of SVM classifier. Second, multi-task training is used to train classifier simultaneously. In Fast R-CNN, the input image and set of object proposals are supplied to the neural network. The neural network produces a convolutional feature map. From convolutional feature map, feature vectors are extracted using Region of Interest Pooling layer. Then, the feature vectors affect into a sequence of fully convolutional layers. The output of fully convolutional layers are branched into K-way Softmax, and K by four real valued bounding box coordinates output. During R-CNN training, the Region of Interests are sampled from training set at random for each mini batch. But for the Fast R-CNN, when different images are in one batch, the computations are expensive for each window. Because, it requires no separate SVM classifier. The convolutional features are extracted from the whole image, the receptive field for the Region of Interest Pooling is very large. In Fast R-CNN, the training becomes much faster compared to the simple R-CNN. Training and test time for the Fast R-CNN is lower than that of R-CNN and SPP net. Accuracy of Fast R-CNN is also higher.

Figure 14. Fast R-CNN Model for moving object detection

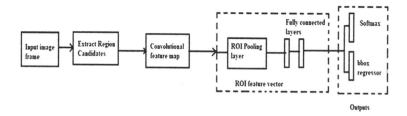

SOLUTIONS AND RECOMMENDATIONS

Building a DNN model involves more complicated parameterization. Here, each layer gives the higher representations to the features of the previous layer. Some model may not be the good starting point. However, the learning of a model with parameter tuning provides good accuracy. In addition to that, adding regularization may lead to over fit and small epoch leads to poor results. Finding good parameters is another major issue in DNN model. To have good parameters, the model needs to do experiment with different classification algorithms to find the best fit. The researcher can try with open sources such as scikit-learn for regular classification. For neural network classification, the deep learning frameworks such as Tensor Flow, Cafe, pytorch, and keras can be used to create, train and evaluate neural network models and these frameworks will provide good support for the real world assignments. These frameworks needs only few line coding parts for the implementation of complex neural network model without in-depth knowledge about mathematical structure. However, it needs collection of high quality training samples, best fitting model and hyper parameters tuning for best results. Further, it is necessary to evaluate the DNN model in order to assess the performance.

Figure 15. Pre-trained model used for food classification

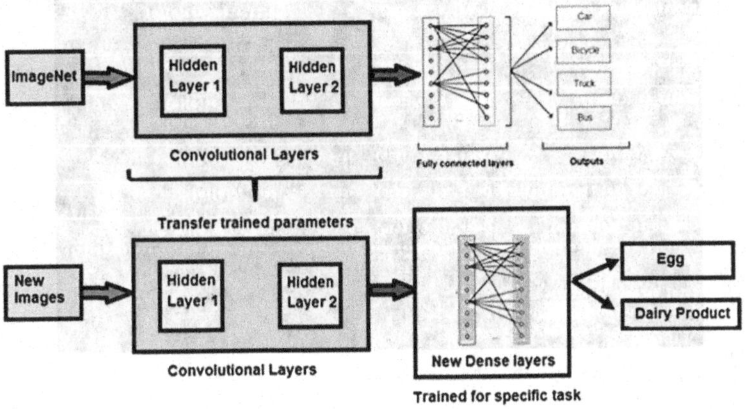

Beneficial of DNN Model in Industries

The DNN model can be used in all industries including food industry, aerospace, automotive industries, electronics industries, manufacturing industries robotics and telecommunications. In food industries, DNN model is trained to predict the type of foods and quality of the foods by analysing the image of the food. In aerospace industries, it is used to predict the component failures, aircraft navigations and path finders. In automotive industries, the DNN model can be deployed for sensor guidance and activity analysis. On the other hand, it can be used in electronics and manufacturing industries to figure out the failures in circuit level as well as chip level and quality analysis visual inspection. In robotics, the DNN is used for vision control as well as motion control. In telecommunication sectors, it is mainly used for banking, network monitoring, signature analysis and object recognition and language processing.

Implementation of Pre-Trained DNN Model in Food Industry

Let us consider the food classification using DNN model. For food classification either, the DNN model can be developed from the scratch or else the pre-trained model can be used. In food industry, a DNN model can be deployed to predict the type of food and to extract the nutrition related information to analyse the quality of the food. Here, the deep learning model can be developed from the scratch or it can be used pre-trained model. If pre-trained model is used, then it can be fine-tuned to improve the performance of the learning model. For pre-trained model, the knowledge from specifically trained model can be transferred to or reused for same kind of task to be done by the other model. This concept is sometimes called as transfer learning. This kind of pre-trained models drastically reduce the computational time when compared to model developed from the scratch. In transfer learning, the DNN model is first trained with the base dataset and then the weights are reused for training the new dataset. The performance of this model is basically determined by the effective usage of weights that can be reused by the new network model.

Figure 16. Model summary of Inceptionresnetv2 pre-trained model

activation_405 (Activation)	(None, 6, 6, 256)	0	batch_normalization_405[0][0]
block8_10_mixed (Concatenate)	(None, 6, 6, 448)	0	activation_402[0][0] activation_405[0][0]
block8_10_conv (Conv2D)	(None, 6, 6, 2080)	933920	block8_10_mixed[0][0]
block8_10 (Lambda)	(None, 6, 6, 2080)	0	block8_9_ac[0][0] block8_10_conv[0][0]
conv_7b (Conv2D)	(None, 6, 6, 1536)	3194880	block8_10[0][0]
conv_7b_bn (BatchNormalization)	(None, 6, 6, 1536)	4608	conv_7b[0][0]
conv_7b_ac (Activation)	(None, 6, 6, 1536)	0	conv_7b_bn[0][0]

```
Total params: 54,336,736
Trainable params: 54,276,192
Non-trainable params: 60,544
```

From the Figure 15, it can be seen that the initial CNN layers are taken from the already trained DNN model (base model) to extract the high level general features and new customized dense layers trained for specific task are used in the output layers for food classification. For food classification using pre-trained model transfer learning, first DNN is initialized with pre-trained weights and the entire DNN network is retrained with very small learning rate. This transfer learning technique provides fast training progress and even it achieves good results for small training dataset.

Building Deep Learning Using Pre-trained Model Inceptionresnetv2

In this example, the Inceptionresnetv2 pre-trained model is used for building DNN to classify the foods in food industry. Figure 16 shows the model summary of Inceptionresnetv2 network which has 54,336,736 parameters out of which there are 54,276,192 trainable parameters and 60,544 non trainable parameters.

Figure 17. Model summary of ResNet50 pre-trained model

conv5_block3_2_conv (Conv2D)	(None, 8, 8, 512)	2359808	conv5_block3_1_relu[0][0]
conv5_block3_2_bn (BatchNormali	(None, 8, 8, 512)	2048	conv5_block3_2_conv[0][0]
conv5_block3_2_relu (Activation	(None, 8, 8, 512)	0	conv5_block3_2_bn[0][0]
conv5_block3_3_conv (Conv2D)	(None, 8, 8, 2048)	1050624	conv5_block3_2_relu[0][0]
conv5_block3_3_bn (BatchNormali	(None, 8, 8, 2048)	8192	conv5_block3_3_conv[0][0]
conv5_block3_add (Add)	(None, 8, 8, 2048)	0	conv5_block2_out[0][0] conv5_block3_3_bn[0][0]
conv5_block3_out (Activation)	(None, 8, 8, 2048)	0	conv5_block3_add[0][0]

```
Total params: 23,587,712
Trainable params: 23,534,592
Non-trainable params: 53,120
```

Figure 18. Training images of food11 sub dataset

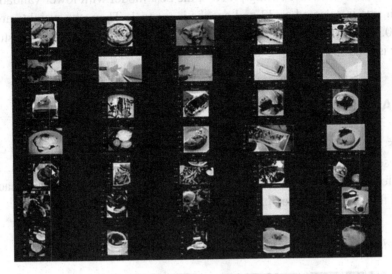

Usually, the base model weights are freeze to avoid the change of weights during training. On the other hand, the ResNet pre-trained model consists of global average pooling 2D layer, flatten layer, dense layer with 256 size, and Relu activation function with dropout of 0.3. This arrangement is followed by second dense layer with 128 size and dropout of 0.3. Finally, the ResNet model has third dense layer which consists of 11 output layers and Softmax activation is used for final classification. The model summary of ResNet50 model is shown in Figure 17. From Figure 17, it is inferred that, the ResNet50 has 23,587,712 parameters out of which 23,534,592 trainable parameters and 53,120 non-trainable parameters.

Figure 19. Number of Images available for 11 food categories

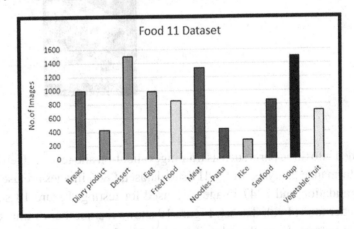

Compile, Train and Fine Tune the Trained Model

In this step, the pre-trained model is fine-tuned with very low learning rate. In this stage, the early stopping is used to exit training if validation loss is not decreasing even after certain epochs to avoid the over fitting problem. After this fine tuning process, the best model with lower validation loss is saved. Initially, the batch size is selected as 32 and epochs is set to 1. Then, the weights are fine-tuned and epochs is set to 10. The learning rate is set to 0.0001, momentum is set to 0.9 and stochastic gradient descent optimizer is used for compiling and training the entire DNN model.

EXPERIMENTAL RESULTS AND ANALYSIS

This section deals with the experimental analysis of pre-trained model that can be deployed in food industry. The dataset CALORIE MAMA is used for training, testing and evaluation. This Dataset has 16643 images of food products belong to 11 categories. The categories include bread, dairy product, dessert, egg, fried food, meat, noodles-pasta, rice, seafood, soup and vegetable-fruit.

Figure 20. (a) Prediction results for 11 food categories; (b) Prediction results for 11 food categories

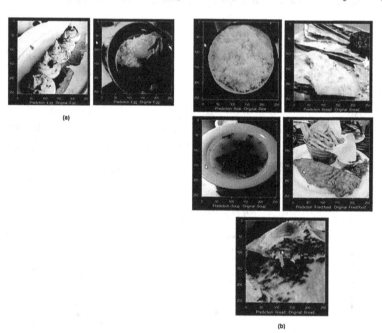

The dataset is divided into three parts such as training, validation and testing. Here, the dataset food11 is selected for the performance analysis. In food11 sub dataset, 9866 images are used for training, 3430 images are used for validation and 3347 images are used for testing. Figure 18 shows the images of different categories under food11 sub dataset. Figure 19 shows the number of images available in each category of food11 sub-dataset. From this plot, it can be seen that some datasets are underrepresented and some are over represented. For effective training of deep neural network, the datasets should be balanced across all the categories. So, it is recommended to perform runtime data augmentation on trianing and testing to generate the data. There are several preprocessing parameters are available for data augmentation including zoom, shear, channel shift, widht and height shifts, rotation,rescale, horizontal flip and vertical flip etc. In this food classification example, the pre-processing such as normalization (1/255), zoom (0.2), horizontal flip and shear (0.2) are used for training. For testing and validation, only normalization is used with image size of 256 by 256 and batch size of 32. Figure 20 (a)-(b) shows the classification results obtained by pre-trained DNN model.

Figure 21. Sample predictions by object tracker: (a) more than 75% overlapping with ground truth region, (b) more than 50% overlapping, (c) less than 50% overlapping with ground truth.
(Source: http://cvlab.hanyang.ac.kr/tracker_benchmark/datasets.html)

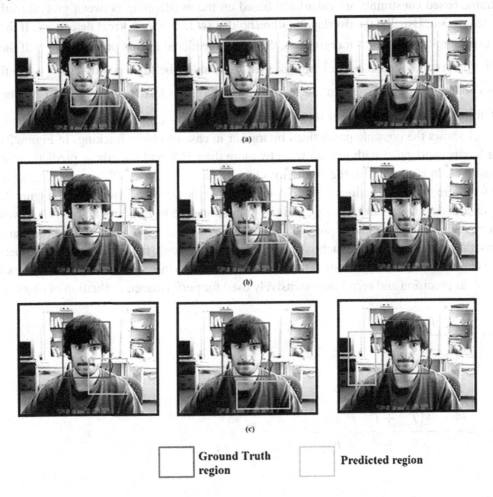

From Figure 20 (a)-(b), it is concluded that the trained model is accurately predicts and classify the type of foods of the given input image. In Figure 20 (a), the egg category foods are predicted as egg products, rice category foods are predicted as rice products. In addition to that bread products, soup, fried-food products are accurately predicted without any classification error (see Figure 20 (b)). These images are not seen by the model and the model is not memorizing the data. Instead, it is actually generalizing on the data.

Performance Evaluation Metrics for Object Detection and Tracking

This section gives an idea about the evaluation metrics used for performance assessment of DNN. In case of object detection, the objective is to detect the presence of object from a certain set of classes and locate the exact position in the image. In this case the objects may be in certain size and shape like cars, bicycles, people, animals, planes. These objects are located in an image with a bounding box. The ground truth bounding box region is compared with the detected bounding box regions in order to validate the numerical results.

The frame based constraints are calculated based on the overlapping between ground truth region and detected region. Usually, the overlapping threshold is set to 0.5 for correct detections. If the tracker detects the foreground objects as foregrounds, then it is considered as true positive (T_{pos}). If the tracker detects the foreground objects as background, then it is said to be false positive (F_{pos}). On the other hand, if no bounding box is present in image, then it is referred as false negative (F_{Neg}) and the correct rejection of non-foreground objects is termed as true negatives (T_{Neg}).

Figure 21 shows the possible predictions by tracker in case of object tracking. In Figure 21(a), the bounding box is overlapped with ground truth by more than 75% and thus these predictions are taken as true positives. In Figure 21(b), the predictions by bounding box have 50% overlapping with ground truth and therefore, these predictions are also considered as true positives. However, in Figure 21(c), the bounding box is deviated from the target and the predictions are having less than 50% of overlapping with ground truth. Therefore, these predictions are referred to false positives. Using the frame based constraints, the evaluation metrics[7] such as precision, accuracy, recall, false alarm rate and F-measure are calculated (refer Eqns. (8)-(12)) to assess the performance of moving object detection and tracking. The metrics such as precision and recall are extensively used for performance evaluation of object detector.

$$Precision = \frac{T_{pos}}{\left(T_{pos} + F_{pos}\right)} \tag{8}$$

$$Accuracy = \frac{\left(T_{pos} + T_{Neg}\right)}{\left(T_{pos} + F_{pos} + T_{Neg} + F_{Neg}\right)} \tag{9}$$

$$False\ Alarm\ Rate = \frac{F_{Pos}}{\left(T_{Pos} + F_{Pos}\right)} \tag{10}$$

$$Recall = \frac{T_{pos}}{\left(T_{pos} + F_{Neg}\right)} \tag{11}$$

Figure 22. Classification report of pre-trained DNN model used for food industry example

	precision	recall	f1-score	support
Bread	0.88	0.89	0.88	368
Dairy product	0.83	0.70	0.76	148
Dessert	0.85	0.86	0.86	500
Egg	0.88	0.87	0.88	335
Fried food	0.91	0.89	0.90	287
Meat	0.91	0.92	0.91	432
Noodles-Pasta	1.00	0.99	0.99	147
Rice	0.95	0.96	0.95	96
Seafood	0.93	0.91	0.92	303
Soup	0.97	0.97	0.97	500
Vegetable-Fruit	0.86	0.96	0.91	231
accuracy			0.90	3347
macro avg	0.91	0.90	0.90	3347
weighted avg	0.90	0.90	0.90	3347

Figure 23. Confusion matrix.

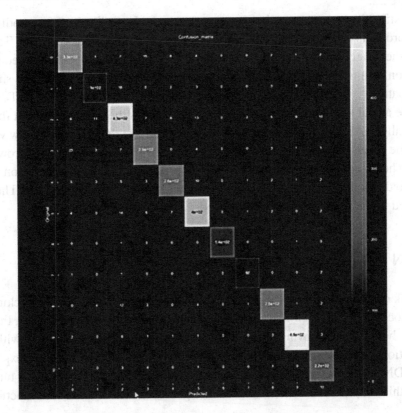

$$F\text{-}measure = \frac{2 \times Precision \times Detection\,Rate}{(Precision + Detection\,Rate)} \tag{12}$$

The precision metric gives the count of correction predictions among the total positive detections whereas, the recall gives an idea about sensitivity of the tracking algorithm. For all testing sequences, the frame based-surveillance metrics are calculated based on the frame based-constraints. Generally, the system with high precision and high recall gets great attention for moving object detection and tracking. The precision and recall can be adjusted by changing the threshold value on the detection score. Based on the precision and recall curve, the performance of two different object detectors can be compared. In case of multiclass detector, the mean average precision is calculated by taking average of average precision across classes. From the precision-recall plot, the best suitable values of precision and recall for particular task can be selected. Generally, the point is selected in such a way that, the precision is maximum. For the object detection, the creation of ground truth annotation is very important. A lot of objects can be missed in ground truth data. This is especially true for the small objects or objects with very similar appearance to the target.

Performance Evaluation of Pre-trained DNN Model for Food Classification

In case of food classification, the trained DNN model predicts the given input image as specified food products. Now, the performance of the trained DNN model is evaluated based on the evaluation metrics such as accuracy, precision, f1-score and recall. The classification report of the pre-trained DNN model is shown in Figure 22.

From the classification report, it can be seen that the model looks like best for noodles soup and it is worse for dairy products. This learning model achieves the overall accuracy of 90%. This model is not developed from the scratch and it is based on the pre-trained model and it is fine-tuned lit bit to get this good classification results. The trained DNN model gives the confusion matrix as in shown Figure 23. The confusion matrix[19-21] is used to assess the performance of trained classification DNN model. This matrix relates the actual and predicted class objects and it gives the clear idea about the classification results. Additionally, it is easy to showcase the prediction results at ready hand to know where the model fails to predict the given dataset. The columns represent the predicted values and rows represent the original values. The diagonal elements indicate correct prediction. From the confusion matrix given in figure, it is inferred that there are lot of zero indicating the model is doing good job. The misclassifications are indicated in the matrix and overall the model predicts really good.

CONCLUSION

Initially, this book chapter introduced the concept of moving object detection and tracking process with basic building blocks and their significance in video surveillance applications. Next, the contributions of various researchers towards moving object detection and tracking are deliberated with pros and cons of their contributions. The building blocks of neural network model and DNN are explained. Further, the notations of DNN, parameters associated with DNN, hyper parameters and their tuning for best fit are discussed in this chapter. The influences of learning rate, choice of activation function, selection of epochs and the process of forward and backward propagation of DNN are introduced. The optimizations of neural model is also discussed. Additionally, the process involved in DNN model for moving object is detection and tracking are illustrated with the guidelines of R-CNN and fast R-CNN models. Finally, the performance metrics used for qualitative and quantitative analysis are deliberated with proper recommendations.

REFERENCES

Almeida, A., & Azkune, G. (2018). Predicting Human Behaviour with Recurrent Neural Networks. *Applied Sciences (Basel, Switzerland)*, 8(2), 305. doi:10.3390/app8020305

Balcilar, M., & Sonmez, A. C. (2013). The effect of color space and block size on foreground detection. In *Proceedings of IEEE Conference on Signal Processing and Communications Applications (SIU)*, (pp. 1-4). 10.1109/SIU.2013.6531583

Barnich, O., & Droogenbroeck, M. V. (2011). ViBe: A Universal Background Subtraction Algorithm for Video Sequences. *IEEE Transactions on Image Processing*, 20(6), 1709–1724. doi:10.1109/TIP.2010.2101613 PMID:21189241

Bhaskar, H., Dwivedi, K., Dogra, D. P., Al-Mualla, M., & Mihaylova, L. (2015). Autonomous detection and tracking under illumination changes, occlusions and moving camera. *Signal Processing*, 117, 343–354. doi:10.1016/j.sigpro.2015.06.003

Chen, S., Zhang, J., Li, Y., & Zhang, J. (2012). A hierarchical model incorporating segmented regions and pixel descriptors for video background subtraction. *IEEE Transactions on Industrial Informatics*, 8(1), 118–127. doi:10.1109/TII.2011.2173202

Cheng, F-c., Huang, S-c., & Ruan, S-j. (2011). Scene Analysis for Object Detection in Advanced Surveillance Systems Using Laplacian. *IEEE Transactions on Systems, Man, and Cybernetics, Part C: Applications and Reviews*, 41(5), 589-598.

Choi, J. Y., Ro, Y. M., & Plataniotis, K. N. (2012). Color local texture features for color face recognition. *IEEE Transactions on Image Processing*, 21(3), 1366–1380. doi:10.1109/TIP.2011.2168413 PMID:21926019

Hossain, S., & Deok-jin, L. (2019). Deep Learning-Based Real-Time Multiple-Object Detection and Tracking from Aerial Imagery via a Flying Robot with GPU-Based Embedded Devices. *Sensors (Basel)*, 19(15), 3371. doi:10.339019153371 PMID:31370336

Kalirajan, K., & Sudha, M. (2017). Moving object detection using median-based scale invariant local ternary pattern for video surveillance system. *Journal of Intelligent & Fuzzy Systems*, 33(3), 1933–1943. doi:10.3233/JIFS-162231

Keck, M., Galup, L., & Stauffer, C. (2013). Real-time tracking of low-resolution vehicles for wide-area persistent surveillance, In *Proceedings of IEEE Workshop on Applications of Computer Vision*, (pp. 441-448). 10.1109/WACV.2013.6475052

Kim, W., & Kim, C. (2012). Background subtraction for dynamic texture scenes using fuzzy color histograms. *IEEE Signal Processing Letters*, *19*(3), 127–130. doi:10.1109/LSP.2011.2182648

Ko, T., Soatto, S., & Estrin, D. (2010). Warping background subtraction. In *Proceedings of 2010 IEEE Conference on Computer Vision and Pattern Recognition (CVPR)* (pp. 1331-1338). 10.1109/CVPR.2010.5539813

Lee, Y., Jung, J., & Kweon, I.-S. (2011). Hierarchical on-line boosting based background subtraction. In *Proceedings of 17th Korea-Japan Joint Workshop on Frontiers of Computer Vision (FCV)*, (pp. 1-5). Academic Press.

Ma, F., & Sang, N. (2013). Background subtraction based on multichannel SILTP, Lecture Notes in Computer Science (including subseries Lecture Notes in Artificial Intelligence and Lecture Notes in Bioinformatics), 7728(1), 73-84.

Sajid, H., & Cheung, S.-C. S. (2015). Background subtraction for static moving camera. In *Proceedings 2015 IEEE International Conference on Image Processing (ICIP)* (pp. 4530-4534). 10.1109/ICIP.2015.7351664

Tsai, D. M., & Luo, J. Y. (2011). Mean shift-based defect detection in multi-crystalline solar wafer surfaces. *IEEE Transactions on Industrial Informatics*, *7*(1), 125–135. doi:10.1109/TII.2010.2092783

Wang, Y., Hu, M., Li, Q., Zhang, X.-P., Zhai, G., & Yao, N. (2020). *Abnormal respiratory patterns classifier may contribute to Large-scale screening of people infected with covid-19 in an accurate and unobtrusive manner.* arXiv:2002.05534v1 [cs.LG]

Wu, H., Liu, N., Luo, X., Su, J., & Chen, L. (2014). Real-time background subtraction-based video surveillance of people by integrating local texture patterns. *Signal, Image and Video Processing*, *8*(4), 665–676. doi:10.100711760-013-0576-5

Zhao, Z., Bouwmans, T., Zhang, X., & Fang, Y. (2012). *A fuzzy background modeling approach for motion detection in dynamic backgrounds.* Multimedia and Signal Processing. doi:10.1007/978-3-642-35286-7_23

Zhou, W., Liu, Y., Zhang, W., Zhuang, L., & Yu, N. (2013). Dynamic background subtraction using spatial-color binary patterns. *IEEE Transactions on Pattern Analysis and Machine Intelligence*, *35*, 597–610. PMID:22689075

Zhu, C., Bichot, C. E., & Chen, L. (2010). Multi-scale color local binary patterns for visual object classes recognition. In *Proceedings of International Conference on Pattern Recognition* (pp. 3065-3068). 10.1109/ICPR.2010.751

KEY TERMS AND DEFINITIONS

Activation Function: It is a transformation function which is used by the neuron to turn on and off the neuron output based on the threshold value.

Deep Neural Network (DNN): It is a network with more than two layers and the word "deep" refers to the number of layers through which the data is transformed.

Epochs: The number of data passes in DNN model is called as epochs.

Mini-Batch: It is the number of samples used to train a model in each iteration.

Moving Object Detection: It is the process of identifying the class objects such as people, vehicle, toy, and human faces in the video sequences.

Neural Network: It is a computing system with interconnected nodes that can recognize hidden patterns and their correlations in input data.

Object Classification: It is the second step in smart video surveillance system. It will classify the objects into people, vehicle, animal, and other targets such as toys, buildings, etc.

Chapter 10
Deep Learning in Social Media Analysis:
Machine and Deep Learning Models for Social Media Analysis in Politics

Vaishali Yogesh Baviskar

G. H. Raisoni Institute of Engineering and Technology, Pune, India

Rachna Yogesh Sable

G. H. Raisoni Institute of Engineering and Technology, Pune, India

ABSTRACT

Social media analytics keep on collecting the information from different media platforms and then calculating the statistical data. Twitter is one of the social network services which has ample amount of data where many users used post significant amounts of data on a regular basis. Handling such a large amount of data using traditional tools and technologies is very complicated. One of the solutions to this problem is the use of machine learning and deep learning approaches. In this chapter, the authors present a case study showing the use of Twitter data for predicting the election result of the political parties.

INTRODUCTION

Use of Social Media

The political background has changed quite a bit within a few decades. The internet has played an outsized role during this change. Social media is specifically, now a significant belief in political movements and within the way, people reflect about issues. Applicants and their followers regularly submit their reviews on Facebook and Twitter. Each party has its pages, from which it indicates propaganda, publicity, and requests for payments and assistance. Social media contains websites like Twitter, Facebook, Instagram, YouTube, WeChat, QQ, Weibo, Quora, LinkedIn, Pinterest, Snapchat Viber, VK, and Viber.

DOI: 10.4018/978-1-7998-7511-6.ch010

Every second, almost 70 million people post on Instagram, 3 million people update the posts, and their status on Facebook, and half a million people on Twitter.

Nowadays, uppermost social media platforms origins marketing channels and at times replace the normal choices like TV commercials and flyers. Political polls are a crucial part of every campaign. Politics usage in social media raises the utilization of online social media platforms in political practices and activities.

People Share Information on Social Media

There are some reasons that individuals share information on social media:

1. Up keeping the issues or causes they sturdily feel about it.
2. To be in-tuned with others, to interact and stay coupled with others
3. Involving within the things happening within the world
4. To shape an image and show for what they stand, who they're by social sharing
5. Develop and nurture relationships.
6. Trying to find attention

Impact of Social Media

Messaging an information technology has improved speedily over the past 20 years with a key expansion being the emergence of social media. Social media is getting used in ways in which it forms politics, world culture, business background, academics sector, inventions, occupations, and lots more. The impact of social media has witnessed heavy growth with the event of mobile technology. People consumed a large share of their time on mobile devices. Mobile devices provide ease to attach with anyone at any place and at any time. This has been a serious reason behind the good upsurge within the use of Social Media.

There are various areas where the impact of social media plays a dynamic role:

1. Costumers depend on social media to monitor and guide their purchases
2. Affects the recruitment and hiring sector heavily.
3. Highly beneficial for general citizens to decide for polling by checking the views on social media and for a politician to build their image by sharing the social work
4. Companies look for candidates' resumes that speak about professional skills and advanced social media techniques.
5. Emerged as a learning platform.
6. For the business to increase awareness of a brand, to keep in mind, showing the human side of the brand, increasing the website traffic, increasing sales
7. Changed the personal relationships, and also affected the general surroundings.

This chapter focuses on the influence of social media in politics:

Impact of Social Media in Politics

Media plays a crucial role in politics because it influences popular opinion and helps to define and take up the problems. Thus, independent media is an efficient check on the government's power and influence over its citizens. Study research from Pew claims that 60 percent of individuals catch their news from social media, with 19 percent doing so fairly often, as matched to other media; social media's impact in political movements has increased immensely. Social networks perform a gradually important role in electoral politics. Social media has been increased in global trends for political communication to attach with their supporters. During the 2019 elections, social media played a crucial role which is used extensively for political campaigning and connecting political leaders and citizens within the country. Within the recent election, social media stands were united into routine political communique since the 2014 elections, because of it, the Bharatiya Janata Party (BJP) picked up power. BJP has established a special way of interactive political message and communication. It's effective usage of social media aimed at political plan building and advertising like *Swacch Bharat Abhiyan* (Clean India) and launching of the Fit India Movement, a national movement, which inspired people to start physical exercise and sports activities in their day-to-day routine. It had been a remarkable success within the 2014 election that prepared other political parties like Congress to take a sit back and take note of the impact of social media.

People started posting their views and opinions on the activities initiated by political parties, which created a huge amount of data on social media. So, here arises the need for data analysis and its interpretation which results in judging the people's views.

Benefits of social media analysis in politics are often of the shape:

- Make the foremost of the latest opportunities
- See where the audience's interests lie
- What is the audience talking about
- What is not so popular amongst prospects
- What problems are they facing?
- What are they expecting?
- Learn from competition
- Build a Fact-Based Social Media Report

BACKGROUND

Introduction to Sentiment Analysis for Machine Learning and Deep Learning Models

Sentiment-Analysis and Role of Knowledge Analysis and Interpretation

Social network analysis (SNA) is an important problem in the data processing. Social Media Analysis may be a broad concept consisting of SNA, Machine learning, Information Retrieval, Data processing, Natural Language Processing, and sentiment analysis.

Data extraction means to retrieve data from poorly structured or unstructured data for further processing and data storage.

Data analysis and interpretation are the procedure of collecting information and determining the inferences, significance, and implications of the findings.

There are two stages to analyze social data.

1. To gather the data produced by users on the sites of people interacting with each other
2. To examine and analyze that data.

Data obtainable can be structured or unstructured.

Structured and Unstructured Data

*   **Structured data**: The data whose patterns are easily searchable. It is a type of data which can be put into rows and column format i.e. spreadsheets and table. It is also known as quantitative data. E.g. numbers of credit card, financial figures, date formats, mobile numbers, Names of products, and addresses
*   **Unstructured data**: A type of data whose patterns are not easily searchable and not organized or properly formatted. The major challenge of such data is to collect, process, and analyze. It is also known as qualitative data as it includes the information which structured data do not include. Unstructured data rapidly grows every year therefore it is difficult to manage such data. E.g. electronic mails, text reports, comments on social media, various audio files, text files, and opinions

Figure 1. Structured data vs unstructured data

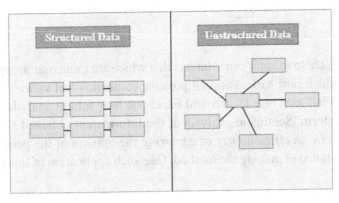

Twitter and Facebook are big data sources that have unstructured data and it's cannot be done directly. Such type of data needs to transform into a somewhat structured format before applying an application of analytics technique. Posting and social comments of people on Facebook and Twitter need to be analyzed to define the sentiments. It involves the process of dissecting the text into words and phrases which can then be categorized from positive to negative including neutral forms, and converted numerically, in a range of +1 to -1. In this way, a set of numeric data can be prepared to analyze. Thus, extracting structured data from unstructured data is an important part of the analysis process. In data extraction, various features are needed to extract from text data.

As our case study deals with political data, so after collecting the huge data related to politics, data analysis and interpretation are to be done. Here comes the role of Social Media Analysis which raises the method of data collection from social media websites and blogs to evaluate the data and to make predictions.

Figure 2. Steps from Data analysis to Data interpretation

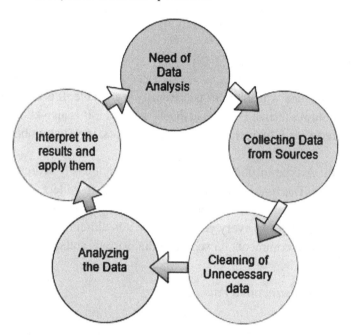

Social media analyses help to know our contents that which are more user accepted. During this way, we get to understand which post had additional positive comments and views and then improve there on the line of content. Platforms like Twitter and Facebook have inbuilt analytics that shows how well our posts make and perform. Sentiment analysis of the information obtained from such social media platforms has proven to be an efficient way of capturing the opinion of the people and predict trends, thereby improving the choice of making the method. One such application of this is often the Prediction of Election Results.

Feature Extraction Technique for Text Classification

Feature extraction of text is the procedure of drawing out a list of words from the textual data and transforming them into a set of features to classify.

Text classification consists of the following stages:

1. **Preparation of Dataset:** It is the primary step that incorporates the loading of a dataset, performing pre-processing, and then categorized into train and test/validation subsets.

2. **Feature Selection and Transformation: It is the su**bsequent step in which flat features are achieved by transforming the raw dataset which may be further utilized for the machine learning model. In this step, new features are formed from the obtainable data.

3. **Training of Model:** The ultimate step is of Model Training and building which consists of machine learning and deep learning model training of a labeled dataset.

4. **Improve Performance of Text Classifier:** Various ways to enhance the result of text classifiers can be considered.

Feature Selection and Transformation

A text data is converted into vectors of features (Alamanda, 2020) and fresh features are formed using the present dataset.

- Bag of words
- Vectors count like features
- TF-IDF vectors of features
  ○ Word level
  ○ N-Gram level
  ○ Character level
- Word Embedding's
- Text / NLP built features
- Topic Models built features
- Sentiment analysis of text

Bag of Words

The bagging of words is that the commonest and therefore the simplest in all the possible feature extraction techniques; it forms a set of features word presence feature set from an instance of all the words. It's referred to as a "bag" of words i.e. the presence of a word in a set of words, the tactic doesn't pay attention to the number of times or order of occurrence of the words. These features are often utilized to train a machine learning model. It is an extremely flexible and straightforward method. It's the representation of textual data which is used to specify usually the occurrence of words in a document and extract the features in several ways.

It includes:

1. A word list
2. An occurrence or the presence of well-known words.

The difficulty of the mentioned model is:

- To determine the score of present acquainted words
- To design the vocabulary document used to words.

Vectors Count Like Features

A matrix representation of the dataset where each tuple symbolizes a document from massive, and column shows a term from a massive amount of data is a vector count. A frequency count for a particular document is represented by each cell.

Word2Vec

It is used to build word embedding. These models are formed by using 2-layer neural networks. Once the model is trained, it reproduces the semantic backgrounds of words. It takes an enormously huge amount of data, as a text taken as an input. It generates a vector space of typical dimensions. Each unique within the massive amount of data is allotted with an equivalent vector within that space. Word2vec can be used among the 2 structural designs: 1. continuous skip-gram and 2. Bag of words (CBOW). Within the first mentioned architecture, the present word is taken in to account to guess the neighboring window of context words. Within the CBOW structural design, architecture, the context words' sequence doesn't influence prediction as the BOW model is used for prediction (Chauhan et al., 2020).

TF-IDF Vectors as Features

A relatively important term in any document is symbolized by the TF-IDF score. It consists of 2 terms: 1. It calculates the standardized Term Frequency, and 2. The Inverse Document Frequency, calculated as a log of a number of the documents divided by the number of documents wherever the appearance of a particular term exists. These are generated at various levels of i/p tokens like characters, words, and n-grams.

In BOW, a bag of words methodology, words with larger frequency turn out to be dominant in the data. This problem is resolved by rescaling the occurrence of the words. As a result of mentioned, this, the frequent words' scores are reduced among all the documents. This manner is termed as TF- IDF.

- TF is the occurrence of the word in an existing document.
- IDF is known as the score of the words in the corpus.

These scores can focus on the words that are identified and signify needful information during an indicated document. So, IDF is low for an infrequent term and high for the frequent term.

1. **TF-IDF at word level:** Matrix representation of tf-idf many of each term in several documents
2. **TF- IDF at N-gram Level:** Matrix representation of tf-idf many N-grams i.e. a mixture of n-terms altogether.
3. **TF-IDF at character level:** Matrix representation of tf-idf many n-grams at character level

Word Embedding's

It is a sort of representation of documents and words having a dense representation of a vector. In vector space, the word position is learned and predicted at what time it's used. These are often generated and trained with the pre-trained embedding of words like Word2Vec, FastText, and Glove.

Features Based on Text/NLP

Here additional features that are text-based are used to improve models based on text classification. Various types are:

1. Counting of words within the documents
2. Counting of characters within the documents
3. Normal Density of the words utilized within the documents
4. Counting of punctuation within the whole essay
5. Counting of capital words within the whole essay
6. Counting of title words within the whole essay
7. Speech distribution Tags: Counting of adjective, noun, pronoun, verb, and adverb

Sentiment analysis is the text classification tool that analyses text messages and predicts the basic sentiment as positive, negative, and neutral (Chen et al., 2020).

Sentiment Analysis

It is also called opinion mining which judges the text opinion. It is used for interpretation and classification by utilizing techniques of text analysis. These models not only specialized in polarity (+ve, -ve, and neutral) but also on emotions and feelings.

The process uses both NLP and ML with predefined labels. After categorizing the posts, the machine learning algorithms can create a public's opinions quantified score supported social media interactions and give predictions (Ahmad et al., 2019).

Types of Sentiment Analysis

Here are a number of the foremost popular sorts of sentiment analysis:

1. **Fine-grained Sentiment Analysis:** If it is important to business, categorization includes: Very positive, positive, neutral, negative, and very negative.
2. **Emotion detection:** It is the type which goals at the detection of emotions such as anger, happiness, sadness, anger and frustration and so many. Most of the emotion detection systems use the lists of words and complicated algorithms of machine learning. One of the problems of using a list of words is that individuals express their emotions.
3. **Sentiment Analysis with Aspect- Based:** While analyzing sentiment texts, need to understand the specific features mentioned in the way of positive, negative, and neutral way.
4. **Sentiment Analysis with Multilingual:** These types of analysis consist of preprocessing which is quite difficult.

Benefits of sentiment analysis include:

1. Arrangement of data at Scale
2. Real-Time Analysis

3.   Steady and Consistent criteria

Working of Sentiment Analysis

The major types include:

- Sentiment analysis is based on Rule-based systems supporting by a collection of automatically created rules.
- Machine learning methods are based on the automatic search from data.
- Combining of rule-based and automatic systems are hybrid systems.

Rule-based Methods

The rule-based methodology utilizes to identify a set of subjectivity, the topic of the views of people, and polarity. These rules consist of a variety of methods of linguistics like:

- Part- of- speech tagging, tokenization, parsing, and tagging
- Wordlist i.e. Lexicons

Figure 3. Typical process of the unstructured source code preprocessing

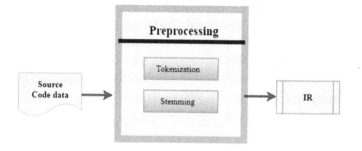

Automatic Methods

Automatic methods which conflict with rule-based systems depend on machine learning techniques instead of mane based rules. Sentiment analysis is particularly modeled as a sorting classification of data where text data is feed and categorized as positive, neutral, and negative.

These classifiers work as shown in the following figure:

Figure 4. The Training and Prediction Process

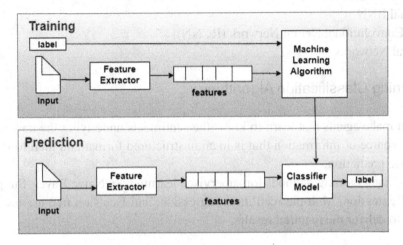

The Training and Prediction Processes

During the training process (a), model studies to map the specific input (i.e. a text) to the equivalent output (tag) supported the test samples used for training. The role of the feature extractor is to transfer the text input to a feature vector. Sets of feature vectors and tags (e.g. *positive*, *negative*, or *neutral*) are served into the machine learning algorithm to get a model.

In the prediction process (b), the feature extractor is engaged in reworking the unseen text inputs into feature vectors. The model's input is the feature vectors, which produces and creates predicted tags (again, *positive*, *negative*, or *neutral*).

Feature Extraction From Text

In machine learning text classifier the first step is to perform rework or text vectorization, and therefore the classical approach such as bag-of-words or bag-of-n grams with their frequency were used but recently, new feature extraction techniques are functional which is supported to word embedding's which is also known as word vector.

Model Building

The Last step within the framework used in text classification is to train a classifier based on the features created. Several choices of machine learning models are as follows:

1. Naïve Linear Classifier
2. Support Vector Machine
3. Bagging & Boosting Models
4. Shallow & Deep Neural Networks
5. Convolutional Neural Network (CNN)
6. Long Short Term Model (LSTM)

7. Gated Recurrent Unit (GRU)
8. Bidirectional RNN
9. Recurrent Convolutional Neural Network (RCNN)
10. Deep Neural Networks

Machine Learning Classification Algorithms

The machine can make agents that learn to know the sentiments underlying the new messages. Social media is that the source of information that is in an unstructured format and therefore the challenge is to form the precise prediction.

Different Machine Learning methods for supervised learning are Naive Bayes, Support Vector Machine, Logistic Regression, Multiple rectilinear regression, and Decision tree are used to extract and analyze the data to deliver the required results.

Naïve Bayes

Naïve Bayes belongs to a family of probabilistic algorithms that makes use of Bayes' Theorem to forecast the category of a text. It can classify binary (two-class) and multiclass classification problems.

The probability model that was formulated by Bayes (1701-1761) is sort of simple yet powerful; and are often written down in simple words as given below:

P(class|data) = (P(data|class) * P(class)) / P(data)

$$(A \mid B) = \frac{P(B \mid A) * P(A)}{P(B)}$$

Figure 5. Naïve Bayes Classifier

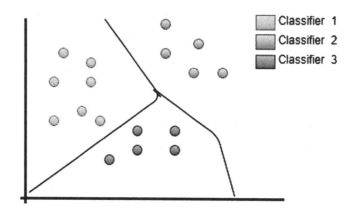

This model is straight forward to create and particularly useful for very large data sets, alongside simplicity. Naive Bayes is well known to outperform even highly sophisticated classification methods.
Pros:

- Very easy to implement
- Less training data is required.
- Used in binary and multiclass classification problems.
- Can handle discrete and continuous data

Cons:

- All attributes are treated equally
- Zero probability
- Assumption of independent predictors

Naive Bayes Algorithm applications are as follows:

- **Real-time Prediction: As** Naive Bayes is a fast and strong learning classifier; it can be used for real-time predictions.
- **Multi-class Prediction:** It can as well predict the probability of multiple classes of the target variable.
- **Text classification/ Spam Filtering/ Sentiment Analysis:** These are mostly used in text classification and perform successfully as equated to other algorithms. it is extensively used in Spam filtering (identify spam e-mail) and Sentiment Analysis (in social media analysis, to spot positive and negative customer sentiments)
- **Recommendation System:** Recommendation systems are constructed using Naive Bayes Classifier and Collaborative Filtering together that makes use of machine learning and data processing, where hidden data is filtered and predicted the choice of user.
- **Linear Classifier:** It is a classification algorithm or classifier that makes the classification depends on a linear predictor function uniting a set of weights and feature vector. To differentiate the two classes, we can draw an arbitrary line, such that all the 'o' are on one side of the line and χ's on the other side of the line. These two classes are called linearly-separable.

Figure 6. Generalized Linear Regression Model for Classification

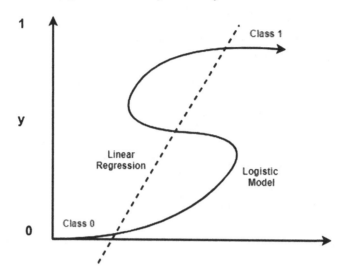

Support Vector Machines

It is a non-probabilistic technique that is non- linear that decides the best decision boundary between the vectors or sample points belongs to a group and not. It can be functional to any kind of vectors and can encode any type of data. For text classification, Text needs to convert into vectors.

Vectors are a list of numbers representing a set of coordinates in some space. SVM selects the hyperplane i.e. best decision boundary in two subspaces.

After encoding the text information, i.e. vector representation, SVM can be applied to text classification which achieves good results.

Figure 7. Support vector machine for text classification

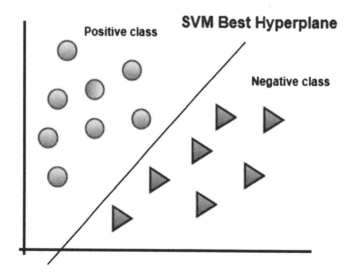

Figure 8. Shallow neural network model

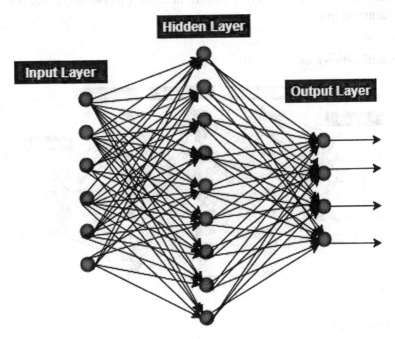

Bagging Model

Bagging is used normally when you want to decrease the variance while retaining the bias. It is possible when you average the predictions in various spaces of the input feature. Bagging is effective as models multiple copies are trained on different sets of data to improve the accuracy of a single model. This method is not recommended on models that have a high bias.

Boosting Model

Another tree-based ensemble model is the Boosting models. It is an algorithm that reduces bias and also variance in supervised machine learning algorithms and converts weak to strong learners. XGBoost is a tree learning algorithm and linear model solver which has a strong capacity to do parallel computation on a single machine. It works 10 times speedily than others, supporting regression, ranking, and classification. XGBoost works only in numeric form, so the need for conversion of other forms in numeric vectors. One hot encoding is such a method.

Deep Learning Classification Algorithms

As an active subset of machine learning, DL is believed to be a powerful tool to deal with Social Media Analysis problems. Deep learning (DL) has become more powerful because of its processing power. Due to the tremendous development and extensive accessibility of digital social media (SM), analyzing this data with the use of traditional tools and technologies is a very tough job. DL is originated as a suitable solution to this problem. Deep Learning extract features and patterns related to the text and concepts available in crisis-related social media posts and use them to provide an overview of the crisis. Deep learning techniques support machines to learn to classify data by themselves. Various deep learning models are Convolutional Neural Networks, Recurrent Neural Networks, Long Short Term Memory networks, Gated recurrent unit.

Figure 9. Deep neural network model

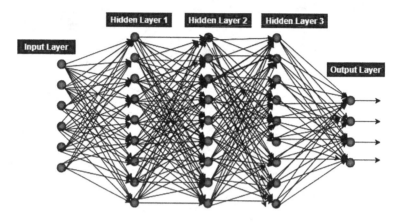

Shallow Neural Networks

A shallow neural network describes NN that typically has only one hidden layer as opposed to deep NN which has numerous hidden layers, often of many types. A shallow neural network has mainly three types of layers – the input layer, hidden layer, and output layer.

Deep Neural Networks

A *deep neural network* is an *artificial neural network* (ANN) with several layers amongst the input and output layers. They are a complex form of neural networks in which the hidden layers are responsible for performing complex operations than simple sigmoid or ReLu activations. Various types of deep learning techniques are functional in text classification problems.

Figure 10. Architecture of Convolutional Neural Network

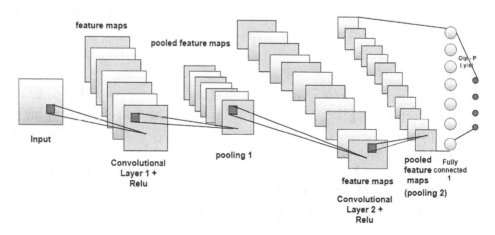

Convolutional Neural Network

Convolutional neural networks (CNN, ConvNet) are a type of deep neural networks that are widely useful in image recognition. An input image is taken and we define a weight matrix. The input is convolved to extract specific features from the image that we provided, without losing the information about its spatial arrangement. This approach reduces the number of parameters from the image that is to be trained.

Recurrent Neural Network – LSTM

The arrangement of a **feed-forward neural network** is such that the movement of information is unidirectional, forward, from the input nodes, through the hidden nodes (if any), and to the output nodes. These networks have no cycles or loops in the network. Such networks are primarily used for pattern recognition. So to successfully handle the sequential data we need to use a recurrent neural network (RNN).

It is a type of artificial neural network normally used in speech recognition and natural language processing (NLP) they are intended to identify a data's sequential characteristics and use patterns to predict the next probable scenario.

The memory state in RNNs gives an advantage over traditional neural networks but it suffers from a problem called Vanishing Gradient. With this problem, it is really hard to learn and tune the parameters of the earlier layers in the network. This problem becomes worse as the number of layers in the architecture increases. To address this problem, a new type of RNNs called LSTMs (Long Short Term Memory) Models has been developed.

Figure 11. Concept of LSTM Network

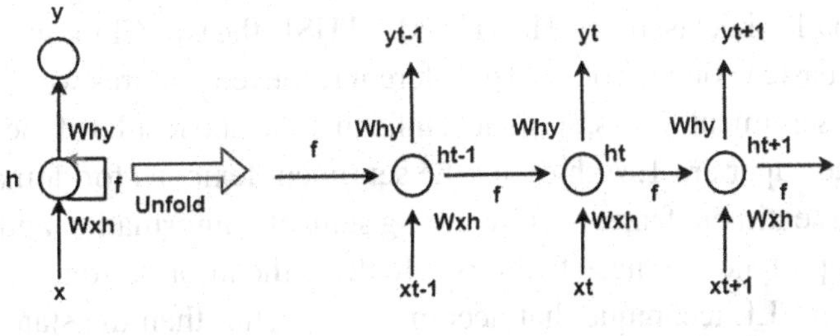

Recurrent Neural Network – GRU

Gated recurrent units -GRUs is a gating mechanism in recurrent neural networks which are like a long short-term memory (LSTM) with a forget gate but have fewer parameters than LSTM, as it lacks an output gate. GRU's performance on polyphonic music modeling, speech signal modeling, and natural language processing are similar to that of LSTM. GRUs exhibit even better performance on certain smaller and less frequent datasets.

Improving Text Classification Models

To achieve good accuracy some improvements can be done in the Text classification framework

1. **Text Cleaning:** It helps to reduce the noise present in text data in the form of stop words, punctuations marks, suffix variations, etc.
2. **Hstacking Text / NLP features with text feature vectors:** Several different feature vectors can be generated and combining them can help to improve the accuracy of the classifier.
3. **Hyperparameter Tuning in modeling:** Parameter tuning is an important step, various parameters such as tree length, leaves, network parameters, etc. can be fine-tuned to get the best fit model.
4. **Ensemble Models:** Stacking dissimilar models and blending their outputs can help to further improve the results.

The case study proposes a machine learning model to predict the number of votes obtained by two major parties namely the Indian National Congress and Bharatiya Janata Party (BJP) for the Lok Sabha Elections of 2019 in India. The data from Twitter for General Elections of 2019 as well as General Elections of 2014 was mined. The mined data was cleaned and relevant data was fed into TextBlob for sentiment analysis. The polarity of tweets obtained was used in a Regression Model. Data about the General Elections of 2014 was used for training the model so that the model can predict the results of the 2019 elections. Prediction is done for each State and the Union Territory of the country and accuracy of the model is obtained by equating the results with the actual number of votes obtained by the two parties in each state in the 2014 polls.

The Literature survey is discussed below:

Kaili Mao, Jianwei Niu (Mao & Niu, 2015), proposed a distinctive sentiment analysis technique that Pools Lexicon-based and Learn-based technique (CLL) to examine the reviews of Chinese product cross-domain sentiment. Three domains were constructed, lexicons based on the basic lexicon and corpus from three domains containing books, hotels, and electronics and used four categories of features (including 16 features in total) to build six classifiers. Howie and NTUSD the two Chinese sentiment lexicons were considered to build the basic lexicon. Totally 16 different retrieved features were classified into four categories named n-Gram, sentiment words, statistical information, and results of the lexicon-based method. The contributions of the paper are 1. Achieving the sentiment lexicons for domains books, hotels, and electronics 2. To offer a sentiment feature set including semantic information and structural information 3. To understand the importance of these features calculates the information entropy to rank features.4. Finally to Recommend a CLL technique that accomplishes better than the state-of-the-art approach in domains of books and hotels. The following four classifiers namely Support Vector Machine (SVM) classifier, Bayes classifier, Decision Tree classifier, and K-Nearest Neighbor (KNN) classifier were used and compared based on the classification accuracy of each classifier.

Adam Bermingham & Alan Smeaton (Bermingham & Smeaton, 2010), discussed Microblogs as a new textual domain that offers a unique proposition for sentiment analysis. As the size of the document in microblogs is short whichever sentiment they hold is compact and explicit. This small length together with the noisy tendency can posture complications for document representation in regular machine learning representations. Sentiment in these short-form documents than in longer form documents can be easily classified this hypothesis was examined in this paper. The dataset considered was taken from Twitter public data API. Support vector machine (SVM) and Multinomial Naïve Bayes (MNB) were the two classifiers considered. The accuracy of Blog classification is considerably lower than for microblogs. It was detected that out of the two supervised classifiers, SVM outpaces MNB for the long-form domains, however, the converse is true in the short-form domains. SVMs balance well with higher vector dimensionality. The total of exclusive terms in the lengthier documents is over three times their shorter counterparts, even when infrequent features have been excluded.

Dipankar Das & Sivaji, (Das & Sivaji, 2010) proposed an annotation task that has been supported out at the sentence level. Bengali blog sentences extracted from a web blog were manually annotated by three annotators, archive with Ekman's six basic emotion tags surprise(Su), anger (A), disgust (D), fear (F), happy (H), sad (Sa). The emotional sentences contained were marked with intensities of three types such as high, general, and low. The sentences identified as neutral and mixed categories were also recognized. The identification of emotional words or phrases and fixing the scope of emotional expressions in the sentences were conceded in the current task. The owner of the emotion and appropriate topics related to the emotional expressions were annotated seeing the punctuation marks, conjuncts, rhetorical structures, and other discourse information. A preliminary experiment was passed out on a small set of 1200 sentences of the annotated blog corpus using Conditional Random Field (CRF). We have used the same corpus and related features for classifying the emotion words using Support Vector Machine (SVM). The outcomes of the automatic emotion classification at the word level show that SVM outperforms CRF significantly. It is seen that the two classifiers failed to identify the emotion words that are enriched by morphological inflections. Though SVM outperforms CRF both of them suffer from sequence labeling and label bias problems with other non - emotional words of a sentence.

Jyoti, Darshan(Ramteke et al., 2016), Focused on the spread of social media to recognize the polarity of the views of the end-users, know the user orientation, and thus make smarter decisions. They discussed the application of social media in politics, where political groups want to know public views and thus regulate their campaigning strategy. A framework comprised of two-stage was used to mine Twitter data without negotiating on features and contextual relevance to produce training data. Lastly, they proposed a scalable machine learning model to forecast the results of the election using two-stage frameworks. Twitter Streaming API was used to get data from Twitter data for two candidates namely Donald Trump and Hillary Clinton for the dates March 16th, 2016, and March 17th, 2016. Multinomial Naive Bayes and Support Vector machines the two algorithms were used to determine the polarity of tweets. SVM delivers the best accuracy for classification.

Parul Sharma and Teng-Sheng Moh (Sharma & Moh, 2016), have come up with a new supervised machine learning approach. They have collected the samples of tweets made by the people about their views for various Indian political parties during the general election in the year 2016. They have applied the Dictionary Based, Naive Bayes, and SVM algorithm to construct a classifier on these collected samples to classify the test data as positive, negative, and neutral. The experiment was done to predict the winning chances of any political party. After experimenting, they have received the winning chances of BJP as 62% using Naïve Bayes, 78% using SVM, and 34% using Dictionary-based. They have also calculated precision and recall for these three approaches and they found the highest value of precision using the SVM algorithm as compared to the other two methodologies. The result of the 2016 election was out of 126 constituencies, BJP got success for 60 places.

Maite Taboada, Julian Brooke et. al (Taboada & Brooke, 2011), proposed a lexicon-based approach for sentiment analysis from text using a semantically oriented calculator (SO-CAL) which uses dictionaries of words with polarity and strength. An input data is classified with positive and negative labels during polarity classification. A mechanical Turk interface collects the results based on dictionary rankings with the words. This work produces better consistency and reliability than the existing methodologies.

Namita Mittal, Basant Agarwal et. al. (Mittal & Agarwal, 2013), has come up with a new idea of HindiSentiWordNet (HSWN) for analyzing the tweets available in the Hindi language. In India, people generally use the Hindi language for communication purposes. It is also found that a lot of news comments, tweets as well as Facebook messages are available in the Hindi language. Therefore, there is a need to study the contents of the Hindi Language to analyze the opinion stated by Indian people. They have used Cohen's Kappa and Fleiss Kappa for developing their model. For experimental research purposes, they have used Hindi Discourses and Hindi movie reviews as a database. With HSWN, the overall accuracy which they have received is 80.21%. They have also suggested that by using Word Sense Disambiguation (WSD) and morphological variants, better accuracy can be obtained for words that have dual nature.

Subhabrata Mukherjee and Pushpak (Mukherjee & Pushpak, 2012), Bhattacharyya performs sentiment analysis in Twitter with lightweight discourse analysis. This work takes noisy, unstructured text as input and it is compared with the collection of words in the dictionary. It ignores discourse elements from the input. To increase the classification rate, relations between the discourse data on the dictionary is analyzed. Some semantic operators like modals and negations are also utilized for their performance. But this work takes more processing time because of using a complex linguistic tool. Also, parsing and tagging processes produce less accuracy in noisy text.

MAIN FOCUS OF THE CHAPTER

- Understanding people's perspective towards the election.
- Understanding what activities should be conducted by the parties participating in elections to avoid losing.
- The understanding sentiment of tweets written in multiple languages restricting to Hindi and English.

SOLUTIONS AND RECOMMENDATIONS

The proposed model can be divided into 5 main stages based on the nature of the task to be performed:

1. Data Collection
2. Data Filtration
3. Analyzing Data
4. Perform Sentiment analysis on Analyzed data
5. Compare Data Sentiment Score
6. Show Result

Figure 12. The System Architecture of the proposed model

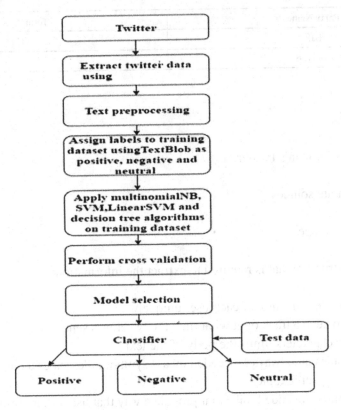

The steps to implement our case study are:

Data Collection From Twitter

One of the powerful tools is the Twitter Developer platform which offers several methods rendering to the objectives and demands of each project. Twitter API Calls are free and upon request can be accessed using two different methods:

- The Streaming API
- The Search API.

Twitter Introduction

For sending posts and messages nowadays, one of the platforms used is Twitter for online news and social networking service.

Table 1. Approximate data for candidates

Party Name	Total Tweets
BJP	3471
Congress	3125

Why Use Twitter?

Following are reasons for using Twitter:

1. Data from disparate sources
2. Embedded content
3. Instantaneous coverage

Elements Tweets structure that is required to extract the information:

- **User Name:** For identification of each user uniquely.
- **Time Stamp:** To keep a track of at what time the tweet was sent.
- **Tweet Text:** 140 characters limits the body of the text.
- **Hashtags:** Hashtags are always proceeded by a # symbol it describes a particular event or can be associated with a specific topic.
- **Links:** Tweets have embedded links that provide a way that users share information.
- **Embedded Media:** tweets hold pictures and videos.
- **Retweets:** When any person shares a tweet with his followers it is called a retweet.
- **Replies** & **Favorites**
- **Latitude/Longitude:** coordinate information is contained in 1% of all tweets.

Getting Data From Twitter Streaming API

To interact with a computer program or web service easily a tool named Application Programming Interface - API is available. To interact with their service several web services offer APIs to developers for programmatically accessing data.

Step 1: Accessing Twitter API Keys

To access Twitter Streaming API from Twitter, 4 elements of information are required namely API key, API secret, Access token, and Access token secret.
    To get the 4 elements to follow the steps given below:

- You need to make a new Twitter account if one doesn't exist.
- Visit link https://apps.twitter.com/ and gain access to login in with your Twitter credentials.
- Take the cursor on the tab named "Create New App"

Table 2. Textblob Sentiment Analysis Examples

Sentence	comp	positive	negative	neutral
He is clever and funny	0.83	0.75	0.0	0.254
A terrible Book	-0.822	0.0	0.79	0.20
It sucks, but I'll be good	0.22	0.274	0.195	0.53

- After filling the complete form, accept the terms and click on the tab "Create your Twitter application"
- You need to click on the "API keys" tab, and copy your "API key" and "API secret".
- Go to the bottom of the page and click on "Create my access token", and after that copy your "Access token" and "Access token secret".

Step 2: Data Downloading and Join to Twitter Streaming API

Tweepy a python library connects the Twitter Streaming API and downloads the data. A new file called twitter_streaming.py is created to copy the code.

You need to add your credentials into access token, access_token_secret, consumer key, and consumer secret.

For this case study, The Search API was optimal and the tweets had to be instigated from Indian Citizens located within India. Twitter data for two parties - namely BJP (Bhartiya Janata Party) and Congress (Indian National Congress) were collected.

Step 3: Data Preprocessing

A huge volume of data is returned by The search API for every tweet. The fields of interest are Tweets Location, Date posted, Tweet's Text, and User's followers count.

The raw data that was collected has to be changed into an understandable format, filtered, and stored in TEXT files.

It included the following steps:

1. **Cleaning of Data -** This process involves filling in missing values, smoothing the noisy data (all the tweets were stripped off special characters like '@' and URLs to overcome noise), resolving inconsistencies in data.
2. **Data Integration –** Data with various representations are placed together and conflicts were resolved.
3. **Data Conversion and reduction -** Data is normalized, aggregated, and generalized. Then it is represented in a reduced form and stored in Dataset (Text file). The python libraries used are:
   a. For parsing, data JSON is used
   b. For data, manipulation pandas are used
   c. For creating charts use matplotlib
   d. Use and re for regular expressions.

Figure 13. Twitter Sentiment Analysis

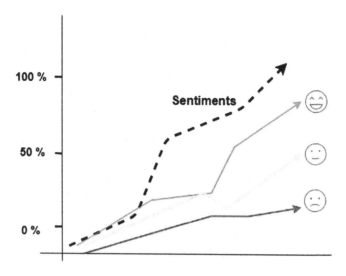

The commands shown below are used for uploading JSON and pandas:

```
import JSON
import pandas as PD
import matplotlib.pyplot as plt
```

4. Then the succeeding step is to get the data in an array which is called tweets.
5. **Mining the tweets:** By using Twitter's API one can perform complex queries like dragging every tweet about a certain topic within the last twenty minutes, or pull a certain user's non-retweeted tweets.
6. **Extracting links from the relevant tweets:** Getting the required tweet.

Step 4: Data Labeling

A tool used precisely in concurrence to sentiments conveyed in social media is TextBlob sentiment analysis. It is a tool that is fundamentally a sentiment intensity polarizer. The sentence is provided as input which returns a percent value for positive, negative, and neutral categories. Polarity values range

Table 3. Example of Training Dataset

Party Name	Sentiment	Total Votes Polled by Parties
BJP	0.75	124721
Cong	0.41	512346
BJP	-0.21	221346

from -1 to 1, where a positive compound value indicates that the overall sentiment expressed in the sentence is positive and vice versa.

Figure 14. Linear and Multiple Linear Regression

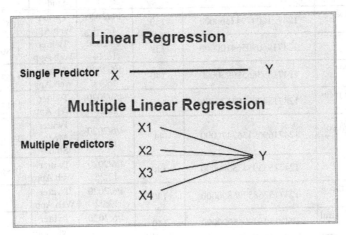

Apart from the polarity value, each tweet has associated with it the Indian State where the tweet was made from and the number of followers of the account from which the tweet was made.

The table shown above depicts three sample examples of investigated sentences using TextBlob. It is observed that the first sentence results as extremely positive, the second sentence is extremely negative in addition to the third sentence which is neutral. To perform the sentiment analysis, the training data set should consist of sentences classified as either positive or negative Thus the method proposed above was used to calculate the polarity of each tweet.

Creating A Training Set

The Dataset for 2014 Elections was used to create our training dataset. From the State Wise Result of 2014 Elections, date related to Total valid votes polled in states and Total valid votes polled by parties was collected and was integrated with our Twitter dataset.

Step 5: Applying Classifier

The sentiment Analysis phase involves attributing the data with its associated polarity value. The final data set created after sentiment analysis and data labeling is fed into a regressor. The regressor is trained on the data collected for the General Elections of 2014 and then is used to predict the results of the 2019 elections.

Multivariate Linear Regression is a type of regressor that predicts the value of one or more responses from a set of forecasters.

To implement the supervised Regression model design, the performance of the Multivariate Linear, and other various regression models like Decision Tree Regression, Cart (Classification and Regression Trees) will be compared.

Table 4. Tweet data with its sentiment classification

Tweets	Id	Length	Date	Source	Likes	Re-tweets	Sentiments
श्री @JPNadda ने भाजपा के 40वें स्थापना दविस क	1247216397081440000	138	4/6/2020 17:35	Twitter Media Studio	1367	237	Neutral
भाजपा राष्ट्रीय अध्यक्ष श्री @JPNadda को भारती	1247216047947560000	140	4/6/2020 17:34	Twitter Web App	1642	207	Neutral
#IndiaFightsCorona \n\ nप्रधानमंत्री, सभी मंत्र...	1247196090564100000	139	4/6/2020 16:14	Twitter Web App	1780	396	Neutral
Leading by example, the Modi government has approved...	1247189386589950000	140	4/6/2020 15:48	Twitter Web App	1760	337	Neutral
PM Shri @narendramodi's 5 pleas to Karyakartas...	1247184702303170000	140	4/6/2020 15:29	Twitter Web App	1114	258	Neutral
Our DNA... #BJPat40 https://t.co/hOgSjbJRcD	1247169691367470000	44	4/6/2020 14:30	Twitter Media Studio	3491	863	Neutral
पीएम श्री @narendramodi के भाजपा के 40वें स्था	1247153395435040000	140	4/6/2020 13:25	Twitter Web App	1954	432	Neutral
RT @narendramodi: During the meeting, highlight	1247152585296890000	140	4/6/2020 13:22	Twitter Web App	0	1858	Positive
RT @narendramodi: Had a fruitful interaction w...	1247152578065900000	140	4/6/2020 13:22	Twitter Web App	0	3921	Neutral
5 अप्रैल को रात 9 बजे, हमने 130 करोड़ देशवासिय...	1247125863776150000	138	4/6/2020 11:35	Twitter Media Studio	2007	417	Neutral
जनसंघ से भाजपा तक, त्याग, तपस्या, बलिदान के आध...	1247124446898310000	140	4/6/2020 11:30	Twitter Media Studio	2905	583	Neutral
समानो मंत्रः समितिः समानी।\ nसमानम् मनः सह चति्...	1247118582258860000	139	4/6/2020 11:06	Twitter Media Studio	1340	307	Neutral
'पीएम मोदी के भाजपा कार्यकर्ताओं से पंच-आग्रह'...	1247093395408860000	138	4/6/2020 9:26	Twitter Media Studio	2294	510	Neutral
RT @rajnathsingh: आज भाजपा का नेतृत्व प्रधानमं...	1247089324618680000	140	4/6/2020 9:10	Twitter Web App	0	436	Neutral
RT @rajnathsingh: अपनी स्थापना के ४० वर्षों मे...	1247089313323420000	139	4/6/2020 9:10	Twitter Web App	0	2016	Neutral
आज हम पार्टी का 40वां स्थापना दविस कोरोना से ल...	1247088710581010000	139	4/6/2020 9:08	Twitter Media Studio	2397	434	Neutral
वैश्विक कोरोना संकट में जिस तरह से प्रधानमंत्र...	1247084268297150000	140	4/6/2020 8:50	Twitter Media Studio	1381	324	Neutral
भाजपा के लिए राष्ट्र सर्वप्रथम होता है। \n\nअं...	1247083230756400000	139	4/6/2020 8:46	Twitter Media Studio	1521	325	Neutral
जनसंघ से जनता पार्टी की यात्रा करते हुए 6 अप्र...	1247082489325030000	140	4/6/2020 8:43	Twitter Media Studio	1540	373	Neutral
RT @JPNadda: ■आरोग्य सेतु एप का अधिकतम डाऊनलो...	1247074939212930000	140	4/6/2020 8:13	Twitter Web App	0	408	Neutral

Table 5. Statistical features for the @BJP4India tweet handle

Mean Tweet Length	Maximum Likes	Maximum Re-tweets
134.8	3491	3921

EXPERIMENTS AND RESULTS

To evaluate the results for social media analysis the Bhartiya Janata Party (BJP, Twitter handle @ *BJP4India*) tweets are fetched. These tweets contain an ID, the tweet length, the actual tweet, and the number of likes & retweets for an individual tweet. This entire data is given to the analytics engine described in the previous section. The engine evaluates the sentiment for each of the tweets and presents the same under the neutral, positive, or negative sentiment. The results of this tweet data are presented in the following table 4,

The average value of the tweet length, maximum number of likes, and the maximum number of retweets are evaluated for this data. The results of this are tabulated in the following table 5,

The data from table 4 is plotted on a timeline, it depicts the performance of the @*BJP4India* Twitter handle over a course of one decade, and it can be observed that during the pre-election period of 2014 there was a major boost in traffic for the handle, which can be considered as one of the causes for victory for BJP.

A similar observation was made for the Indian National Congress (INC, Twitter handle @*INCIndia*). The sentiment analysis results can be observed from table 6, wherein it can be observed that the majority of sentiments were negative for INC during the recent pandemic situation.

Similarly, statistical analysis was done on the tweets, and the following results were observed,

Similar looking trends were observed for @*INCIndia* during the pre-election period, but most of the tweet analysis showcased that there was a negative sentiment towards INC during the election period. This data can be observed in figure 16, wherein the result of likes and retweets are showcased.

Figure 15. Statistical results of one side Party Tweets

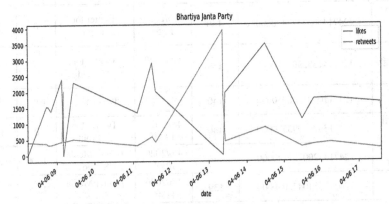

Table 6. Sentiment analysis for Indian National Congress (INC)

Tweets	Id	Length	Date	Source	Likes	Re-tweets	Sentiments
Had the government started planning to procure…	1247192340600510000	144	4/6/2020 16:00	TweetDeck	1301	447	Neutral
Media's role to question the Govt & to hold…	1247186197459250000	143	4/6/2020 15:35	Twitter Media Studio	2243	797	Neutral
The govt needs to share inf…	1247184791893490000	144	4/6/2020 15:30	TweetDeck	659	227	Positive
RT @INCUttarPradesh: कांग्रेस महासचिव श्रीमती …	1247181612657160000	140	4/6/2020 15:17	Twitter for Android	0	481	Neutral
RT @priyankagandhi: इस नाज़ुक समय में डाक्टर, स…	1247181323682200000	140	4/6/2020 15:16	Twitter for Android	0	2167	Neutral
RT @TS_SinghDeo: लॉकडाउन के चलते किसी को भूखा …	1247179512082620000	140	4/6/2020 15:09	Twitter Web App	0	201	Neutral
RT @capt_amarinder: I am happy to share that w…	1247179071705890000	144	4/6/2020 15:07	Twitter Web App	0	339	Positive
Our demand for sharing the great benefits &amp…	1247177240514900000	143	4/6/2020 15:00	TweetDeck	488	166	Positive
Why is the govt profiteering and not profit sh…	1247173466190760000	140	4/6/2020 14:45	TweetDeck	640	225	Negative
In the middle of a health crisis, BJP leaders …	1247169691531070000	140	4/6/2020 14:30	TweetDeck	2194	658	Negative
Our government in Chhattisgarh took several me…	1247162142530440000	140	4/6/2020 14:00	TweetDeck	457	180	Neutral
RT @RahulGandhi: #Covid19 के इस कठिन समय में ह…	1247158869022780000	140	4/6/2020 13:47	Twitter Web App	0	7547	Neutral
Our nation was founded on the principles and I…	1247154591587650000	140	4/6/2020 13:30	Twitter Media Studio	1242	453	Neutral
AICC General Secretary I/c Organisation Shri @…	1247149709979840000	140	4/6/2020 13:10	TweetDeck	473	171	Negative
RT @INCSandesh: Govt should share part of Rs 2…	1247145004373420000	140	4/6/2020 12:51	Twitter for Android	0	183	Positive
RT @AjayLalluINC: उत्तर प्रदेश कांग्रेस कमेटी …	1247141595905840000	139	4/6/2020 12:38	Twitter for Android	0	293	Neutral
कोरोना से निपटने के लिये अधिक से अधिक टेस्ट कि…	1247140621506050000	140	4/6/2020 12:34	TweetDeck	1081	288	Neutral
RT @rssurjewala: सांसदों की सैलरी पर कट ज़रूर …	1247136982993520000	140	4/6/2020 12:20	Twitter for Android	0	1110	Neutral
सोनिया गांधी जी ने 7500 रूपये की आर्थिक सहायता…	1247133200721240000	140	4/6/2020 12:05	Twitter Media Studio	1000	348	Neutral
अंतरराष्ट्रीय बाज़ार में कच्चे तेल की कीमतों मे…	1247128540476080000	139	4/6/2020 11:46	Twitter Media Studio	1383	441	Neutral

Table 7. Statistical analysis of Twitter data for @INCIndia

Mean Tweet Length	Maximum Likes	Maximum Retweets
140.8	2243	7547

Figure 16. Statistical results of other side party tweets

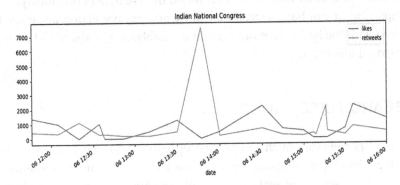

Figure 17. Sentiment polarity Tweets results of both the parties

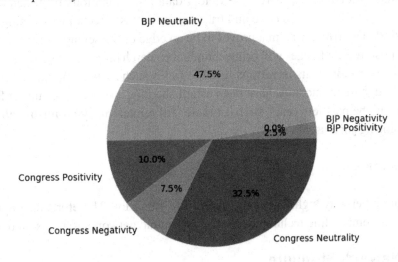

Table 8. Accuracy results of the proposed algorithm

Twitter Handle	Work in (Mao & Niu, 2015)	Work in (Ramteke et al., 2016)	This Work
@BJP4India	84%	86%	95%
@INCIndia	79%	88%	96%
@realDonaldTrump	86%	88%	95%
@JoeBiden	88%	85%	94%
@JPNadda	74%	79%	89%

But recently there has been a lot of negativity for BJP, while INC is gaining popularity. This can be observed from the trend analysis showcased in figure 17, which is done on the recent (6-month tweets) data. INC almost leads with a 7.5% more positive sentiment than BJP. These numbers can change during the pre-election period (2022-23), and upon analysis, the winning party can be predicted.

The discussed algorithm outperforms some of the standard algorithms for sentiment prediction for social media analysis. The accuracy for the prediction of the proposed algorithm along with some standard algorithms is depicted in table 8, wherein it can be observed that the proposed algorithm is at least 8% more accurate than the standard algorithms proposed by researchers previously.

From the comparison, it can be observed that the sentiment prediction accuracy for social media analysis is improved with the help of not only sentiment analysis, but also trend prediction on Twitter data using the proposed algorithm.

FUTURE RESEARCH DIRECTIONS

Social media platforms present various challenges to deep learning. The DL based models have substantial power to learn valued data representations from multi-domain social media podiums such as behavior analysis, business analysis, sentiment analysis, anomaly detection, and many more. however, the aspects including powerful resource requirement to deal with the data heaps, improving productivity and putting down the computational costs, learning efficient data representations from heterogeneous social data sources and so on, still, need effective and trustworthy dl based techniques. Using DL, these tasks need to be addressed in a official way that proves to be an edge or the scientific community. We have to believe that these postured challenges will bring abundant research projections to the dl community. also, they will deliver key developments in various real-life fields such as education, business, e-commerce, medicine etc. Although many methods have been established for a varied spectrum of Social Networks Analysis problems in the past few years, we trust there still remain many promising guidelines that are worth further exploring such as:

Dynamic Networks

Social networks are inherently highly dynamic in real-life scenarios. Therefore, how to design effective and efficient network embedding techniques for truly dynamic networks remains an open question.

Hierarchical Network Structure

How to design effective network embedding methods that are capable of preserving hierarchical structures of networks is a promising direction for further work.

Heterogeneous Networks

Existing network embedding methods mainly deal with homogeneous networks. Learning embedding's for heterogeneous networks is still at the early stage, and more comprehensive techniques are required to fully capture the relations between different types of network elements, toward modeling more complex real systems.

CONCLUSION

- Netizens use social media platforms to express their emotions for a particular event.
- These emotions are used for psephology.
- This helps us to predict the maximum likelihood for a party to win an election.
- It also helps us to analyze how events happening in a particular geographic location ends up affecting a party standing for election.

ACKNOWLEDGMENT

This work would not have been possible without the motivation and moral support of our Principal Dr. R. D. Kharadkar who has always been our teacher and mentor, he has taught us more than we could ever give him credit for here. We are especially indebted to our students Mr. Patrick D'Souza and Mr. Ayush Chhajer for helping us in this book chapter. We are grateful to all of those with whom we have had the pleasure to work during this and other related projects. We would like to thank our parents, our family members whose love and guidance are with us in whatever we pursue.

REFERENCES

Ahmad, S., Asghar, M. Z., Alotaibi, F. M., & Awan, I. (2019). Detection and classification of social media-based extremist affiliations using sentiment analysis techniques. *Hum. Cent. Comput. Inf. Sci.*, 9(1), 24. doi:10.118613673-019-0185-6

Alamanda, M. S. (2020). Aspect-based sentiment analysis search engine for social media data. *CSIT*, 8(2), 193–197. doi:10.100740012-020-00295-3

Bermingham & Smeaton. (2010). *Classifying Sentiment in Microblogs: Is Brevity an Advantage?* In CIKM'10, Toronto, Ontario, Canada.

Chauhan, P., Sharma, N., & Sikka, G. (2020). *The emergence of social media data and sentiment analysis in election prediction. J Ambient Intell Human Comput.* doi:10.100712652-020-02423-y

Chen, L., Lee, C., & Chen, M. (2020). Exploration of social media for sentiment analysis using deep learning. *Soft Computing*, 24(11), 8187–8197. doi:10.100700500-019-04402-8

Das & Sivaji. (2010). Labeling Emotion in Bengali Blog Corpus – A Fine-Grained Tagging at Sentence Level. *Proceedings of the 8th Workshop on Asian Language Resources*, 47–55.

Mao, K., & Niu, J. (2015). Cross-Domain Sentiment Analysis of Product Reviews by Combining Lexicon-based and Learn-based Techniques. *IEEE 17th International Conference on High-Performance Computing and Communications.*

Mittal, N., & Agarwal, B. (2013). Sentiment Analysis of Hindi Review based on Negation and Discourse Relation. *International Joint Conference on Natural Language Processing*, 45–50.

Mukherjee, & Pushpak. (2012). Sentiment Analysis in Twitter with Lightweight Discourse Analysis. *Proceedings of COLING 2012: Technical Papers*, 1847–1864.

Ramteke, J., Godhia, D., Shah, S., & Shaikh, A. (2016). Election Result Prediction Using Twitter sentiment Analysis. *Conference: 2016 International Conference on Inventive Computation Technologies (ICICT)*.

Sharma & Moh. (2016). Prediction of Indian Election Using Sentiment Analysis on Hindi Twitter. *IEEE International Conference on Big Data (Big Data)*.

Taboada & Brooke. (2011). Lexicon-Based Methods for Sentiment Analysis. *Association for Computational Linguistics, 37*(2).

Chapter 11
The Replacement of HMI (Human–Machine Interface) in Industry Using Single Interface Through IoT

Pradnya Sulas Borkar
Jhulelal Institute of Technology, Nagpur University, Nagpur, India

Prachi U. Chanana
Jhulelal Institute of Technology, Nagpur University, Nagpur, India

Simranjeet Kaur Atwal

Jhulelal Institute of Technology, Nagpur University, Nagpur, India

Tanvi G. Londe
Jhulelal Institute of Technology, Nagpur University, Nagpur, India

Yash D. Dalal
Jhulelal Institute of Technology, Nagpur University, Nagpur, India

ABSTRACT

The new era of computing is internet of things (IoT). Internet of things (IoT) represents the ability of network devices to sense and collect data from around the world and then share that data across the internet where it can be processed and utilize for different converging systems. Most of the organisation and industries needs up-to-date data and information about the hardware machines. In most industries, HMI (human-machine interface) is used mostly for connecting the hardware devices. In many manufacturing industries, HMI is the only way to access information about the configuration and performance of machine. It is difficult to take the history of data or data analysis of HMI automatically. HMI is used once per machine which is quite hard to handle. Due to frequent use of HMI, it leads to loss of time, high costs, and fragility, and it needs to be replaced, which was found to be costlier. An internet of things (IOT) is a good platform where all the machines in the industry are able to be handled from a single IoT-based web portal.

DOI: 10.4018/978-1-7998-7511-6.ch011

1. INTRODUCTION

This chapter focuses on the implementation of single interface for handling multiple hardware devices in industry from remote places. Generally HMI enables the operator to interact with the machine. But this HMI need to be repair/ replace frequently which is found to be costlier and therefore one interface should be needed to operate(i.e. to access data for data analysis and access status of machines) the industrial machines through portal and this portal can be accessed from remote places.

This chapter is divided into different sections i) Introduction to Industry 4.0 ii)Introduction to HMI iii)Introduction to Internet of Things iv)Literature Review v) Methodology vi)Data Analysis vii)Description of Portal

1.1 Industry 4.0

The conventional manufacturing in industrial platforms and practices has been empowered with smart technology that is called as Industry 4.0. This fourth revolution focuses on the implementation of Internet of Things(IOT) to provide automation, machine communication and monitoring that can analyse the various technical issues without interfering human. The connected Enterprise, smart manufacturing, manufacturing 4.0, Internet of Everything, Smart Factory, Industrial Internet of things(IIOT) etc. can be collectively called as Industry 4.0. This industry 4.0 is nothing but inclination towards automation and analysis as well as exchange of data in manufacturing technologies. These smart manufacturing technologies includes cloud computing, cognitive computing and artificial intelligence. Industry 4.0 can also endow with predictive maintenance with the help of IoT sensors and technology. This predictive maintenance can identify issues in real time which uses to perform cost-effective maintenance and helps to detect it(if there is any issue) before the machinery fails or gets damaged. It means that any equipment get observed by any person sitting anywhere in the world and can identify whether that equipment needed to be repaired or not. This speed of technological development impacts on socio-economic and infrastructural transformations which marks a transition to a new time era. In industries, the operator interacts with machine interface and it is the only way to interact with the machine, this is called Human Machine Interface (HMI).

1.2 Human Machine Interface (HMI)

The Human Machine Interface (HMI), sometime also frequently referred to the Operator Interface Terminal (OIT) or Man Machine Interface (MMI), is the bit of the machine that grasp human interaction. The HMI in a constructing or process control system which is the user interface that provides control, monitoring and visualization between a human and a machine

Automation is carried out in number of industrial plants without any connection and interaction between the machines and the operator. This makes it more difficult for the operator to handle the state of the industrial machines and the immediate actions taking place in the machines. The operator requires the flexibility and transparency for working in the industrial environment where the processes are getting more complex and requirements for machine is increasing. Nowadays many of the companies are turned to automatic working principle which gave a good efficiency by using Human Machine Interface (HMI).

An interface or dashboard which creates a bridge between human beings and machines or device to connect them is known as Human-Machine Interface (HMI). Technically, the user interface helps in performing operations with the machine or the device. HMI is widely used in the field of textiles industry process. Sometimes HMI is referred as Man-Machine Interface (MMI), Operator Interface Terminal (OIT), Local Operator Interface (LOI) or Operator Terminal (OT) as HMI is very common in use. To optimize the industrial processes HMI technology is used by almost all industrial sectors as well as huge range of other companies.

Figure 1. Block diagram of HMI

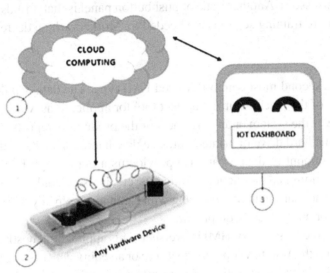

HMI are used to optimize an industrial process and also communicate with Programmable Logic Controllers (PLCs) and input/output sensors. It optimizes the process by digitizing and centralizing data for a viewer and the sensors are used to get and display information for users to view.

By holding HMI, operators can see important information displayed in graphs, charts or digital dashboards and also view and manage alarms, and connect with SCADA and MES systems. HMI screen can also be used for single function, like monitoring, tracking, etc, it can also perform more sophisticated operations, like switching machines off or increasing production speed, depending on how they are implemented.

In industrial settings, HMIs can be used to:

- Visually display data
- Track production time, trends, and tags
- Oversee KPIs
- Monitor machine inputs and outputs
- And more

1.2.1 Types of HMI

There are three basic types of HMI available in the market.

A. Pushbutton

It is central control panel containing of numerous buttons, among which each has particular function. Most of the industrial factories use the pushbutton replacers for better planning and production. Mostly Pushbutton panel is used for simple systems with few pieces of equipments. Different commands are executed by workers on various machines through the use of single appropriate interface. When the sections of equipment started to grow, pushbutton panel was started to show defect. The issues arises when various machines are in operation and not clear which machine is running at any given time and this makes the diagnosis issues. Another issue of pushbutton panel is that it finds difficult for new workers and therefore the more training sessions are needed for workers which decreases the productivity.

B. Data Handler

The data handler is the second most commonly used HMI type. The data handler is basically used for harvesting information of the machine, it is a perfect tool for applications which requires constant feedback from the machine or the system or any printouts of the production reports, depending on the user's command it also sent the hard drive or printed out. The data handlers are basically used in applications which involve a huge amount of data it can also provide us a big enough HMI screen for things like graphs,visual representations and production summaries, etc. It also includes functions like recipes, data trending, data logging and alarm handling/logging which can also help any industry to collect information from the machine or any piece of equipment.

The third last but not the least type of HMI is overseer, This application mostly required a full-fledged industrial PC that runs on the Windows operating system or an equivalent operating system and also have some Ethernets ports for further connections these ports run at minimum of 100Mb, which is required for network segmentation to control network traffic speeds.

C. Overseer

Overseer takes more and clear visual approach to interact between a human operator and machine, allowing for a graphical interface via an electronic display or touchscreen display which provide high desirability to hand data of company on mobile or any other electronic display. This type of HMI also same the overall costs by reducing the number of HMIs needed to operate the equipment but this type of HMI is costly and quite difficult to maintain around. The functions like data warehousing, database transactions, and interfacing with an enterprise-type system requires SCADA or even MES (manufacturing execution system) applications for this an overseer HMI is highly beneficial to be used.

But the consequences of using HMI came in front. It leads to loss of time, expensive and delicate to handle. We cannot be able to take the history of data or data analysis of HMI automatically. The only thing is that it will be showing the runtime data of the machine. HMI is used for once per machine which is quite hard to handle. So, to overcome the consequences, Internet of Things can be used.

1.3 Internet of Things

Kelvin Ashton came up with the term IOT in 1999. Internet of Things(IOT) is the general notion in which network devices are able to collect data from all over around the world and this shared data can be utilised for diversified purposes. The term IOT is also called as "Universal Global Neural Network".

Web-enabled Smart Devices which uses embedded systems like processors, sensors and communication devices that acts on data collected from various environments are included in IoT systems. IoT Gateway or other edge devices acts as connecting devices through which IoT devices share the sensed data that is either sent to the cloud to be analysed or analysed locally.

Generally the devices in IoT act on the information received from other related devices The operator or people in the industry interact with the machines just for instance to set them up, to give them instructions or access the data as the devices in IoT do most of the work without human. Depending on the specific IoT applications deployed, the connectivity, networking and communication protocols are used for web-enabled devices. IoT is the interrelated system in which the various computing devices, objects, digital machines, mechanical machines, animals or the people are included and these are able to transfer the data over a network without requiring human-to-human or the human-to-computer interaction.

In today's scenario, internet of things is everywhere in people lives. With respect to offering smart devices to automate homes, IoT is also important for business. IoT supports business by means of offering real time look into how their systems really work, it provides the perception right from the performance of machines to supply chain and logistics operations.

IoT enables companies to simplify processes and reduce labor costs. It reduces waste and improves service quality, making it less costly to produce and supply products. As such IoT is daily life's most relevant innovations and it will continue to pick up momentum as more businesses understand the ability of connected devices to keep them competitive.

It also cuts down on waste and improves service delivery, making it less expensive to manufacture and deliver goods, as well as offering transparency into customer transactions. As such, IoT is one of the most important technologies of everyday life, and it will continue to pick up steam as more businesses realize the potential of connected devices to keep them competitive. The IoT (Internet of Things) gives numerous benefits to industries. Some benefits are industry specific, and some are applicable across multiple industries.

2. LITERATURE SURVEY

Amruta P Bauskar & Kanchan Pujari (2016) describes the system that deals with the authority of corporal hardware devices above the internet which is developed using IOT or internet of things. The Developers created this system to control the appliances of the industries and machines above the internet. They have demonstrated this structure using 2 packs i.e. machines or industrial appliances and an industrial motor. An Arduino is used to process all the WIFI-modem and user commands is settled in to join the internet and to accept commands from the user. While dispatching commands by the internet they are firstly accepted by the Wi-Fi modem and then the modem decrypt data and passes it to the Arduino microcontroller for another processing. The microcontroller shows the system situation on an LCD display. This how the developers automate whole industry using online GUI for simple industry automation. They have used the Wi-Fi IP address to join with the folio. For changing of accessible power of one set of attributes of power supply unit is used to meet up the requirements. To increase operational efficiency, this industrial automation systems make use of wireless communication to connect remote and local provision. In this suggested system Wi-Fi modem ESP8266 was used. The ESP8266 Wi-Fi Module which is liberated System on Chip and is Unsegregated with TCP/IP protocol stack that gives the microcontroller entry to the Wi-Fi network. The ESP8266 module is an expensive beam with a large, and rising, community.

This module used in this system has a strong sufficient processing and storage capacity which permit it to be integrated with the sensors and other petition specific devices through its GPIOs with least development and loading during runtime. Minimal external circuitry is allowed by its high degree of on-chip integration, including the front-end module, is designed to occupy minimal PCB area.

A "Water Quality Monitoring System" developed by Vaishnavi V. Daigavane and Dr. M.A Gaikwad (2017) which is based on IOT. The System includes the hardware and software part. The hardware includes a core controller i.e. Arduino and various sensors like temperature, pH, turbidity, flow which are connected to it. The data transferred to the internet by the core controller which access the sensor value and display the sensor data over the internet WIFI system. The pH sensor checks the acidity and alkalinity of the water or can say the solution. To check the cloudiness and flow of water the turbidity sensor and the flow sensor is used respectively. The flow basically comprises of a rotor, a valve body made up of plastic, and a Hall Effect sensor. The valve and the speed of the water/liquid flow through it will be directly proportional to the flow rate when the pinwheel rotor rotates. With each revolution of the pinwheel rotor the Hall Effect sensor will be given to an electrical pulse. This System also consists of an Arduino Uno and anESO8266 WIFI Module. Arduino Uno has multiple input/output pins including a USB connection, a power jack, a reset button and an ICP header and it is the ATmega328P based microcontroller board. In a series of USB Arduino boards first was the UNO board. The WIFI module can give authority to the microcontroller to access the WIFI network. Using all this hardware components this system is developed including the software part, the hardware helps to measure the real time values and Arduino ATmega328 converts the analog values to digital values and they are displayed on the LCD. The connection between the hardware and the software is given by the WIFI module. The software programming is done with the embedded C language. The kit, Arduino and WIFI gets on when the dc current flows through it when the system get started. The parameter of water is tested one by one and their result are given to the LCD display. The application provided with hotspot gives the exact value as on LCD display shows on kit. Hence, such as this when the kit is detected on any certain water body and WIFI is given by which we can see its real time value on the android phone anywhere.

A better smart home automation system using the IOT .i.e. Internet of Things the most popular technology used today. In this system Bijay Shrestha et.al.(2017) have used different type of components and modules like LDR, Motion Sensors, Temperature Sensors etc. which are connected to the Arduino board and more hardware like light, LCD, etc. To indicate the change in the environment the sensors in the sensor unit are placed, which then report back to the Arduino board. The programming of the Arduino board is done in a way like that if the LDR sensor senses less light intensity then the light glows on. The system includes the android andweb application too, to give commands to the hardware. On receiving commands from the application, the hardware processes and acts to turn on or off. One more module i.e. the WIFImodule plays a major part in this system. It acts as a bridge between the UI and the Arduino. The connectivity is done with the help of the IP address using the ESP8266 WIFI module in this proposed system. The hardware components like the sensors, fan, LCD display, etc arejoined to the Arduino board. These sensors read the data and forward it to the Arduino to check the given condition as a program. The respective appliance is controlled if the given condition gets matched and the controlling can be done with the help of application as well as web pages. To display the humidity and temperature LCD issued.

In the current studies Joseph Nuamah & Younho Seong (2017) tried to find the highlighted human-in-the-loop problems in the systems and in specific IOT systems along with evaluating applicable literature from various outlooks. Most of the matter are probably spotlighted including information imagination, perception and the human faith in the intelligent systems. Keven Ashton was the first used to the term "The Internet of Things" in the supply chain management domains. Nowadays IOT has covered up the large range of domains as well as transportation, healthcare, utilities and logistics, etc. The IOT domains are arranged into classes according to their network availability, scale, user participation, heterogeneity and effect. The technologies that enables the IOT includes recognition and noticing technologies e.g., Radio Frequency Identification (RFID) and Wireless Sensor Networks (WSNs), middleware, cloud computing and IOT application software. Humans play a significant role in the IOT systems. Some of the issues are raised in the circumstances of human-automation interaction and by extending human IOT interaction. Marco Brambilla, Eric Umuhoza and Roberto Acerbis (2017) proposed a system on Model-driven development of user interfaces for IoT systems via domain-specific components and patterns in which they have given a brief discussion as Internet of Things technologies and the application is developing widely and gaining the traction in all the fields like environments, homes, cities, services, industry and commercial enterprises. Then also many problems are there which have to be addressed for example, the IOT vision is mainly focusing on the technological, infrastructure, aspects, management and analysis of the large amount of the generated data.

The user interaction plays a critical role in a large class of software and systems. Nowadays lot of research has been focusing on the scenario related to the industrial use of the IOT, machine-to-machine or sensor-to-sensor communication. In the particular area, the solutions proposed mainly focus on the extending standard IFML Language adopted by the Object Management Group (OMG). There are set of design patterns for the common user interactions for those applications. Along the formal definition of the IOT extensions to the IFML language and the modelling of UI design patterns for the IOT.

3. BACKGOUND AND MOTIVATION

The traditional way of interacting with machines is through Interface that is called as Human Machine Interface(HMI). To optimize the industrial processes HMI technology is used by almost all industrial sectors as well as huge range of other companies.

But the consequences of using HMI came in front. It leads to loss of time, expensive and delicate to handle. We cannot be able to take the history of data or data analysis of HMI automatically. The only thing is that it will be showing the runtime data of the machine. HMI is used for once per machine which is quite hard to handle. Similarly in the world of automation it is also advantageous, if anybody can switch on/ off or monitor the machines from remote place. To overcome the consequences of HMI as well as to implement the concept of automation, There is a need to design an Interface through which it can be possible to monitor machines remotely.

4. METHODOLOGY

An interface or dashboard which creates a bridge between human beings and machines or device to connect them is known as Human-Machine Interface (HMI). Technically, the user interface helps in performing operations with the machine or the device. HMI is widely used in the field of textiles industry process. Sometimes HMI is referred as Man-Machine Interface (MMI), Operator Interface Terminal (OIT), Local Operator Interface (LOI) or Operator Terminal (OT) as HMI is very common in use. To optimize the industrial processes HMI technology is used by almost all industrial sectors as well as huge range of other companies.

HMI is in great use but the consequences of using HMI are that we have to work manually, we need to set the readings or parameters for each individual machine. For every individual machine we require individual HMI. Using this includes the high maintenance cost and every individual HMI cost higher. By using HMI, the user or operator cannot set the reading flexibly.

So to overcome all these issues of HMI, a portal has been designed through which user can handle the machines by online devices. It can be possible to set the parameters of the machines online from anywhere using this device. This portal will also include the history of the machines and its readings. All parameters can update regarding machines online only. It will reduce the maintenance cost as well the hardware cost. The user can continuously monitor the data of the machines from any device. The User has overall rights over the system and can moderate and delete any connected device over the portal.

Figure 2. Overall Architecture of single interface to handle data of multiple machines using IoT.

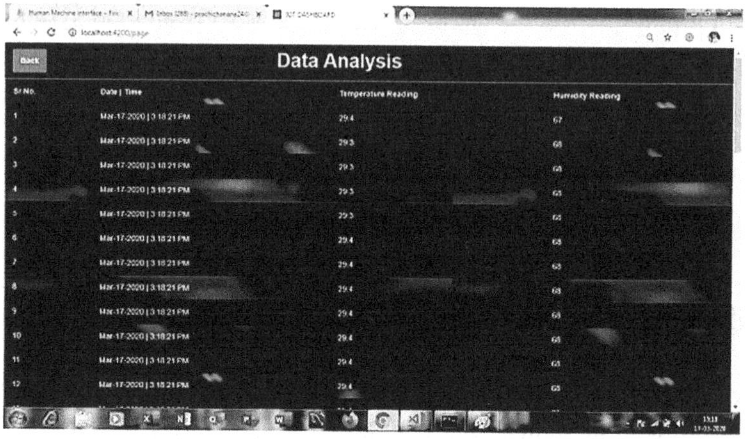

The above block diagram consists of overall architecture of Single Interface to Handle Data of Multiple Machines using IoT. It mainly has three parts hardware, database and IoT dashboard.

- Firebase is a Realtime database (considered as cloud) which is used to store the data fetched from the hardware.
- Hardware Device has many tools like arduino, microcontroller, node MCU, current sensor, voltage sensor, temperature sensor, power supply, PCB, connector for fetching the data from machine.
- IoT Dashboard is online web portal where the user can interact with hardware device by using it. It has a unique user ID and password for accessing it. The user can handle the hardware devices online only by using this web portal.

The terms depicted in above figure can be explained as follows.

Table 1. Input/output type

Input	100-240 VAC 50/60 Hz
Output Type	DC

4.1 Cloud Computing

• Traditionally business world (computing) requires hardware, operating system, application software and infrastructure. All these facilities require a specific well-trained staff worker to install, configure and maintain the system data and machine i.e. the hardware to overcome this need of expert staff, we developed a portal to do all these tasks of the expert to vanish its need. The data or the parameters which are set by the expert will later on get flexible the whole working of HMI will become remote with decrease in cost and space.

• The purpose of cloud computing is to store the run-time data in the cloud .So, for this purpose we are using the Firebase real-time database cloud storing which will store all the reading fetched form the hardware device via Wi-Fi module .The current run-time stored data then fetched by the IoT portal using Key-Value pairs.

• We are using Firebase real-time database as a cloud because it provides security to the data. It is the cloud which is developed by the Google so it is highly secure to store or retrieve any data from it.

4.2 The Hardware Device

In general the hardware device can be any machine in the industry which has to be connected with IOT dashboard. For implementation purpose, the hardware module is considered which consists of many tools such as:

1. Arduino: It is a prototype which is used to develop interactive hardware objects.
2. lC 7805: Voltage may differ or may have fluctuations and can lead to varying voltage outputs. The maintenance of output voltage at a fixed value is done by the voltage regulator IC . A member of 78xx series of fixed linear voltage regulators, i.e, 7805 IC, used to maintain such varying voltage fluctuations. The xx in 78xx points the voltage it provides.
3. LED: A semiconductor light source that emits light when current flows through it is known as light-emitting diode (LED) .
4. DHT 11: It is low-cost digital temperature and humidity sensor. To measure the surrounding air it uses a capacitive humidity sensor and a thermistor, and spits out a digital signal on the data pin.
5. Node MCU: It is an open-source development kit and firmware that helps to prototype or build loT products . The firmware runs on the ESP8266 Wi -Fi SoC if Systems, and hardware parts is based on t he ESP- 12 module.

12 V 1A DC Adapter is shown in Table 1.

4.3 IoT Dashboard

IOT dashboard is the key HMI (Human Machine Interface) component that organizes and presents digital information from our physical world into a simply understood display on a computer or mobile device.

- Here, the IOT dashboard works as the only medium to turn on/off the components (temperature or humidity) to load data, to change parameters, to analyze data, etc.
- As it is a single machine interface which can handle data of multiple machines, it is able to add new devices in the dashboard and also, we can run it on any device which increases the flexibility of the system for the user.
- The software portal is developed to retrieve information of the hardware from the cloud to the IoT dashboard which is not only use to display the data but also use to analyze the current active hardware device
- This portal provides you various options/pages to analyze the data such as add device, widgets, result and history.
- The add device page in the dashboard is use to add various devices of the hardware in the portal like temperature sensor, humidity sensor etc.
- The widgets page in the dashboard is use to view the various components that we have added through add device page. So now can have a display of current reading of that hardware with the help of gauge.
- The result page in the dashboard is use to show which hardware device is currently sending data to the portal that is which device is currently active or not.
- The history page in the dashboard is use to analyze the current data of the hardware that is which reading is actively fetched by the software and also store the history of previous readings with a particular date and time of change for the same.

4.4 Data Analysis

The data analysis part includes the data processing and handling function. The data processing and handling is done with the help of Firebase Real-time Database. A database of the hardware is pushed on the cloud with the help of the Wi-Fi module included in IoT. With the help of firebase real-time database, the data is fetched on the IoT portal using a key generated by firebase. The database includes all the current and previous data and the same data is displayed on the IoT dashboard.

4.5 Description About Working of Portal

- Everytime a user login on the IoT dashboard authentication is done with the help of firebase realtime database. If a user is not registered new registration have to be done by the user. The user data while registering on the portal is saved on the database of firebase.
- After logging in on the IoT dashboard all the features Like Home, add devices, History, and result is there.
- In add devices page there are number of widgets through which we can add multiple components at a time After adding components all the monitoring and analysis is done here.

- During this adding of devices or components, they can be turned on or off according to the need of the user. When the Widgets of the components are enabled along with the hardware connectivity the current reading of the devices is displayed. When the components disabled they show the previous readings .
- A History page is there which is used to keep track of the previous data of the devices when they are enabled and on which date and day. This helps the user to change the parameters accordingly.
- Lastly, result page displays the overall activity of the components and which device is on.

The core functions which are described here as follows:

1. Add Devices

The Add devices function is a function which is used by the owner or the one who is handling the IOT dashboard of the hardware.

To implement this function Angular 6+ is used as a front end developer and firebase realtime database as a backend tool.

The major dependencies to implement this are:

```
fixture = TestBed.createComponent(AdddeviceComponent);
component = fixture.componentInstance;
fixture.detectChanges();
```

This function helps the admin to add types of devices according to the need of the user and the machines. Therefore add devices plays a vital role in implementation of any new device.

2. Add Widgets

The Add Widgets is the page where the user can add features of their device in the IoT dashboard. To implement this function Angular 6+ is used as a front end developer and firebase realtime database as a backend tool .

The major dependencies to implement this project are:

```
1. import { CircularGaugeComponent, ILoadedEventArgs, GaugeTheme } from '@syncfusion/ej2-angular-circulargauge';
2. import { Slider, SliderChangeEventArgs } from '@syncfusion/ej2-inputs';
```

These dependences plays a major role to implement the widgets on the portal. The **syncfusion/ej2** is the core dependency which help us to implement the necessary widgets which is required for hardware analysis and adjustment .

Through this dependency the user can now see the widgets on the portal and andand also make changes on the module and have current reading of the hardware device such as temperature, humidity, battery and switch to on/off a particular component of machine.

Figure 3. Device Status

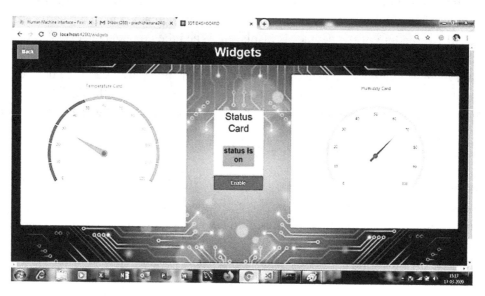

As shown in above fig 3, the user can see the status of machine that is which is currently active and which is not. Similarly it notifies the device status in Table 2.

Table 2. Device Status (Active/ Inactive)

Sr. No	Name	IP Address	Status
1	Iot Advance	198.162.13.02	Active
2	Arduino	198.162.13.12	Deactivate

3. Data Analysis Page

In data analysis, the user can have a watch on pervious as well as current reading of the hardware .This page will provide the user to access the runtime data analysis of the machine. To implement this function we have used Angular 6+ as a front end developing tool and firebase realtime database as a backend tool .

The data is been fetched form the cloud that is the firebase realtime database using a key value pair of the following data which is been stored in the database through the cloud.

The key value pairs are present in the database as:

```
Ex: DHT111
- Device
-M2Gp00_uHRBkA2oq-Y9
-humidity:67
-temperature:29.4
```

Table 3 shows how data will be displayed.

Table 3. Analysis Table (Readings)

Sr No	Date	Time	Temperature Reading	Humidity Reading
1.	Mar-5-2020 |05:02:03 AM	23	66
2.	Mar-5-2020 |08:19:05 AM	25	75
3.	Mar-6-2020 |12:11:01 PM	26.3	65
4.	Mar-6-2020 |12:45:15 PM	27	80

The data analysis page depicts the readings of machines. For developing this application only two parameters were considered but more parameters can also be added. Table 3 shows the temperature and humidity timely status of the machines.

SUMMARY

Creating an interface using IOT is used to reduce the cost of HMI. This will also increase the flexibility of operating machines from any where the user is or the user will be. The users can operate the machines using the application and is able to send the commands like on or off with the help of Internet. The wi-fi module of IOT plays the major role of sending and receiving the data. This system will also help the users to have a record of the past data and the parameters of the machines. Using this the users can observe the readings and also they can check which parameters they have to change to let the machine work better than before. As the use of this system increase, the need of HMI will be going to be vanished and as a result a flexible cost-effective system will come into existence.

REFERENCES

Al-Fuqaha, Guizani, Mohammadi, Aledhari, & Ayyash. (2015). Internet of Things: A Survey onEnabling Technologies, Protocols and Applications. *IEEE Communications Surveys & Tutorials*.

Bauskar & Pujari. (2016). A Review on Industrial Automation Using IOT. *International Research Journal of Engineering and Technology, 3*(12).

Brambilla, M., Umuhoza, E., & Acerbis, R. (2017). Model-driven development of user interfaces for IoT systems via domain-specific components and patterns. *Journal of Internet Services and Applications, 8*(1), 14. doi:10.118613174-017-0064-1

Ektapure & Ingale. (2016). Android based interactive Home Automation System through Internet of Things. *International Journal of Advanced Research in Electronics and Communication Engineering, 5*(4).

Gubbi, J., Buyya, R., Marusic, S., & Palaniswami, M. (2013). Internet ofThings (IoT): A vision, architectural elements, and future directions. *Future Generation Computer Systems, 29*(7), 1645–1660. doi:10.1016/j.future.2013.01.010

Normanyo, Husinu, & Agyare. (2014). Developing a Human Machine Interface (HMI) for Industrial Automated Systems using Siemens Simatic WinCC Flexible Advanced Software. *Journal of Emerging Trends in Computing and Information Sciences, 5*(2).

Nuamah, J. (2017, June). Human Machine Interface in the Internet of Things (IoT). *International Journal of Latest Technology in Engineering, Management & Applied Sciences.*

Patole, Shide, Salve, Kaushik, & Puri. (2017). IOT based Vehicle Tracking & Vehicular Emergency System- A Case Study and Review. *International Journal of Advanced Research in Electrical, Electronics and Instrumentation Engineering, 6*(10).

Sharma & Tiwari. (2016). A review paper on "IOT" & It's Smart Applications. *International Journal of Science, Engineering and Technology Research, 5*(2).

Shrestha, Mali, Joseph, Singh, & Raj. (2017). Web and Android based Automation using IoT. *International Journal of Latest Technology in Engineering, Management & Applied Science, 6*(5).

Sruthi & Kavitha. (2016). A survey on IoT platform. *International Journal of Scientific Research and Modern Education, 1*(1).

Vaishnavi & Gaikwad. (2017). Water Quality Monitoring System Based onIOT. *Advances in Wireless and Mobile Communications, 10*(5).

Chapter 12
An Investigation for Cellular Automata–Based Lightweight Data Security Model Towards Possible Uses in Fog Networks

Arnab Mitra

iD https://orcid.org/0000-0002-7382-089X
Siksha 'O' Anusandhan (Deemed), India

Sayantan Saha

iD https://orcid.org/0000-0003-4854-4704
Siksha 'O' Anusandhan (Deemed), India

ABSTRACT

A lightweight data security model is of much importance in view of security and privacy of data in several networks (e.g., fog networks) where available computing units at edge nodes are often constrained with low computing capacity and limited storage/availability of energy. To facilitate lightweight data security at such constrained scenarios, cellular automata (CA)-based lightweight data security model is presented in this chapter to enable low-cost physical implementation. For this reason, a detailed investigation is presented in this chapter to explore the potential capabilities of CA-based scheme towards the design of lightweight data security model. Further, a comparison among several existing lightweight data security models ensure the effectiveness for proposed CA-based lightweight data security model. Thus, application suitability in view of fog networks is explored for the proposed CA-based model which has further potential for easy training of a reservoir of computers towards uses in IoT (internet of things)-based multiple industry applications.

DOI: 10.4018/978-1-7998-7511-6.ch012

1. INTRODUCTION

With the advances in computing technologies, the simple computing by a single computing unit has been transformed into today's advanced computing technologies, which are often being performed by several computing devices in a co-operation and may be situated over different locations. Among several advanced computing paradigms, Fog Computing has recently gained attention and popularity among researchers and practitioners for its potential advantages towards modelling of several IoT (Internet of Things)-based real life and industry applications (Mitra et al., 2019). The concept of Fog Computing describes it as a distributed computing where "resources and application services are used in logically efficient places from data source to cloud" (Saha et al., 2019a). As presented in (Saha et al., 2019b), it is found that the MEC (Mobile Edge computing, is used to process task over cloud by running a cloud server), MCC (Mobile Cloud computing, where mobile Cloud Applications store data in cloud (i.e., outer side with reference to the mobile device) after data processing) etc are similar concepts with reference to the concept of Fog Computing. A typical workflow between the Fog, Cloud and Computing Devices is presented in Figure 1 (Figure 1 is inspired from (Saha et al., 2019a)).

Figure 1. Typical workflow between the Fog, Cloud and Computing Devices

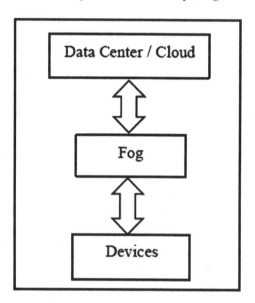

As mentioned earlier, several researchers at present days have focused on the enhanced design of Fog computing network to enhance the efficiency and service quality. In our studies we found research have focused on several aspects in Fog networks e.g., on the design of an enhanced Fog network architecture (Bonomi et al., 2012; Khakimov et al., 2012; and Saha et al., 2019b), data security (Suo et al., 2012; Ni et al., 2017; and Mitra et al., 2019), design of energy optimized algorithm (Saha et al., 2019a) etc. Further the role of Fog computing in IoT-based applications was examined in (Bonomi et al., 2012) by Bonomi et al. Though several research areas are present, we focused on data security in Fog network.

In our studies we found that conventional data security (authentication and cryptography) approaches are not well suited for IoT/ Fog computing-based applications. Conventional data security approaches require a high power of computation and hence requires a high amount of power and high volume of memory (Mitra et al., 2019). Previously with the same focus, uses of lightweight cryptography in lieu of existing conventional cryptography were described in (Eisenbarth et al., 2007; and Buchanan et al., 2017), several lightweight authentications were presented in (Vajda et al., 2003; Gilbart et al., 2005) towards IoT/Fog computing-based applications.

At the same time, Green Computing and sustainability is one of major concern among researchers, which primarily focus on the minimization of energy consumption. Several approaches towards Green Computing in Cloud may be found in (Mitra et al., 2017b; Mitra 2019). To facilitate, energy efficient physical modelling researchers have presented Cellular Automata (CA) (Chaudhuri et al., 1997) based design (Nandi et al., 1994; Chaudhuri et al., 1997; Vajda et al. 2003; Gilbart et al., 2005; Mitra et al., 2017b; and Mitra, 2019) towards several engineering applications in Distributed Computing environment. In our studies, we found that CA-based several lightweight cryptosystems were investigated in (Nandi et al., 1994; Ojha et al., 2009; Tripathy et al., 2009; and Mitra et al. 2017a), further several lightweight CA-based authentications were investigated and presented in (Shemaili et al., 2014; and Mariot et al., 2019). A brief discussion on CA is presented next.

CA is a dynamic modelling tool which advance over discrete time and discrete space. Elementary CA (ECA) are known as simple CA configuration consisting three cells in single-dimension, three neighbourhood (left and right neighbour and self-cell) at fixed / periodic boundary condition (Chaudhuri et al., 1997). The next state of a cell in ECA configuration at time t is determined by a function (known as CA rule, also known as Wolfram CA rules, total 256 rules), $x_i^{t+1} = f\left(x_{i-1}^t, x_i^t, x_{i+1}^t\right)$ where at time t, x_{i-1}^t indicates value at left cell, x_i^t indicates value at self-cell, x_{i+1}^t value at right cell and x_i^{t+1} indicates the value of a cell at time $\left(t+1\right)$ (Chaudhuri et al., 1997). A typical ECA configuration is presented in Figure 2.

Figure 2. Schematic diagram for ECA configuration

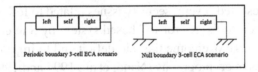

The reader(s) of this chapter is(are) requested to go through (Chaudhuri et al., 1997) to have more details of CA and its dynamics.

In our studies, we found several lightweight cryptography and authentication approaches were presented by researchers. Unfortunately, we have not found any literature towards the implementation of complete lightweight data security involving both authentication and cryptography approaches in an energy efficient low-cost physical modelling for multiple users (available several computing units in any interconnected architecture). We trust that a low energy consuming and simple modelling towards lightweight data security at low-cost physical implementation capability should always have a privilege towards implementation of Green Computing in Fog Networks. For this reason, we further investigated the CA based modelling towards lightweight data security in Fog Networks of (Mitra et al., 2019) to explore its true potential for the consideration as a Green approach.

Major contributions of this chapter are as followed.

1. A theoretical background is presented to explore the inherent efficiencies (if any) for CA-based modelling of complete data security in Fog networks;
2. complete data security scheme involves authentication and cryptography;
3. an easy and cost-efficient CA based multi-user authentication scheme as a lightweight authentication approach is presented and analysed;
4. a simple CA based cryptography scheme as a lightweight cryptography approach is presented and analysed;
5. low-energy requirement for CA based data security modelling in Fog Networks is confirmed.

Rest of the chapter organization is as followed. State-of-the-art literatures are briefly discussed in Section 2; background is briefly presented in Section 3; proposed work and an empirical analysis are presented in Section 4; experimental result and analytical discussions are in Section 5; finally concluding remarks are presented in Section 6.

2. RELATED WORKS

Fog Computing is most frequently considered as a progress of Cloud Computing to help location recognition, heterogeneity, low-latency, mobility, real-time uses etc. with the help of an exceptionally large number of components (nodes). Hence, quite a lot of IoT-based applications such as Smart City applications, Smart Grids, wireless sensor and actuators networks (WSANs)-based applications, industry applications etc. are often well suited to be modelled with Fog Computing (Khakimov et al., 2012; and Mitra et al., 2019). In IoT and Fog computing, data mobility plays a significant role. Unfortunately, at the same time data mobility between several nodes of such network potentially strive from data security and privacy issues (Bonomi et al., 2012; Khakimov et al., 2012; and Mitra et al., 2019). To deal with such scenario, researchers presented several security issues related to IoT. Among numerous efforts, we found a detailed survey on security issues for IoT-based system by Suo et al. in (Suo et al., 2012), and by Ni et al. in (Ni et al., 2017). To overcome the said deficit and to improve data security and privacy, researchers suggested the uses of cryptography (Nandi et al., 1994 and 1997) and authentication (Mitra et al., 2017a) schemes. Though we found that conventional data security and authentication approaches are not well suited for IoT / Fog Computing networks (Vajda et al., 2003; and Buchanan et al., 2017) "due to a high constraint on limited availability of power (from energy source) and processing power" (Mitra et al., 2019). To overcome the said restriction researchers have presented lightweight cryptography (Eisenbarth et al., 2007; and Buchanan et al., 2017) and lightweight authentication scheme (Vajda et al., 2003; and Gilbert et al., 2005).

On the other hand, CA-based dynamic modelling is quite popular among researchers. Several CA-based models were presented by researchers since past for many complex and dynamic problems (Nandi et al., 1994; Chaudhuri et al., 1997; Nandi et al., 1997; Mitra et al., 2017a and b; Mitra, 2019). CA-based cryptography was presented in (Nandi et al., 1994 and 1997); CA-based multi-user authentication was also presented in (Mitra et al., 2017a). We further found, "CA-based components are regular, modular and cascadeable structures the proposed scheme can be easily realized in hardware" (Tripathy et al., 2009). Thus, several researchers have presented several CA-based lightweight cryptographies, CA-based lightweight authentication schemes. Among several others, LCASE (Lightweight CA-based Symmetric-key Encryption) model was presented in (Tripathy et al., 2009), "TWIS" (Ojha et al, 2009) model (an enhanced version over existing "CLEFIA" (Ojha et al, 2009)) was presented in (Ojha et al, 2009). Another CA-based lightweight stream cipher was presented in (Shemaili et al., 2014) to "enhance LFSR (Linear Feedback Shift Register), Feed Carry Shift Register (FCSR) within the Shrinking Generator stream cipher" (Shemaili et al., 2014).

A regular inspection of the CA-based S-box cryptographic properties was presented in (Mariot et al., 2019). Besides the efforts on CA-based lightweight cryptographies, we also find efforts by researchers towards lightweight authentications (Mihaljevic et al., 2008; and Shin et al., 2012). CA-based multi-user authentication scheme using OTP (one-time password) was presented in (Shin et al., 2012). In our studies (Mihaljevic et al., 2008; Katagi et al., 2008; Ojha et al., 2009; Tripathy et al., 2009; Morrell, 2012; Shin et al., 2012; Shemaili et al., 2014; Mariot et al., 2019; and Mitra et al., 2017a), we found that randomness and prime number may play a crucial role in lightweight cryptography and lightweight authentication. Hence, few efforts towards CA-based models towards the data security and privacy is presented next.

Cost-effective CA-based Prime (randomly distributed set of Primes) generation was presented in (Mitra et al., 2013) which was further used to enhance the data security and privacy (Mitra et al., 2015; and Mitra, 2018). A detailed investigation in (Mitra et al., 2015) concluded that the sequence behaves as "more or less uniform noise" (Mitra et al., 2015) "with a tendency of "weak periodicity" ..." (Mitra et al., 2015). Besides, the investigations of (Mitra et al., 2017b; and Mitra, 2019) explored the true potential of CA as a green model in Cloud environment. Based on the reference works of (Oskuii, 2004; Mehta et al., 2011), it was concluded in (Mitra et al., 2017b; and Mitra, 2019) that CA-based model (D flip-flops (FFs)) requires a very low-power consumption. Power consumption for FFs at $1.0\, v_{dd}$ in $0.13\mu m$ CMOS technology as discussed in (Mitra et al., 2017b; and Mitra, 2019) is presented in following Figure 3.

Figure 3. Range of power consumption for CA blocks (FFs) at physical level

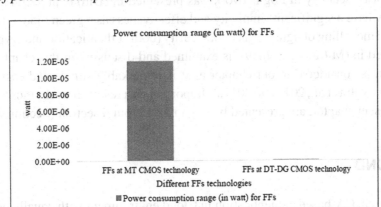

From Figure 3 and (Mitra et al., 2017b; and Mitra, 2019), it is observed that minimum and maximum power consumption ranges from $1.17E-07$ watt to $1.20E-05$ watt for different CMOS technology based FFs, which is very low with respect to the total amount of power consumption.

On the other hand, now a days Deep Learning technique are quite popular among researchers. Several applications have been developed by researchers using deep learning techniques. Among several others security and privacy applications with deep learning techniques are particularly interesting (Abeshu et al., 2018; and Liao et al., 2019): a distributed deep learning approach towards cyber-attacks detection was presented in (Abeshu et al., 2018); further a deep learning-based authentication framework in physical layer was presented in (Liao et al., 2019). Besides, integration of CA with deep learning approaches have also been presented by researchers to enhance the efficiencies for several scientific applications (Nichele et al., 2017; He et al., 2018; Babson et al., 2019; Ou et al., 2019; Tangsakul et al., 2020; and Xing et al, 2020). Designs for CA-based reservoirs towards reservoir computing (which facilitates deep learning approaches) were presented in (Nichile et al., 2017; and Babson et al., 2019). Besides several integration of CAs with supervised and or, unsupervised deep learning approach were presented in (He et al., 2018; Ou et al., 2019; Tangsakul et al., 2020; and Xing et al., 2020). In our studies we have found that though deep learning techniques with or, without combination with CAs may enhance results and efficiencies at a significant level. On the other hand, layerd (deep) Reservoir computers (i.e., CAs as presented in (Nichile et al., 2017; and Babson et al., 2019)) are easy to train and further it is having an advantage towards on-chip implementation at tiny sized IoT modules/nodes (please recall that CAs are VLSI (Very Large-Scale Integration) compatible (Chaudhuri et al., 1997)).

On conclusion, we realized that a low power consuming physical modelling of lightweight data security technique may have advantages in Fog Network. Irrespective of our hard efforts we have not found literature(s) focused on the physical modelling of an energy-efficient and complete data security (i.e., inclusion of both authentication and cryptography in same design) in Fog Network. Though, CA-based lightweight cryptography and OTP-based authentication using CA was presented in (Mitra et al., 2017a) and (Shin et al., 2012) respectively, we found equally populated set of random OTPs for multi-user authentication was not presented in (Shin et al., 2012); further prime number-based a simple cryptography was not found in (Mitra et al., 2019). Besides, several other lightweight security models were presented by researchers (Lee et al., 2014; Diro et al., 2017; and Lu et al., 2017); among those efforts, an elliptic curve-based security in Fog network was presented in (Diro et al., 2017). We believe, said considerations may have a significant simplicity and effectiveness as a green model. For this reason, an alternate CA-based modelling of lightweight data security (both authentication and cryptography in same design) as presented in (Mitra et al., 2019), is examined and discussed in this chapter. Null-boundary ECA configuration is considered in our chapter as it is remarkably simple and easy to implement in physical modelling (Mitra et al., 2013 and 2017a). Important past research works those have significantly influenced our present chapter, are presented briefly in background section (Section 3).

3. BACKGROUND

In a different research, CA-based authentication in Cloud environment with equally populated and randomly distributed set of OTPs (one-time passwords) was offered in (Mitra et al., 2017a). An analysis verified that the characteristics polynomial involved towards the generation of OTPs was primitive or, primitive-recursive in nature (characteristics polynomial was $(1 + x)$ or, $(1 + x)^n$). Further p-value analysis obtained from statistical RUNs test confirmed the presence of randomness in all produced set of OTPs using CA. In an additional research, generation of set of Primes (randomly populated) was presented with CA (Mitra et al., 2013 and 2017a). In (Mitra et al., 2015), time complexity involved with the generation of set of Primes was found to be $O\big(n\big) + O\big(k * \log^2 n\big)$. With the involvement of existing CA-based authentication as presented in (Mitra et al., 2017a) and set of primes generation (Mitra et al., 2013), a lightweight data security model was further presented in (Mitra et al., 2019). The lightweight data security of (Mitra et al., 2019) is explained briefly next.

The lightweight complete data security in Fog networks in (Mitra et al., 2019) is modularized into two modules: i) an equally populated set of OTP-based multi-user authentication with a null-boundary ECA scenario, and ii) a prime number (achieved from CA-based randomly populated set of Primes)-based cryptography. Proposed authentication approach authenticates sender(s) using one OTP at each time strap (dependent on internal clock of the system). Only authenticated sender(s) is(are) then allowed to encrypt message using one key (a prime number selected from the randomly populated set of Primes based again on internal clock of the system). Encrypted message along with time strap value is transferred to the receiver side and receiver finds the decryption key from the randomly populated set of Primes using received time value; and performs the decryption. The simple lightweight data security model as presented in (Mitra et al., 2019) is diagrammatically presented in following Figure 4.

Figure 4. An overview for CA-based lightweight data security

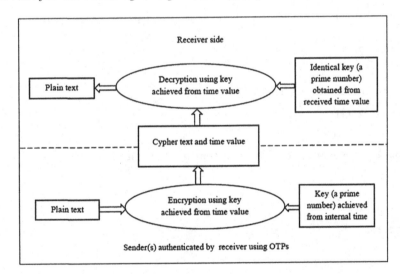

We found that a lightweight data security approach in Fog network using CA, involving both authentication and cryptography was introduced in (Mitra et al., 2019). Unfortunately, a detailed investigation is still required to explore its true potential to be considered as a green model in Fog network. Hence, an empirical analysis is presented next.

Algorithm 1. CA-based_lightweight_complete_data_security

```
Input: Number of CA cells (n), CA rules (r)
Output: Equally populated set of OTPs (m), randomly distributed set of Primes (p)
void CA-based_lightweight_ data_security ()
{
    CA_cells = n; // Initialize the number of cells for CA configuration
/* Equally populated set of OTPs generation and distribution for authentication*/
OTPs = Authentication(n, m);
for (i = 1; i < = m; i ++)
{
message[i] = OTPs[i]; //Assign one OTP set to one message
for (j = 1; j < = (n - m); j ++)
{
OTP[j] = OTP_list[i]; // Assign OTPs at sender and receiver
}
}
t = clock(); //present system clock value
OTP_authenticate(OTP, t);
/* Randomly distributed set of Primes generation and distribution for cryptography*/
key = primes(n)
for (i=0; i<n; i++)
{
key[i] = primes[n];
}
for (i = 1; i < = n; i ++)
{
key[i] = primes[i]; //Assign keys to sender and receiver
}
t = clock(); //Receive present system clock value
encryption (); //Encryption of message using prime number based on t
communicate (encrypted message, t);
decryption_at_receiver (); //Decryption of message using prime number based on t
}

void Authentication (n, m)
{
    for (i = 1; i < = n; i ++)
{
CA_cell [i] = r; // Initialize CA rules
q = pow(2, n);
for (q = 1; q < = n; q ++)
{
for (m = 1; m < = (n-1); m ++)
{
temp_states = pow(2, m) * pow(2, (q - m)) // Generate OTP sets
}
}
if (temp_states = = q)
{
for (i = 1; i < = m; i ++)
{
return (temp_states);
}
}
}
}

void Primes (n)
{
    for (i = 1; i < = n; i ++)
{
CA_cell [i] = r; // Initialize CA rules
q = pow(2, n);
for (q = 1; q < = n; q ++)
{
for (m = 1; m < = (n-1); m ++)
{
temp_states = set_of_primes(n) // Generate Primes set
}
}
return (temp_states);
}
}
```

Table 1. A detailed comparison between several CA-based authentication

CA-based Lightweight Authentication	Support for Multi-user	Support for Multisession	Number of Set of OTPs	Number of OTPs in Each Set	Time Complexity	Assurance for Randomness Among OTPs
HB#-like low complexity authentication scheme (Mihaljevic et al., 2008).	Not available.	Not available.	Not available.	Not available.	Not found, it was mentioned that the time complexity of HB#-like is higher than of the time complexity of original HB#.	Uses of response vector consisting effective bits and dummy bits embedded in pseudorandom way, ensured randomness.
CA-based a multi-user authentication scheme (Shin et al., 2012).	Yes.	Not available.	Not available.	Not available.	Not available	Diehard test results were provided to ensure randomness.
CA-based equally populated and randomly distributed set of OTP-based authentication scheme (Mitra et al., 2017 a).	Yes.	Yes.	Controllable.	Controllable.	$\sum O(m_i)$ where i stands for number of OTP set and m denotes the number of members in each set.	Characteristics polynomial for generation of set of OTPs found to primitive (or, recursive-primitive) which ensures randomness. Additionally, statistical results involving RUNs test, Diehard tests were also presented in (Mitra et al., 2017a).

4. PROPOSED WORK AND EMPIRICAL ANALYSIS

It was already presented that CA-based design towards Reservoir computers enjoys the advantage of easy training for layered (deep) networks (Nichile et al., 2017; and Babson et al., 2019). Thus, proposed CA-based design should also be easily used towards deep architecture-based trainings. A new algorithm (Algorithm 1) was designed to facilitate CA-based complete lightweight data security in Fog Networks. Algorithm 1 is inspired from (Mitra et al., 2017a).

For simplicity, we only presented algorithmic part involving CA-based patterns only; for encryption and decryption we followed available standard process.

It is already presented, several CA-based lightweight cryptographies (Ojha et al., 2009; Tripathy et al., 2009; Shemaili et al., 2014; and Mariot et al., 2019) and CA-based lightweight authentication approaches (Mihaljevic et al., 2008; and Shin et al., 2012) may be found in literature. Unfortunately, the approaches as presented in (Ojha et al., 2009; Tripathy et al., 2009; Shemaili et al., 2014; and Mariot et al., 2019; Mihaljevic et al., 2008; and Shin et al., 2012) were considering either lightweight cryptography or the lightweight authentication for a system. For this reason, a lightweight complete data security system involving both authentication and cryptography was proposed in (Mitra et al., 2019) which uses CA generated patterns for OTP based multi-user authentication for multisession, and a simple prime number-based cryptography (refer Figure 4). A detailed analysis related to the inherent efficiencies for the model of (Mitra et al., 2019) is presented next in following three sub sections.

4.1. An Investigation on Different CA-based Lightweight Authentications

Comparative results as explored from the studies of several CA-based lightweight authentication are presented in Table 1.

It is observed from Table 1 that the time complexity associated with OTP based authentication of (Mitra et al., 2017a) is $\sum O\left(m_i\right)$; further the same technique is capable to produce equally populated set of random OTPs which is capable to be used for multi-user authentication at multi-sessions and easy to be physically modelled to achieve low power consumption.

4.2. An Investigation Towards Different CA-based Lightweight Cryptography Approaches

Comparative results as explored from the studies of several CA-based lightweight cryptographic approaches are presented in Table 2.

Table 2. An overview for several CA-based lightweight cryptographies

CA-based Lightweight Cryptographic Approach	Remarks
LCASE model was presented in (Tripathy et al., 2009).	A lightweight block cipher scheme towards AES (Advanced Encryption Standard).
TWIS model was presented in (Ojha et al., 2009).	An enhanced version over existing CLEFIA model.
CA-based lightweight stream cipher (Shemaili et al., 2014).	It was presented to improve LFSR (Linear Feedback Shift Register), Feed Carry Shift Register (FCSR).
CA-based S-box cryptography techniques (Mariot et al., 2019).	A survey paper towards several S-box cryptographic approaches.

It is observed from Table 2 that existing CA-based lightweight cryptography approaches are primarily focused towards block and stream cipher. Unfortunately, lightweight cryptography using prime number has not been considered in (Ojha et al., 2009; Tripathy et al., 2009; Shemaili et al., 2014; and Mariot et al., 2019; Mihaljevic et al., 2008; and Shin et al., 2012). Elliptic curve-based security in Fog network was presented in (Diro et al., 2017). As elliptic curve-based security concerns with large Prime was

Table 3. A comparison between approaches towards generation of Prime number

Prime Number Finding Approach	Physical Modelling Compatibility	Time Complexity
Elliptic Curves based Prime finding was presented in (Morrell, 2012).	Not addressed.	$O\left(n^4\right)$
Randomly distributed set of Primes presented in (Mitra et al., 2013).	Yes, with D FFs as it was an approach with CA.	$O\left(n\right) + O\left(k * \log^2 n\right)$

presented in (Diro et al., 2017), hence a brief discussion related to different prime finding approaches are presented in next subsection.

Table 4. Data achieved with CA simulation towards Algorithm 1

	Automata Size	Rule	Set Members (in Sequence)	Remarks
Randomly distributed set of Primes towards uses in lightweight cryptography	3	<110, 110, 204>	{3, 7, 5}	One set of randomly sequenced primes with 3 distinct prime numbers as cryptographic keys for 3 different sessions.
	4	<110, 110, 110, 204>	{3, 7, 13, 11}	One set of randomly sequenced primes with 4 distinct prime numbers as cryptographic keys for 4 different sessions.
Set of OTPs towards OTP-based authentications (multi-users, multi-sessions lightweight authentication)	3	<153, 153, 153>	{0, 7, 6, 5} {1, 4, 3, 2}	Two different sets of randomly sequenced OTPs with 4 distinct passwords for 4 different sessions for 2 distinct users.
	4	<153, 153, 153, 153>	{0, 15, 14, 13, 8, 7, 6, 5} {1, 12, 11, 2, 9, 4, 3, 10}	Two different sets of randomly sequenced OTPs with 8 distinct passwords for 8 different sessions for 2 distinct users.
	3	<51, 51, 51>	{0, 7} {1, 6} {2, 5} {3, 4}	Four different sets of randomly sequenced OTPs with 2 distinct passwords for 2 different sessions for 4 distinct users.
	4	<51, 51, 51, 51>	{0, 15} {1, 14} {2, 13} {3, 12} {4, 11} {5, 10} {6, 9} {7, 8}	Eight different sets of randomly sequenced OTPs with 2 distinct passwords for 2 different sessions for 8 distinct users.

4.3. An Investigation on Different Prime Number Finding Approaches

Comparative results as explored from the studies of several prime number finding approaches are presented in Table 3.

It is observed from Table 3 that randomly distributed set of primes generation as presented in (Mitra et al., 2013) is benefited with better time complexity with reference to the elliptic curve based prime finding approach of (Morrell, 2012); and further it is capable to be modelled with FFs to achieve low power consumption.

5. EXPERIMENTAL RESULTS AND ANALYTICAL DISCUSSIONS

A simulation result towards Algorithm 1 is presented next. For simplicity, we have reported the simulation result in following Table 4 for automata size 3 and 4 (as an instance for odd and even size) only.

Pseudo-randomness (randomness) for achieved patterns from CAs towards uses in lightweight data security were presented in following Figure 5. For simplicity, we considered patterns obtained from several CA sizes (from CA size 3 to CA size 7); both types of patterns (i.e. patterns from CAs with characteristics polynomial $(1+x)$ and patterns from CAs with characteristics polynomial $\left[(1+x)^n\right]$ were considered in our analysis. We considered uniform (homogeneous) CAs with rule 51 towards CAs with characteristics polynomial $(1+x)$ and uniform (homogeneous) CAs with rule 195 towards CAs with characteristics polynomial $(1+x)^n$ in our analysis. In Figure 5, X-axis represents number of states and Y-axis represents state values in decimal number.

Figure 5. Pseudo-randomness in CA generated patterns at several CA size

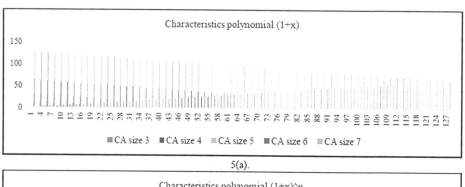

5(a).

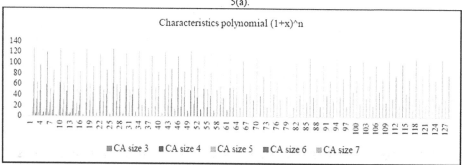

5(b).

Achieved patterns from CAs towards uses in lightweight data security were further investigated through RUNs test (a statistical test suit to achieve the quality/degree of randomness for an associated pattern) (Mitra et al., 2017a; "http://www.statstutor.ac.uk/resources/uploaded/pearsons.pdf" and "https://home.ubalt.edu/ntsbarsh/business-stat/otherapplets/Randomness.htm"). The Runs test results in (Mitra et al., 2017a) showed that randomness was presented in generated set of OTPs; further the characteristics polynomial for the CA-based multi-user authentication using linear CA rules as discussed in (Mitra et

Figure 6. Time complexity for CA-based lightweight data security

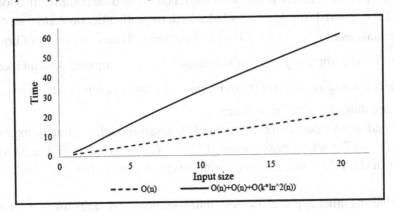

al., 2017a) was found to be a primitive or, recursive-primitive in nature, which is a necessary criterion for randomness in generated pattern at $\sum O\left(m_i\right)$ time complexity (Mitra et al., 2017a). The characteristics polynomial as found in (Mitra et al., 2017a) is $\left(1+x\right)$ or, $\left(1+x\right)^n$. It is confirmed in "https://mathworld.wolfram.com/PrimitivePolynomial.html" that the irreducible (primitive) polynomial over $GF\left(2\right)$ may be used to produce pseudo-random bit from n former ones. Hence, randomness is assured in generated set of OTPs. Additionally, the correlation and FFT (Fast Fourier Transform) spectrum analysis in (Mitra, 2016) ensures that the same type sequence is potentially capable to be used as an efficient pseudo-random noise generator (PRNG). In our studies, we did not find presence of other method(s) to generate equally populated set of OTPs / patterns. Hence, performance of such patterns was compared with several other hardware-based approaches (e.g., linear feed-back shift register (LFSR), CA-based maximum length cycle (MaxCA) pattern) and found to be superior in quality with comparison to the said approaches (Mitra, 2016). Please recall that only a single cycle of length $\left(2^n-1\right)$ may be achieved with LFSR or, MaxCA, which might be used as a single set of random OTPs /patterns. Reader(s) may further go through the detailed analysis of (Mitra, 2016) to know further. Thus, a high quality of randomness may be assured with such set of OTPs.

On the other hand, the randomly distributed set of Primes generation in ECA scenario was presented in (Mitra et al., 2013; Mitra, 2018) with a time complexity of $O\left(n\right)+O\left(k*\log^2 n\right)$ (Mitra et al., 2015). Quality of the prime generating CA pattern was explored in (Mitra et al., 2015) using several signal analysis techniques and found to be a source for uniform noise. Thus, said patterns may be used in case of data security. Unfortunately, we did not find other CA-based approach(es) towards generation of set of Primes with random distribution. Hence, we were unable to proceed performance comparison with respect to generation of randomly distributed set of Primes.

It is explored from Section 4 that, total time complexity associated with proposed CA-based lightweight data security involving both authentication and cryptography includes the time complexities of (Mitra et al., 2017a) and (Mitra et al., 2013), i.e., the total time complexity $f\left(t\right)$ is,

$$f\left(t\right)=\sum O\left(m_i\right)+O\left(n\right)+O\left(k*\log^2 n\right) \tag{1}$$

We believe, is very much acceptable one with reference to the time complexities for other approaches (refer Table 1, Table 2 and Table 3) as it includes both the authentication and data cryptography. For simplification, we considered $\sum O(m_i) \approx O(n)$ in Equation 1. Time complexity of Equation 1 is further shown in Figure 6. Time complexity $f(t)$ of Equation 1 is also compared with an ideal time complexity $O(n)$ in Figure 6, and explored that $f(t)$ of Equation 1 is most similar to the growth as $O(n)$, which is most desirable and thus, describes its efficiency.

On the other hand, power consumption for the CA-based model, is already explored in the range (minimum of $1.17E - 07$ watt to maximum of $1.20E - 05$ watt) (refer Figure 3). Hence, an energy modelling is confirmed for the said CA-based complete data security approach involving authentication a cryptography.

As we did not find any other approach towards multi-sessions and multi-users compatible lightweight complete data security (i.e., involving both authentication and cryptography) model at low-cost physical modelling capability, we have not presented any comparative data related to its performance.

6. CONCLUSION AND FUTURE WORK

Presented empirical analyses explore that proposed CA-based architectures towards multi-user authentications in multi-sessions and cryptography, both enjoy a competitive time-complexity as compared to several other existing approaches. Further, power consumption at the physical implementation level of the CA-based architecture is predicted to be very low (only in the range of $1.17E - 07$ watt to $1.20E - 05$ watt). Thus, based on the presented advantageous points it may be concluded that CA-based proposed lightweight data security model has several inherent advantages for the possible uses as a green model towards data security in Fog Computing architecture and has further potential for easy training of Reservoir computers towards uses in IoT (Internet of Things)-based multiple industry applications.

We found an existing literature on lightweight security approaches in Industry 4.0 (Katsikeas et al., 2017). In future we have a plan to extend our research and investigate the scope for our proposed model for possible uses in Industry 4.0.

ACKNOWLEDGMENT

Authors sincerely acknowledge the review comments received from anonymous reviewers which have significantly helped to enhance the quality of the chapter.

REFERENCES

Abeshu, A., & Chilamkurti, N. (2018). Deep learning: The frontier for distributed attack detection in fog-to-things computing. *IEEE Communications Magazine*, *56*(2), 169–175. doi:10.1109/MCOM.2018.1700332

Babson, N., & Teuscher, C. (2019). Reservoir Computing with Complex Cellular Automata. *Complex Systems*, *28*(4), 433–455. doi:10.25088/ComplexSystems.28.4.433

Bonomi, F., Milito, R., Zhu, J., & Addepalli, S. (2012, August). Fog computing and its role in the internet of things. In *Proceedings of the first edition of the MCC workshop on Mobile cloud computing* (pp. 13-16). 10.1145/2342509.2342513

Buchanan, W. J., Li, S., & Asif, R. (2017). Lightweight cryptography methods. *Journal of Cyber Security Technology*, *1*(3-4), 187–201. doi:10.1080/23742917.2017.1384917

Chaudhuri, P. P., Chowdhury, D. R., Nandi, S., & Chattopadhyay, S. (1997). *Additive cellular automata: theory and applications* (Vol. 1). John Wiley & Sons.

Diro, A. A., Chilamkurti, N., & Kumar, N. (2017). Lightweight cybersecurity schemes using elliptic curve cryptography in publish-subscribe fog computing. *Mobile Networks and Applications*, *22*(5), 848–858. doi:10.100711036-017-0851-8

Eisenbarth, T., Kumar, S., Paar, C., Poschmann, A., & Uhsadel, L. (2007). A survey of lightweight-cryptography implementations. *IEEE Design & Test of Computers*, *24*(6), 522–533. doi:10.1109/MDT.2007.178

Gilbert, H., Robshaw, M., & Sibert, H. (2005). Active attack against HB/sup+: A provavly secure lightweight authentication protocol. *Electronics Letters*, *41*(21), 1169–1170. doi:10.1049/el:20052622

He, J., Li, X., Yao, Y., Hong, Y., & Jinbao, Z. (2018). Mining transition rules of cellular automata for simulating urban expansion by using deep learning techniques. *International Journal of Geographical Information Science*, *32*(10), 2076–2097. doi:10.1080/13658816.2018.1480783

Katagi, M., & Moriai, S. (2008). Lightweight cryptography for the internet of things. *Sony Corporation*, *2008*, 7–10.

Katsikeas, S., Fysarakis, K., Miaoudakis, A., Van Bemten, A., Askoxylakis, I., Papaefstathiou, I., & Plemenos, A. (2017, July). Lightweight & secure industrial IoT communications via the MQ telemetry transport protocol. In *2017 IEEE Symposium on Computers and Communications (ISCC)* (pp. 1193-1200). IEEE. 10.1109/ISCC.2017.8024687

Khakimov, A., Muthanna, A., & Muthanna, M. S. A. (2012, August). Study of fog computing structure. In *2018 IEEE Conference of Russian Young Researchers in Electrical and Electronic Engineering (EIConRus)* (pp. 51-54). IEEE.

Lee, J. Y., Lin, W. C., & Huang, Y. H. (2014, May). A lightweight authentication protocol for internet of things. In *2014 International Symposium on Next-Generation Electronics* (ISNE), pp. 1-2. IEEE. 10.1109/ISNE.2014.6839375

Liao, R. F., Wen, H., Wu, J., Pan, F., Xu, A., Jiang, Y., Xie, F., & Cao, M. (2019). Deep-learning-based physical layer authentication for industrial wireless sensor networks. *Sensors (Basel)*, *19*(11), 2440. doi:10.339019112440 PMID:31142016

Lu, R., Heung, K., Lashkari, A. H., & Ghorbani, A. A. (2017). A lightweight privacy-preserving data aggregation scheme for fog computing-enhanced IoT. *IEEE Access: Practical Innovations, Open Solutions*, *5*, 3302–3312. doi:10.1109/ACCESS.2017.2677520

Mariot, L., Picek, S., Leporati, A., & Jakobovic, D. (2019). Cellular Automata based S-boxes. *Cryptography and Communications: Discrete Structures, Boolean Functions and Sequences, 11*(1), 41–62. doi:10.100712095-018-0311-8

Mehta, K., Arora, N., & Singh, B. P. (2011). Low power efficient D flip flop circuit. In *International Symposium on Devices MEMS, Intelligent Systems & Communication (ISDMISC)* (pp. 16-19). IJCA.

Mihaljevic, M. J., Watanabe, H., & Imai, H. (2008, December). A cellular automata based HB#-like low complexity authentication technique. In *2008 International Symposium on Information Theory and its Applications* (pp. 1-6). IEEE. 10.1109/ISITA.2008.4895617

Mitra, A. (2016). On the selection of Cellular Automata based PRNG in Code Division Multiple Access Communications. *Studies in Informatics and Control, 25*(2), 218–227. doi:10.24846/v25i2y201609

Mitra, A. (2018, September). Selection of cost-effective prime source towards possible uses in Fog Computing. In *2018 2nd International Conference on Data Science and Business Analytics (ICDSBA)* (pp. 19-24). IEEE. 10.1109/ICDSBA.2018.00011

Mitra, A. (2019). On Investigating Energy Stability for Cellular Automata Based PageRank Validation Model in Green Cloud. *International Journal of Cloud Applications and Computing, 9*(4), 66–85. doi:10.4018/IJCAC.2019100104

Mitra, A., & Kundu, A. (2013). Cost optimized set of Primes Generation with Cellular Automata for Stress Testing in Distributed Computing. *Procedia Technology, 10*, 365–372. doi:10.1016/j.protcy.2013.12.372

Mitra, A., & Kundu, A. (2015, October). Analysis of sequences generated by ELCA-type cellular automata targeting noise generation. In *19th International Conference on System Theory, Control and Computing (ICSTCC)* (pp. 883-888). IEEE. 10.1109/ICSTCC.2015.7321406

Mitra, A., & Kundu, A. (2017b). Energy Efficient CA based Page Rank Validation Model: A Green Approach in Cloud. *International Journal of Green Computing, 8*(2), 59–76. doi:10.4018/IJGC.2017070104

Mitra, A., Kundu, A., Chattopadhyay, M., & Chattopadhyay, S. (2017a). A cost-efficient one time password-based authentication in cloud environment using equal length cellular automata. *Journal of Industrial Information Integration, 5*, 17–25. doi:10.1016/j.jii.2016.11.002

Mitra, A., & Saha, S. (2019, December). A design towards an energy-efficient and lightweight data security model in Fog Networks. In *2019 International Conference on Intelligent and Cloud Computing (pp. 227-236)*. Springer Nature. 10.1007/978-981-15-5971-6_25

Morrell, T. (2012, June). Computability and Complexity in Elliptic Curves and Cryptography: An Algorithm for Finding Elliptic Curves of Prime Order over Fp. *AAAS Pacific Division Conference*. Accessed from https://math.boisestate.edu/reu/publications/AAASTomMorrell.PDF

Nandi, S., & Chaudhuri, P. P. (1997). Reply to comments on theory and applications of cellular automata in cryptography. *IEEE Transactions on Computers, 46*(5), 638–639. doi:10.1109/TC.1997.589246

Nandi, S., Kar, B. K., & Chaudhuri, P. P. (1994). Theory and applications of cellular automata in cryptography. *IEEE Transactions on Computers, 43*(12), 1346–1357. doi:10.1109/12.338094

Ni, J., Zhang, K., Lin, X., & Shen, X. S. (2017). Securing fog computing for internet of things applications: Challenges and solutions. *IEEE Communications Surveys and Tutorials*, *20*(1), 601–628. doi:10.1109/COMST.2017.2762345

Nichele, S., & Molund, A. (2017). Deep learning with cellular automaton-based reservoir computing. *Complex Systems*, *26*(4), 319–339. doi:10.25088/ComplexSystems.26.4.319

Ojha, S. K., Kumar, N., & Jain, K. (2009, December). TWIS-a lightweight block cipher. In *International Conference on Information Systems Security* (pp. 280-291). Springer. 10.1007/978-3-642-10772-6_21

Oskuii, S. T. (2004). *Comparative study on low-power high-performance flip-flops* (Unpublished Master of Technology Thesis). Linköping University. Accessed from http://www.divaportal.org/smash/get/diva2:19406/FULLTEXT01.pdf

Ou, C., Yang, J., Du, Z., Zhang, X., & Zhu, D. (2019). Integrating Cellular Automata with Unsupervised Deep-Learning Algorithms: A Case Study of Urban-Sprawl Simulation in the Jingjintang Urban Agglomeration, China. *Sustainability*, *11*(9), 24–64. doi:10.3390u11092464

Pearson's Correlation. (n.d.). Accessed from http://www.statstutor.ac.uk/resources/uploaded/pearsons.pdf

Randomness of statistical sampling: the runs' test. (n.d.). Accessed from https://home.ubalt.edu/ntsbarsh/business-stat/otherapplets/Randomness.htm

Saha, S., & Mitra, A. (2019a, January). Towards Exploration of Green Computing in Energy Efficient Optimized Algorithm for Uses in Fog Computing. In *International Conference on Intelligent Computing and Communication Technologies* (pp. 628-636). Springer Nature. 10.1007/978-981-13-8461-5_72

Saha, S., & Mitra, A. (2019b, December). An energy-efficient data routing in weight-balanced tree-based Fog Network. In *2019 International Conference on Intelligent and Cloud Computing* (pp. 3-11). Springer Nature. 10.1007/978-981-15-6202-0_1

Shemaili, M. A. B., Yeun, C. Y., Zemerly, M. J., & Mubarak, K. (2014). A novel cellular automata based cipher system for internet of things. In *Future information technology* (pp. 269–276). Springer. doi:10.1007/978-3-642-40861-8_40

Shin, S. H., Kim, D. H., & Yoo, Y. (November 2012). A light-weight multi-user authentication scheme based on cellular automata in cloud environment., In *2012 IEEE 1ˢᵗ International Conference on Cloud Networking (CLOUDNET)* (pp. 176-178). IEEE.

Suo, H., Wan, J., Zou, C., & Liu, J. (2012, March). *Security in the internet of things: a review. In 2012 international conference on computer science and electronics engineering*. IEEE.

Tangsakul, S., & Wongthanavasu, S. (2020). Single Image Haze Removal Using Deep Cellular Automata Learning. *IEEE Access: Practical Innovations, Open Solutions*, *8*, 103181–103199. doi:10.1109/ACCESS.2020.2999076

Tripathy, S., & Nandi, S. (2009). Lightweight Cellular Automata-based Symmetric-Key Encryption. *International Journal of Network Security*, *8*(3), 243–252.

Vajda, I., & Buttyan, L. (2003, October). Lightweight authentication protocols for low-cost RFID tags. *Second workshop on Security in Ubiquitous Computing*.

Weisstein, E. W. (n.d.). *Primitive Polynomial. MathWorld-A Wolfram Web Resource.* Accessed from https://mathworld.wolfram.com/PrimitivePolynomial.html

Xing, W., Qian, Y., Guan, X., Yang, T., & Wu, H. (2020). A novel cellular automata model integrated with deep learning for dynamic spatio-temporal land use change simulation. *Computers & Geosciences, 137*, 104430. doi:10.1016/j.cageo.2020.104430

Chapter 13
Automated Hydroponic System Integrated With an Android Smartphone Application

Nnamdi Nwulu

iD https://orcid.org/0000-0003-2607-7439
University of Johannesburg, South Africa

Darshal Suka
University of Johannesburg, South Africa

Eustace Dogo
University of Johannesburg, South Africa

ABSTRACT

Hydroponics farming is fast gaining acceptance globally as an alternative and viable method of farming, instigated by the contemporary challenges posed by climate change, exploding population growth, and global food insecurity. Hydroponics farming can be greatly improved by leveraging on innovative technological advances that will allow for the effective and efficient utiliza-tion of limited natural resources such as water, energy (sunlight), and dwindling agricultural farmlands, consequently resulting in higher yields. This paper presents the design and implementation of an automated flood and drain hydroponic system with internet of things and Android application functionalities. The design is an integrated and automatic plant-watering, water level, and pH measurement and control system using Android application with wi-fi communication technology. Tests carried out proved the worka-bility of the system in line with expected design considerations.

DOI: 10.4018/978-1-7998-7511-6.ch013

INTRODUCTION

Hydroponics is a method of growing plants using nutrient-enriched water solution to feed the plants, without the need for soil as a medium for growing them (Fleming, 2019). The word 'Hydroponics' is derived from two Greek words hydro, meaning 'water' and ponein, meaning 'to labour or to toil' (Fleming, 2019). In this method, plants are grown with their roots immersed in a nutrient-rich solution and fibrous compounds such as rockwool, vermiculite, coconut shells or clay pellets (depending on the plant's root structure) that serve as a physical support structure to the plant root. These compounds are also able to retain a large amount of water and air needed for the plant growth. The process is achieved through a flooding process using a submerged pump in the reservoir connected to a timer unit to flood the grow bed with nutrient solution, which is then circulated back to the reservoir using a drain tube (Resh, 2013).

BACKGROUND

There are different methods of hydroponics namely; wick culture, ebb and flow or flood and drain, deep-water culture, nutrient film technique, and the drip method (Resh, 2013). The hydroponic method could also be regarded as passive, with no mechanical movements, such wick culture method or active, with mechanical movements, such as the ebb and flow method. Several automated hydroponic systems have been developed leveraging on sensor and IoT technologies, as well as using different microcontroller platforms for controlling the system (Lundin & Olli, 2017) (Atmadja, Liawatimena, Lukas, Putra Leo Nata, & Alexander, 2017) (Domingues, Takahashi, Camara, & Nixdorf, 2012) (Saaid, Yahya, Noor, & Ali, 2013). Some works have also proposed integrating the hydroponics system with a smartphone application for remotely controlling commands of the microcontrollers. A review of similar proposed works also shows some limitations, such as unnecessary complexities, with no means of controlling the pH levels and overall cost of system design.

MAIN FOCUS OF THE CHAPTER

This paper aims to automate the original/traditional ebb and flow system, leveraging on sensor technology for monitoring and android application for water level, pH and nutrients concentration measurement and control, with minimal human intervention. This is done by explaining current world problems and background research on several hydroponic methods.

Issues, Controversies, Problems

Rural to urban migration is increasing; many countries, especially in the developing regions are gradually adopting the concepts of smart cities and 4IR (Dogo, Salami, Aigbavboa, & Nkonyana, 2019). The consequent effect of this paradigm shift will require a vast amount of land to build basic infrastructures such roads, schools, hospitals, and airports, this will affect negatively on agricultural farmlands needed for food production. In no distant future, more food will have to be produced by farmers to feed the exploding global population, with a limited amount of natural resources and under harsh economic conditions (Barrios, Ouattara, & Strobl, 2008). Hence, food insecurity is turning out to be one of the global challenges today. The method of hydroponics crop production is a viable means that will help to address some of these aforementioned problems, in tandem with enabling and innovative technological advancements. This will be critical in meeting the sustainable development goal (SGD) object 2 on zero hunger as we approach the year 2030 SGD target year.

SOLUTIONS AND RECOMMENDATIONS

There are many advantages associated with hydroponic farming. They include, minimal space require-ment, low water usage, better control of the environment which makes pest/disease control easier to deal with, can be set up nearly anywhere indoors and outdoors, and minimal labour requirement (Barrios, Ouattara, & Strobl, 2008) (Jones Jr, 2004).

This section describes the proposed system. The aim of this paper is to proffer solution to the problem associated Geoponic (conventional farming) namely, the issue of growing space, high labour/maintenance and high consumption of water for growing crops. Whereby homeowners could implement their small-scaled hydroponics systems to grow their vegetables by utilizing their home space more effectively. The process would be automated to reduce the amount of maintenance and allow the system to be controlled remotely if the owner is away from their plants. The water usage is minimal as water is only refilled once levels are very low and the same water flows from the tank to tank. Since growing of crops can be done in people's homes, by aggregation, the load on commercial farms could be less and allowing less water usage on commercial farms as well as making people self-sufficient. There is a slight cost of measuring pH levels in the water. However, if a big demand for pH sensors is created, the market could explode with cheaper variants of sensors, which can help decrease the cost of pH measurement components.

An ebb and flow system is an active system and therefore there are a few moving parts in this system. This system includes two tanks of which one contains the nutrient solution and the other contains the plants. The nutrient solution is pumped from the reservoir tank to the main tank that contains the plants. These nutrients are pumped according to the timer that is connected to the pump. The water flows into the grow tank as illustrated in Figure 1 until it soaks the roots and once it reaches the overflow, the water drains back out to recirculate again later.

It is important to note that the plant-tank is placed above the water nutrient tank so that the water can flow back into the nutrient tank through gravity (Jones Jr, 2004). To put everything into context, the process diagram of the system is depicted in Figure 2.

After completing the literature review and getting a better understanding of the theories and compo-nents appropriateness, selection of the hardware components was made using criteria based on ease of use, cost, functionality, accessibility and availability. The final components selected for this study are summarized in Table 1.

Description of Hardware Components

The conceptual system design is depicted in Figure 7 consisting of all the interconnected units, while the physical circuit layout diagram is shown in Figure 8. The power requirement for the pumps is all 220V AC. The NodeMCU utilizes power from a 5v source. The hardware components selected are briefly described as follows:

Figure 1. Ebb and flow hydroponic system with a timer on the water pump

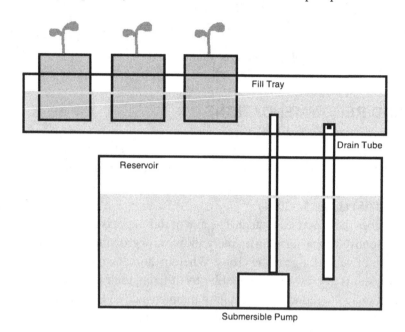

NodeMCU ESP12-E With Wi-Fi Module

The NodeMCU chip is a derivation of the ESP8266-01 with a Wi-Fi module. The Wi-Fi module is compatible with the NodeMCU chip and conforms to the IEEE802.1b/g/n standard. Thus, NodeMCU consist of a microcontroller with digital outputs, RAM, flash memory, processor and analogue to digital pin configuration. The NodeMCU layout is depicted in Figure 3.

Table 2 shows the technical specifications of the ESP12-E based NodeMCU microcontroller with a Wi-Fi module.

Wi-Fi is one of the most commonly used communication technologies in comparison to Bluetooth and GSM and conforms to IEEE802.11 protocol standard (IEEE, 2016). Wi-Fi comes with many advantages such as low power consumption, less wired connections requirement, good signal range, and fast and secure. Depending on the frequency band (2.4GHz spectrum more commonly used), Wi-Fi can operate at an indoor range of 46 meters and up to 92 meters outdoors (Mitchell, 2019).

pH Sensor - SEN0161

The SEN0161 pH sensor was selected because of its cost which is much lower when compared to the other available sensors. Nevertheless, most importantly this sensor suited the prototype design consideration for cheaper and easily available components. Resulting in lowering the overall implementation cost of the system. The technical specification of the pH sensor is summarized in Table 3.

Figure 2. Process diagram of the system

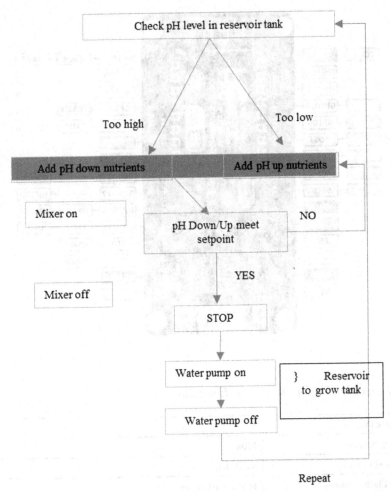

Table 1. Final component selection

Component	Sensor Type
Microcontroller	NodeMCU ESP-12E
pH sensor	SEN-0161
Water level sensor	HC-SR04 ultrasonic sensor
Temperature and humidity sensor	DHT11
Pumps	Peristaltic pump
Communication technology	Wi-Fi

Figure 3. NodeMCU microcontroller with Wi-Fi module

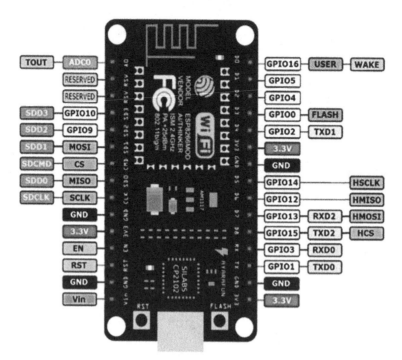

Table 2. Technical specification of the ESP12-E module

Voltage (VCC)	5V
Running Current	170mA
Wi-Fi Standard	802.11b/g/n
Available Flash Memory	16MB Flash Memory
Network	Integrated TCP/IP
Processor	Tensilica L106, 32-bit
RAM	64 KB instruction, 96 KB data, 64 K boot
Output Power	19.5dBm (802.11b) 0.5W

Table 3. Specifications of the SEN0161 pH sensor

Specification	SEN0161 pH Sensor
pH scale range	0-14
Measuring temperature range	0-60
Accuracy	+/- 0.1
Life expectancy (continuous use)	~6months
Submersible	Not fully submersible
Continuous testing in water	No
Availability	Available locally

Figure 4. DHT11 temperature and humidity sensor

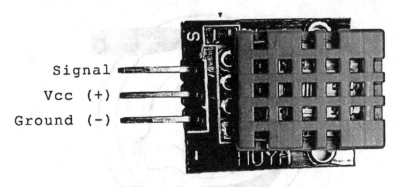

Signal

Vcc (+)

Ground (-)

Temperature and Humidity Sensor

The DHT11 temperature and humidity sensor module are shown in Figure 4. It operates at a voltage of between 3.5V - 5.5V and outputs both the temperature and humidity signal through a serial data. The DHT11 temperature sensor used is a thermistor, meaning the temperature is calculated by correlating the resistance of the element (Beaty & Fink, 2013). The DHT11 sensor has a temperature range of 0-50°C and an error of +/- 2°C. Its humidity range is 20-90% with an error of +/-5% (DHT11 Temperature and Humidity Sensor, 2016).

Water Level Sensor HC-SR04 Ultrasonic Sensor

The HC-SR04 is an ultrasonic sensor shown in Figure 5 that transmits an ultrasonic wave and receives the wave reflected off the object. The distance is calculated by measuring the time taken to send and receive the wave, based on the formula in equation 1.

$$D = \frac{1}{2} * T * C \tag{1}$$

Where, T = time between the transmission and reception, C = speed of sound which is 343m/s. It has a range of between 2cm to 400cm and does not need to be submerged in water for it to work (McComb, 2013).

Figure 5. HC-SR04 ultrasonic sensor

Figure 6. Peristaltic pump

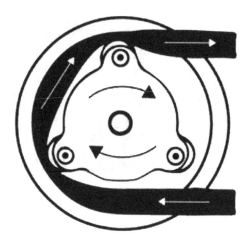

Peristaltic Pumps

The peristaltic pump shown in Figure 6, is operated with a DC motor, and is used to transport liquid from one place to another with aid of an internal roller that pushes against a tube (Avallone, Baumeister III, & Sadegh, 2007). The liquid flows through the tube while the roller is connected to the DC motor for rotation.

With reference to Figure 6, when the roller turns, the part where the tube is squeezed forces the liquid in the tube to move through the tube (Avallone, Baumeister III, & Sadegh, 2007). With the help of the moving roller, the liquid is transferred from one point to another. The specific purpose of the peristaltic pump in this study is for adding the pH nutrients in small doses into the water reservoir.

Figure 7. Conceptual design of the system

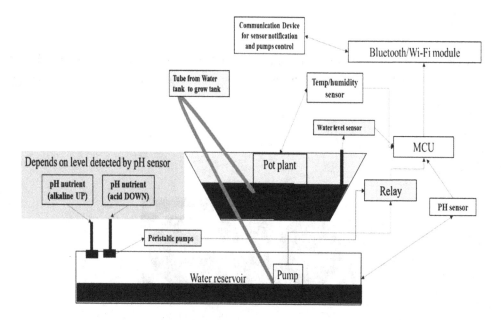

Figure 8. Circuit layout of the system

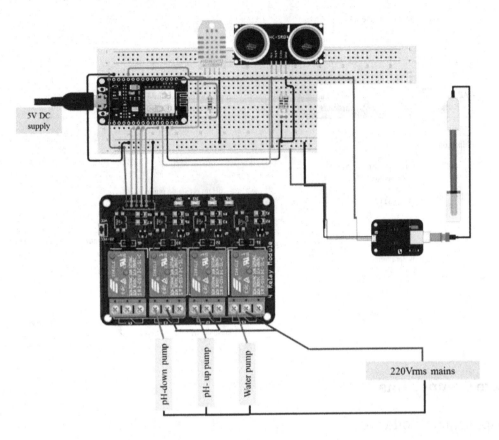

Figure 9. Blynk Communication Structure

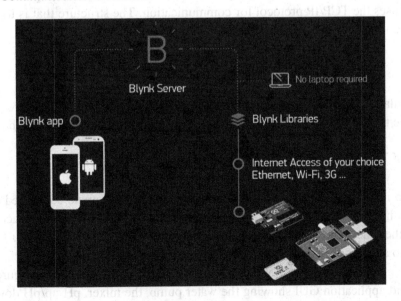

Figure 10. System process of operation

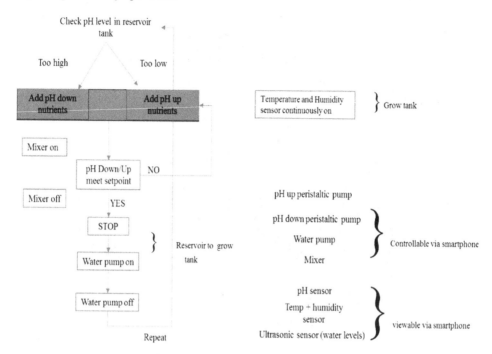

Software Components

Blynk Application Software

The NodeMCU is used to communicate the system to the user's smartphone device or any device that has access to Wi-Fi. This is achieved by leveraging on the Blynk (BLYNK, 2020) open-source application software. Blynk uses the TCP/IP protocol for communication. The structure that is used by the Blynk application for communication is depicted in Figure 9.

Fritzing

Fritzing is a simulation software that allows the user to design and organize hardware peripherals onto a virtual interface to give the user an idea of how the connection would function in the real world.

The Internet of Things (IoT) Platform

The IoT platform is a software that allows a user to manage and automate connected devices such as sensors and other hardware that are connected to the internet. This allows for remote access, control and management of these devices (Smart farming and smart agriculture solutions, 2019). The IoT platform was configured to assist in the wireless control of the hydroponic system.

Depicted in Figure 10 is the layout of the system process of operation. While Figure 11 depicts the developed android application GUI showing the water pump, the mixer, pH up/pH down, temperature and humidity measurement and control knobs for autoregulation of the system with a smartphone through a Wi-Fi connection.

Figure 11. The developed mobile application interface

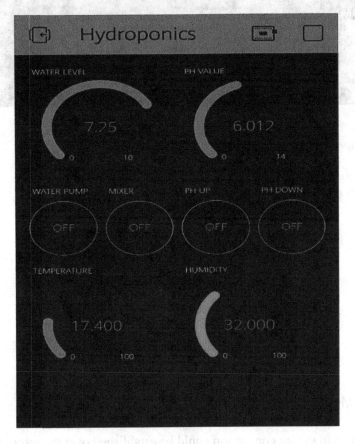

Testing and Analysis of Designed System

Series of tests were conducted for each component to ascertain their expected working condition, leading to the final integrated working system. These tests are described below.

Figure 12. Wi-Fi connection test

```
15:31:10.866 -> Connecting to NETGEAR-G ...
15:31:10.866 ->
15:31:10.866 ->
15:31:10.866 -> Connection Established
15:31:10.866 -> IP address:     192.168.0.5
```

Figure 13. Successful packet transfer

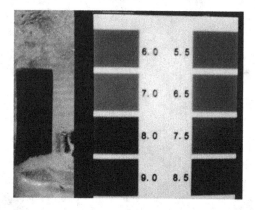

Figure 14. Litmus paper measuring pH level

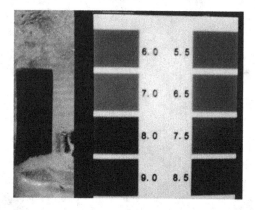

NodeMCU Wi-Fi Module Test

This test was performed to ensure connection could be established over the internet through the Wi-Fi network. The results were printed onto the serial port of the Arduino IDE, as illustrated in Figure 12.

The connection was successfully made, and the IP address was printed. Thereafter, communication from the command prompt of the laptop to the NodeMCU was made to make sure that data could be sent and received. As illustrated in Figure 13, ICMP ping test via command prompt was initiated and four (4) packets of data were sent and received from the laptop to the NodeMCU at an average round trip time of 33ms with 0% packets loss.

Figure 15. Bleach bottle indicating pH level

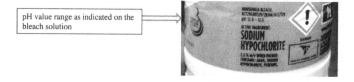

pH Sensor Test

Three tests were performed for the pH sensor. The first test was to measure an acidic solution, the second was to measure a neutral solution and the last was to measure an alkaline solution. Vinegar was chosen as the acidic solution, water as the neutral and bleach as the alkaline solution. For each test, 1000 measurements were taken.

For the test in the acidic solution, the known pH of vinegar is approximately 2.4. When the probe was immersed in the vinegar, the average measurements was approximately 2.41. The known ideal value of water on the pH scale is 7.0; however, the probe produced an average value of 7.52. This value was not exactly 7.0 but further measurement test with a litmus paper shown in Figure 14 indicated a value of 7.5.

Finally, the probe was placed in an alkaline solution of bleach, which has a known pH of between 12.0 to 12.5 as indicated on the bleach bottle shown in Figure 15.

The measurements produced from the pH sensor were approximately 11.55 as shown in Figure 16. For this measurement, the pH value was off by 0.5.

Figure 16. pH measurement of bleach solution

```
22:39:38.365 -> Voltage:3.30    pH value: 11.55
22:39:38.365 -> Voltage:3.30    pH value: 11.55
22:39:38.365 -> Voltage:3.30    pH value: 11.55
22:39:38.365 -> Voltage:3.30    pH value: 11.55
22:39:38.399 -> Voltage:3.30    pH value: 11.55
22:39:38.399 -> Voltage:3.30    pH value: 11.55
```

The pH probe measured three types of solutions and was accurate as the measurements had a very low deviation (0.028, 0.009 and 0.0187 for acid, neutral and base respectively) indicating that the measurements were close to their respective averages.

Figure 17. pH levels of acidic, neutral and basic solutions

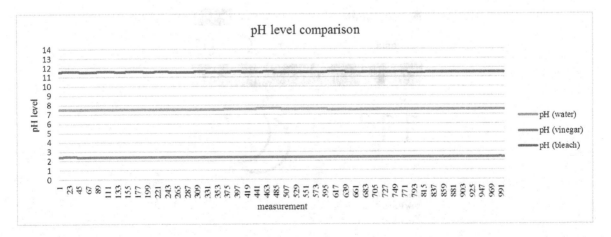

Figure 18. DHT11 sensor placed in ice

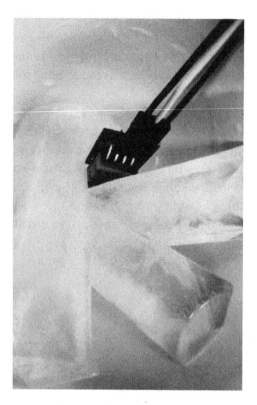

Figure 17 indicates the pH levels of the 3 solutions tested (acid, neutral and basic). After 1000 samples obtained for each solution test that the readings did not fluctuate very much. This concludes that the sensor was reliable and can be used for the project to maintain the pH level of the water.

Figure 19. The ambient temperature at 10:26 pm

Temperature and Humidity Sensor Test

The DHT11 was placed in a cup filled with ice to measure the temperature drop of the sensor as shown in Figure 18.

The environmental ambient temperature at the time taking the readings was 11°C as indicated on a South African weather website captured as shown in Figure 19.

Figure 20. Temperature vs Time graph

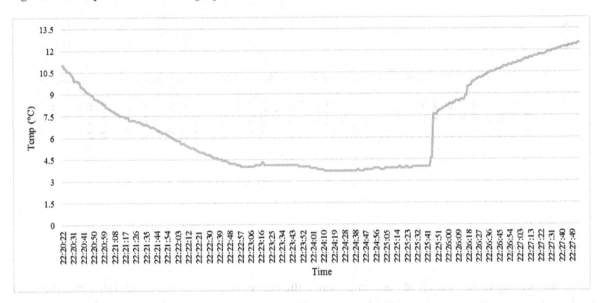

The sensor dropped down to a low of 3.9°C. It was expected to drop to at least 0°C because that is the freezing point of water. It did not reach 0°C because the ice already started melting as soon as it was taken out of the fridge. The sensor could also not be placed on any of the ice-cubes as the water would damage the sensor. The graph in figure 20 shows the temperature readings measured by the DHT11 from the time it was placed in the ice until the ice melted to the ambient temperature of the room. These results indicate that the sensor was within 2° of the actual measurement indicating that the sensor is acceptable for use.

Ultrasonic Sensor Distance Test

The ultrasonic sensor distance test was carried out by placing an object in front of the sensor at a given distance and comparing the difference between the actual distance and the distance measured by the sensor. The test was carried out at distances of 15 and 30cm away from the sensor. For each of the distance measurements, 454 samples were taken. The average for the 15cm measurement was 15.36cm, while that of 30cm measurement was 30.66cm. Both measurements had very low variances, 0.047 and 0.051 for the 15cm and 30cm measurements respectively. This indicated that the values were close to the average and therefore concludes that the sensor is accurate and within the manufacturer's error specification of 3mm. The data collected for measurements at 15cm and 30cm are shown in figure 21.

Figure 21. Measurement data for distance tests

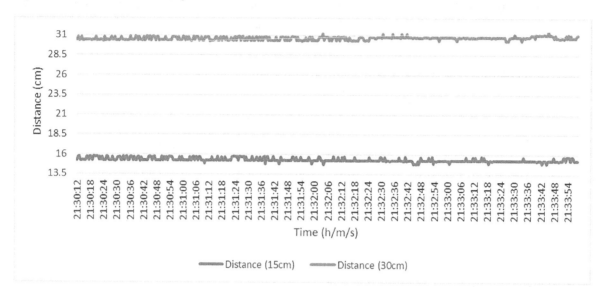

Integration of System

After performing tests for each of the components, the sub-systems were then integrated into the final packaged product. When the NodeMCU executed the code, the mixer turned on to mix the water whilst the pH sensor measured the pH level of the water. A threshold of 6.5 and 7.5 was set to maintain the pH at that level. If the water was between that level, only then would the water be pumped into the grow tank. The HC-SR04 was programmed to detect the water level of the plant grow tank and when the water reached to a level that could wet the rockwool fibre, the water pump would stop as the sensor would indicate that it has reached its threshold level. The water would then siphon back into the reservoir tank until when the whole process is to be repeated.

A step-by-step operation of the system is as follows:

Figure 22. Sied view of final packaged protoype

Figure 23. Top view of final packaged protoype

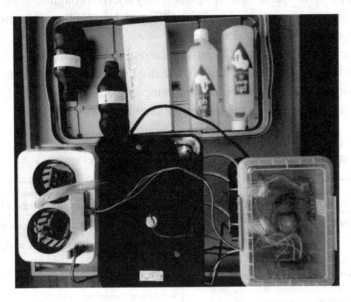

Figure 24. The Final packaged system

1. The pH level, temperature, humidity and water level are constantly displayed on the mobile application.
2. The peristaltic pumps switch ON if the pH value is below the range of 6.5 and 7.5.

3. The submersible pump was set to water the plants every hourly throughout the day. This was achieved by configuring the pumping interval to 3600000L which is 3600ms (60 minutes and therefore a 1-hour interval), defined as a long datatype.
4. The mixer can be switched ON and OFF using the mobile application.
5. Figure 19, 20 and 21 show different views of the final integrated system. The blue enclosure held the electronic components and the peristaltic pumps. The reservoir is the black container in the middle and the plant grow tank is the white container at the bottom.

Table 4. Distinction between previous studies and this current paper

Title: **Automated pH Controller System for Hydroponic Cultivation**	Reference: **(Saaid, Sanuddin, Megat Ali, & M, 2015)**
Technology Used	**Distinction/Improvement**
1. A servo motor is used to drop the nutrients. 2. The *deep-water culture* method of hydroponics is used. - This contributes to more fluctuations in pH and nutrient concentration. 3. The sensor data is only monitored via smartphone (android application).	1. A peristaltic pump is used to efficiently dose and maintain the pH level of the water. 2. The *ebb and flow* method is used. – Allows water to continuously flow in and out of the grow tank containing the plants. This method is able to maintain the pH levels of the water before allowing it to make contact with the plant. 3. Sensor data is monitored, and the pumps and pH levels are controlled via smartphone (android application).
Title: **Automated Hydroponics Nutrition Plants Systems Using Arduino Uno Microcontroller Based on Android**	Reference: **(Sihombing, Karina, Tarigan, & Syarif, 2017)**
Technology Used	**Distinction/ Improvement**
1. Use of a Temperature sensor (LM35), Ultrasonic sensor (HC-SR04). 2. LCD Display and data displayed on the phone through a Wi-Fi module	1. DHT11 sensor (temperature and humidity) used instead of LM35 sensor (temperature sensor only). 2. Data is displayed on a smartphone through a Wi-Fi module to control and display the system as opposed to viewing the data on an LCD display at the plant's location.
Title: **Hydroponic System Design With Real Time OS Based on ARM Cortex-M Microcontroller**	Reference: **(Atmadja, Liawatimena, Lukas, Putra Leo Nata, & Alexander, 2017)**
Technology Used	**Distinction/Improvement**
1. Monitors C02, temperature, pH and light intensity. A grow light is used to provide light to the plant. 2. The system can't be controlled remotely. It requires the user to control the system locally.	1. Monitors Temperature and Humidity only. Plant is placed in area with maximum sunlight during the day, therefore does not require grow lights and light intensity sensors. 2. Data is displayed on a smartphone through Wi-Fi module remotely as opposed to viewing the data on an LCD display at the plant's location.
Title: **Applied Internet of Things for Smart Hydroponic Farming Ecosystem**	Reference: **(Ruengittinun, Phongsamsuan, & Sureeratanakorn, 2017)**
Technology Used	**Distinction/Improvement**
1. The water pump was switched on when the temperature was in the correct threshold. (Pump on based on temperature of the system). 2. A solenoid valve was to add pH nutrients to the system.	1. The HC-SR04 distance sensor detected a shortage of water and would prompt the water pump to switch on. (Pump on based on water level). 2. A Peristaltic pump was used to add pH nutrient to the system. It is more accurate in terms of dosing because the pH level could be controlled by adding very little nutrient at a time as opposed to the solenoid valve which opens and closes fully and is also not as responsive as the peristaltic pump.

COMPARATIVE ANALYSIS

Table 4 indicates the technology used by previous studies and a distinction/improvement between their system and the current system belonging to this research paper.

The main improvements to the studies that were discussed above is that the system can be viewed remotely and uses a peristaltic pump to insert the pH nutrient into the solution to maintain the pH level of the system. An advantage to having a remotely controlled and viewed system is that the user can continue with their daily activities without having to closely monitor the system every day, because the entire process of watering the plant and maintaining the pH level of the plant is automated. An advantage to using a peristaltic pump as mentioned earlier is that nutrient is accurately added to the system without causing big fluctuations in the pH level of the system. The fluctuations of the pH level in the solution is what causes stress to the plant which will eventually result in the plant dying.

FUTURE RESEARCH DIRECTIONS

In future work, in order to improve the system reliability, a back-up wireless communication or GSM module could be incorporated alongside the Wi-Fi module for redundancy.

The GSM module could send details of the pH levels, temperature and humidity and water levels. The GSM module could also receive commands from the user to switch the pumps on.

A PCB can be designed to have easier component connection and better aesthetics. A higher quality pH probe could be utilized

CONCLUSION

In this paper, the design and implementation of a flood and drain hydroponics system with IoT and android application is presented. Information from the sensors (ultrasonic for water level, temperature, humidity and pH level) was gathered and displayed on the mobile application. The pumps and mixer were automated and controlled from the App each time they were required to be switched ON. The submersible pump switches ON the and water the plant. The peristaltic pumps switches ON each time the pH value is not within the configured threshold. The mixer would mix the water in the reservoir after the pH nutrient was inserted into the tank. Notifications were received from the smartphone via the App. In future work, in order to improve the system reliability, a back-up wireless communication or GSM module could be incorporated alongside the Wi-Fi module for redundancy.

ACKNOWLEDGMENT

The authors would like to thank the University of Johannesburg for funding and making the resources available to complete this work.

REFERENCES

Advanced Nutrients. (2016, December 15). *How to Start Growing With Hydroponics For Beginners.* Retrieved from Advanced Nutrients: https://www.advancednutrients.com/articles/easy-hydroponics-beginners-guide/

Atmadja, W., Liawatimena, S., Lukas, J., Putra Leo Nata, E., & Alexander, I. (2017). Hydroponic system design with real time OS based on ARM Cortex-M microcontroller. *IOP Conference Series. Earth and Environmental Science, 109*, 012017. doi:10.1088/1755-1315/109/1/012017

Avallone, E. A., Baumeister, T. III, & Sadegh, A. (2007). *Mark's Standard Handbook for Mechanical Engineers.* McGraw-Hill Professional.

Barrios, S., Ouattara, B., & Strobl, E. (2008). The Impact of Climatic Change on Agricultural Production: Is it Different for Africa? *Food Policy, 33*(4), 287–298. doi:10.1016/j.foodpol.2008.01.003

Beaty, H. W., & Fink, D. G. (2013). *Standard Handbook for Electrical Engineers.* McGraw-Hill Professional.

D'Anna, C. (2019, March 8). *Wick System Hydroponic Gardens.* Retrieved from The Spruce: https://www.thespruce.com/hydroponic-gardens-wick-system-1939222

DHT11 Temperature and Humidity Sensor. (2016). Retrieved from Keyestudio: https://www.keyestudio.com/free-shipping-keyestudio-dht11-temperature-humidity-moisture-sensor-detection-module-for-arduino-p0374-p0374.html

Dogo, E. M., Salami, A. F., Aigbavboa, C. O., & Nkonyana, T. (2019). Taking Cloud Computing to the Extreme Edge: A Review of Mist Computing for Smart Cities and Industry 4.0 in Africa. In *Edge Computing: From Hype to Reality* (pp. 107–132). Springer. doi:10.1007/978-3-319-99061-3_7

Domingues, D. S., Takahashi, H. W., Camara, C. P., & Nixdorf, S. L. (2012, June). Automated System Developed to Control pH and Concentration of Nutrient Solution Evaluated in Hydroponic Lettuce Production. *Computers and Electronics in Agriculture, 84*, 53–61. doi:10.1016/j.compag.2012.02.006

Fleming, S. (2019, February 5). *What is hydroponics - and is it the future of farming?* Retrieved from World Economic Forum: https://www.weforum.org/agenda/2019/02/hydroponics-future-of-farming

IEEE. (2016, December 14). *802.11-2016 - IEEE Standard for Information technology--Telecommunications and information exchange between systems Local and metropolitan area networks--Specific requirements - Part 11: Wireless LAN Medium Access Control (MAC) and Physical Layer (PHY) Sp.* Retrieved from IEEE Standards Association: https://standards.ieee.org/standard/802_11-2016.html#Standard

Jones, J. B. Jr. (2004). *Hydroponics: A Practical Guide for the Soilless Grower.* CRC Press. doi:10.1201/9780849331671

Lundin, K., & Olli, O. (2017). *Automated hydroponics: Regulation of pH and Nutrients.* KTH Royal Institute of Technology, Bsc thesis in Mechatronics, Stockholm.

McComb, G. (2013). *Arduino Robot Bonanza.* McGraw-Hill Professional.

Mitchell, B. (2019, November 10). *What is the Range of a Typical WiFi Network*. Retrieved from Lifewire: https://www.lifewire.com/range-of-typical-wifi-network-816564#:~:text=A%20general%20rule%20of%20thumb,one%2Dthird%20of%20these%20distances

Resh, H. M. (2013). *Hobby Hydroponics*. CRC Publisher. doi:10.1201/b13737

Roberto, K. (2003). *How-to Hydroponics*. The Futuregarden Press.

Ruengittinun, S., Phongsamsuan, S., & Sureeratanakorn, P. (2017). Applied Internet of Things for Smart Hydroponic Farming Ecosystem. *10th International Conference on Ubi-Media Computing and Workshops*. Pattaya, Thailand: IEEE. 10.1109/UMEDIA.2017.8074148

Saaid, M. F., Sanuddin, A., Megat Ali, M. S., & M, Y. I. (2015). *Automated pH Controller System for Hydroponic Cultivation*. IEEE.

Saaid, M. F., Yahya, N. A., Noor, M. Z., & Ali, M. A. (2013). A development of an Automatic Microcontroller System for Deep Water Culture (DWC). In *IEEE 9th International Colloquium on Signal Processing and its Applications* (pp. 328-332). Kuala Lumpur: IEEE. 10.1109/CSPA.2013.6530066

Saraswathi, D., Manibharathy, P., Gokulnath, R., Sureshkumar, E., & Karthikeyan, K. (2018). Automation of Hydroponics Green House Farming. *2018 IEEE International Conference on System, Computation, Automation and Networking (ICSCA)*. Pondicherry, India: IEEE. 10.1109/ICSCAN.2018.8541251

Shavrukov, Y., Genc, Y., & Hayes, J. C. (2012). *The Use of Hydroponics in Abiotic Stress Tolerance Research*. Academic Press.

Sihombing, P., Karina, N. A., Tarigan, J. T., & Syarif, M. I. (2017). Automated Hydroponics Nutrition Plants Systems Using Arduino Uno Microcontroller Based on Android. In *2nd International Conference on Computing and Applied Informatics*. Medan, Indonesia: IOP Publishing Ltd.

Smart farming and smart agriculture solutions. (2019). Retrieved from ThingsBoard: https://thingsboard.io/smart-farming/

Smith, C., & Collins, D. (2002). *3G Wireless Networks*. McGraw-Hill Professional.

ADDITIONAL READING

Advanced Nutrients. (2016, December 15). *How to Start Growing With Hydroponics For Beginners*. Retrieved from Advanced Nutrients: https://www.advancednutrients.com/articles/easy-hydroponics-beginners-guide/

D'Anna, C. (2019, March 8). *Wick System Hydroponic Gardens*. Retrieved from The Spruce: https://www.thespruce.com/hydroponic-gardens-wick-system-1939222

Roberto, K. (2003). *How-to Hydroponics*. The Futuregarden Press.

Shavrukov, Y., Genc, Y., & Hayes, J. C. (2012). *The Use of Hydroponics in Abiotic Stress Tolerance Research*.

Smith, C., & Collins, D. (2002). *3G Wireless Networks*. New York: McGraw-Hill Professional.

KEY TERMS AND DEFINITIONS

4IR: The fourth industrial revolution, which has also been referred to as 4IR or Industry 4.0, describes the age of intelligence and encompasses technologies like artificial intelligence, augmented reality, 3D printing and cloud computing.

Automation: The use or introduction of automatic equipment in a manufacturing or other process or facility.

Hydroponics: The process of growing plants in sand, gravel, or liquid, with added nutrients but without soil.

IoT: The internet of things is a network of Internet connected objects able to collect and exchange data.

Chapter 14
CSAP:
Cyber Security Asynchronous Programming With C++20 and C# 8 for Internet of Things and Embedded Software Systems

Marius Iulian Mihailescu
https://orcid.org/0000-0001-9655-9666
Spiru Haret University, Romania

Stefania Loredana Nita
University of Bucharest, Romania

ABSTRACT

The current proposal of C++20 features suggests that the coroutines will have dedicated support for the native language. This chapter will provide an analysis that is performed based on a comprehensive survey of coroutines that are used in the development process of the embedded systems and how they are used on dedicated platforms based on their constrained resources. Another important aspect of the work consists of analyzing the performance of designing and implementation of coroutines in software applications related to IoT and embedded devices focusing on the security vulnerabilities of the devices within an IoT ecosystem. The research analysis that forms the basis of the current work is based on metrics, such as software and hardware platform requirements, computation power, scenarios, advantages, and designing user interfaces based on the programming language used. The current work will be completed by adding a comparison with C# 8 programming language and C++20.

DOI: 10.4018/978-1-7998-7511-6.ch014

INTRODUCTION

Internet-of-Things (IoT) is one of the most challenging and technology from nowadays with a very bright future, with a higher number of devices that will be attached to the IoT ecosystem or a wide network.

IoT is one of the promising directions to be focused on when applications for devices that are found within the IoT environment are developed. In this way the best from the network that has multiple devices inter-connected with them will be get out, being treated as *things*.

The objectives of this chapter are as follows:

- **Asynchronous Programming Guide from IoT perspective (see Section *Asynchronous Programming*).** The chapter will cover the asynchronous programming framework for C++20 and C# 8.0 and it will be demonstrated how to embed asynchronous source code on (complex) embedded software systems.
- **Cyber Security Threats (see Section *Cyber Security Threats*, Section *IoT Taxonomy for Security Classification*, Section *Important Security Incidents*, and *Cyber Security Attacks*).** Asynchronous programming has its advantages and disadvantages. One of the disadvantages consists in the way how the data are passed and processed during the code execution.
- **Coroutines (see Section *Asynchronous Programming*).** Another important objective is utilizing coroutines, such as to *await* and *async* to protect the security of the data.

The chapter structure is as follows and covers the most important security threats of IoT devices and their applications within the network in which they are deployed. The chapter structure is:

- **Background.** The section provides a short analysis of the sources for security issues and discusses the security aspects that are demanded on three different levels;
- **Cyber Security Threats.** The section covers the most significant safety threats for different reasons and the advantages of IoT, IIoT, and IoMT. The second purpose of the section is to give a presentation of the most common hackers and their ways of compromising and damaging the IoT, IIoT, and IoMT devices.
- **IoT Taxonomy for Security Classification.** The section will discuss an important way of grading security using seven important taxonomies.
- **Important Security Incidents.** The section will cover the most important security incidents that happened to start with 2009 and until now.
- **Cyber Security Attacks.** For each of the security incidents, the current section will cover the most important attacks and different IoT devices and how the hackers are proceeding to gain access.
- **Asynchronous Programming.** The section will present a framework that can be used by developers when developing applications for IoT devices. The framework is focusing on two of the most powerful programming language (C# and C++) and their new features brought with C# 8.0 and C++20, with respect for security and cryptography algorithms.

In business and personal environments, Internet-enabled devices are rapidly evolving. They sometimes go unnoticed, simply emerging inside network infrastructures, using wired or wireless networks, and widening the scope of an assault on businesses.

Besides, businesses are more likely to have more Internet of Things (IoT) devices on their networks than conventional endpoints – according to Armis, by 2021, more than 90 percent of business devices would not be manageable by conventional IT protection tools. IBM projected that the world will reach 25 billion connected devices by 2020, a number which is likely to continue to rise in the future.

A successful threat management system needs to discover, classify, and evaluate all forms of unmanaged and managed IoT devices that are connected to enterprise infrastructure, adapting the past threat environment to the reality of today. The first step is to passively identify unknown types of products, gathering product information such as size, model, supplier, the operating system installed, and applications.

BACKGROUND

Internet of Things (IoT) is focused on the billions of devices and their existence in the entire world within the way of how they are connected to the Internet, collecting and exchanging data through a component called a chip. From a commercial point of view, the IoT devices improve the Quality of Life (QoL), making easier the daily responsibilities of the peoples, while from an industrial point of view, the IoT devices are revolutionizing the market through the interconnection between the devices. The combining between the devices' interconnectivity and systems' automatization permits collecting the information, analyzing it, and making a decision based on the analysis result.

Moreover, the IoT allows both the communication in a private network and communication in a public network, leading to an interconnected world. The benefits of IoT for the companies are different according to the needs and implementation techniques. However, a common benefit is that the companies have access to more data about their products and internal systems, leading to a better ability to make decisions. For individuals, the IoT benefit is that the environment (houses, cars, personal devices, etc.) becomes smarter and easier to measure and maintain. The IoT ecosystem can be included everywhere, from smart houses to smart cities or healthcare areas.

The Internet of Things is closely related to embedded systems. An embedded system is a component of a larger system that has a determined task (or tasks) and it can incorporate hardware elements and the corresponding software or it can have a specific capability or the ability to be programmable. Examples of things that can include embedded systems are medical tools, industrial machines, airplanes, mobile devices, etc.

The IoT has the potential to transform the world, but how secure is it? The improvements and the growth of the technology showed over time that (almost) always there are cybersecurity concerns. IoT is not an exception, even more, it seeks to interconnect different devices from different domains. According to (Hassan, 2017), some of the sources for security issues in IoT are:

- Vulnerable points: Any device connected to the internet is natively exposed, especially the devices that have an old or outdated operating system or software. These old versions can authorize illegitimate access because of the weak encryption or backdoors.
- Side-channels: The communication from the IoT devices to the internet is made through specific signals that reveal at any moment the amount of power consumption, named side channels. These are vulnerable to attacks because a malicious user can falsify the amount of power consumption to redirect the signals. An example of a side-channel attack is DDoS (Distributed Denial of Service)

that the route of the messages is compromised, by refusing to create a root or by redirecting the messages to the wrong place.

- Hardware: It is more vulnerable especially in systems that have different types of components, such as sensors, smart cards, RFID tags, etc. A common attack here is the physical attack, where can be different targets: to drain the battery of a device, to damage a device, to exploit physical ports to achieve unauthorized access to the system.

For an IoT system, several security aspects are demanded at three different levels, as follows (Fremantle & Scott, 2017; Weber, 2010):

- Information level, where the integrity, the anonymity and the confidentiality of the data should be guaranteed;
- Access level, where access control, an authentication and authorization processes should be implemented;
- Functional level, where resilience and self-organization for the IoT device should be guaranteed. Here, resilience is related to the network, such that it should have the proper capacity to assure the security of the connected devices.

As the IoT devices are connected to the internet, three layers of communication in the IoT architecture can be differentiated (Pielli et al., 2015). The first layer is Edge and it is related to the physical components of the communication, providing capabilities for MACs and the physical part of the communication of a local network. The second layer is composed of Access whose purpose is to link the device with the external networks and Middleware that is an intermediary sub-layer between the device and the external networks. The third and last layer is Application, which is related to software and services that interact with the IoT device. For each of the above layers, there are specific security issues or attacks. The Edge layer is vulnerable to side-channel attacks (Singh et al., 2008) denial-of-service attacks, or hardware trojans (El-hajj, 2017), which exploit the information about the physical components or make them unavailable. The second layer is vulnerable to sniffing, packets injection, or routing attacks (Ammar et al., 2017). The attacks over the third layer of the IoT architecture are related to data integrity because the targets of the attacks are the software and the services used by the IoT devices.

However, the IoT devices are implemented several protection mechanisms. The followings can be mentioned:

- Pseudo-random number generators (PRNG) – these are used in different protocols to provide randomness in their implementation. Moreover, some solutions provide specific PRNGs for IoT devices with limited resources (Bakiri et al., 2018).
- Secured hardware – a solution that can be included on the hardware level of the IoT infrastructure is represented by the Physically Unclonable Functions that work with the chip's fabric characteristics (Halak et al., 2016).
- Encryption and standard encryption techniques – encryption represents an important part of securing the data, as it ensures the confidentiality of the data. The encryption systems that can be divided into symmetric (that use a private key for both encryption and decryption) and asymmetric (that use a public key for encryption and a private key for decryption). Examples of well-known encryption schemes are AES (Rijmen & Daemen, 2011) and RSA (Rivest et al., 1983).

- Intrusion detection systems (IDS) – these are mostly specialized to prevent the attacks, basically by analyzing the configured system parameters, for example, memory consumption on an IoT device. Specific IDS for IoT devices with limited resources are proposed in (Sedjelmaci et al., 2017; Li et al., 2019).

CYBERSECURITY THREATS

The Internet of Things (IoT) phenomenon, has in its structure other types of devices, such as the Industrial Internet of Things (IIoT) and the Internet of Medical Things (IoMT), will have a high explosion of devices and applications in 2020 and beyond. These devices continue to provide real security risks based on their advantages for both categories, end-users, and business side, particularly because they can be easily hacked and can lead to larger breaches, data exfiltration, and other issues.

But now all IoT, IIoT and IoMT systems pose very real – very significant – safety threats for a variety of reasons for all their advantages:

- The common and traditional best practices for offering data protection are not sufficient – or efficient for IoT Health devices. On IoT Health devices the attention needs to be special and dedicated and treated with maximum responsibility.
- Credentials are hard-coded within the device in most of the cases, and may not be a unique device to device, making it easy for hackers to exploit.
- Most of the IoT devices are typically closed or poses limited memory or processing power. This makes extremely difficult the process of installing endpoint detection and response software (EDR) or other security tools.

The growing number of IoT devices are now able to "walk" to the network and are practically invisible to security teams. Which include wearable devices, BYOD technology, and even patient devices such as pacemakers or insulin pumps which are internally embedded. For example, if an IoT system is hacked and the hacker has access to travel laterally through the internal network, current IoT security solutions will not be able to stop it because they don't have visibility in network traffic to the east.

That all adds to a surprising amount of risk. For example, here are five ways that hackers can compromise devices such as IoT, IIoT, and IoMT and damage your organization:

- Enable an IoT computer, and use it as a proxy to travel around the network laterally and connect to other critical devices. However, most monitoring tools actually cannot have real-time insight into east-west network traffic, rendering such risks long-term "invisible." In many of the biggest cyber-attacks, this element alone plays a part.
- Using a compromised IoT platform to hack other computers, systems, and applications. For example, Verizon provided the example of a major university that suffered a botnet attack resulting from more than 5,000 connected devices in its 2017 Data Breach Digest report, almost all of which were on the university's network.
- Attack network systems and trigger the shutdown of the entire system. To cite another recent example, an HVAC controller in a Finnish apartment complex was successfully compromised, allowing hackers to shut down several different HVAC systems.

- The systems are interrupted to cause further damage. In healthcare settings, hackers inside compromised hospital networks can reset IoMT devices such as pacemakers and insulin pumps. This example is particularly scary as these compromised IoMT devices may affect the safety and health of patients.
- Let the IoT computer back. Hackers can take over and transform IoT devices against your company; for example, by using them to compromise other devices or exfiltrate data.

IoT TAXONOMY FOR SECURITY CLASSIFICATION

In IoT, security classification is critical for both users and the producers, because this makes things better decisions to select, grow, and sustain IoT apparatus. IoT security can be graded using the seven taxonomies listed below.

Access Control

In (El-Hajj et al., 2017) the access control tests the functionality of the device within the IoT network and/or the IoT app tools. One of the advantages of IoT is its ability to share data and resources among other devices. This leads to health issues and therefore underlines the require an IoT Access Control System (Al-Halabi et al., 2017).

Encryption Implementation and Confidentiality Assurance

Software encryption includes algorithms for the application of encrypting data and between multiple communication devices (Yousefi & Jameii, 2017). RSA algorithm is the agreed standard for protecting the public key encryption on Internet communication but in resource-constrained IoT devices, this is not feasible. Because of this infeasibility, many developers started to prefer and adopt in their projects the private key, such as the AES cryptosystem (Tsai, 2018). IoT systems are based on dynamic routes and they are dividing their load on multiple physical networks. This information that is ongoing through communication channels needs to be secured against malicious users (Hoogendoorn & Kottke, 2014).

Availability

The concept of being or having availability levels in IoT systems is defined as the availability of the device when a user needs it (El-hajj, 2017). This aspect is very important when a user wishes to replace an old device with a new one. The new device has to be capable to access or to download the history of data.

Authentication Process

Authentication is one of the most exposed and vulnerable points or modules of a device/software application/process/service of a device within an IoT system. As a process, the authentication represents the confirmation of a user and its identity during the process of gaining access to a device or network. The identity can be seen as proof of the user identity. In this case, the authentication is based on "something that the user known". It is recommended that the authentication could be composed of multiple factors, such as 2FA (Two-Factor Authentication), 3FA (Three-Factor Authentication), or MFA (Multi-Factor Authentication). This can be translated into *"something that the user is"*, *"something that the user has"*, or *"something that the user knows"* (Shah et al., 2009).

Authorization

The *authorization process* represents the process that determines if a user or device (who is already authenticated) has the permission to access the resources available on the network (Kim & Lee, 2017). The authorization process represents a complex activity and if it is not well designed and implemented it can be devastating for a real IoT environment. A good and reliable authorization plan includes groups and roles which contain permissions and privileges.

Integrity

The *integrity process* represents the process of making sure that only the entitled user can modify the data and only the right members have the privilege to work with it (El-hajj, 2017).

Non-Repudiation

The process of non-repudiation helps in the law process and the court to identify the users who are in charge and takes responsibility for their actions within an IoT device (Alrababah et al., 2017; Tsai, 2019).

Communication Security

One of the IoT's principal pros is the devices' ability to share data and services. For these devices, communication patterns include telemetry, inquiries, notification, and commands (Hoogendoorn & Kottke, 2014). To protect the privacy and confidentiality of the shared data (whether the contact is machine-to-machine, human-to-human, or human-to-machine), these contact patterns need to be protected.

IMPORTANT SECURITY INCIDENTS

This section covers the most important security incidents that happened to start with 2009 until now. In Table 1 are listed the most important security incidents and it is reviewed their impact on the IoT devices and network itself.

Table 1. Security incidents starting with 2009 until 2020

Security Incident	Description of the Incident / Areas Affected	Reference(s)
University	In 2017, the Security Team from Verizon Wireless has reported a botnet attack on a university for which the name was not disclosed. The effect was quite a disaster, 5000 of IoT devices being affected by the attack. The attack was launched as malware, is designed to change the passwords for each of the devices within the IoT ecosystem. In this situation, the administrators of the devices didn't have access anymore.	(Verizon, 2017)
Energy and Power	Starting with 2010 and by the end of 2014, the National Nuclear Security Administration from United Stated has suffered from 21attacks which managed with success to corrupt the entire system that was in charge of the protection of the nuclear weapons warehouse.	(Macaulay, 2016)
Business and Internet	In 2016 a DDoS attack occurred on Dyn, the largest provider of DNS. The attackers used a powerful botnet called Mirai, intending to penetrate the IoT devices that were used by 100 popular web sites, such as Twitter, Box, Spotify, and PayPal. The purpose of the attack was to make those websites unavailable.	(Capgemini Consulting)
Smart Buildings	Starting with 2012, the thermostats of a government institution were hacked. During the attack, the hackers managed to exploit with success the vulnerabilities within the heating system and to change the temperature from the buildings.	(Macaulay, 2016)
Smart Homes	In 2013 the IP wireless camera from Foscam has been hacked in different places around the world. A successful attack will take control of the audio and mobility of the camera.	(Hill, 2013)
Healthcare	In 2015, the United States Food and Drug Administration has brought to the hospital attention the possibility of being accessed remotely the Symbiq Infusion from Hospira. This attack gives the possibility to the hackers to allow users with no authorization to get control over the device and to modify the quantity of the pumps. This is crucial and vital for the patients.	(Kovacs, 2015)
Transport	In 2015 some cars were remotely hacked. In a video of Miller C. and Valasek C., they demonstrate how it is possible to gain access over the car remotely.	(Greenberg, 2015)

CYBERSECURITY ATTACKS

Table 2 is listed as the most common IoT devices which are already in use in different areas, such as business, medical, transportation, or education institutions. Most of the attacks are successful on IoT devices and networks due to the lack of a proper taxonomy. A proper taxonomy should include a wide review of the most important cases in which the attacks were successful and to underline the lessons learned.

It is very important to understand the security threats within the most popular IoT devices. Table 3 will list for each of the IoT technology from Table 2 the attacks to which are vulnerable.

ASYNCHRONOUS PROGRAMMING

The Task Asynchronous Programming model (TAP) represents one of the most powerful abstraction models used over the asynchronous code. The statements and codes are written using a specific logic and order. In some of the cases and scenarios, several tasks are needed to run at the same time. Once each of the tasks is reaching to its end of the execution, the program will continue with other statements that are ready to be executed.

Table 2. Cyber Security Taxonomy

IoT #	IoT Devices	Cyber Security Taxonomy and Their Lacking's							References
		X_1	X_2	X_3	X_4	X_5	X_6	X_7	
1	Toys for children's	X	X	X		X	X	X	(Chu et al., 2019)
2	Smart locks	X	X	X	X			X	(Ye at al, 2017; Ho et al., 2016)
3	Assistant activation based on voice	X	X	X		X			(Yuan et al., 2018)
4	Thermostat with IoT technology	X	X	X	X	X	X	X	(Feamster, 2016)
5	Medical computers and machines based on IoT technology	X	X		X	X	X		(Halperin et al., 2008; Nextgen, 2018)
6	Camera-based on IoT technology	X	X	X	X	X	X		(Seralathan, 2018)
7	Sensors for improving the quality of air	X	X		X	X	X		(Kapadia et al., 2009)
8	RFID[1] Tags	X	X		X	X	X		(Khattab et al., 2016; Kulkami et al., 2014)
9	Smart Watches	X	X			X	X		(Venable, 2017)
10	UPnP[2] Devices	X	X		X	X	X	X	(Ling et al., 2017)
11	IoT Devices for Industrial Technologies	X	X	X		X	X	X	(Longley, 2016; Sadeghi et al., 2015)

X1 – Authentication; X2 – Integrity and authorization; X3 – Access Control; X4-Availability; X5 – Confidentiality and Encryption; X6 – Secure Communication; X7 – Non-repudiation

It is important to fully understand the process of running the tasks in a specific order. For this is better to start with simple examples and scenarios such as driving a car or preparing breakfast. The code instructions will need to be written with respect for the asynchronous programming model, following the order of the actions or instructions (see Table 4).

For both examples let's consider the standard implementation in Code Example 1 in C# which is a bad implementation especially if those events will occur in an IoT environment or complex ecosystems.

In Source Code Example 2, the messages that are passed as parameters are encrypted using RSA.

In Code Example 3, the code will be updated in such a way that the threads will not block the tasks that are running.

In some of the situations, such as multiple devices that are connected to the IoT ecosystem, one of the goals that are needed to be achieved is to start several tasks independently and immediately at the same time. As soon as each task will get to the end of its execution, the program will jump to the next task or tasks that are ready for execution. By analyzing the two analogies listed above, driving a car, or making breakfast, it is observed that this is the proper way of doing it fast.

Table 3. Security attacks on IoT devices

IoT #	IoT Devices	Security Attack
1	Toys for children's	Replay attack Spoofing Eavesdropping Sniffing
2	Smart locks	Spoofing Relay Attack Eavesdropping Sniffing MitM[3]Attack
3	Assistant activation based on voice	DOS[4] Spoofing
4	Thermostat with IoT technology	Attack through DoS MitM Attack Sniffing Eavesdropping
5	Medical computers and machines based on IoT technology	Replay attack Spoofing MitM attack Eavesdropping Sniffing
6	Camera-based on IoT technology	DoS Spoofing Eavesdropping Sniffing MitM attack
7	Sensors for improving the quality of air	Sniffing MitM attack DoS attack Spoofing Sniffing
8	RFID Tags	Cloning Eavesdropping Sniffing MitM attack DoS attack Cloning Tracking Replay attack
9	Smart Watches	MitM attack Sniffing Eavesdropping
10	UPnP Devices	MitM attack DoS attack Eavesdropping Sniffing Relay attack
11	IoT Devices for Industrial Technologies	MitM attack DoS attack Eavesdropping Sniffing Relay attack Spoofing

Table 4. Examples for asynchronous programming

Example 1 – Preparing the Breakfast	Example 2 – Driving Car[5]
Step 1: Prepare a coup with coffee by pouring it; **Step 2:** Heat a pan and fry three eggs; **Step 3:** Prepare two slices of bacon and fry them; **Step 4:** Take two slices of bread and toast them; **Step 5:** On the toasted bread add butter and jam; **Step 6:** Take a glass and add orange juice.	**Step 1:** Open the car door using a remote controller; **Step 2:** Open the door; **Step 3:** Push down the hand brake and put the gear in "dead point"; **Step 4:** Insert the key and start the engine; **Step 5:** Push the clutch pedal **Step 6:** Put the gear in the first step; **Step 7:** Push acceleration pedal and drive.

To work with tasks that are in progress, for C# it has to be imported System. Threading.Tasks namespace and class Task. This will give the possibility to write code that will be processed simultaneously, cooking breakfast, fry eggs, bacon, and toast at the same time. Each of the code lines represents a specific action to take place, the attention needs to be focused and to use await for other actions that need to be executed. When the implementation occurs in a real IoT environment on a specific device is very important to start a specific task and to protect the Task object because it represents the work. For each of the tasks, it is necessary to use await before executing and focus on its output.

Code Example 1. C# standard (normal) implementation

```
static void Breakfast()
{
        Coffee pourCoffeeCup = PourCoffee();
        MessageBox.Show("The coffee is ready to be served");


Egg friedEggs = FryEggs(2);
        MessageBox.Show("The eggs are fried with success.");


Bacon cookedBacon = FryBacon(3);
        MessageBox.Show("The bacon is ready to be served");


Toast toast = ToastTheBread(2);
        MessageBox.Show("The toasted bread is ready");


PutButter(toast);
        PutJam(toast);
        MessageBox.Show("The toast is ready to be served");


Juice orangeJuice = PourOrangeJuice();
        MessageBox.Show("Orange juice is ready to be served");


        MessageBox.Show("Breakfast is ready to be served");

}
```

Code Example 2. C# data encryption using RSA

```
using System;
using System.Security.Cryptography;
using System.Text;
class BreakfastExample
{
    static void Main()
    {
        try
        {
            //** declare a UnicodeEncoder object and use it to make the
                //** conversion between a byte array and a string.
            UnicodeEncoding converter_to_byte = new UnicodeEncoding();
            //** Hold the real encrypted and decrypted data
                //** using byte arrays.
            byte[] data_to_be_encrypted = converter_to_byte.GetBytes
                                                            ("Data to Encrypt");
            byte[] data_encrypted;
            byte[] data_decrypted;
            //** To generate a public and a private key a new
                //** instance of RSACryptoServiceProvider is declared
            using (RSACryptoServiceProvider encryptionUsingRSA = new
                                            RSACryptoServiceProvider())
            {
                //** the data is passed for encryption together with the
                    //** public key and a flag used as Boolean (true or false).
                //** The Boolean flag is used as OAEP padding
                data_encrypted = EncryptionWithRSA(data_to_be_encrypted,
                            encryptionUsingRSA.ExportParameters(false), false);
                //** the data is passed for decryption together with the
                    //** public key and a flag used as Boolean (true or false).
                //** The Boolean flag is used as OAEP padding
                data_decrypted = DecryptionWithRSA(data_encrypted,
                            encryptionUsingRSA.ExportParameters(true), false);
                //** show the decrypted text in the console
                Console.WriteLine("The decrypted text is: {0}",
                                    converter_to_byte.GetString(data_decrypted));
            }
        }
        catch (ArgumentNullException)
        {
            //** this exception is thrown when something
                //** went wrong with the encryption
            Console.WriteLine("Something went wrong with the encryption.");
        }
    }
    public static byte[] EncryptionWithRSA(byte[] data_to_be_encrypted,
                        RSAParameters rsa_key_info, bool do_oaep_padding)
    {
        try
        {
            byte[] data_encrypted;
            //** declare a new object of RSACryptoServiceProvider.
            using (RSACryptoServiceProvider encryptionUsingRSA = new
                                            RSACryptoServiceProvider())
            {
                //** Import the RSA Key information. To do this is sufficient
                    //** to have included the information about the public key.
                encryptionUsingRSA.ImportParameters(RSAKeyInfo);
                //** mention the OAEP padding and encrypt the bye array
                data_encrypted =
                            encryptionUsingRSA.Encrypt(data_to_be_encrypted,
                                                            do_oaep_padding);
            }
            return data_encrypted;
        }
        //** If there are any exceptions during the process, throw
            //** and catch the Cryptographic Exception and show it in the console
        catch (CryptographicException cryptoExcept)
        {
            Console.WriteLine(cryptoExcept.Message);
            return null;
        }
    }
    public static byte[] DecryptionWithRSA(byte[] data_to_be_decrypted,
                        RSAParameters rsa_key_info, bool do_oaep_padding)
    {
        try
        {
            byte[] data_decrypted;
            //** declare a new object instance of RSACryptoServiceProvider.
            using (RSACryptoServiceProvider decryptionUsingRSA = new
                                            RSACryptoServiceProvider())
            {
                //** The RSA key information has to be imported.
                decryptionUsingRSA.ImportParameters(rsa_key_info);

                //** mention the OAEP padding and encrypt the bye array
                data_decrypted = RSA.Decrypt(DataToDecrypt, DoOAEPPadding);
            }
            return data_decrypted;
        }
        //** If there are any exceptions during the process, throw
            //** and catch the Cryptographic Exception and show it in the console
        catch (CryptographicException cryptoExcept)
        {
            Console.WriteLine(cryptoExcept.ToString());
            return null;
        }
    }
}
```

Code Example 3. C# implementation using async task and encryption

```
static async Task Main(string[] args)
{
BreakfastExample be = new BreakfastExample();

Coffee pourCoffeeCup = PourCoffee();
        MessageBox.Show(be.EncryptionWithRSA("The coffee is ready to be
served", encryptionUsingRSA.ExportParameters(false), false));


Egg friedEggs = FryEggs(2);
        MessageBox.Show(be.EncryptionWithRSA("The eggs are fried with
success.", encryptionUsingRSA.ExportParameters(false), false));

Bacon cookedBacon = FryBacon(3);
        MessageBox.Show(be.EncryptionWithRSA("The bacon is ready to be
served",
encryptionUsingRSA.ExportParameters(false), false));


Toast toast = ToastTheBread(2);

PutButter(toast);
        PutJam(toast);
        MessageBox.Show(be.EncryptionWithRSA("The toast bread is ready",
encryptionUsingRSA.ExportParameters(false), false));

Juice orangeJuice = PourOrangeJuice();
        MessageBox.Show(be.EncryptionWithRSA("Orange juice is ready to be
served", encryptionUsingRSA.ExportParameters(false), false));

        MessageBox.Show(be.EncryptionWithRSA("Breakfast is ready to be
served.", encryptionUsingRSA.ExportParameters(false), false));
}
```

For the above examples (see Code Example 1 and Code Example 2) the source code should be modified to store the operations that will follow to be executed once they start, rather than wait (*await*) for them (Code Example 4).

The source code from above will work better. All the asynchronous tasks will start at once. Each task will be in the awaited state as the outputs will be necessary for further processing. The same code from above can be very useful if there is a web application being developed and it makes requests for microservice, in the end, the results being combined on a single web page. The requests in the web ap-

Code Example 4. Using task class from C#

```
Coffee pourCoffeeCup = PourCoffee();
MessageBox.Show(be.EncryptionWithRSA("The coffee is ready to be served",
encryptionUsingRSA.ExportParameters(false), false));

Task<Egg> taskEggs = FryEggs(2);
Egg eggs = await taskEggs;
MessageBox.Show(be.EncryptionWithRSA("The eggs are fried with success.",
encryptionUsingRSA.ExportParameters(false), false));

Task<Bacon> taskBacon = FryBacon(3);
Bacon cookedBacon = await taskBacon;
MessageBox.Show(be.EncryptionWithRSA("The bacon is ready to be served.",
encryptionUsingRSA.ExportParameters(false), false));

Task<Toast> taskToastingBread = ToastTheBread(2);
Toast toast = await taskToastingBread;
PutButter(toast);
PutJam(toast);
MessageBox.Show(be.EncryptionWithRSA("The toast bread is ready.",
encryptionUsingRSA.ExportParameters(false), false));

Juice orangeJuice = PourOrangeJuice();
MessageBox.Show(be.EncryptionWithRSA("Orange juice is ready to be served.",
encryptionUsingRSA.ExportParameters(false), false));

MessageBox.Show(be.EncryptionWithRSA("Breakfast is ready to be served.",
encryptionUsingRSA.ExportParameters(false), false));
```

plication will be done immediately and with the help of await the rest of the tasks will be in standby mode and the web page displayed to the user will be populated accordingly.

In C++ the things are a little different and the mechanism of providing asynchronous programming coroutines and assuring the security of the data have a different representation comparing with C++.

Consider Code Example 5 to fetch the data that should be synchronized and later to assure their security.

To use cryptography primitives within an IoT source code, Code Example 6 represents an adjustment of the Code Example 5. For this is necessary and sufficient to modify the functions data_fetching and data_fetching_from_file.

Code Example 5. Using threads synchronization in C++20

```cpp
#include <string>
#include <thread>

std::string data_fetching(std::string data_to_be_fetched)
{
        //** set the time for 5 second to be sure
        //** that the function will be completed
        std::this_thread::sleep_for(seconds(5));

        //** format the string to be returned
        return "Data: " + data_to_be_fetched;
}


std::string data_fetching_from_file (std::string data_to_be_fetched)
{
        //** set the time for 5 second to be sure
        //** that the function will be completed
        std::this_thread::sleep_for(seconds(5));

        //** format the string to be returned
        return "Data from File: " + data_to_be_fetched;
}


int main()
{
        //** start timing
        system_clock::time_point startTime = system_clock::now();

        //** fetch normal data (but not hard coded)
        std::string fetched_data = data_fetching ("Data");

        //** fetch the data available in the files
        std::string fetched_data_from_file = data_fetching_from_file("Data");

        //** stop the time and save the end time
        auto endTime = system_clock::now();

        auto differenceTime = duration_cast < std::chrono::seconds >
                                            (endTime - startTime).count();
        std::cout << "The amount of total time consumed is = "
                                            << diff << " Seconds" << std::endl;

        //** combine both sources of data
        std::string combinedDataSources = fetched_data +
                                            ":: " + fetched_data_from_file;

        //** displaying the combination of both data sources
        std::cout << "The final data is = " <<
                                            combinedDataSources << std::endl;

        return 0;
}
```

Code Example 6. Using threads synchronization with cryptography primitives, such as RSA[6] in C++20

```cpp
std::string data_fetching(std::string data_to_be_fetched)
{
        //** set the time for 5 second to be sure
        //** that the function will be completed
        std::this_thread::sleep_for(seconds(5));

        //** format the string to be returned
        return "Data: " + RSAEncrypt(data_to_be_fetched);
}

std::string data_fetching_from_file (std::string data_to_be_fetched)
{
        //** set the time for 5 second to be sure
        //** that the function will be completed
        std::this_thread::sleep_for(seconds(5));

        //** format the string to be returned
        return "Data from File: " + RSADecrypt(data_to_be_fetched);
}
```

FUTURE RESEARCH DIRECTIONS

A promising research direction is integrating IoT with Artificial Intelligence (AI) and Machine Learning (ML). In this research direction, the AI will have an increasing role in the security of the IoT devices. The new generation systems will need different types of authentication (for example, authentication of an IoT device in a network), dynamic authorization processes, or behavior analysis processes specialized on individual device behavior analysis, but also the network behavior analysis, whose purpose is to detect the security threats. Other candidates that includes the research direction of integrating IoT and AI/ML are the smart cities and the industry. Regarding the smart cities, there already are different sensors or cameras mounted across the cities. Analyzing the data received from these devices could have many benefits, from which pollution reduction, energy saving, or smart management systems (for example, a parking system that manages and finds parking places) can be mentioned. Regarding industry, one of the immediately benefits is the smart maintenance of the machines. Having different IoT devices connected through a network, the management of the production system can be optimized. For example, when the temperature of a machine is too high, the system can make decisions such that the work to not be interrupted by this incident.

CONCLUSION

The current chapter underlined the importance and the role that security guarantees for the creation of a secure infrastructure and not making it susceptible to external attacks. It is very important to have a classification of security threats in IoT technologies and ecosystems. Based on the review of the most important security threats a framework (CSAP) has been proposed to be used for developing applications that run on IoT devices. The proposed framework is using two powerful programming languages, C# 9 and C++20. The framework has been developed and proposed using the new features of the programming languages, in this way the integrity and authentication mechanisms will be using new advanced programming concepts that can guarantee a higher level of security performance of the applications.

Security taxonomies are very important for developing IoT applications. If the IoT devices are used for different sectors, such as industry, medical, transport, smart homes, government, or education, the security taxonomies need to be done properly. The security attacks and vulnerabilities should be analyzed accordingly and in-depth research has to be done before the IoT devices are deployed and applications/services installed accordingly within a secure network. A secured IoT device connected to an unsecured network and an unsecured IoT device connected to a secured network will result in an unsecured system or network. If one of the two scenarios exists, the hackers will take advantage of the unsecured system to gain access to the network and to use their abilities for gaining personal advantages.

Having an infiltrated network or a penetrated IoT device, an attacker will have the possibility to infest other servers and IoT devices from the network or Internet.

A solution to the missing security features reported in Table 2, is to introduce standard security characteristics for all the IoT devices from a network. The security threats listed in Table 3 represents the most common threats experienced in most of the IoT devices. The developers are encouraged to create tests used for verifying and checking the vulnerabilities of the IoT device for such threats. The collected data will determine the security level of the device.

All the device types mentioned in Table 2 and Table are proprietary devices. As a result, it is very difficult for the users to be aware and know the source code of the applications that are running and the security taxonomy is supported.

REFERENCES

Al-Halabi, Y., Raeq, N., & Abu-Dabaseh, F. (2017). Study on access control approaches in the context of the Internet of Things: A survey. *International Conference on Engineering and Technology (ICET)*, 1-7. 10.1109/ICEngTechnol.2017.8308153

Alrababah, D., Al-Shammari, E., & Alsuht, A. (2017). A Survey: Authentication Protocols for Wireless Sensor Network in the Internet of Things. *Keys and Attacks. In International Conference on New Trends in Computing Sciences (ICTCS)*, 270-276. 10.1109/ICTCS.2017.34

Ammar, M., Russello, G., & Crispo, B. (2018). Internet of Things: A survey on the security of IoT frameworks. *Journal of Information Security and Applications, 38,* 8–27. doi:10.1016/j.jisa.2017.11.002

Bakiri, M., Guyeux, C., Couchot, J. F., Marangio, L., & Galatolo, S. (2018). Hardware and secure pseudorandom generator for constrained devices. *IEEE Transactions on Industrial Informatics, 14*(8), 3754–3765. doi:10.1109/TII.2018.2815985

Capgemini Consulting. (n.d.). *Securing the Internet of Things Opportunity: Putting Cybersecurity at the Heart of IoT.* Author.

Chi-Ren, T. (2020). *Non-Repudiation in Practice. Paper.* Citigroup Information Security Office. Available http://citeseerx.ist.psu.edu/viewdoc/download?doi=10.1.1.106.6685&rep=rep1&type=pdf

Chu, G., Apthorpe, N., & Feamster, N. (2019, February). Security and Privacy Analyses of Internet of Things Children's Toys. *IEEE Internet of Things Journal, 6*(1), 978–985. doi:10.1109/JIOT.2018.2866423

El-hajj, M., Chamoun, M., Fadlallah, A., & Serrhouchni, A. (2017). Taxonomy of authentication techniques in the Internet of Things (IoT). *IEEE 15th Student Conference on Research and Development (SCOReD),* 67-71.

Feamster, N. (2016). *Who Will Secure the Internet of Things?* Available: https://freedom-to-tinker. com/2016/01/19/who -will -secure-the-internet-of-things/

Fremantle, P., & Scott, P. (2017). A survey of secure middleware for the Internet of Things. *PeerJ. Computer Science, 3,* e114. doi:10.7717/peerj-cs.114

Greenberg. (2015). *Hackers Remotely Kill a Jeep on a Highway.* YouTube.

Halak, B., Zwolinski, M., & Mispan, M. S. (2016, October). Overview of PUF-based hardware security solutions for the Internet of Things. *2016 IEEE 59th International Midwest Symposium on Circuits and Systems (MWSCAS),* 1-4.

Halperin, D. (2008). Pacemakers and Implantable Cardiac Defibrillators: *Software Radio Attacks and Zero-Power Defenses. IEEE Symposium on Security and Privacy,* 129-142.

Hassan, W. H. (2019). Current research on the Internet of Things (IoT) security: A survey. *Computer Networks, 148,* 283–294. doi:10.1016/j.comnet.2018.11.025

Hill, K. (2013). *Baby Monitor Hack Could Happen to 40,000 Other Foscam Users.* Available: https:// www.forbes.com/sites/kashmirhill/2013/08/27/baby-monitor-hack-could-happen-to-40000-other-foscam-users/#75ffc8f558b5

Ho, Leung, Mishra, Hosseini, Song, & Wagner. (2016). Smart Locks: Lessons for Securing Commodity Internet of Things Devices. In *Proceedings of the 11th ACM on Asia Conference on Computer and Communications Security (ASIA CCS '16).* Association for Computing Machinery. 10.1145/2897845.2897886

Hoogendoorn, M., & Kottke, M. (2014). *Building the Internet of Things.* Available: http://cdn2.hubspot. net/hub/444534/file-2491337246-df/Building_the_Internet_of_Things.pdf?t=1424896250151

Kapadia, A., Kotz, D., & Triandopoulos, N. (2009). Opportunistic sensing: Security challenges for the new paradigm. First International Communication Systems and Networks and Workshops, 1-10.

Khattab, Jeddi, Amini, & Bayoumi. (2016). *RFID Security: A Lightweight Paradigm.* Springer International Publishing.

Kim, H., & Lee, E. A. (2017). Authentication and Authorization for the Internet of Things. *IT Professional, 19*(5), 27–33. doi:10.1109/MITP.2017.3680960

Kovacs, E. (2015). *FDA Issues Alert Over Vulnerable Hospira Drug Pumps*. Available: https://www.securityweek.com/fdaissues-alert-over-vulnerable-hospira-drug-pumps/

Kulkarni, G., Shelke, R., Sutar, R., & Mohite, S. (2014). RFID security issues & challenges. *International Conference on Electronics and Communication Systems (ICECS)*, 1-4.

Li, F., Shinde, A., Shi, Y., Ye, J., Li, X. Y., & Song, W. (2019). System statistics learning-based IoT security: Feasibility and suitability. *IEEE Internet of Things Journal, 6*(4), 6396–6403. doi:10.1109/JIOT.2019.2897063

Ling, Z., Luo, J., Xu, Y., Gao, C., Wu, K., & Fu, X. (2017). Security Vulnerabilities of the Internet of Things: A Case Study of the Smart Plug System. *IEEE Internet of Things Journal, 4*(6), 1899–1909. doi:10.1109/JIOT.2017.2707465

Longley, G. (2016). *The Security Challenges Facing Industrial IoT*. Available: https://www.itproportal.com/2016/04/11/thesecurity-challenges-facing-industrial-iot/

Macaulay, T. (2016). *RIoT Control: Understanding and Managing Risks and the Internet of Things*. Todd Green.

NextGen. (2018). *IoT Medical Devices Security Vulnerabilities on WiFi Networks*. Available: https://www.nextgenexecsearch.com/iot-medical-devices-security

Pielli, C., Zucchetto, D., Zanella, A., Vangelista, L., & Zorzi, M. (2015). Platforms and Protocols for the Internet of Things. *EAI Endorsed Trans. Internet Things, 15*(1), e5. doi:10.4108/eai.26-10-2015.150599

Rijmen, V., & Daemen, J. (2001). Advanced encryption standard. In Proceedings of Federal Information Processing Standards Publications. National Institute of Standards and Technology.

Rivest, R. L., Shamir, A., & Adleman, L. M. (1983). *U.S. Patent No. 4,405,829*. Washington, DC: U.S. Patent and Trademark Office.

Sadeghi, A., Wachsmann, C., & Waidner, M. (2015). Security and privacy challenges in the industrial Internet of Things. *52nd ACM/EDAC/IEEE Design Automation Conference (DAC)*, 1-6. 10.1145/2744769.2747942

Sedjelmaci, H., Senouci, S. M., & Taleb, T. (2017). An accurate security game for low-resource IoT devices. *IEEE Transactions on Vehicular Technology, 66*(10), 9381–9393. doi:10.1109/TVT.2017.2701551

Seralathan, Y. (2018). IoT security vulnerability: A case study of a Web camera. *20th International Conference on Advanced Communication Technology (ICACT)*, 1–2.

Shah, Fazl-e-Hadi, & Minhas. (2009). New Factor of Authentication: Something You Process. *International Conference on Future Computer and Communication*, 102-106.

Singh, A., Chawla, N., Ko, J. H., Kar, M., & Mukhopadhyay, S. (2018). Energy-efficient and side-channel secure cryptographic hardware for IoT-edge nodes. *IEEE Internet of Things Journal, 6*(1), 421–434. doi:10.1109/JIOT.2018.2861324

Tsai, K., Huang, Y., Leu, F., You, I., Huang, Y., & Tsa, C. (2018). AES-128 Based Secure Low Power Communication for LoRaWAN IoT Environments. *IEEE Access: Practical Innovations, Open Solutions, 6*, 45325–45334. doi:10.1109/ACCESS.2018.2852563

Venable, J. (2017). *Child safety smartwatches 'easy' to hack, watchdog says*. Available: https://www.bbc.com/news/technology-41652742

Verizon. (2017). *IoT Calamity: The Panda Monium*. Available: http://www.verizonenterprise.com/resources/rp_data-breach-digest-2017-sneak-peek_xg_en.pdf

Weber, R. H. (2010). Internet of Things–New security and privacy challenges. *Computer Law & Security Review, 26*(1), 23–30. doi:10.1016/j.clsr.2009.11.008

Ye, M., Jiang, N., Yang, H., & Yan, Q. (2017). Security analysis of Internet-of-Things: A case study of the smart lock. *IEEE Conference on Computer Communications Workshops (INFOCOM WKSHPS)*, 499-504. 10.1109/INFCOMW.2017.8116427

Yousefi, A., & Jameii, S. M. (2017). Improving the security of the Internet of things using encryption algorithms. *International Conference on IoT and Application (ICIOT)*, 1-5. 10.1109/ICIOTA.2017.8073627

Yuan, X. (2018). All Your Alexa Are Belong to Us: A Remote Voice Control Attack against Echo. *IEEE Global Communications Conference (GLOBECOM)*, 1-6. 10.1109/GLOCOM.2018.8647762

ADDITIONAL READING

Dehghantahna, A., & Choo, K. K. R. (Eds.). (2019). *Handbook of Big Data and IoT Security*. Springer International Publishing. doi:10.1007/978-3-030-10543-3

Gilchrist, A. (2017). *IoT Security Issues*. De Gruyter. doi:10.1515/9781501505775

KEY TERMS AND DEFINITIONS

Authentication: Represents the process of identifying a user within a computer system, software, or web application.

Confidentiality: Is the process to assure that nobody is able to get into the possession of the data and read it without the legitimate user.

Cracker: Represents the individual who is trying to gain access to computer systems without being authorized.

Cryptanalysis: Represents the art of studying and analyzing the information systems with the goal to study the way of how the information and data are hidden.

Cryptography: Represents the art of studying techniques in order to obtain a secure communication knowing that third-parties are participating in order to obtain the real nature of secure communication.

Cryptology: The art of studying *cryptography* and *cryptanalysis* with their techniques in order to create a secure communication.

Cyber Security: Deals with the protection of networks and computer systems with the goal to protect them against attackers and their possible damages on the hardware, software, or electronic data.

Ethical Hacker: Is a legal person, sometimes known as an information security expert, who is hired by a company with the goal to test their network infrastructure and applications for vulnerabilities and report them in order to take action and to improve the security measures.

Integrity: Deals with protecting the information from not being modified by attackers which play the role of an unauthorized party.

ENDNOTES

[1]   RFID = Radio-Frequency Identification

[2]   UPnP = Universal Plug and Play

[3]   MitM = Man-in-the-Middle

[4]   DoS = Denial of Service

[5]   This example is listed as an analogy. This example will not be treated within this chapter.

[6]   C++ Program for RSA Algorithm Implementation, https://www.sanfoundry.com/cpp-program-implement-rsa-algorithm/

Compilation of References

Goap, A., Sharma, D., Shukla, A. K., & Krishna, C. R. (2018). An IoT based smart irrigation management system using Machine learning and open source technologies. *Computers and Electronics in Agriculture*, *155*, 41–49. doi:10.1016/j.compag.2018.09.040

Shaikh, J. (2020). Role of Artificial Intelligence in Prevention and Detection of Covid-19. *International Journal of Advanced Science and Technology*, *29*(9), 45–54.

Goodfellow, I., Bengio, Y., & Courville, A. (2016). *Deep learning*. MIT Press.

Vaishya, R., Javaid, M., Khan, I. H., & Haleem, A. (2020). Artificial Intelligence (AI) applications for COVID-19 pandemic. *Diabetes & Metabolic Syndrome*, *14*(4), 337–339. doi:10.1016/j.dsx.2020.04.012 PMID:32305024

Alamanda, M. S. (2020). Aspect-based sentiment analysis search engine for social media data. *CSIT*, *8*(2), 193–197. doi:10.100740012-020-00295-3

Kamaruddin, F., Abd Malik, N. N. N., Murad, N. A., Latiff, N. M. A. A., Yusof, S. K. S., & Hamzah, S. A. (2019). IoT-based intelligent irrigation management and monitoring system using Arduino. *Telkomnika*, *17*(5), 2378–2388. doi:10.12928/telkomnika.v17i5.12818

OECD. (2020). *Using Artificial Intelligence to Help Combat COVID-19*, in *OECD*. http://www.oecd.org/coronavirus/policy-responses/using-artificial-intelligence-to-help-combat-covid-19-ae4c5c21/

Chauhan, P., Sharma, N., & Sikka, G. (2020). *The emergence of social media data and sentiment analysis in election prediction. J Ambient Intell Human Comput*. doi:10.100712652-020-02423-y

LeCun, Y., Bottou, L., Bengio, Y., & Haffner, P. (1998). Gradient-based learning applied to document recognition. *Proceedings of the IEEE*, *86*(11), 2278–2324. doi:10.1109/5.726791

Wu, J. (2020). *How Artificial Intelligence Can Help Fight Coronavirus*. Academic Press.

Chen, L., Lee, C., & Chen, M. (2020). Exploration of social media for sentiment analysis using deep learning. *Soft Computing*, *24*(11), 8187–8197. doi:10.100700500-019-04402-8

Kent, J. (2020). *Artificial Intelligence Identifies High-Risk COVID-19 Patients*. Academic Press.

Minerva, R., Biru, A., & Rotondi, D. (2015). Towards a definition of the Internet of Things (IoT). *IEEE Internet Initiative*, *1*(1), 1–86.

Ahmad, S., Asghar, M. Z., Alotaibi, F. M., & Awan, I. (2019). Detection and classification of social media-based extremist affiliations using sentiment analysis techniques. *Hum. Cent. Comput. Inf. Sci.*, *9*(1), 24. doi:10.118613673-019-0185-6

Deep Mind. (n.d.). https://deepmind.com/research/open-source/computational-predictions-of-protein-structures-associated-with-COVID-19

Mungale, S. C., Sankar, M., Khot, D., Parvathi, R., & Mudgal, D. N. (2020, February). An Effiecient Smart Irrigation System for Solar System by using PIC and GSM. In *2020 International Conference on Inventive Computation Technologies (ICICT)* (pp. 973-976). IEEE. 10.1109/ICICT48043.2020.9112431

Namala, K. K., & AV, K. K. PMath, AKumari, AKulkarni, S. (2016, December). Smart irrigation with embedded system. In *2016 IEEE Bombay Section Symposium (IBSS)* (pp. 1-5). IEEE.

Tahamtan, A., & Ardebili, A. (2020). Real-time RT-PCR in COVID-19 detection: Issues affecting the results. *Expert Review of Molecular Diagnostics, 20*(5), 453–454. doi:10.1080/14737159.2020.1757437 PMID:32297805

Lee, K.-F. (2020). *Covid-19 Will Accelerate the AI Health Care Revolution.* Available from: https://www.wired.com/story/covid-19-will-accelerate-ai-health-care-revolution/

National Geographic. (2020). *Resource Library.* Accessed February 20, 2020, at https://www.nationalgeographic.org/encyclopedia

Oregon State University. (2020). *Describe the importance of irrigation in producing forages.* Accessed February 18, 2020, at https://forages.oregonstate.edu/nfgc/eo/onlineforagecurriculum/instructormaterials/availabletopics/irrigation/importance

Salman, F. M. (2020). COVID-19 Detection using Artificial Intelligence. *International Journal of Academic Engineering Research, 4*(3), 18–25.

Pezol, N. S., Adnan, R., & Tajjudin, M. (2020, June). Design of an Internet of Things (IoT) Based Smart Irrigation and Fertilization System Using Fuzzy Logic for Chili Plant. In *2020 IEEE International Conference on Automatic Control and Intelligent Systems (I2CACIS)* (pp. 69-73). IEEE. 10.1109/I2CACIS49202.2020.9140199

Zhang, J. (2020). *COVID-19 Screening on Chest X-ray Images Using Deep Learning based Anomaly Detection.* arXiv preprint arXiv:2003

Abba, S., Wadumi Namkusong, J., Lee, J. A., & Liz Crespo, M. (2019). Design and Performance Evaluation of a Low-Cost Autonomous Sensor Interface for a Smart IoT-Based Irrigation Monitoring and Control System. *Sensors (Basel), 19*(17), 3643. doi:10.339019173643 PMID:31438597

Mao, K., & Niu, J. (2015). Cross-Domain Sentiment Analysis of Product Reviews by Combining Lexicon-based and Learn-based Techniques. *IEEE 17th International Conference on High-Performance Computing and Communications.*

Medical News Today. (n.d.). https://www.medicalnewstoday.com/articles/novel-coronavirus-your-questions-answered

Reghukumar, A., & Vijayakumar, V. (2019). Smart Plant Watering System with Cloud Analysis and Plant Health Prediction. *Procedia Computer Science, 165,* 126–135. doi:10.1016/j.procs.2020.01.088

Zhang, M. (2020). *Application of artificial intelligence image-assisted diagnosis system in chest CT examination of COVID-19.* Nuclear Medicine & Medical Imaging.

Narin, A., Kaya, C., & Pamuk, Z. (2020). Automatic Detection of Coronavirus Disease (COVID-19) Using X-ray Images and Deep Convolutional Neural Networks. arXiv preprint arXiv

Rumelhart, D. E., Hinton, G. E., & Williams, R. J. (1985). *Learning internal representations by error propagation* (No. ICS-8506). California Univ San Diego La Jolla Inst for Cognitive Science.

Akwu, S., Bature, U. I., Jahun, K. I., Baba, M. A., & Nasir, A. Y. (2020). Automatic plant Irrigation Control System Using Arduino and GSM Module. *International Journal of Engineering and Manufacturing*, *10*(3), 12–26. doi:10.5815/ijem.2020.03.02

Hemdan, Shouman, & Karar. (2020). *COVIDX-Net: A Framework of Deep Learning Classifiers to Diagnose COVID-19 in X-Ray Images*. arXiv preprint arXiv, 2020.2003.11055

Salakhutdinov, R., & Hinton, G. (2009, April). Deep Boltzmann machines. In Artificial intelligence and statistics (pp. 448-455). Academic Press.

Sethy, P. K. (2020). *Detection of Coronavirus Disease (COVID-19)*. Based on Deep Features and Support Vector Machine. Preprints.

Abdulla, A. (2020). Project IDentif.AI: Harnessing Artificial Intelligence to Rapidly Optimize Combination Therapy Development for Infectious Disease Intervention. Advanced Therapeutics.

Selmani, A., Outanoute, M., Alaoui, M. A., El Khayat, M., Guerbaoui, M., Ed-Dahhak, A., . . . Bouchikhi, B. (2018, April). Multithreading design for an embedded irrigation system running on solar power. In *2018 4th International Conference on Optimization and Applications (ICOA)* (pp. 1-5). IEEE. 10.1109/ICOA.2018.8370519

My Gov. (n.d.). https://www.mygov.in/aarogya-setu-app/

Singh, G., Sharma, D., Goap, A., Sehgal, S., Shukla, A. K., & Kumar, S. (2019, October). Machine Learning based soil moisture prediction for the Internet of Things based Smart Irrigation System. In *2019 5th International Conference on Signal Processing, Computing and Control (ISPCC)* (pp. 175-180). IEEE. 10.1109/ISPCC48220.2019.8988313

Google Play. (n.d.). https://play.google.com/store/apps/details?id=org.nic.covidcarekannur&hl=en_IN&showAllReviews=true

Singh, P., & Saikia, S. (2016, December). *Arduino-based smart irrigation using water flow sensor, soil moisture sensor, temperature sensor and ESP8266 WiFi module. In 2016 IEEE Region 10 Humanitarian Technology Conference (R10-HTC)*. IEEE.

Thakare, S., & Bhagat, P. H. (2018, June). Arduino-based smart irrigation using sensors and ESP8266 WiFi module. In *2018 Second International Conference on Intelligent Computing and Control Systems (ICICCS)* (pp. 1-5). IEEE. 10.1109/ICCONS.2018.8663041

Trace Together. (n.d.). https://www.tracetogether.gov.sg/

Covid Watch. (n.d.). https://covid-watch.org/

Vincent, P., Larochelle, H., Lajoie, I., Bengio, Y., Manzagol, P. A., & Bottou, L. (2010). Stacked denoising autoencoders: Learning useful representations in a deep network with a local denoising criterion. *Journal of Machine Learning Research*, *11*(12).

Govextra. (n.d.). https://govextra.gov.il/ministry-of-health/hamagen-app/

Aggarwal, S., & Kumar, A. (2019, March). A Smart Irrigation System to Automate Irrigation Process Using IOT and Artificial Neural Network. In *2019 2nd International Conference on Signal Processing and Communication (ICSPC)* (pp. 310-314). IEEE. 10.1109/ICSPC46172.2019.8976631

Bermingham & Smeaton. (2010). *Classifying Sentiment in Microblogs: Is Brevity an Advantage?* In CIKM'10, Toronto, Ontario, Canada.

Zheng, Y.-Y., Ma, Y.-T., Zhang, J.-Y., & Xie, X. (2020). COVID-19 and the cardiovascular system. *Nature Reviews. Cardiology, 17*(5), 259–260. doi:10.103841569-020-0360-5 PMID:32139904

Reuters. (n.d.). https://in.reuters.com/article/health-coronavirus-germany-tech/germany-launches-smartwatch-app-to-monitor-coronavirus-spread-idINKBN21P1US

Bartoletti, I. (2019). AI in Healthcare: Ethical and Privacy Challenges. In Artificial Intelligence in Medicine. AIME 2019. Springer. doi:10.1007/978-3-030-21642-9_2

Wahl, B., Cossy-Gantner, A., Germann, S., & Schwalbe, N. R. (2018). Artificial intelligence (AI) and global health: How can AI contribute to health in resource-poor settings? *BMJ Global Health, 3*(4), e000798. doi:10.1136/bmjgh-2018-000798 PMID:30233828

Ahamed, T. (2019). *Deep learning and IoT-based pump systems for precision irrigation.* Accessed August 8, 2020, at https://www.apo-tokyo.org/resources/articles/deep-learning-and-iot-based-pump-systems-for-precision-irrigation/

Das & Sivaji. (2010). Labeling Emotion in Bengali Blog Corpus – A Fine-Grained Tagging at Sentence Level. *Proceedings of the 8th Workshop on Asian Language Resources*, 47–55.

Mei, X., Lee, H.-C., Diao, K., Huang, M., Lin, B., Liu, C., Xie, Z., Ma, Y., Robson, P. M., Chung, M., Bernheim, A., Mani, V., Calcagno, C., Li, K., Li, S., Shan, H., Lv, J., Zhao, T., Xia, J., ... Yang, Y. (2020). Artificial intelligence–enabled rapid diagnosis of patients with COVID-19. *Nature Medicine, 26*(8), 1224–1228. doi:10.103841591-020-0931-3 PMID:32427924

Alomar, B., & Alazzam, A. (2018, November). A smart irrigation system using IoT and fuzzy logic controller. In 2018 Fifth HCT Information Technology Trends (ITT) (pp. 175-179). IEEE. doi:10.1109/CTIT.2018.8649531

Huang, C., Wang, Y., Li, X., Ren, L., Zhao, J., Hu, Y., Zhang, L., Fan, G., Xu, J., Gu, X., Cheng, Z., Yu, T., Xia, J., Wei, Y., Wu, W., Xie, X., Yin, W., Li, H., Liu, M., ... Cao, B. (2020). Clinical features of patients infected with 2019 novel coronavirus in Wuhan, China. *Lancet, 395*(10223), 497–506. doi:10.1016/S0140-6736(20)30183-5 PMID:31986264

Ramteke, J., Godhia, D., Shah, S., & Shaikh, A. (2016). Election Result Prediction Using Twitter sentiment Analysis. *Conference: 2016 International Conference on Inventive Computation Technologies (ICICT).*

Arvindan, A. N., & Keerthika, D. (2016, March). Experimental investigation of remote control via Android smartphone of Arduino-based automated irrigation system using moisture sensor. In *2016 3rd International Conference on Electrical Energy Systems (ICEES)* (pp. 168-175). IEEE.

Rothan, H. A., & Byrareddy, S. N. (2020). The epidemiology and pathogenesis of coronavirus disease (COVID-19) outbreak. *Journal of Autoimmunity, 109*, 102433. doi:10.1016/j.jaut.2020.102433 PMID:32113704

Sharma & Moh. (2016). Prediction of Indian Election Using Sentiment Analysis on Hindi Twitter. *IEEE International Conference on Big Data (Big Data).*

Assiri, A., Al-Tawfiq, J. A., Al-Rabeeah, A. A., Al-Rabiah, F. A., Al-Hajjar, S., Al-Barrak, A., Flemban, H., Al-Nassir, W. N., Balkhy, H. H., Al-Hakeem, R. F., Makhdoom, H. Q., Zumla, A. I., & Memish, Z. A. (2013). Epidemiological, demographic, and clinical characteristics of 47 cases of Middle East respiratory syndrome coronavirus disease from Saudi Arabia: A descriptive study. *The Lancet. Infectious Diseases, 13*(9), 752–761. doi:10.1016/S1473-3099(13)70204-4 PMID:23891402

Atzori, L., Iera, A., & Morabito, G. (2017). Understanding the Internet of Things: Definition, potentials, and societal role of a fast evolving paradigm. *Ad Hoc Networks, 56*, 122–140. doi:10.1016/j.adhoc.2016.12.004

Taboada & Brooke. (2011). Lexicon-Based Methods for Sentiment Analysis. *Association for Computational Linguistics, 37*(2).

Chang, Y. C., Huang, T. W., & Huang, N. F. (2019, September). A Machine Learning Based Smart Irrigation System with LoRa P2P Networks. In *2019 20th Asia-Pacific Network Operations and Management Symposium (APNOMS)* (pp. 1-4). IEEE. 10.23919/APNOMS.2019.8893034

Mittal, N., & Agarwal, B. (2013). Sentiment Analysis of Hindi Review based on Negation and Discourse Relation. *International Joint Conference on Natural Language Processing*, 45–50.

Ren, L.-L., Wang, Y.-M., Wu, Z.-Q., Xiang, Z.-C., Guo, L., Xu, T., Jiang, Y.-Z., Xiong, Y., Li, Y.-J., Li, X.-W., Li, H., Fan, G.-H., Gu, X.-Y., Xiao, Y., Gao, H., Xu, J.-Y., Yang, F., Wang, X.-M., Wu, C., ... Wang, J.-W. (2020). Identification of a novel coronavirus causing severe pneumonia in human: A descriptive study. *Chinese Medical Journal, 133*(9), 1015–1024. doi:10.1097/CM9.0000000000000722 PMID:32004165

Dogo, E. M., Salami, A. F., Nwulu, N. I., & Aigbavboa, C. O. (2019). Blockchain and internet of things-based technologies for intelligent water management system. In *Artificial intelligence in IoT* (pp. 129–150). Springer. doi:10.1007/978-3-030-04110-6_7

Dong, E., Du, H., & Gardner, L. (2020). An interactive web-based dashboard to track COVID-19 in real time. *The Lancet. Infectious Diseases, 20*(5), 533–534. doi:10.1016/S1473-3099(20)30120-1 PMID:32087114

Mukherjee, & Pushpak. (2012). Sentiment Analysis in Twitter with Lightweight Discourse Analysis. *Proceedings of COLING 2012: Technical Papers*, 1847–1864.

Hinton, G. E., Osindero, S., & Teh, Y. W. (2006). A fast learning algorithm for deep belief nets. *Neural Computation, 18*(7), 1527–1554. doi:10.1162/neco.2006.18.7.1527 PMID:16764513

Kamel Boulos, M. N., & Geraghty, E. M. (2020). Geographical tracking and mapping of coronavirus disease COVID-19/severe acute respiratory syndrome coronavirus 2 (SARS-CoV-2) epidemic and associated events around the world: How 21st century GIS technologies are supporting the global fight against outbreaks and epidemics. *International Journal of Health Geographics, 19*(1), 8. doi:10.118612942-020-00202-8 PMID:32160889

Abd-ellah, M. K., Ismail, A., Khalaf, A. A. M., & Hamed, H. F. A. (2019). A review on brain tumor diagnosis from MRI images : Practical implications, key achievements, and lessons learned. *Magnetic Resonance Imaging, 61*(May), 300–318. doi:10.1016/j.mri.2019.05.028 PMID:31173851

Abdullahi, U. S., Nyabam, M., Orisekeh, K., Umar, S., Sani, B., David, E., & Umoru, A. A. (2019). *Exploiting iot and lorawan technologies for effective livestock monitoring in Nigeria*. Academic Press.

Aberman, K., Shi, M., Liao, J., Lischinski, D., Chen, B., & Cohen-Or, D. (2019, May). Deep Video-Based Performance Cloning. *Computer Graphics Forum, 38*(2), 219–233. doi:10.1111/cgf.13632

Abeshu, A., & Chilamkurti, N. (2018). Deep learning: The frontier for distributed attack detection in fog-to-things computing. *IEEE Communications Magazine, 56*(2), 169–175. doi:10.1109/MCOM.2018.1700332

Abibullaev & An. (2012). *Decision Support Algorithm for Diagnosis of ADHD Using Electroencephalograms*. Academic Press.

Abraham, Dohmatob, Thirion, Samaras, Abraham, Dohmatob, Thirion, Samaras, Varoquaux, Abraham, Dohmatob, & Thirion. (2014). *Extracting Brain Regions from Rest FMRI with Total-Variation Constrained Dictionary Learning To Cite This Version : HAL Id : Hal-00853242 Extracting Brain Regions from Rest FMRI with Total-Variation Constrained Dictionary Learning*. Academic Press.

Advanced Nutrients. (2016, December 15). *How to Start Growing With Hydroponics For Beginners*. Retrieved from Advanced Nutrients: https://www.advancednutrients.com/articles/easy-hydroponics-beginners-guide/

Agrawal, R., & Gupta, N. (Eds.). (2018). *Extracting Knowledge from Opinion Mining*. IGI Global.

Albayrak, A., & Bilgin, G. (2017). Mitosis detection using convolutional neural network based features. *CINTI 2016 - 17th IEEE International Symposium on Computational Intelligence and Informatics: Proceedings*, 335–340. 10.1109/CINTI.2016.7846429

Al-Fuqaha, Guizani, Mohammadi, Aledhari, & Ayyash. (2015). Internet of Things: A Survey onEnabling Technologies, Protocols and Applications. *IEEE Communications Surveys & Tutorials*.

Al-Halabi, Y., Raeq, N., & Abu-Dabaseh, F. (2017). Study on access control approaches in the context of the Internet of Things: A survey. *International Conference on Engineering and Technology (ICET)*, 1-7. 10.1109/ICEngTechnol.2017.8308153

Almeida, A., & Azkune, G. (2018). Predicting Human Behaviour with Recurrent Neural Networks. *Applied Sciences (Basel, Switzerland)*, *8*(2), 305. doi:10.3390/app8020305

Alp Güler, R., Neverova, N., & Kokkinos, I. (2018). Densepose: Dense human pose estimation in the wild. In *Proceedings of the IEEE Conference on Computer Vision and Pattern Recognition* (pp. 7297-7306). IEEE.

Alrababah, D., Al-Shammari, E., & Alsuht, A. (2017). A Survey: Authentication Protocols for Wireless Sensor Network in the Internet of Things. *Keys and Attacks. In International Conference on New Trends in Computing Sciences (ICTCS)*, 270-276. 10.1109/ICTCS.2017.34

American Cancer Society center (US). (2020). *Brain cancer statics*. Author.

Amin, J., Sharif, M., Anjum, M. A., Raza, M., & Bukhari, S. A. C. (2020). Convolutional neural network with batch normalization for glioma and stroke lesion detection using MRI. *Cognitive Systems Research*, *59*, 304–311. doi:10.1016/j.cogsys.2019.10.002

Ammar, M., Russello, G., & Crispo, B. (2018). Internet of Things: A survey on the security of IoT frameworks. *Journal of Information Security and Applications*, *38*, 8–27. doi:10.1016/j.jisa.2017.11.002

Anwar, S. M., Majid, M., Qayyum, A., Awais, M., Alnowami, M., & Khan, M. K. (2018). Medical Image Analysis using Convolutional Neural Networks: A Review. *Journal of Medical Systems*, *42*(11), 226. Advance online publication. doi:10.100710916-018-1088-1 PMID:30298337

Aradhya, A. M. S. (2017). *Deep Transformation Method for Discriminant Analysis of Multi-Channel Resting State FMRI*. Academic Press.

Aradhya, A. M. S., & Ashfahani, A. (2019). Deep Network Optimization for Rs-FMRI Classification. *IEEE International Conference on Data Mining Workshops, ICDMW*, 77–82.

Arel, I., Rose, D. C., & Karnowski, T. P. (2010). Deep machine learning-a new frontier in artificial intelligence research. *IEEE Computational Intelligence Magazine*, *5*(4), 13–18. doi:10.1109/MCI.2010.938364

Ariza-Colpas, P., Morales-Ortega, R., Piñeres-Melo, M. A., Melendez-Pertuz, F., Serrano-Torné, G., Hernandez-Sanchez, G., & Martínez-Osorio, H. (2019, September). Teleagro: iot applications for the georeferencing and detection of zeal in cattle. In *IFIP International Conference on Computer Information Systems and Industrial Management* (pp. 232-239). Springer. 10.1007/978-3-030-28957-7_19

Arnold, L., Rebecchi, S., Chevallier, S., & Paugam-Moisy, H. (2011) An Introduction to Deep Learning. *ESANN 2011 Proceedings, European Symposium on Artificial Neural Networks, Computational Intelligence and Machine Learning*, 477-488.

Atmadja, W., Liawatimena, S., Lukas, J., Putra Leo Nata, E., & Alexander, I. (2017). Hydroponic system design with real time OS based on ARM Cortex-M microcontroller. *IOP Conference Series. Earth and Environmental Science, 109*, 012017. doi:10.1088/1755-1315/109/1/012017

Avallone, E. A., Baumeister, T. III, & Sadegh, A. (2007). *Mark's Standard Handbook for Mechanical Engineers*. McGraw-Hill Professional.

Averbuch-Elor, H., Cohen-Or, D., Kopf, J., & Cohen, M. F. (2017). Bringing portraits to life. *ACM Transactions on Graphics, 36*(6), 196. doi:10.1145/3130800.3130818

Babson, N., & Teuscher, C. (2019). Reservoir Computing with Complex Cellular Automata. *Complex Systems, 28*(4), 433–455. doi:10.25088/ComplexSystems.28.4.433

Bakiri, M., Guyeux, C., Couchot, J. F., Marangio, L., & Galatolo, S. (2018). Hardware and secure pseudorandom generator for constrained devices. *IEEE Transactions on Industrial Informatics, 14*(8), 3754–3765. doi:10.1109/TII.2018.2815985

Balakrishnan, G., Zhao, A., Dalca, A. V., Durand, F., & Guttag, J. (2018). Synthesizing images of humans in unseen poses. In *Proceedings of the IEEE Conference on Computer Vision and Pattern Recognition* (pp. 8340-8348). 10.1109/CVPR.2018.00870

Balcilar, M., & Sonmez, A. C. (2013). The effect of color space and block size on foreground detection. In *Proceedings of IEEE Conference on Signal Processing and Communications Applications (SIU)*, (pp. 1-4). 10.1109/SIU.2013.6531583

Barnich, O., & Droogenbroeck, M. V. (2011). ViBe: A Universal Background Subtraction Algorithm for Video Sequences. *IEEE Transactions on Image Processing, 20*(6), 1709–1724. doi:10.1109/TIP.2010.2101613 PMID:21189241

Barrios, S., Ouattara, B., & Strobl, E. (2008). The Impact of Climatic Change on Agricultural Production: Is it Different for Africa? *Food Policy, 33*(4), 287–298. doi:10.1016/j.foodpol.2008.01.003

Bauskar & Pujari. (2016). A Review on Industrial Automation Using IOT. *International Research Journal of Engineering and Technology, 3*(12).

Beaty, H. W., & Fink, D. G. (2013). *Standard Handbook for Electrical Engineers*. McGraw-Hill Professional.

Bhaskar, H., Dwivedi, K., Dogra, D. P., Al-Mualla, M., & Mihaylova, L. (2015). Autonomous detection and tracking under illumination changes, occlusions and moving camera. *Signal Processing, 117*, 343–354. doi:10.1016/j.sigpro.2015.06.003

Blanco, Ojala, Kariniemi, Per, Niinim, & Tervonen. (2005). *Interventional and Intraoperative MRI at Low Field Scanner – a Review*. Academic Press.

Bonomi, F., Milito, R., Zhu, J., & Addepalli, S. (2012, August). Fog computing and its role in the internet of things. In *Proceedings of the first edition of the MCC workshop on Mobile cloud computing* (pp. 13-16). 10.1145/2342509.2342513

Boon, H. J. (2020). What Do ADHD Neuroimaging Studies Reveal for Teachers, Teacher Educators and Inclusive Education? *Child and Youth Care Forum, 49*(4), 0123456789. doi:10.100710566-019-09542-4

Boutraa, T., Akhkha, A., Alshuaibi, A., & Atta, R. (2011). Evaluation of the effectiveness of an automated irrigation system using wheat crops. *Agriculture and Biology Journal of North America, 2*(1), 80–88.

Brambilla, M., Umuhoza, E., & Acerbis, R. (2017). Model-driven development of user interfaces for IoT systems via domain-specific components and patterns. *Journal of Internet Services and Applications, 8*(1), 14. doi:10.118613174-017-0064-1

Bregler, C., Covell, M., & Slaney, M. (1997, August). Video rewrite: Driving visual speech with audio. In *Proceedings of the 24th annual conference on Computer graphics and interactive techniques* (pp. 353-360). 10.1145/258734.258880

Brock, A., Donahue, J., & Simonyan, K. (2018). *Large scale gan training for high fidelity natural image synthesis.* arXiv preprint arXiv:1809.11096

Buchanan, W. J., Li, S., & Asif, R. (2017). Lightweight cryptography methods. *Journal of Cyber Security Technology, 1*(3-4), 187–201. doi:10.1080/23742917.2017.1384917

Bulten, W., Pinckaers, H., van Boven, H., Vink, R., de Bel, T., van Ginneken, B., van der Laak, J., Hulsbergen-van de Kaa, C., & Litjens, G. (2020). Automated deep-learning system for Gleason grading of prostate cancer using biopsies: A diagnostic study. *The Lancet. Oncology, 21*(2), 233–241. doi:10.1016/S1470-2045(19)30739-9 PMID:31926805

Bush, G. (2011). Cingulate, Frontal, and Parietal Cortical Dysfunction in Attention-Deficit/Hyperactivity Disorder. *Biological Psychiatry, 69*(12), 1160–1167. doi:10.1016/j.biopsych.2011.01.022 PMID:21489409

Capgemini Consulting. (n.d.). *Securing the Internet of Things Opportunity: Putting Cybersecurity at the Heart of IoT.* Author.

Chan, C., Ginosar, S., Zhou, T., & Efros, A. A. (2019). Everybody dance now. In *Proceedings of the IEEE International Conference on Computer Vision* (pp. 5933-5942). IEEE.

Chang, C. W., Ho, C. C., & Chen, J. H. (2012, August). ADHD Classification by a Texture Analysis of Anatomical Brain MRI Data. *Frontiers in Systems Neuroscience, 6*, 1–35. doi:10.3389/fnsys.2012.00066 PMID:23024630

Chaudhuri, P. P., Chowdhury, D. R., Nandi, S., & Chattopadhyay, S. (1997). *Additive cellular automata: theory and applications* (Vol. 1). John Wiley & Sons.

Chen, M. (2019). *A Multichannel Deep Neural Network Model Analyzing Multiscale Functional Brain Connectome Data for Attention.* Academic Press.

Cheng, F-c., Huang, S-c., & Ruan, S-j. (2011). Scene Analysis for Object Detection in Advanced Surveillance Systems Using Laplacian. *IEEE Transactions on Systems, Man, and Cybernetics, Part C: Applications and Reviews, 41*(5), 589-598.

Cheng, Z., Sun, H., Takeuchi, M., & Katto, J. (2018). Deep Convolutional AutoEncoder-based Lossy Image Compression. *2018 Picture Coding Symposium, PCS 2018 - Proceedings*, 253–257. 10.1109/PCS.2018.8456308

Chen, Q., & Koltun, V. (2017). Photographic image synthesis with cascaded refinement networks. In *Proceedings of the IEEE international conference on computer vision* (pp. 1511-1520). 10.1109/ICCV.2017.168

Chen, S., Zhang, J., Li, Y., & Zhang, J. (2012). A hierarchical model incorporating segmented regions and pixel descriptors for video background subtraction. *IEEE Transactions on Industrial Informatics, 8*(1), 118–127. doi:10.1109/TII.2011.2173202

Chen, Y., Tang, Y., Wang, C., Liu, X., & Zhao, L. (2019). ADHD Classification by Dual Subspace Learning Using Resting-State Functional Connectivity. *Artificial Intelligence in Medicine*, 101786. PMID:32143793

Chheda-varma, B. (2010). *Attention Deficit Hyperactivity Disorder (ADHD): A Case Study and Exploration of Causes and Interventions Symptoms of ADHD.* Springer International Publishing.

Chi-Ren, T. (2020). *Non-Repudiation in Practice. Paper.* Citigroup Information Security Office. Available http://citeseerx. ist.psu.edu/viewdoc/download?doi=10.1.1.106.6685&rep=rep1&type=pdf

Choi, Y., Uh, Y., Yoo, J., & Ha, J. W. (2019). *StarGAN v2: Diverse Image Synthesis for Multiple Domains.* arXiv preprint arXiv:1912.01865.

Choi, J. Y., Ro, Y. M., & Plataniotis, K. N. (2012). Color local texture features for color face recognition. *IEEE Transactions on Image Processing, 21*(3), 1366–1380. doi:10.1109/TIP.2011.2168413 PMID:21926019

Choi, Y., Choi, M., Kim, M., Ha, J. W., Kim, S., & Choo, J. (2018). Stargan: Unified generative adversarial networks for multi-domain image-to-image translation. In *Proceedings of the IEEE conference on computer vision and pattern recognition* (pp. 8789-8797). 10.1109/CVPR.2018.00916

Chu, G., Apthorpe, N., & Feamster, N. (2019, February). Security and Privacy Analyses of Internet of Things Children's Toys. *IEEE Internet of Things Journal, 6*(1), 978–985. doi:10.1109/JIOT.2018.2866423

Citoni, B., Fioranelli, F., Imran, M. A., & Abbasi, Q. H. (2019). Internet of Things and LoRaWAN-Enabled Future Smart Farming. *IEEE Internet of Things Magazine, 2*(4), 14–19. doi:10.1109/IOTM.0001.1900043

Codella, N. C. F., Pankanti, S., Gutman, D. A., Helba, B., Halpern, A. C., Smith, J. R., & States, U. (2017). Deep learning ensembles for melanoma recognition in dermoscopy images. *IBM Journal of Research and Development, 61*(4–5), 1–15. doi:10.1147/JRD.2017.2708299

Cornou, C. (2009). Automation systems for farm animals: Potential impacts on the human—animal relationship and on animal welfare. *Anthrozoos, 22*(3), 213–220. doi:10.2752/175303709X457568

Cubillo & Rubia. (2010). *Structural and Functional Brain Imaging in Adult Attention- Deficit / Hyperactivity Disorder.* Academic Press.

D'Anna, C. (2019, March 8). *Wick System Hydroponic Gardens.* Retrieved from The Spruce: https://www.thespruce. com/hydroponic-gardens-wick-system-1939222

Danaee, P., Ghaeini, R., & Hendrix, D. A. (2017). A deep learning approach for cancer detection and relevant gene identification. *Pacific Symposium on Biocomputing, 0*(212679), 219–229. doi:10.1142/9789813207813_0022 PMID:27896977

Day, M., & Lee, C. (2016). *Deep Learning for Financial Sentiment Analysis on Finance News Providers.* Academic Press.

Degiorgi, M., Garzotto, F., Gelsomini, M., Leonardi, G., Penati, S., Ramuzat, N., Silvestri, J., Clasadonte, F., & Kinoe, Y. (2017). Puffy - An Inflatable Robotic Companion for Pre-Schoolers. *RO-MAN 2017 - 26th IEEE International Symposium on Robot and Human Interactive Communication,* 35–41. 10.1109/ROMAN.2017.8172277

Demanuele, C., James, C. J., Sonuga-Barke, E. J. S., & Capilla, A. (2008). Low Frequency Phase Synchronisation Analysis of MEG Recordings from Children with ADHD and Controls Using Single Channel ICA. *IET Conference Publications.* 10.1049/cp:20080428

Denton, E. L. (2017). Unsupervised learning of disentangled representations from video. In Advances in neural information processing systems (pp. 4414-4423). Academic Press.

Denton, E. L., Chintala, S., & Fergus, R. (2015). Deep generative image models using a laplacian pyramid of adversarial networks. In Advances in neural information processing systems (pp. 1486-1494). Academic Press.

Deshpande, G., Wang, P., Rangaprakash, D., & Wilamowski, B. (2015). Fully Connected Cascade Artificial Neural Network Architecture for Attention Deficit Hyperactivity Disorder Classification from Functional Magnetic Resonance Imaging Data. *IEEE Transactions on Cybernetics, 45*(12), 2668–2679. doi:10.1109/TCYB.2014.2379621 PMID:25576588

DHT11 Temperature and Humidity Sensor. (2016). Retrieved from Keyestudio: https://www.keyestudio.com/free-shipping-keyestudio-dht11-temperature-humidity-moisture-sensor-detection-module-for-arduino-p0374-p0374.html

Dhungel, N., Carneiro, G., & Bradley, A. P. (2015). *Automated Mass Detection in Mammograms using Cascaded Deep Learning and Random Forests*. Academic Press.

Ding & Yuan. (2011). *Simultaneous EEG and MEG Source Reconstruction in Sparse Electromagnetic Source Imaging*. Academic Press.

Ding, Z. (2020). Imitation Learning. In *Deep Reinforcement Learning* (pp. 273–306). Springer. doi:10.1007/978-981-15-4095-0_8

Diro, A. A., Chilamkurti, N., & Kumar, N. (2017). Lightweight cybersecurity schemes using elliptic curve cryptography in publish-subscribe fog computing. *Mobile Networks and Applications*, 22(5), 848–858. doi:10.100711036-017-0851-8

Dogo, E. M., Salami, A. F., Aigbavboa, C. O., & Nkonyana, T. (2019). Taking Cloud Computing to the Extreme Edge: A Review of Mist Computing for Smart Cities and Industry 4.0 in Africa. In *Edge Computing: From Hype to Reality* (pp. 107–132). Springer. doi:10.1007/978-3-319-99061-3_7

Domingues, D. S., Takahashi, H. W., Camara, C. P., & Nixdorf, S. L. (2012, June). Automated System Developed to Control pH and Concentration of Nutrient Solution Evaluated in Hydroponic Lettuce Production. *Computers and Electronics in Agriculture*, 84, 53–61. doi:10.1016/j.compag.2012.02.006

Dorj, U. O., Lee, K. K., Choi, J. Y., & Lee, M. (2018). The skin cancer classification using deep convolutional neural network. *Multimedia Tools and Applications*, 77(8), 9909–9924. doi:10.100711042-018-5714-1

DSM-V. (2013). *A.P.A., Diagnostic and Statistical Manual of Mental Disorders, 5th Ed.* Arlington, VA: American Psychiatric Association.

Dubreuil-vall, Ruffini, & Camprodon. (2019). *A Deep Learning Approach with Event-Related Spectral EEG Data in Attentional Deficit Hyperactivity Disorder*. Academic Press.

Durston, S. (2003). A Review f the Biological Bases of ADHD: What Have We Learned from Imaging Studies? *Mental Retardation and Developmental Disabilities Research Reviews*, 9(3), 184–195. doi:10.1002/mrdd.10079 PMID:12953298

Ebg, F. G. (2016). Breast Cancer Histopathological Image Classification using Convolutional. *Neural Networks*, 2560–2567.

Efros, A. A., Berg, A. C., Mori, G., & Malik, J. (2003, October). Recognizing action at a distance. In Null (p. 726). IEEE. doi:10.1109/ICCV.2003.1238420

Eisenbarth, T., Kumar, S., Paar, C., Poschmann, A., & Uhsadel, L. (2007). A survey of lightweight-cryptography implementations. *IEEE Design & Test of Computers*, 24(6), 522–533. doi:10.1109/MDT.2007.178

Ektapure & Ingale. (2016). Android based interactive Home Automation System through Internet of Things. *International Journal of Advanced Research in Electronics and Communication Engineering*, 5(4).

El-hajj, M., Chamoun, M., Fadlallah, A., & Serhrouchni, A. (2017). Taxonomy of authentication techniques in the Internet of Things (IoT). *IEEE 15th Student Conference on Research and Development (SCOReD)*, 67-71.

Erden, B., Gamboa, N., & Wood, S. (n.d.). *3D Convolutional Neural Network for Brain Tumor Segmentation*. Academic Press.

Eslami, T., & Saeed, F. (2018). Similarity Based Classification of ADHD Using Singular Value Decomposition. *2018 ACM International Conference on Computing Frontiers, CF 2018 – Proceedings*, 19–25. 10.1145/3203217.3203239

Esser, P., Sutter, E., & Ommer, B. (2018). A variational u-net for conditional appearance and shape generation. In *Proceedings of the IEEE Conference on Computer Vision and Pattern Recognition* (pp. 8857-8866). 10.1109/CVPR.2018.00923

Faye, R. M., Mora-Camino, F., Sawadogo, S., & Niang, A. (1998, October). An intelligent decision support system for irrigation system management. In *SMC'98 Conference Proceedings. 1998 IEEE International Conference on Systems, Man, and Cybernetics (Cat. No. 98CH36218)* (Vol. 4, pp. 3908-3913). IEEE. 10.1109/ICSMC.1998.726698

Feamster, N. (2016). *Who Will Secure the Internet of Things?* Available: https://freedom-to-tinker.com/2016/01/19/who -will -secure-the-internet-of-things/

Felisa, Bernabel, Dufresne, & Sood. (2020). Deep Learning for Mental Illness Detection Using Brain SPECT Imaging. *Medical Imaging and Computer-Aided Diagnosis.*

Finn, C., Goodfellow, I., & Levine, S. (2016). Unsupervised learning for physical interaction through video prediction. In Advances in neural information processing systems (pp. 64-72). Academic Press.

Fleming, S. (2019, February 5). *What is hydroponics - and is it the future of farming?* Retrieved from World Economic Forum: https://www.weforum.org/agenda/2019/02/hydroponics-future-of-farming

Fremantle, P., & Scott, P. (2017). A survey of secure middleware for the Internet of Things. *PeerJ. Computer Science, 3*, e114. doi:10.7717/peerj-cs.114

Garcia Ricardez, G. A., Koganti, N., Yang, P. C., Okada, S., Uriguen Eljuri, P. M., Yasuda, A., El Hafi, L., Yamamoto, M., Takamatsu, J., & Ogasawara, T. (2020). Adaptive motion generation using imitation learning and highly compliant end effector for autonomous cleaning. *Advanced Robotics, 34*(3-4), 189–201. doi:10.1080/01691864.2019.1698461

Garg, D., Khan, S., & Alam, M. (2020). Integrative Use of IoT and Deep Learning for Agricultural Applications. *Proceedings of ICETIT, 2019*, 521–531. doi:10.1007/978-3-030-30577-2_46

Germani, L., Mecarelli, V., Baruffa, G., Rugini, L., & Frescura, F. (2019). An IoT Architecture for Continuous Livestock Monitoring Using LoRa LPWAN. *Electronics (Basel), 8*(12), 1435. doi:10.3390/electronics8121435

Gezahegn, Y. G. (2020). *Breast Cancer detection using Convolutional Neural Network.* Academic Press.

Ghassemi, N., Shoeibi, A., & Rouhani, M. (2020). Deep neural network with generative adversarial networks pre-training for brain tumor classification based on MR images. *Biomedical Signal Processing and Control, 57*, 101678. doi:10.1016/j.bspc.2019.101678

Gilbert, H., Robshaw, M., & Sibert, H. (2005). Active attack against HB/sup+: A provavly secure lightweight authentication protocol. *Electronics Letters, 41*(21), 1169–1170. doi:10.1049/el:20052622

Girshick, R. (2015). Fast R-CNN. *Proceedings of the IEEE International Conference on Computer Vision, 2015 Inter*, 1440–1448. 10.1109/ICCV.2015.169

Goodfellow, I. J., Pouget-abadie, J., Mirza, M., Xu, B., & Warde-farley, D. (2014). *Generative Adversarial Nets.* Academic Press.

Goodfellow, I., Pouget-Abadie, J., Mirza, M., Xu, B., Warde-Farley, D., Ozair, S., Courville, A., & Bengio, Y. (2014). Generative adversarial nets. *Proceedings of the International Conference on Neural Information Processing Systems*, 2672–2680.

Greenberg. (2015). *Hackers Remotely Kill a Jeep on a Highway.* YouTube.

Greenway, C. W., & Edwards, A. R. (2020). Knowledge and Attitudes towards Attention-Deficit Hyperactivity Disorder (ADHD): A Comparison of Teachers and Teaching Assistants Teaching Assistants. *Australian Journal of Learning Difficulties*, *00*(00), 1–19. doi:10.1080/19404158.2019.1709875

Guan, S. (2019). Breast cancer detection using synthetic mammograms from generative adversarial networks in convolutional neural networks. *Journal of Medical Imaging (Bellingham, Wash.)*, *6*(03), 1. doi:10.1117/1.JMI.6.3.031411 PMID:30915386

Gubbi, J., Buyya, R., Marusic, S., & Palaniswami, M. (2013). Internet of Things (IoT): A vision, architectural elements, and future directions. *Future Generation Computer Systems*, *29*(7), 1645–1660. doi:10.1016/j.future.2013.01.010

Gupta, N., & Agrawal, R. (2017). Challenges and Security Issues of Distributed Databases. In *NoSQL* (pp. 265–284). Chapman and Hall/CRC.

Gupta, N., & Agrawal, R. (2020). Application and Techniques of Opinion Mining. In *Hybrid Computational Intelligence*. Elsevier. doi:10.1016/B978-0-12-818699-2.00001-9

Gupta, N., & Verma, S. (2019). Tools of Opinion Mining. In *Extracting Knowledge From Opinion Mining* (pp. 179–203). IGI Global. doi:10.4018/978-1-5225-6117-0.ch009

Hai, Z., Chang, K., Kim, J. J., & Yang, C. C. (2013). Identifying features in opinion mining via intrinsic and extrinsic domain relevance. *IEEE Transactions on Knowledge and Data Engineering*, *26*(3), 623–634. doi:10.1109/TKDE.2013.26 doi:10.1109/TKDE.2013.26

Halak, B., Zwolinski, M., & Mispan, M. S. (2016, October). Overview of PUF-based hardware security solutions for the Internet of Things. *2016 IEEE 59th International Midwest Symposium on Circuits and Systems (MWSCAS)*, 1-4.

Halperin, D. (2008). Pacemakers and Implantable Cardiac Defibrillators: *Software Radio Attacks and Zero-Power Defenses. IEEE Symposium on Security and Privacy*, 129-142.

Hamilton, A. W., Davison, C., Tachtatzis, C., Andonovic, I., Michie, C., Ferguson, H. J., & Jonsson, N. N. (2019). Identification of the rumination in cattle using support vector machines with motion-sensitive bolus sensors. *Sensors (Basel)*, *19*(5), 1165. doi:10.339019051165 PMID:30866541

Hassan, W. H. (2019). Current research on the Internet of Things (IoT) security: A survey. *Computer Networks*, *148*, 283–294. doi:10.1016/j.comnet.2018.11.025

He, J., Li, X., Yao, Y., Hong, Y., & Jinbao, Z. (2018). Mining transition rules of cellular automata for simulating urban expansion by using deep learning techniques. *International Journal of Geographical Information Science*, *32*(10), 2076–2097. doi:10.1080/13658816.2018.1480783

Helenius, P., Laasonen, M., Hokkanen, L., Paetau, R., & Niemivirta, M. (2011). *Neuropsychologia Impaired Engagement of the Ventral Attentional Pathway in ADHD*. Academic Press.

Hesamian, M. H., Jia, W., He, X., & Kennedy, P. (2019). Deep Learning Techniques for Medical Image Segmentation: Achievements and Challenges. *Journal of Digital Imaging*, *32*(4), 582–596. doi:10.100710278-019-00227-x PMID:31144149

He, Z., Kan, M., Shan, S., & Chen, X. (2019). S2GAN: Share Aging Factors Across Ages and Share Aging Trends Among Individuals. In *Proceedings of the IEEE International Conference on Computer Vision* (pp. 9440-9449). 10.1109/ICCV.2019.00953

Hill, K. (2013). *Baby Monitor Hack Could Happen to 40,000 Other Foscam Users*. Available: https://www.forbes.com/sites/kashmirhill/2013/08/27/baby-monitor-hack-could-happen-to-40000-other-foscam-users/#75ffc8f558b5

Ho, Leung, Mishra, Hosseini, Song, & Wagner. (2016). Smart Locks: Lessons for Securing Commodity Internet of Things Devices. In *Proceedings of the 11th ACM on Asia Conference on Computer and Communications Security (ASIA CCS '16)*. Association for Computing Machinery. 10.1145/2897845.2897886

Hoogendoorn, M., & Kottke, M. (2014). *Building the Internet of Things*. Available: http://cdn2.hubspot.net/hub/444534/file-2491337246-df/Building_the_Internet_of_Things.pdf?t=1424896250151

Hossain, S., & Deok-jin, L. (2019). Deep Learning-Based Real-Time Multiple-Object Detection and Tracking from Aerial Imagery via a Flying Robot with GPU-Based Embedded Devices. *Sensors (Basel)*, *19*(15), 3371. doi:10.339019153371 PMID:31370336

Huang, X., Liu, M. Y., Belongie, S., & Kautz, J. (2018). Multimodal unsupervised image-to-image translation. In *Proceedings of the European Conference on Computer Vision (ECCV)* (pp. 172-189). Academic Press.

Hwang, Kim, Kang, Seo, & Paeng. (2018). *Improving Accuracy of Simultaneously Reconstructed Activity and Attenuation Maps Using Deep Learning*. Academic Press.

IEEE. (2016, December 14). *802.11-2016 - IEEE Standard for Information technology--Telecommunications and information exchange between systems Local and metropolitan area networks--Specific requirements - Part 11: Wireless LAN Medium Access Control (MAC) and Physical Layer (PHY) Sp*. Retrieved from IEEE Standards Association: https://standards.ieee.org/standard/802_11-2016.html#Standard

Ikhsan, M. G., Saputro, M. Y. A., Arji, D. A., Harwahyu, R., & Sari, R. F. (2018, November). Mobile LoRa Gateway for Smart Livestock Monitoring System. In *2018 IEEE International Conference on Internet of Things and Intelligence System (IOTAIS)* (pp. 46-51). IEEE. 10.1109/IOTAIS.2018.8600842

Isola, P., Zhu, J. Y., Zhou, T., & Efros, A. A. (2017). Image-to-image translation with conditional adversarial networks. In *Proceedings of the IEEE conference on computer vision and pattern recognition* (pp. 1125-1134). IEEE.

Jadhav, S., & Hambarde, S. (2015). Automated Irrigation System using Wireless Sensor Network and Raspberry Pi. *International Journal of science and research, 4*(12), 2056-2058.

Jafari, M. H., Karimi, N., Nasr-Esfahani, E., Samavi, S., Soroushmehr, S. M. R., Ward, K., & Najarian, K. (2016). Skin lesion segmentation in clinical images using deep learning. *Proceedings - International Conference on Pattern Recognition, 0*, 337–342. 10.1109/ICPR.2016.7899656

Jalota, C., & Agrawal, R. (2019). Ontology-Based Opinion Mining. In Extracting Knowledge From Opinion Mining (pp. 84-103). IGI Global. doi:10.4018/978-1-5225-6117-0.ch005 doi:10.4018/978-1-5225-6117-0.ch005

Jones, J. B. Jr. (2004). *Hydroponics: A Practical Guide for the Soilless Grower*. CRC Press. doi:10.1201/9780849331671

Kadampur, M. A., & Al Riyaee, S. (2020). Skin cancer detection: Applying a deep learning based model driven architecture in the cloud for classifying dermal cell images. *Informatics in Medicine Unlocked, 18*(November), 100282. doi:10.1016/j.imu.2019.100282

Kaewmard, N., & Saiyod, S. (2014, October). Sensor data collection and irrigation control on vegetable crop using smart phone and wireless sensor networks for smart farm. In *2014 IEEE Conference on Wireless Sensors (ICWiSE)* (pp. 106-112). IEEE.

Kalchbrenner, N., Grefenstette, E., & Blunsom, P. (2014). *A convolutional neural network for modelling sentences*. arXiv preprint arXiv:1404.2188. doi:10.3115/v1/P14-1062

Kalchbrenner, N., van den Oord, A., Simonyan, K., Danihelka, I., Vinyals, O., Graves, A., & Kavukcuoglu, K. (2017, August). Video pixel networks. In *Proceedings of the 34th International Conference on Machine Learning-Volume 70* (pp. 1771-1779). JMLR. org.

Kaldera, H. N. T. K., Gunasekara, S. R., & DIssanayake, M. B. (2019). Brain tumor Classification and Segmentation using Faster R-CNN. *2019 Advances in Science and Engineering Technology International Conferences, ASET 2019*, 1–6. doi:10.1109/ICASET.2019.8714263

Kalirajan, K., & Sudha, M. (2017). Moving object detection using median-based scale invariant local ternary pattern for video surveillance system. *Journal of Intelligent & Fuzzy Systems, 33*(3), 1933–1943. doi:10.3233/JIFS-162231

Kalra, V., & Aggarwal, R. (2017). Importance of Text Data Preprocessing & Implementation in RapidMiner. In *Proceedings of the First International Conference on Information Technology and Knowledge Management–New Dehli, India* (Vol. 14, pp. 71-75). 10.15439/2017KM46

Kalra, V., & Agrawal, R. (2019). Challenges of Text Analytics in Opinion Mining. In *Extracting Knowledge From Opinion Mining* (pp. 268–282). IGI Global. doi:10.4018/978-1-5225-6117-0.ch012

Kamilaris, A., & Prenafeta-Boldú, F. X. (2018). Deep learning in agriculture: A survey. *Computers and Electronics in Agriculture, 147*, 70–90. doi:10.1016/j.compag.2018.02.016

Kamnitsas, K., Ledig, C., Newcombe, V. F. J., Simpson, J. P., Kane, A. D., Menon, D. K., Rueckert, D., & Glocker, B. (2017). Efficient multi-scale 3D CNN with fully connected CRF for accurate brain lesion segmentation. *Medical Image Analysis, 36*, 61–78. doi:10.1016/j.media.2016.10.004 PMID:27865153

Kansara, K., Zaveri, V., Shah, S., Delwadkar, S., & Jani, K. (2015). Sensor based automated irrigation system with IOT: A technical review. *International Journal of Computer Science and Information Technologies, 6*(6), 5331–5333.

Kapadia, A., Kotz, D., & Triandopoulos, N. (2009). Opportunistic sensing: Security challenges for the new paradigm. First International Communication Systems and Networks and Workshops, 1-10.

Karras, T., Aila, T., Laine, S., & Lehtinen, J. (2017). *Progressive growing of gans for improved quality, stability, and variation.* arXiv preprint arXiv:1710.10196.

Karras, T., Laine, S., & Aila, T. (2019). A style-based generator architecture for generative adversarial networks. In *Proceedings of the IEEE Conference on Computer Vision and Pattern Recognition* (pp. 4401-4410). 10.1109/CVPR.2019.00453

Katagi, M., & Moriai, S. (2008). Lightweight cryptography for the internet of things. *Sony Corporation, 2008*, 7–10.

Katsikeas, S., Fysarakis, K., Miaoudakis, A., Van Bemten, A., Askoxylakis, I., Papaefstathiou, I., & Plemenos, A. (2017, July). Lightweight & secure industrial IoT communications via the MQ telemetry transport protocol. In *2017 IEEE Symposium on Computers and Communications (ISCC)* (pp. 1193-1200). IEEE. 10.1109/ISCC.2017.8024687

Kaur, S., & Agrawal, R. (2018). A Detailed Analysis of Core NLP for Information Extraction. *International Journal of Machine Learning and Networked Collaborative Engineering, 1*(01), 33–47. doi:10.30991/IJMLNCE.2017v01i01.005

Kautzky, A., Vanicek, T., Philippe, C., Kranz, G. S., Wadsak, W., Mitterhauser, M., Hartmann, A., Hahn, A., Hacker, M., Rujescu, D., Kasper, S., & Lanzenberger, R. (2020). Machine Learning Classification of ADHD and HC by Multimodal Serotonergic Data. *Translational Psychiatry, 10*(1), 104. doi:10.103841398-020-0781-2 PMID:32265436

Keck, M., Galup, L., & Stauffer, C. (2013). Real-time tracking of low-resolution vehicles for wide-area persistent surveillance, In *Proceedings of IEEE Workshop on Applications of Computer Vision*, (pp. 441-448). 10.1109/WACV.2013.6475052

Khakimov, A., Muthanna, A., & Muthanna, M. S. A. (2012, August). Study of fog computing structure. In *2018 IEEE Conference of Russian Young Researchers in Electrical and Electronic Engineering (EIConRus)* (pp. 51-54). IEEE.

Khamaysa Hajaya, M., Samarasinghe, S., Kulasiri, G. D., & Lopez Benavides, M. (2019). *Detection of dairy cattle Mastitis: modelling of milking features using deep neural networks.* Academic Press.

Khattab, Jeddi, Amini, & Bayoumi. (2016). *RFID Security: A Lightweight Paradigm.* Springer International Publishing.

Khullar, V., Singh, H. P., & Bala, M. (2019a). Autism Spectrum Disorders : A Systematic Review from the Perspective of Computer Assisted Developments. In S. P. And & C. Subudhi (Eds.), *Psycho-Social Perspectives on Mental Health and Well-Being.* IGI Global.

Khullar, V., Singh, H. P., & Bala, M. (2019b). IoT Based Assistive Companion for Hypersensitive Individuals (ACHI) with Autism Spectrum Disorder. *Asian Journal of Psychiatry, 46*, 92–102. doi:10.1016/j.ajp.2019.09.030 PMID:31639556

Kim, T., Cha, M., Kim, H., Lee, J. K., & Kim, J. (2017, August). Learning to discover cross-domain relations with generative adversarial networks. In *Proceedings of the 34th International Conference on Machine Learning-Volume 70* (pp. 1857-1865). JMLR. org.

Kim, Y. (2014). *Convolutional neural networks for sentence classification.* arXiv preprint arXiv:1408.5882. doi:10.3115/v1/D14-1181

Kim, H., Garrido, P., Tewari, A., Xu, W., Thies, J., Nießner, M., Pérez, P., Richardt, C., Zollhöfer, M., & Theobalt, C. (2018). Deep video portraits. *ACM Transactions on Graphics, 37*(4), 1–14. doi:10.1145/3197517.3201283

Kim, H., & Lee, E. A. (2017). Authentication and Authorization for the Internet of Things. *IT Professional, 19*(5), 27–33. doi:10.1109/MITP.2017.3680960

Kim, W., & Kim, C. (2012). Background subtraction for dynamic texture scenes using fuzzy color histograms. *IEEE Signal Processing Letters, 19*(3), 127–130. doi:10.1109/LSP.2011.2182648

Kingma, D. P., & Ba, J. (2017). *Adam: A method for stochastic optimization.* Available at: https://arxiv.org/abs/1412.6980v9

Klein, A. M., Onnink, M., Van, M., Wolfers, T., Harich, B., Shi, Y., Dammers, J., & Arias-va, A. (2017). Brain Imaging Genetics in ADHD and beyond – Mapping Pathways from Gene to Disorder at Different Levels of Complexity. *Neuroscience and Biobehavioral Reviews, 80*, 115–155. doi:10.1016/j.neubiorev.2017.01.013 PMID:28159610

Ko, T., Soatto, S., & Estrin, D. (2010). Warping background subtraction. In *Proceedings of 2010 IEEE Conference on Computer Vision and Pattern Recognition (CVPR)* (pp. 1331-1338). 10.1109/CVPR.2010.5539813

Kovacs, E. (2015). *FDA Issues Alert Over Vulnerable Hospira Drug Pumps.* Available: https://www.securityweek.com/fdaissues-alert-over-vulnerable-hospira-drug-pumps/

Krain, A. L., & Xavier Castellanos, F. (2006). *Brain Development and ADHD.* Academic Press.

Krishnan, R. S., Julie, E. G., Robinson, Y. H., Raja, S., Kumar, R., & Thong, P. H. (2020). Fuzzy Logic based Smart Irrigation System using Internet of Things. *Journal of Cleaner Production, 252*, 119902.

Kuang, D. (2014). *Classification on ADHD with Deep Learning.* Academic Press.

Kulkarni, G., Shelke, R., Sutar, R., & Mohite, S. (2014). RFID security issues & challenges. *International Conference on Electronics and Communication Systems (ICECS)*, 1-4.

Kwok, J., & Sun, Y. (2018, January). A smart iot-based irrigation system with automated plant recognition using deep learning. In *Proceedings of the 10th International Conference on Computer Modeling and Simulation* (pp. 87-91). 10.1145/3177457.3177506

Lakshmanaprabu, S. K., Mohanty, S. N., Shankar, K., Arunkumar, N., & Ramirez, G. (2019). Optimal deep learning model for classification of lung cancer on CT images. *Future Generation Computer Systems*, *92*, 374–382. doi:10.1016/j.future.2018.10.009

Laufs, H. (2012). NeuroImage A Personalized History of EEG – FMRI Integration. *NeuroImage*, *62*(2), 1056–1067. doi:10.1016/j.neuroimage.2012.01.039 PMID:22266176

LeCun, Y., Bengio, Y., & Hinton, G. (2015). Deep learning. *Nature, 521*(7553), 436-444.

Lee, A. X., Zhang, R., Ebert, F., Abbeel, P., Finn, C., & Levine, S. (2018). *Stochastic adversarial video prediction.* arXiv preprint arXiv:1804.01523.

Lee, H. Y., Tseng, H. Y., Huang, J. B., Singh, M., & Yang, M. H. (2018). Diverse image-to-image translation via disentangled representations. In *Proceedings of the European conference on computer vision (ECCV)* (pp. 35-51). Academic Press.

Lee, M. (2018). *IoT Livestock Estrus Monitoring System based on Machine Learning.* Academic Press.

Lee, Y., Jung, J., & Kweon, I.-S. (2011). Hierarchical on-line boosting based background subtraction. In *Proceedings of 17th Korea-Japan Joint Workshop on Frontiers of Computer Vision (FCV)*, (pp. 1-5). Academic Press.

Lee, H. Y., Tseng, H. Y., Mao, Q., Huang, J. B., Lu, Y. D., Singh, M., & Yang, M. H. (2020). Drit++: Diverse image-to-image translation via disentangled representations. *International Journal of Computer Vision*, *128*(10-11), 1–16. doi:10.100711263-019-01284-z

Lee, J. Y., Lin, W. C., & Huang, Y. H. (2014, May). A lightweight authentication protocol for internet of things. In *2014 International Symposium on Next-Generation Electronics* (ISNE), pp. 1-2. IEEE. 10.1109/ISNE.2014.6839375

Li, P., Hu, Y., Li, Q., He, R., & Sun, Z. (2018, August). Global and local consistent age generative adversarial networks. In *2018 24th International Conference on Pattern Recognition (ICPR)* (pp. 1073-1078). IEEE. 10.1109/ICPR.2018.8545119

Liang, X., Lee, L., Dai, W., & Xing, E. P. (2017). Dual motion GAN for future-flow embedded video prediction. In *Proceedings of the IEEE International Conference on Computer Vision* (pp. 1744-1752). 10.1109/ICCV.2017.194

Liao, R. F., Wen, H., Wu, J., Pan, F., Xu, A., Jiang, Y., Xie, F., & Cao, M. (2019). Deep-learning-based physical layer authentication for industrial wireless sensor networks. *Sensors (Basel)*, *19*(11), 2440. doi:10.339019112440 PMID:31142016

Li, F., Shinde, A., Shi, Y., Ye, J., Li, X. Y., & Song, W. (2019). System statistics learning-based IoT security: Feasibility and suitability. *IEEE Internet of Things Journal*, *6*(4), 6396–6403. doi:10.1109/JIOT.2019.2897063

Li, H., Li, A., & Wang, M. (2019). A novel end-to-end brain tumor segmentation method using improved fully convolutional networks. *Computers in Biology and Medicine*, *108*, 150–160. doi:10.1016/j.compbiomed.2019.03.014 PMID:31005007

Ling, Z., Luo, J., Xu, Y., Gao, C., Wu, K., & Fu, X. (2017). Security Vulnerabilities of the Internet of Things: A Case Study of the Smart Plug System. *IEEE Internet of Things Journal*, *4*(6), 1899–1909. doi:10.1109/JIOT.2017.2707465

Liu, B. (2006). Mining comparative sentences and relations. In AAAI (Vol. 22). Academic Press.

Liu, L., Xu, W., Zollhoefer, M., Kim, H., Bernard, F., Habermann, M., . . . Theobalt, C. (2018). *Neural Rendering and Reenactment of Human Actor Videos.* arXiv preprint arXiv:1809.03658.

Liu, M. Y., & Tuzel, O. (2016). Coupled generative adversarial networks. In Advances in neural information processing systems (pp. 469-477). Academic Press.

Liu, M. Y., Breuel, T., & Kautz, J. (2017). Unsupervised image-to-image translation networks. In Advances in neural information processing systems (pp. 700-708). Academic Press.

Liu, G., Bao, H., & Han, B. (2018). A Stacked Autoencoder-Based Deep Neural Network for Achieving Gearbox Fault Diagnosis. *Mathematical Problems in Engineering, 2018*, 1–10. Advance online publication. doi:10.1155/2018/5105709

Liu, J., Pan, Y., Li, M., Chen, Z., Tang, L., Lu, C., & Wang, J. (2018). Applications of Deep Learning to MRI Images W. *Survey (London, England), 1*(1), 1–18.

Liu, M. Y., Huang, X., Mallya, A., Karras, T., Aila, T., Lehtinen, J., & Kautz, J. (2019). Few-shot unsupervised image-to-image translation. In *Proceedings of the IEEE International Conference on Computer Vision* (pp. 10551-10560). IEEE.

Liu, S., Zheng, H., Feng, Y., & Li, W. (2017). Prostate cancer diagnosis using deep learning with 3D multiparametric MRI. *Medical Imaging 2017. Computer-Aided Diagnosis, 10134*, 1013428. doi:10.1117/12.2277121

Liu, Y., Li, Q., & Sun, Z. (2019). Attribute-aware face aging with wavelet-based generative adversarial networks. In *Proceedings of the IEEE Conference on Computer Vision and Pattern Recognition* (pp. 11877-11886). 10.1109/CVPR.2019.01215

Liu, Y., Zhang, W., Pan, S., Li, Y., & Chen, Y. (2020). Analyzing the robotic behavior in a smart city with deep enforcement and imitation learning using IoRT. *Computer Communications, 150*, 346–356. doi:10.1016/j.comcom.2019.11.031

Lo, C., Chen, Y., Weng, R., & Hsieh, K. L. (n.d.). *Applied sciences Intelligent Glioma Grading Based on Deep Transfer Learning of MRI Radiomic Features*. Academic Press.

Longley, G. (2016). *The Security Challenges Facing Industrial IoT*. Available: https://www.itproportal.com/2016/04/11/thesecurity-challenges-facing-industrial-iot/

Lotter, W., Kreiman, G., & Cox, D. (2016). *Deep predictive coding networks for video prediction and unsupervised learning*. arXiv preprint arXiv:1605.08104.

Lundin, K., & Olli, O. (2017). *Automated hydroponics: Regulation of pH and Nutrients*. KTH Royal Institute of Technology, Bsc thesis in Mechatronics, Stockholm.

Lu, R., Heung, K., Lashkari, A. H., & Ghorbani, A. A. (2017). A lightweight privacy-preserving data aggregation scheme for fog computing-enhanced IoT. *IEEE Access: Practical Innovations, Open Solutions, 5*, 3302–3312. doi:10.1109/ACCESS.2017.2677520

Ma, F., & Sang, N. (2013). Background subtraction based on multichannel SILTP, Lecture Notes in Computer Science (including subseries Lecture Notes in Artificial Intelligence and Lecture Notes in Bioinformatics), 7728(1), 73-84.

Ma, L., Jia, X., Sun, Q., Schiele, B., Tuytelaars, T., & Van Gool, L. (2017). Pose guided person image generation. In Advances in Neural Information Processing Systems (pp. 406-416). Academic Press.

Macaulay, T. (2016). *RIoT Control: Understanding and Managing Risks and the Internet of Things*. Todd Green.

Mahanand, Savitha, & Suresh. (2013). *Computer Aided Diagnosis of ADHD Using Brain Magnetic Resonance Images*. Academic Press.

Maina, C. (2017, May). IoT at the grassroots—Exploring the use of sensors for livestock monitoring. In 2017 IST-Africa Week Conference (IST-Africa) (pp. 1-8). IEEE.

Ma, L., Sun, Q., Georgoulis, S., Van Gool, L., Schiele, B., & Fritz, M. (2018). Disentangled person image generation. In *Proceedings of the IEEE Conference on Computer Vision and Pattern Recognition* (pp. 99-108). IEEE.

Mariot, L., Picek, S., Leporati, A., & Jakobovic, D. (2019). Cellular Automata based S-boxes. *Cryptography and Communications: Discrete Structures, Boolean Functions and Sequences, 11*(1), 41–62. doi:10.100712095-018-0311-8

Mathieu, M., Couprie, C., & LeCun, Y. (2015). *Deep multi-scale video prediction beyond mean square error.* arXiv preprint arXiv:1511.05440.

McComb, G. (2013). *Arduino Robot Bonanza*. McGraw-Hill Professional.

Medhat, W., Hassan, A., & Korashy, H. (2014). Sentiment analysis algorithms and applications: A survey. *Ain Shams Engineering Journal, 5*(4), 1093–1113. doi:10.1016/j.asej.2014.04.011

Mediun. (2020). *Convolutional Neural Network*. Author.

Mehta, K., Arora, N., & Singh, B. P. (2011). Low power efficient D flip flop circuit. In *International Symposium on Devices MEMS, Intelligent Systems & Communication (ISDMISC)* (pp. 16-19). IJCA.

Mihaljevic, M. J., Watanabe, H., & Imai, H. (2008, December). A cellular automata based HB#-like low complexity authentication technique. In *2008 International Symposium on Information Theory and its Applications* (pp. 1-6). IEEE. 10.1109/ISITA.2008.4895617

Mikolov, T., Chen, K., Corrado, G., & Dean, J. (2013). *Efficient estimation of word representations in vector space.* arXiv preprint arXiv:1301.3781.

Milletari, F., Navab, N., & Ahmadi, S. A. (2016). V-Net: Fully convolutional neural networks for volumetric medical image segmentation. *Proceedings - 2016 4th International Conference on 3D Vision, 3DV 2016*, 565–571. 10.1109/3DV.2016.79

Mirza, M., & Osindero, S. (2014). *Conditional generative adversarial nets.* arXiv preprint arXiv:1411.1784.

Mitchell, B. (2019, November 10). *What is the Range of a Typical WiFi Network*. Retrieved from Lifewire: https://www.lifewire.com/range-of-typical-wifi-network-816564#:~:text=A%20general%20rule%20of%20thumb,one%2Dthird%20of%20these%20distances

Mitra, A. (2018, September). Selection of cost-effective prime source towards possible uses in Fog Computing. In *2018 2nd International Conference on Data Science and Business Analytics (ICDSBA)* (pp. 19-24). IEEE. 10.1109/ICDSBA.2018.00011

Mitra, A. (2016). On the selection of Cellular Automata based PRNG in Code Division Multiple Access Communications. *Studies in Informatics and Control, 25*(2), 218–227. doi:10.24846/v25i2y201609

Mitra, A. (2019). On Investigating Energy Stability for Cellular Automata Based PageRank Validation Model in Green Cloud. *International Journal of Cloud Applications and Computing, 9*(4), 66–85. doi:10.4018/IJCAC.2019100104

Mitra, A., & Kundu, A. (2013). Cost optimized set of Primes Generation with Cellular Automata for Stress Testing in Distributed Computing. *Procedia Technology, 10*, 365–372. doi:10.1016/j.protcy.2013.12.372

Mitra, A., & Kundu, A. (2015, October). Analysis of sequences generated by ELCA-type cellular automata targeting noise generation. In *19th International Conference on System Theory, Control and Computing (ICSTCC)* (pp. 883-888). IEEE. 10.1109/ICSTCC.2015.7321406

Mitra, A., & Kundu, A. (2017b). Energy Efficient CA based Page Rank Validation Model: A Green Approach in Cloud. *International Journal of Green Computing, 8*(2), 59–76. doi:10.4018/IJGC.2017070104

Mitra, A., Kundu, A., Chattopadhyay, M., & Chattopadhyay, S. (2017a). A cost-efficient one time password-based authentication in cloud environment using equal length cellular automata. *Journal of Industrial Information Integration*, 5, 17–25. doi:10.1016/j.jii.2016.11.002

Mitra, A., & Saha, S. (2019, December). A design towards an energy-efficient and lightweight data security model in Fog Networks. In *2019 International Conference on Intelligent and Cloud Computing (pp. 227-236)*. Springer Nature. 10.1007/978-981-15-5971-6_25

Mittal, M., Goyal, L. M., Kaur, S., Kaur, I., Verma, A., & Hemanth, D. J. (2019). Deep learning based enhanced tumor segmentation approach for MR brain images. *Applied Soft Computing*, 78, 346–354. doi:10.1016/j.asoc.2019.02.036

Miyato, T., & Koyama, M. (2018). *cGANs with projection discriminator.* arXiv preprint arXiv:1802.05637.

Mohammadi, Khaleghi, Nasrabadi, Rafieivand, & Begol. (2016). *EEG Classification of ADHD and Normal Children Using Non-Linear Features and Neural Network.* Academic Press.

Mori, G., Berg, A., Efros, A., Eden, A., & Malik, J. (2004). Video based motion synthesis by splicing and morphing. *Computer Science.*

Morrell, T. (2012, June). Computability and Complexity in Elliptic Curves and Cryptography: An Algorithm for Finding Elliptic Curves of Prime Order over Fp. *AAAS Pacific Division Conference.* Accessed from https://math.boisestate.edu/reu/publications/AAASTomMorrell.PDF

Mostapha, M., & Styner, M. (2019). Role of Deep Learning in Infant Brain MRI Analysis. *Magnetic Resonance Imaging*, 64, 171–189. doi:10.1016/j.mri.2019.06.009 PMID:31229667

Mueller, A., Candrian, G., Kropotov, J. D., Ponomarev, V. A., & Baschera, G. M. (2010). Classification of ADHD Patients on the Basis of Independent ERP Components Using a Machine Learning System. *Nonlinear Biomedical Physics*, 4(S1), 1–12. doi:10.1186/1753-4631-4-S1-S1 PMID:20522259

Müller, A., Vetsch, S., Pershin, I., Candrian, G., Kropotov, J., Kasper, J., & Abdel Rehim, H. (2019). EEG/ERP-Based Biomarker/Neuroalgorithms in Adults with ADHD: Development, Reliability, and Application in Clinical Practice. *The World Journal of Biological Psychiatry*, 172–182. PMID:30990349

Munir, K., Elahi, H., Ayub, A., Frezza, F., & Rizzi, A. (2019). Cancer diagnosis using deep learning: A bibliographic review. *Cancers (Basel)*, 11(9), 1–36. doi:10.3390/cancers11091235 PMID:31450799

Naghedifar, S. M., Ziaei, A. N., & Ansari, H. (2020). Numerical Analysis of Sensor-Based Flood-Floor Ebb-and-Flow Sub-irrigation System with Saline Water. *Archives of Agronomy and Soil Science.*

Nandi, S., & Chaudhuri, P. P. (1997). Reply to comments on theory and applications of cellular automata in cryptography. *IEEE Transactions on Computers*, 46(5), 638–639. doi:10.1109/TC.1997.589246

Nandi, S., Kar, B. K., & Chaudhuri, P. P. (1994). Theory and applications of cellular automata in cryptography. *IEEE Transactions on Computers*, 43(12), 1346–1357. doi:10.1109/12.338094

Naveed, Qureshi, Min, Jo, & Lee. (2016). *Multiclass Classification for the Differential Diagnosis on the ADHD Subtypes Using Recursive Feature Elimination and Hierarchical Extreme Learning Machine : Structural MRI Study.* Academic Press.

Neverova, N., Alp Guler, R., & Kokkinos, I. (2018). Dense pose transfer. In *Proceedings of the European conference on computer vision (ECCV)* (pp. 123-138). Academic Press.

NextGen. (2018). *IoT Medical Devices Security Vulnerabilities on WiFi Networks.* Available: https://www.nextgenexecsearch.com/iot-medical-devices-security

Niazi, M., & Hussain, A. (2009). Agent-based tools for modeling and simulation of self-organization in peer-to-peer, ad hoc, and other complex networks. *IEEE Communications Magazine, 47*(3), 166–173. doi:10.1109/MCOM.2009.4804403

Nichele, S., & Molund, A. (2017). Deep learning with cellular automaton-based reservoir computing. *Complex Systems, 26*(4), 319–339. doi:10.25088/ComplexSystems.26.4.319

NIH National Cancer. (2020). Cancer Facts & Figures 2020. *CA: a Cancer Journal for Clinicians*, 1–76.

Ni, J., Zhang, K., Lin, X., & Shen, X. S. (2017). Securing fog computing for internet of things applications: Challenges and solutions. *IEEE Communications Surveys and Tutorials, 20*(1), 601–628. doi:10.1109/COMST.2017.2762345

Nikolaou, G., Neocleous, D., Christou, A., Kitta, E., & Katsoulas, N. (2020). Implementing Sustainable Irrigation in Water-Scarce Regions under the Impact of Climate Change. *Agronomy (Basel), 10*(8), 1120. doi:10.3390/agronomy10081120

Normanyo, Husinu, & Agyare. (2014). Developing a Human Machine Interface (HMI) for Industrial Automated Systems using Siemens Simatic WinCC Flexible Advanced Software. *Journal of Emerging Trends in Computing and Information Sciences, 5*(2).

Nuamah, J. (2017, June). Human Machine Interface in the Internet of Things (IoT). *International Journal of Latest Technology in Engineering, Management & Applied Sciences*.

Nvidia. (2016). *Deep learning Breast Cancer Diagnosis*. Author.

Odena, A., Olah, C., & Shlens, J. (2017, August). Conditional image synthesis with auxiliary classifier gans. In *Proceedings of the 34th International Conference on Machine Learning-Volume 70* (pp. 2642-2651). JMLR. org.

Oh, J., Sim, O., Cho, B., Lee, K., & Oh, J. H. (2020). Online Delayed Reference Generation for a Humanoid Imitating Human Walking Motion. *IEEE/ASME Transactions on Mechatronics*, 1. doi:10.1109/TMECH.2020.3002396

Oj, Elmose, Skoog, Hansen, Simonsen, Pedersen, Tendal, He, Faltinsen, & Gluud. (2019). *Social Skills Training for Attention Deficit Hyperactivity Disorder (ADHD) in Children Aged 5 to 18 Years (Review)*. Academic Press.

Ojha, S. K., Kumar, N., & Jain, K. (2009, December). TWIS-a lightweight block cipher. In *International Conference on Information Systems Security* (pp. 280-291). Springer. 10.1007/978-3-642-10772-6_21

Oskuii, S. T. (2004). *Comparative study on low-power high-performance flip-flops* (Unpublished Master of Technology Thesis). Linköping University. Accessed from http://www.divaportal.org/smash/get/diva2:19406/FULLTEXT01.pdf

Ou, C., Yang, J., Du, Z., Zhang, X., & Zhu, D. (2019). Integrating Cellular Automata with Unsupervised Deep-Learning Algorithms: A Case Study of Urban-Sprawl Simulation in the Jingjintang Urban Agglomeration, China. *Sustainability, 11*(9), 24–64. doi:10.3390u11092464

Ouyang, X., Zhou, P., Li, C. H., & Liu, L. (2015). *Sentiment analysis using convolutional neural network. In 2015 IEEE international conference on computer and information technology; ubiquitous computing and communications; dependable, autonomic and secure computing; pervasive intelligence and computing*. IEEE.

Pang, B., & Lee, L. (2008). Opinion mining and sentiment analysis. *Foundations and Trends in Information Retrieval, 2*(1–2), 1–135. doi:10.1561/1500000011

Park, T., Liu, M. Y., Wang, T. C., & Zhu, J. Y. (2019). Semantic image synthesis with spatially-adaptive normalization. In *Proceedings of the IEEE Conference on Computer Vision and Pattern Recognition* (pp. 2337-2346). IEEE.

Patel, K. K., & Patel, S. M. (2016). Internet of things-IOT: definition, characteristics, architecture, enabling technologies, application & future challenges. *International Journal of Engineering Science and Computing, 6*(5), 6122-6131.

Patole, Shide, Salve, Kaushik, & Puri. (2017). IOT based Vehicle Tracking & Vehicular Emergency System- A Case Study and Review. *International Journal of Advanced Research in Electrical, Electronics and Instrumentation Engineering, 6*(10).

Pearson's Correlation. (n.d.). Accessed from http://www.statstutor.ac.uk/resources/uploaded/pearsons.pdf

Peng, Lin, Zhang, & Wang. (2013). *Extreme Learning Machine-Based Classification of ADHD Using Brain Structural MRI Data.* Academic Press.

Pereira, S., Pinto, A., Alves, V., & Silva, C. A. (2016). *Brain Tumor Segmentation Using Convolutional Neural Networks in MRI Images.* Academic Press.

Pielli, C., Zucchetto, D., Zanella, A., Vangelista, L., & Zorzi, M. (2015). Platforms and Protocols for the Internet of Things. *EAI Endorsed Trans. Internet Things, 15*(1), e5. doi:10.4108/eai.26-10-2015.150599

Poria, S., Gelbukh, A., Hussain, A., Howard, N., Das, D., & Bandyopadhyay, S. (2013). Enhanced SenticNet with affective labels for concept-based opinion mining. *IEEE Intelligent Systems, 28*(2), 31–38. doi:10.1109/MIS.2013.4

Qiao, Y., Su, D., Kong, H., Sukkarieh, S., Lomax, S., & Clark, C. (2019). Individual Cattle Identification Using a Deep Learning Based Framework. *IFAC-PapersOnLine, 52*(30), 318–323. doi:10.1016/j.ifacol.2019.12.558

Qureshi, M. N. I., Oh, J., Min, B., Jo, H. J., & Lee, B. (2017). Multi-Class Discrimination of ADHD with Hierarchical Feature Extraction and Extreme Learning Machine Using Structural and Functional Brain MRI. *Frontiers in Human Neuroscience, 11*(157), 1–16.

Radford, A., Metz, L., & Chintala, S. (2015). *Unsupervised representation learning with deep convolutional generative adversarial networks.* arXiv preprint arXiv:1511.06434.

Raj, A., Sangkloy, P., Chang, H., Hays, J., Ceylan, D., & Lu, J. (2018, September). Swapnet: Image based garment transfer. In *European Conference on Computer Vision* (pp. 679-695). Springer.

Randomness of statistical sampling: the runs' test. (n.d.). Accessed from https://home.ubalt.edu/ntsbarsh/business-stat/otherapplets/Randomness.htm

Rao, R. N., & Sridhar, B. (2018, January). IoT based smart crop-field monitoring and automation irrigation system. In *2018 2nd International Conference on Inventive Systems and Control (ICISC)* (pp. 478-483). IEEE. 10.1109/ICISC.2018.8399118

Razzak, M. I., Naz, S., & Zaib, A. (2018). Deep learning for medical image processing: Overview, challenges and the future. *Lecture Notes in Computational Vision and Biomechanics, 26*, 323–350. doi:10.1007/978-3-319-65981-7_12

Reda, I., Khalil, A., Elmogy, M., El-Fetouh, A. A., Shalaby, A., El-Ghar, M. A., ... El-Baz, A. (2018). Deep learning role in early diagnosis of prostate cancer. *Technology in Cancer Research & Treatment, 17*, 1–11. doi:10.1177/1533034618775530 PMID:29804518

Reed, S., Akata, Z., Yan, X., Logeswaran, L., Schiele, B., & Lee, H. (2016). *Generative adversarial text to image synthesis.* arXiv preprint arXiv:1605.05396.

Reiter, S., Sattlecker, G., Lidauer, L., Kickinger, F., Öhlschuster, M., Auer, W., & Iwersen, M. (2018). Evaluation of an ear-tag-based accelerometer for monitoring rumination in dairy cows. *Journal of Dairy Science, 101*(4), 3398–3411. doi:10.3168/jds.2017-12686 PMID:29395141

Ren, S., He, K., Girshick, R., & Sun, J. (2017). Faster R-CNN: Towards Real-Time Object Detection with Region Proposal Networks. *IEEE Transactions on Pattern Analysis and Machine Intelligence, 39*(6), 1137–1149. doi:10.1109/TPAMI.2016.2577031 PMID:27295650

Resh, H. M. (2013). *Hobby Hydroponics*. CRC Publisher. doi:10.1201/b13737

Riaz, A., Asad, M., Alonso, E., & Slabaugh, G. (2019). DeepFMRI: End-to-End Deep Learning for Functional Connectivity and Classification of ADHD Using FMRI. *Journal of Neuroscience Methods*. PMID:32001294

Richard, A. E., Lajiness-O'Neill, R. R., & Bowyer, S. M. (2013). Impaired Prefrontal Gamma Band Synchrony in Autism Spectrum Disorders during Gaze Cueing. *Neuroreport*, *24*(16), 894–897. doi:10.1097/WNR.0000000000000015 PMID:24077557

Rijmen, V., & Daemen, J. (2001). Advanced encryption standard. In Proceedings of Federal Information Processing Standards Publications. National Institute of Standards and Technology.

Rim, B., Min, S., & Hong, M. (2020). Deep Learning in Physiological Signal Data. *Survey (London, England)*. PMID:32054042

Rivest, R. L., Shamir, A., & Adleman, L. M. (1983). *U.S. Patent No. 4,405,829*. Washington, DC: U.S. Patent and Trademark Office.

Roberto, K. (2003). *How-to Hydroponics*. The Futuregarden Press.

Rodríguez-martínez, E. I., Angulo-ruiz, B. Y., Arjona-valladares, A., Rufo, M., Gómez-gonzález, J., & Gómez, C. M. (2019, October). Research in Developmental Disabilities Frequency Coupling of Low and High Frequencies in the EEG of ADHD Children and Adolescents in Closed and Open Eyes Conditions. *Research in Developmental Disabilities*, *96*, 103520. doi:10.1016/j.ridd.2019.103520 PMID:31783276

Ronneberger, O., Fischer, P., & Brox, T. (2015). U-net: Convolutional networks for biomedical image segmentation. Lecture Notes in Computer Science (Including Subseries Lecture Notes in Artificial Intelligence and Lecture Notes in Bioinformatics), 9351, 234–241. doi:10.1007/978-3-319-24574-4_28

Rostain & Ramsay. (2006). *A Combined Treatment Approach for Adults With ADHD — Results of an Open Study of 43 Patients*. Academic Press.

Ruengittinun, S., Phongsamsuan, S., & Sureeratanakorn, P. (2017). Applied Internet of Things for Smart Hydroponic Farming Ecosystem. *10th International Conference on Ubi-Media Computing and Workshops*. Pattaya, Thailand: IEEE. 10.1109/UMEDIA.2017.8074148

Saaid, M. F., Sanuddin, A., Megat Ali, M. S., & M, Y. I. (2015). *Automated pH Controller System for Hydroponic Cultivation*. IEEE.

Saaid, M. F., Yahya, N. A., Noor, M. Z., & Ali, M. A. (2013). A development of an Automatic Microcontroller System for Deep Water Culture (DWC). In *IEEE 9th International Colloquium on Signal Processing and its Applications* (pp. 328-332). Kuala Lumpur: IEEE. 10.1109/CSPA.2013.6530066

Saba, T. (2019). Automated lung nodule detection and classification based on multiple classifiers voting. *Microscopy Research and Technique*, *82*(9), 1601–1609. doi:10.1002/jemt.23326 PMID:31243869

Sadeghi, A., Wachsmann, C., & Waidner, M. (2015). Security and privacy challenges in the industrial Internet of Things. *52nd ACM/EDAC/IEEE Design Automation Conference (DAC)*, 1-6. 10.1145/2744769.2747942

Saha, S., & Mitra, A. (2019a, January). Towards Exploration of Green Computing in Energy Efficient Optimized Algorithm for Uses in Fog Computing. In *International Conference on Intelligent Computing and Communication Technologies* (pp. 628-636). Springer Nature. 10.1007/978-981-13-8461-5_72

Saha, S., & Mitra, A. (2019b, December). An energy-efficient data routing in weight-balanced tree-based Fog Network. In *2019 International Conference on Intelligent and Cloud Computing* (pp. 3-11). Springer Nature. 10.1007/978-981-15-6202-0_1

Sajid, H., & Cheung, S.-C. S. (2015). Background subtraction for static moving camera. In *Proceedings 2015 IEEE International Conference on Image Processing (ICIP)* (pp. 4530-4534). 10.1109/ICIP.2015.7351664

Saraswathi, D., Manibharathy, P., Gokulnath, R., Sureshkumar, E., & Karthikeyan, K. (2018). Automation of Hydroponics Green House Farming. *2018 IEEE International Conference on System, Computation, Automation and Networking (ICSCA).* Pondicherry, India: IEEE. 10.1109/ICSCAN.2018.8541251

Schelb, P., Kohl, S., Radtke, J. P., Wiesenfarth, M., Kickingereder, P., Bickelhaupt, S., Kuder, T. A., Stenzinger, A., Hohenfellner, M., Schlemmer, H.-P., Maier-Hein, K. H., & Bonekamp, D. (2019). Classification of cancer at prostate MRI: Deep Learning versus Clinical PI-RADS Assessment. *Radiology, 293*(3), 607–617. doi:10.1148/radiol.2019190938 PMID:31592731

Sedjelmaci, H., Senouci, S. M., & Taleb, T. (2017). An accurate security game for low-resource IoT devices. *IEEE Transactions on Vehicular Technology, 66*(10), 9381–9393. doi:10.1109/TVT.2017.2701551

Seetha, J., & Raja, S. S. (2018). Brain Tumor Classification Using Convolutional. *Neural Networks, 11*(September), 1457–1461.

Sen, Borle, Greiner, & Brown. (2018). *A General Prediction Model for the Detection of ADHD and Autism Using Structural and Functional MRI.* Academic Press.

Seralathan, Y. (2018). IoT security vulnerability: A case study of a Web camera. *20th International Conference on Advanced Communication Technology (ICACT),* 1–2.

Sethi, P., & Sarangi, S. R. (2017). Internet of things: Architectures, protocols, and applications. *Journal of Electrical and Computer Engineering, 2017,* 1–25. doi:10.1155/2017/9324035

Shah, Fazl-e-Hadi, & Minhas. (2009). New Factor of Authentication: Something You Process. *International Conference on Future Computer and Communication,* 102-106.

Shahzadi, I., Meriadeau, F., Tang, T. B., & Quyyum, A. (2019). CNN-LSTM: Cascaded framework for brain tumour classification. *2018 IEEE EMBS Conference on Biomedical Engineering and Sciences, IECBES 2018 - Proceedings,* (March), 633–637. 10.1109/IECBES.2018.8626704

Sharma & Tiwari. (2016). A review paper on "IOT" & It's Smart Applications. *International Journal of Science, Engineering and Technology Research, 5*(2).

Shavrukov, Y., Genc, Y., & Hayes, J. C. (2012). *The Use of Hydroponics in Abiotic Stress Tolerance Research.* Academic Press.

Shekhar, Y., Dagur, E., Mishra, S., & Sankaranarayanan, S. (2017). Intelligent IoT based automated irrigation system. *International Journal of Applied Engineering Research: IJAER, 12*(18), 7306–7320.

Shemaili, M. A. B., Yeun, C. Y., Zemerly, M. J., & Mubarak, K. (2014). A novel cellular automata based cipher system for internet of things. In *Future information technology* (pp. 269–276). Springer. doi:10.1007/978-3-642-40861-8_40

Shin, S. H., Kim, D. H., & Yoo, Y. (November 2012). A light-weight multi-user authentication scheme based on cellular automata in cloud environment., In *2012 IEEE 1ˢᵗ International Conference on Cloud Networking (CLOUDNET)* (pp. 176-178). IEEE.

Shirsath, P. B., & Singh, A. K. (2010). A comparative study of daily pan evaporation estimation using ANN, regression and climate based models. *Water Resources Management, 24*(8), 1571–1581. doi:10.100711269-009-9514-2

Shrestha, Mali, Joseph, Singh, & Raj. (2017). Web and Android based Automation using IoT. *International Journal of Latest Technology in Engineering, Management & Applied Science, 6*(5).

Shysheya, A., Zakharov, E., Aliev, K. A., Bashirov, R., Burkov, E., Iskakov, K., Ivakhnenko, A., Malkov, Y., Pasechnik, I., Ulyanov, D., & Vakhitov, A. (2019). Textured neural avatars. In *Proceedings of the IEEE Conference on Computer Vision and Pattern Recognition* (pp. 2387-2397). IEEE.

Siarohin, A., Sangineto, E., Lathuilière, S., & Sebe, N. (2018). Deformable gans for pose-based human image generation. In *Proceedings of the IEEE Conference on Computer Vision and Pattern Recognition* (pp. 3408-3416). 10.1109/CVPR.2018.00359

Sihombing, P., Karina, N. A., Tarigan, J. T., & Syarif, M. I. (2017). Automated Hydroponics Nutrition Plants Systems Using Arduino Uno Microcontroller Based on Android. In *2nd International Conference on Computing and Applied Informatics*. Medan, Indonesia: IOP Publishing Ltd.

Silverstein, Faraone, Leon, Biederman, Spencer, & Adler. (2018). *The Relationship Between Executive Function Deficits and DSM -5-Defined ADHD Symptoms*. Academic Press.

Singh, A., Chawla, N., Ko, J. H., Kar, M., & Mukhopadhyay, S. (2018). Energy-efficient and side-channel secure cryptographic hardware for IoT-edge nodes. *IEEE Internet of Things Journal, 6*(1), 421–434. doi:10.1109/JIOT.2018.2861324

Singh, S., Pandey, S. K., Pawar, U., & Janghel, R. R. (2018). Classification of ECG Arrhythmia using Recurrent Neural Networks. *Procedia Computer Science, 132*(1), 1290–1297. doi:10.1016/j.procs.2018.05.045

Smart farming and smart agriculture solutions. (2019). Retrieved from ThingsBoard: https://thingsboard.io/smart-farming/

Smith, C., & Collins, D. (2002). *3G Wireless Networks*. McGraw-Hill Professional.

Socher, R., Lin, C. C., Manning, C., & Ng, A. Y. (2011). Parsing natural scenes and natural language with recursive neural networks. In *Proceedings of the 28th international conference on machine learning (ICML-11)* (pp. 129-136). Academic Press.

Song, J., Zhang, J., Gao, L., Liu, X., & Shen, H. T. (2018, July). Dual Conditional GANs for Face Aging and Rejuvenation. In IJCAI (pp. 899-905). doi:10.24963/ijcai.2018/125

Sruthi & Kavitha. (2016). A survey on IoT platform. *International Journal of Scientific Research and Modern Education, 1*(1).

Sun, Q. (2018). Deep Learning for Image-based Cancer Detection and Diagnosis— A Survey. *Pattern Recognition, 83*, 134–149. Advance online publication. doi:10.1016/j.patcog.2018.05.014

Suo, H., Wan, J., Zou, C., & Liu, J. (2012, March). *Security in the internet of things: a review. In 2012 international conference on computer science and electronics engineering*. IEEE.

Suparwito, H., Wong, K. W., Xie, H., Rai, S., & Thomas, D. (2019, November). A hierarchical classification method used to classify livestock behaviour from sensor data. In *International Conference on Multi-disciplinary Trends in Artificial Intelligence* (pp. 204-215). Springer. 10.1007/978-3-030-33709-4_18

Swiderski, B., Kurek, J., Osowski, S., Kruk, M., & Barhoumi, W. (2017). Deep Learning and Non-Negative Matrix Factorization in Recognition of Mammograms. *Icgip 2016*, 1–7. doi:10.1117/12.2266335

Tan, Qiu, Liu, Yan, Hai, Mei, Meng, Huang, Yu, He, & Liao. (2019). *Alterations of Cerebral Perfusion and Functional Brain Connectivity in Medication - Naïve Male Adults with Attention - Deficit / Hyperactivity Disorder.* Academic Press.

Tandel, G. S., Biswas, M., Kakde, O. G., Tiwari, A., Suri, H. S., Turk, M., Laird, J., Asare, C., Ankrah, A. A., Khanna, N. N., Madhusudhan, B. K., Saba, L., & Suri, J. S. (2019). A review on a deep learning perspective in brain cancer classification. *Cancers (Basel)*, *11*(1), 111. Advance online publication. doi:10.3390/cancers11010111 PMID:30669406

Tangsakul, S., & Wongthanavasu, S. (2020). Single Image Haze Removal Using Deep Cellular Automata Learning. *IEEE Access: Practical Innovations, Open Solutions*, *8*, 103181–103199. doi:10.1109/ACCESS.2020.2999076

Tenev, A., Markovska-simoska, S., Kocarev, L., Pop-jordanov, J., Müller, A., & Candrian, G. (2013). Machine Learning Approach for Classi Fi Cation of ADHD Adults. *International Journal of Psychophysiology*, 1–5. PMID:23361114

Thapar, Cooper, Eyre, & Langley. (2012). *Practitioner Review : What Have We Learnt about the Causes of ADHD?* Academic Press.

Thies, J., Zollhofer, M., Stamminger, M., Theobalt, C., & Nießner, M. (2016). Face2face: Real-time face capture and reenactment of rgb videos. In *Proceedings of the IEEE conference on computer vision and pattern recognition* (pp. 2387-2395). 10.1145/2929464.2929475

Tikade, R., & Rajeswari, P. D. K. (2018). Lung Cancer Detection and Classification using Deep learning. IEEE, 4, 5–9.

Townsend, Beyer, & Blodgett. (2003). *PET/CT Scanners: A Hardware Approach to Image Fusion.* Academic Press.

Tran, K., & Wu, J. (2019). Case Report : Neuroimaging Analysis of Pediatric ADHD-Related Symptoms Secondary to Hypoxic Brain Injury. *Brain Injury: [BI]*, *33*(10), 1402–1407. doi:10.1080/02699052.2019.1641744 PMID:31307241

Tripathy, S., & Nandi, S. (2009). Lightweight Cellular Automata-based Symmetric-Key Encryption. *International Journal of Network Security*, *8*(3), 243–252.

Tsai, A. C. R., Wu, C. E., Tsai, R. T. H., & Hsu, J. Y. J. (2013). Building a concept-level sentiment dictionary based on commonsense knowledge. *IEEE Intelligent Systems*, *28*(2), 22–30. doi:10.1109/MIS.2013.25

Tsai, D. M., & Luo, J. Y. (2011). Mean shift-based defect detection in multi-crystalline solar wafer surfaces. *IEEE Transactions on Industrial Informatics*, *7*(1), 125–135. doi:10.1109/TII.2010.2092783

Tsai, K., Huang, Y., Leu, F., You, I., Huang, Y., & Tsa, C. (2018). AES-128 Based Secure Low Power Communication for LoRaWAN IoT Environments. *IEEE Access: Practical Innovations, Open Solutions*, *6*, 45325–45334. doi:10.1109/ACCESS.2018.2852563

Turkki, R., Linder, N., Kovanen, P. E., Pellinen, T., & Lundin, J. (2016). Antibody-supervised deep learning for quantification of tumor-infiltrating immune cells in hematoxylin and eosin stained breast cancer samples. *Journal of Pathology Informatics*, *7*(1), 38. Advance online publication. doi:10.4103/2153-3539.189703 PMID:27688929

Uddin, J., Reza, S. T., Newaz, Q., Uddin, J., Islam, T., & Kim, J. M. (2012, December). Automated irrigation system using solar power. In *2012 7th International Conference on Electrical and Computer Engineering* (pp. 228-231). IEEE.

Umair, S. M., & Usman, R. (2010). Automation of irrigation system using ANN based controller. *International Journal of Electrical & Computer Sciences IJECS-IJENS*, *10*(02), 41–47.

Ünal, Z. (2020). Smart Farming Becomes Even Smarter With Deep Learning—A Bibliographical Analysis. *IEEE Access : Practical Innovations, Open Solutions*, *8*, 105587–105609.

Vahid, Bluschke, Roessner, & Stober. (2019). *Deep Learning Based on Event-Related EEG Di Ff Erentiates Children with ADHD from Healthy Controls.* Academic Press.

Vaishali, S., Suraj, S., Vignesh, G., Dhivya, S., & Udhayakumar, S. (2017, April). Mobile integrated smart irrigation management and monitoring system using IOT. In *2017 International Conference on Communication and Signal Processing (ICCSP)* (pp. 2164-2167). IEEE.

Vaishnavi & Gaikwad. (2017). Water Quality Monitoring System Based onIOT. *Advances in Wireless and Mobile Communications, 10*(5).

Vajda, I., & Buttyan, L. (2003, October). Lightweight authentication protocols for low-cost RFID tags. *Second workshop on Security in Ubiquitous Computing.*

Vasconcelos, C. N., & Vasconcelos, B. N. (2017). Experiments using deep learning for dermoscopy image analysis. *Pattern Recognition Letters, 0,* 1–9. doi:10.1016/j.patrec.2017.11.005

Vateekul, P., & Koomsubha, T. (2016). A Study of Sentiment Analysis Using Deep Learning Techniques on Thai Twitter Data. *13th International Joint Conference on Computer Science and Software Engineering (JCSSE),* 1-6. 10.1109/JCSSE.2016.7748849

Vaughan, J., Green, P. M., Salter, M., Grieve, B., & Ozanyan, K. B. (2017). *Floor sensors of animal weight and gait for precision livestock farming. In 2017 IEEE SENSORS.* IEEE.

Velmurugan, S. (2020). *An IOT based Smart Irrigation System using Soil Moisture and Weather Prediction.* Academic Press.

Venable, J. (2017). *Child safety smartwatches 'easy' to hack, watchdog says.* Available: https://www.bbc.com/news/technology-41652742

Verizon. (2017). *IoT Calamity: The Panda Monium.* Available: http://www.verizonenterprise.com/resources/rp_data-breach-digest-2017-sneak-peek_xg_en.pdf

Verma, V. K., & Jain, T. (2019). Soft-Computing-Based Approaches for Plant Leaf Disease Detection: Machine-Learning-Based Study. In Applications of Image Processing and Soft Computing Systems in Agriculture (pp. 100-113). IGI Global.

Verma, S., Bhatia, A., Chug, A., & Singh, A. P. (2020). Recent Advancements in Multimedia Big Data Computing for IOT Applications in Precision Agriculture: Opportunities, Issues, and Challenges. In *Multimedia Big Data Computing for IOT Applications* (pp. 391–416). Springer. doi:10.1007/978-981-13-8759-3_15

Villegas, R., Yang, J., Hong, S., Lin, X., & Lee, H. (2017). *Decomposing motion and content for natural video sequence prediction.* arXiv preprint arXiv:1706.08033.

Villegas, R., Yang, J., Ceylan, D., & Lee, H. (2018). Neural kinematic networks for unsupervised motion retargeting. In *Proceedings of the IEEE Conference on Computer Vision and Pattern Recognition* (pp. 8639-8648). 10.1109/CVPR.2018.00901

Walker, J., Doersch, C., Gupta, A., & Hebert, M. (2016, October). An uncertain future: Forecasting from static images using variational autoencoders. In *European Conference on Computer Vision* (pp. 835-851). Springer. 10.1007/978-3-319-46478-7_51

Walker, J., Marino, K., Gupta, A., & Hebert, M. (2017). The pose knows: Video forecasting by generating pose futures. In *Proceedings of the IEEE international conference on computer vision* (pp. 3332-3341). 10.1109/ICCV.2017.361

Wang, T. C., Liu, M. Y., Zhu, J. Y., Liu, G., Tao, A., Kautz, J., & Catanzaro, B. (2018). *Video-to-video synthesis.* arXiv preprint arXiv:1808.06601.

Wang, Y., Hu, M., Li, Q., Zhang, X.-P., Zhai, G., & Yao, N. (2020). *Abnormal respiratory patterns classifier may contribute to Large-scale screening of people infected with covid-19 in an accurate and unobtrusive manner.* arXiv:2002.05534v1 [cs.LG]

Wang, Z., Bovik, A. C., Sheikh, H. R., & Simoncelli, E. P. (2004). Image quality assessment: From error visibility to structural similarity. *IEEE Transactions on Image Processing*, *13*(4), 600–612. doi:10.1109/TIP.2003.819861 PMID:15376593

Wang, Z., Tang, X., Luo, W., & Gao, S. (2018). Face aging with identity-preserved conditional generative adversarial networks. In *Proceedings of the IEEE Conference on Computer Vision and Pattern Recognition* (pp. 7939-7947). IEEE.

Weber, R. H. (2010). Internet of Things–New security and privacy challenges. *Computer Law & Security Review*, *26*(1), 23–30. doi:10.1016/j.clsr.2009.11.008

Weisstein, E. W. (n.d.). *Primitive Polynomial. MathWorld-A Wolfram Web Resource.* Accessed from https://mathworld.wolfram.com/PrimitivePolynomial.html

Welch, S. (2018). *How To Determine When A Cow Is In Heat - Farm And Dairy.* https://www.farmanddairy.com/top-stories/how-to-determine-when-a-cow-is-in-heat/464746.html

Wenz, J. R., Moore, D. A., & Kasimanickam, R. (2011). Factors associated with the rectal temperature of Holstein dairy cows during the first 10 days in milk. *Journal of Dairy Science*, *94*(4), 1864–1872.

WHO. (2020).. . *Cancer.*

Wu, H., Liu, N., Luo, X., Su, J., & Chen, L. (2014). Real-time background subtraction-based video surveillance of people by integrating local texture patterns. *Signal, Image and Video Processing*, *8*(4), 665–676. doi:10.100711760-013-0576-5

Xing, W., Qian, Y., Guan, X., Yang, T., & Wu, H. (2020). A novel cellular automata model integrated with deep learning for dynamic spatio-temporal land use change simulation. *Computers & Geosciences*, *137*, 104430. doi:10.1016/j.cageo.2020.104430

Xu, B., Wang, N., Chen, T., & Li, M. (2015). *Empirical Evaluation of Rectified Activations in Convolutional Network.* Retrieved from https://arxiv.org/abs/1505.00853

Xu, B., Wang, W., Falzon, G., Kwan, P., Guo, L., Sun, Z., & Li, C. (2020). Livestock classification and counting in quadcopter aerial images using Mask R-CNN. *International Journal of Remote Sensing*, • • •, 1–22.

Xue, T., Wu, J., Bouman, K., & Freeman, B. (2016). Visual dynamics: Probabilistic future frame synthesis via cross convolutional networks. In Advances in neural information processing systems (pp. 91-99). Academic Press.

Xu, W., Chatterjee, A., Zollhöfer, M., Rhodin, H., Mehta, D., Seidel, H. P., & Theobalt, C. (2018). Monoperfcap: Human performance capture from monocular video. *ACM Transactions on Graphics*, *37*(2), 1–15. doi:10.1145/3181973

Yang, H., Huang, D., Wang, Y., & Jain, A. K. (2019). Learning continuous face age progression: A pyramid of gans. *IEEE Transactions on Pattern Analysis and Machine Intelligence*, 1. doi:10.1109/TPAMI.2019.2930985 PMID:31352335

Ye, M., Jiang, N., Yang, H., & Yan, Q. (2017). Security analysis of Internet-of-Things: A case study of the smart lock. *IEEE Conference on Computer Communications Workshops (INFOCOM WKSHPS)*, 499-504. 10.1109/INFOCOMW.2017.8116427

Ye, Q., Zhang, Z., & Law, R. (2009). Sentiment classification of online reviews to travel destinations by supervised machine learning approaches. *Expert Systems with Applications*, *36*(3), 6527–6535. doi:10.1016/j.eswa.2008.07.035

Yi, Z., Zhang, H., Tan, P., & Gong, M. (2017). Dualgan: Unsupervised dual learning for image-to-image translation. In *Proceedings of the IEEE international conference on computer vision* (pp. 2849-2857). 10.1109/ICCV.2017.310

Yoo, S., Gujrathi, I., Haider, M. A., & Khalvati, F. (2019). Prostate Cancer Detection using Deep Convolutional Neural Networks. *Scientific Reports*, *9*(1), 1–10. doi:10.103841598-019-55972-4 PMID:31863034

Yousefi, A., & Jameii, S. M. (2017). Improving the security of the Internet of things using encryption algorithms. *International Conference on IoT and Application (ICIOT)*, 1-5. 10.1109/ICIOTA.2017.8073627

Yuan, X. (2018). All Your Alexa Are Belong to Us: A Remote Voice Control Attack against Echo. *IEEE Global Communications Conference (GLOBECOM)*, 1-6. 10.1109/GLOCOM.2018.8647762

Zanfir, M., Popa, A. I., Zanfir, A., & Sminchisescu, C. (2018). Human appearance transfer. In *Proceedings of the IEEE Conference on Computer Vision and Pattern Recognition* (pp. 5391-5399). IEEE.

Zhang, C., Xiao, D., Yang, Q., Wen, Z., & Lv, L. (2020). Application of Infrared Thermography in Livestock Monitoring. *Transactions of the ASABE*, *63*(2), 389–399.

Zhang, H., Xu, T., Li, H., Zhang, S., Wang, X., Huang, X., & Metaxas, D. N. (2017). Stackgan: Text to photo-realistic image synthesis with stacked generative adversarial networks. In *Proceedings of the IEEE international conference on computer vision* (pp. 5907-5915). 10.1109/ICCV.2017.629

Zhang, N., Ding, S., Zhang, J., & Xue, Y. (2018). An overview on Restricted Boltzmann Machines. *Neurocomputing*, *275*, 1186–1199. doi:10.1016/j.neucom.2017.09.065

Zhang, R., Isola, P., Efros, A. A., Shechtman, E., & Wang, O. (2018). The unreasonable effectiveness of deep features as a perceptual metric. In *Proceedings of the IEEE conference on computer vision and pattern recognition* (pp. 586-595). 10.1109/CVPR.2018.00068

Zhang, Z., Song, Y., & Qi, H. (2017). Age progression/regression by conditional adversarial autoencoder. In *Proceedings of the IEEE conference on computer vision and pattern recognition* (pp. 5810-5818). 10.1109/CVPR.2017.463

Zhao, B., Wu, X., Cheng, Z. Q., Liu, H., Jie, Z., & Feng, J. (2018, October). Multi-view image generation from a single-view. In *Proceedings of the 26th ACM international conference on Multimedia* (pp. 383-391). ACM.

Zhao, Z., Bouwmans, T., Zhang, X., & Fang, Y. (2012). *A fuzzy background modeling approach for motion detection in dynamic backgrounds*. Multimedia and Signal Processing. doi:10.1007/978-3-642-35286-7_23

Zhou, Y., Wang, Z., Fang, C., Bui, T., & Berg, T. (2019). Dance dance generation: Motion transfer for internet videos. In *Proceedings of the IEEE International Conference on Computer Vision Workshops* (pp. 0-0). IEEE.

Zhou, W., Liu, Y., Zhang, W., Zhuang, L., & Yu, N. (2013). Dynamic background subtraction using spatial-color binary patterns. *IEEE Transactions on Pattern Analysis and Machine Intelligence*, *35*, 597–610. PMID:22689075

Zhu, J. Y., Zhang, R., Pathak, D., Darrell, T., Efros, A. A., Wang, O., & Shechtman, E. (2017). Toward multimodal image-to-image translation. In Advances in neural information processing systems (pp. 465-476). Academic Press.

Zhu, C., Bichot, C. E., & Chen, L. (2010). Multi-scale color local binary patterns for visual object classes recognition. In *Proceedings of International Conference on Pattern Recognition* (pp. 3065-3068). 10.1109/ICPR.2010.751

Zhu, H., Su, H., Wang, P., Cao, X., & Yang, R. (2018). View extrapolation of human body from a single image. In *Proceedings of the IEEE Conference on Computer Vision and Pattern Recognition* (pp. 4450-4459). 10.1109/CVPR.2018.00468

Zhu, J. Y., Park, T., Isola, P., & Efros, A. A. (2017). Unpaired image-to-image translation using cycle-consistent adversarial networks. In *Proceedings of the IEEE international conference on computer vision* (pp. 2223-2232). 10.1109/ICCV.2017.244

Zuo, G., Chen, K., Lu, J., & Huang, X. (2020). Deterministic generative adversarial imitation learning. *Neurocomputing*, *388*, 60–69. doi:10.1016/j.neucom.2020.01.016

About the Contributors

Roshani Raut has obtained her BE degree in Computer Science and Engineering from Rashta Sant Tukdoji Maharaj, Nagpur University, India and ME in Computer Science and Engineering from Savitribai Phule Pune University, India. She has completed her doctorate in Computer Science and Engineering from Sant Gadge Baba Amravati University, Amravati, India. She has more than 16 years of experience and currently she is working as a Associate Professor in the Department of Computer Engineering of Vishwakarma Institute of Information Technology, Pune, India. She worked as a TPC member and She worked as a Reviewer for various conference including IEEE-ICCUBEA-2016, IEEE-ICCUBEA-2017, She also worked as a convener for BCUD sponsored workshops, national and international conferences. She has been selected for Outstanding woman in Engineeirng Award by VIWA.

Albena Dimitrova Mihovska, PhD (2008), is an Associate Professor at Aarhus University, Department of Business Development and Technologies, where she is with the CTIF Global Capsule and MBIT research group. Her main activities relate to research in the area of smart dense connectivity and related applications; 5G ultradense access networks, Internet of Things technologies for healthcare and smart grid, and most recently, holographic communications, digital technologies and their impact on business.

* * *

Venugopal D. completed his B.E in ECE from University of Madras in 2001 and M.E in optical communication from Anna University in 2005 and Ph. D in medical image processing in 2016. He has teaching experience of 16 years and published 17 international journals and 20 conference papers. Reviewer for sci and Scopus indexed journals.

Eustace Dogo is currently pursuing his PhD at the Department of Electrical and Electronic Engineering Science, University of Johannesburg. Eustace's current research interest is in applied machine learning and intelligent systems.

Anshul Garg is working as an Assistant Professor in Chandigarh Group of Colleges, Landran, Mohali, Punjab, India. She had done her M.Tech(Computer Science and Engineering) from Kurukshetra University, Haryana, India. She is pursuing her Ph.D. in Computer Applications From Chandigarh University, Gharuan, Punjab, Mohali. Her research interest includes Machine Learning, Big Data, and image processing.

Neha Gupta is currently working as an Associate professor, Faculty of Computer Applications at Manav Rachna International Institute of Research and Studies, Faridabad campus. She has completed her PhD from Manav Rachna International University and has done R&D Project in CDAC-Noida. She has total of 12+ year of experience in teaching and research. She is a Life Member of ACM CSTA, Tech Republic and Professional Member of IEEE. She has authored and coauthored 30 research papers in SCI/SCOPUS/Peer Reviewed Journals (Scopus indexed) and IEEE/IET Conference proceedings in areas of Web Content Mining, Mobile Computing, and Web Content Adaptation. She is a technical programme committee (TPC) member in various conferences across globe. She is an active reviewer for International Journal of Computer and Information Technology and in various IEEE Conferences around the world. She is one of the Editorial and review board members in International Journal of Research in Engineering and Technology.

Balaji K. completed his B.E in ECE from Anna University and M.E in Computer Science Engineering from Anna University. He has teaching experience of 8 years and published papers in various international journals and conference.

Kalirajan K. received his BE degree in ECE from Manonmanium Sundaranar University in 2003, ME in VLSI design from Anna University in 2009 and his PhD degree in Image and Video Processing from Anna University, Chennai in 2017. He has published research articles in various peer reviewed journals and he is a recognized supervisor at Anna University, Chennai.

Suyeb Khan is working as Director at Baba Kuma Singh Ji Group of Institute, Amritsar, India. Present area of research is Voice over Internet Protocol and Wireless Sensor Network.

Vikas Khullar is working as Assistant Professor in the Department of Computer Science and Engineering at Chitkara University Institute of Engineering and Technology, India. My present area of research is computer-assisted interventions to support the individuals with Autism Spectrum Disorder.

Raju Kumar is working as an associate professor with Chandigarh University, Mohali, India. He has expertise in regular and online teaching, administration, and research activities. He received his doctorate in Computer Science from Gurukula Kangri Vishwavidyalaya, Haridwar, India. He did his master's degree from Dr. Bhimrao Ambedkar University, Agra, India. He qualified UGC-NET in Computer Science and Applications. He is member of several professional societies including IAENG, IACSIT, CSTA, and IAOIP. His research interest includes distributed database, data science, machine learning, and ICT. He published several research papers in international and national journals and conferences. He has written and reviewed many Self Learning Material books for U.G. and P.G. programmes.

Mathaphelo Makana completed her Honours' degree with an emphasis in Electrical and Electronic Engineering at the University of Johannesburg. She strongly believes in continuous learning and sees herself as an individual who can tackle any challenge brought to her. Her Honours research focused on the application of Microcontroller technologies to automate watering systems in various sectors.

Marius Iulian Mihailescu, PhD, is CEO of Dapyx Solution Ltd., a company focused on security- and cryptography-related research and Associate Professor at "Spiru Haret" University, Romania. He has authored and co-authored more than 50 articles, journal contributions, and conference proceedings, and three books related to security and cryptography, including the International Journal of Applied Cryptography. He lectures at well-known national and international universities, teaching courses on programming, cryptography, information security, and other technical topics. He holds a PhD (thesis on applied cryptography over biometrics data) and two MSc in information security and software engineering.

Arnab Mitra has received B.E. (Information Technology) from University of North Bengal, India, M.Tech (Computer Science and Engineering) from West Bengal University of Technology, India, and Ph.D. (Engineering) from Jadavpur University, India. He was also an Erasmus Mundus visiting doctoral researcher at "Ghoerghe Asachi" Technical University of Iasi, Romania. His research interests include Cellular Automata, Distributed Computing, Cloud Applications.

Stefania Loredana Nita, PhD, is a software developer and researcher at the Institute for Computers. Prior to that she was an assistant lecturer at the University of Bucharest, where she taught courses on advanced programming techniques, simulation methods, and operating systems. She has authored and co-authored more than 15 papers and journals, most recently Advanced Cryptography and Its Future: Searchable and Homomorphic Encryption, as well as two books. She holds a PhD (thesis on advanced cryptographic schemes using searchable encryption and homomorphic encryption), an MSc in software engineering and two BSc in computer science and mathematics.

Sayantan Saha received his M.Tech. degree from the Indian Institute of Technology, Kharagpur, India, in 2016. His research interests include cloud computing, fog computing, and machine learning.

Karuna Salgotra is a Research Scholar in the Department of Computer Science and Engineering at CT Institute of Engineering, Management & Technology, India.

Harjit Pal Singh is working as Associate Professor in the Department of Electronics and Communication Engineering at CT Institute of Engineering, Management & Technology, India. Present area of research is to computer-assisted intervention support for individuals with Autism Spectrum Disorder.

Pradeep Kumar Tiwari is an Assistant Professor at the Computer and Communication Engineering department of the Manipal University Jaipur, India. Dr. Tiwari completed his Bachelor's and Master's degrees in Computer Application and M.Phil with Computer Science. Under his Ph.D. studies, Dr. Tiwari is actively involved in research on Load Balancing in Cloud Computing using, Virtual Machine Migrations, Distributed System, IOT and Machine learning. Dr Tiwari has Six high indexed journal publications and Ten international conferences. He is a also frequent reviewer for research conferences and journals Reviewer, The Computer Journal – An Oxford University Journal(ACM, SCIE), International Journal of Information Technologies and Systems Approach, International Journal of Measurement Technologies and Instrumentation Engineering (IJMTIE-IGI Global-ACM-ESCI), SCIRP Research Group (Scientific Research Publishing Group with 200 Open access journals) Irvine, CA, USA.

Seetha V. completed her B.E in EEE from PSG college of Technology, Coimbatore and M.Tech in Applied Electronics and Ph. D in ICE from Anna University in 2015. She has teaching experience of 20 years and published various international journals and conference papers. Her research interest is Wireless Sensor and Adhoc Networks and Routing.

Vivek Verma is an experienced Assistant Professor with a demonstrated history of working in the Technical education industry. Skilled in Research, E-Learning, Lecturing, Teaching, and Higher Education. Strong education professional with a Doctor of Philosophy (Ph.D.) focused in Natural Language Processing from Manipal University Jaipur. Working as Assistant Professor at the School of Computing & Information Technology Manipal University Jaipur.

Index

Ensure Quality Research is Introduced to the Academic Community

Become an IGI Global Reviewer for Authored Book Projects

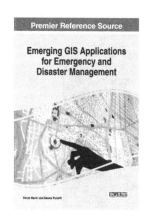

Premier Reference Source

Emerging GIS Applications for Emergency and Disaster Management

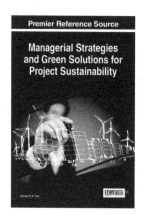

Premier Reference Source

Managerial Strategies and Green Solutions for Project Sustainability

Premier Reference Source

Comparative Approaches to Using R and Python for Statistical Data Analysis

Premier Reference Source

Solutions for High-Touch Communications in a High-Tech World

The overall success of an authored book project is dependent on quality and timely reviews.

In this competitive age of scholarly publishing, constructive and timely feedback significantly expedites the turnaround time of manuscripts from submission to acceptance, allowing the publication and discovery of forward-thinking research at a much more expeditious rate. Several IGI Global authored book projects are currently seeking highly-qualified experts in the field to fill vacancies on their respective editorial review boards:

Applications and Inquiries may be sent to:
development@igi-global.com

Applicants must have a doctorate (or an equivalent degree) as well as publishing and reviewing experience. Reviewers are asked to complete the open-ended evaluation questions with as much detail as possible in a timely, collegial, and constructive manner. All reviewers' tenures run for one-year terms on the editorial review boards and are expected to complete at least three reviews per term. Upon successful completion of this term, reviewers can be considered for an additional term.

If you have a colleague that may be interested in this opportunity,
we encourage you to share this information with them.

IGI Global Proudly Partners With eContent Pro International

Receive a 25% Discount on all Editorial Services

Editorial Services

IGI Global expects all final manuscripts submitted for publication to be in their final form. This means they must be reviewed, revised, and professionally copy edited prior to their final submission. Not only does this support with accelerating the publication process, but it also ensures that the highest quality scholarly work can be disseminated.

English Language Copy Editing

Let eContent Pro International's expert copy editors perform edits on your manuscript to resolve spelling, punctuaion, grammar, syntax, flow, formatting issues and more.

Scientific and Scholarly Editing

Allow colleagues in your research area to examine the content of your manuscript and provide you with valuable feedback and suggestions before submission.

Figure, Table, Chart & Equation Conversions

Do you have poor quality figures? Do you need visual elements in your manuscript created or converted? A design expert can help!

Translation

Need your documjent translated into English? eContent Pro International's expert translators are fluent in English and more than 40 different languages.

Hear What Your Colleagues are Saying About Editorial Services Supported by IGI Global

"The service was very fast, very thorough, and very helpful in ensuring our chapter meets the criteria and requirements of the book's editors. I was quite impressed and happy with your service."

– Prof. Tom Brinthaupt,
Middle Tennessee State University, USA

"I found the work actually spectacular. The editing, formatting, and other checks were very thorough. The turnaround time was great as well. I will definitely use eContent Pro in the future."

– Nickanor Amwata, Lecturer,
University of Kurdistan Hawler, Iraq

"I was impressed that it was done timely, and wherever the content was not clear for the reader, the paper was improved with better readability for the audience."

– Prof. James Chilembwe,
Mzuzu University, Malawi

Email: customerservice@econtentpro.com   www.igi-global.com/editorial-service-partners

 www.igi-global.com

Celebrating Over 30 Years of Scholarly Knowledge Creation & Dissemination

InfoSci®-Books

A Database of Over 5,300+ Reference Books Containing Over 100,000+ Chapters Focusing on Emerging Research

GAIN ACCESS TO **THOUSANDS** OF REFERENCE BOOKS AT **A FRACTION** OF THEIR INDIVIDUAL LIST **PRICE**.

InfoSci®-Books Database

The **InfoSci®-Books** database is a collection of over 5,300+ IGI Global single and multi-volume reference books, handbooks of research, and encyclopedias, encompassing groundbreaking research from prominent experts worldwide that span over 350+ topics in 11 core subject areas including business, computer science, education, science and engineering, social sciences and more.

Open Access Fee Waiver (Offset Model) Initiative

For any library that invests in IGI Global's InfoSci-Journals and/or InfoSci-Books databases, IGI Global will match the library's investment with a fund of equal value to go toward **subsidizing the OA article processing charges (APCs) for their students, faculty, and staff** at that institution when their work is submitted and accepted under OA into an IGI Global journal.*

INFOSCI® PLATFORM FEATURES

- No DRM
- No Set-Up or Maintenance Fees
- A Guarantee of No More Than a 5% Annual Increase
- Full-Text HTML and PDF Viewing Options
- Downloadable MARC Records
- Unlimited Simultaneous Access
- COUNTER 5 Compliant Reports
- Formatted Citations With Ability to Export to RefWorks and EasyBib
- No Embargo of Content (Research is Available Months in Advance of the Print Release)

*The fund will be offered on an annual basis and expire at the end of the subscription period. The fund would renew as the subscription is renewed for each year thereafter. The open access fees will be waived after the student, faculty, or staff's paper has been vetted and accepted into an IGI Global journal and the fund can only be used toward publishing OA in an IGI Global journal. Libraries in developing countries will have the match on their investment doubled.

To Learn More or To Purchase This Database:
www.igi-global.com/infosci-books

eresources@igi-global.com • Toll Free: 1-866-342-6657 ext. 100 • Phone: 717-533-8845 x100

 www.igi-global.com

Printed in the United States
By Bookmasters